ON THE BRINK

ON THE BRINK

*Inside the Race to Stop the Collapse
of the Global Financial System*

HENRY M. PAULSON, JR.

**BUSINESS
PLUS**

NEW YORK   BOSTON

Business Plus
Hachette Book Group
237 Park Avenue
New York, NY 10017

www.HachetteBookGroup.com

Business Plus is an imprint of Grand Central Publishing.
The Business Plus name and logo are trademarks of Hachette Book
Group, Inc.

Printed in the United States of America

First Edition: February 2010

10 9 8 7 6 5 4 3 2 1

ISBN: 978-0-446-56193-8
LCCN: 2009939043

For Wendy

MAIN CAST OF CHARACTERS
(in Alphabetical Order)

CONGRESS

REP. SPENCER BACHUS (R-Alabama), ranking Republican on the House Committee on Financial Services

SEN. MAX BAUCUS (D-Montana), chairman of the Senate Committee on Finance

REP. ROY BLUNT (R-Missouri), House minority whip

REP. JOHN BOEHNER (R-Ohio), House minority leader

SEN. JIM BUNNING (R-Kentucky), member of the Senate Committee on Banking, Housing, and Urban Affairs

SEN. HILLARY RODHAM CLINTON (D–New York)

SEN. CHRISTOPHER DODD (D-Connecticut), chairman of the Senate Committee on Banking, Housing, and Urban Affairs

REP. RAHM EMANUEL (D-Illinois), chairman of the House Democratic Caucus; later chosen as chief of staff by President-elect Barack Obama

REP. BARNEY FRANK (D-Massachusetts), chairman of the House Committee on Financial Services

SEN. LINDSEY GRAHAM (R–South Carolina), national campaign co-chairman for Sen. John McCain

SEN. JUDD GREGG (R–New Hampshire), ranking Republican on the Senate Committee on the Budget

SEN. MITCH MCCONNELL (R-Kentucky), Senate minority leader

REP. NANCY PELOSI (D-California), Speaker of the House

SEN. HARRY REID (D-Nevada), Senate majority leader

SEN. CHARLES SCHUMER (D–New York), vice chairman of the Senate Democratic Conference

SEN. RICHARD SHELBY (R-Alabama), ranking Republican on the Senate Committee on Banking, Housing, and Urban Affairs

FINANCIAL LEADERS AND THEIR ADVISERS

JOSEF ACKERMANN, chairman of the management board and CEO of Deutsche Bank

HERBERT ALLISON, JR., chairman and CEO of TIAA-CREF; later president and CEO of Fannie Mae

LLOYD BLANKFEIN, chairman and CEO of Goldman Sachs

WARREN BUFFETT, chairman and CEO of Berkshire Hathaway

H. RODGIN COHEN, chairman of Sullivan & Cromwell

MERVYN DAVIES, chairman of Standard Chartered Bank

JAMES DIMON, chairman and CEO of JPMorgan Chase

J. CHRISTOPHER FLOWERS, CEO of J.C. Flowers & Company

RICHARD FULD, chairman and CEO of Lehman Brothers

EDWARD HERLIHY, co-chairman of the executive committee of Wachtell, Lipton, Rosen & Katz

JEFFREY IMMELT, chairman and CEO of General Electric

ROBERT KELLY, chairman and CEO of Bank of New York Mellon

RICHARD KOVACEVICH, chairman of Wells Fargo

KENNETH LEWIS, chairman and CEO of Bank of America

EDWARD LIDDY, chairman and CEO of AIG

JOHN MACK, chairman and CEO of Morgan Stanley

HERBERT (BART) MCDADE III, president of Lehman Brothers

DANIEL MUDD, president and CEO of Fannie Mae

VIKRAM PANDIT, CEO of Citigroup

ROBERT RUBIN, former secretary of the Treasury; director and
senior counselor of Citigroup

ALAN SCHWARTZ, CEO of Bear Stearns

ROBERT SCULLY, vice chairman of Morgan Stanley

LAWRENCE SUMMERS, former secretary of the Treasury; chosen as
director of the National Economic Council by President-elect
Barack Obama

RICHARD SYRON, chairman and CEO of Freddie Mac

JOHN THAIN, chairman and CEO of Merrill Lynch

ROBERT WILLUMSTAD, CEO of AIG

FINANCIAL REGULATORS

SHEILA BAIR, chairman of the Federal Deposit Insurance
Corporation

BEN BERNANKE, chairman of the Federal Reserve Board

CHRISTOPHER COX, chairman of the Securities and Exchange
Commission

JOHN DUGAN, comptroller of the currency

TIMOTHY GEITHNER, president of the Federal Reserve Bank of New
York; later nominated for secretary of the Treasury by
President-elect Barack Obama

DONALD KOHN, vice chairman of the Federal Reserve Board

JAMES LOCKHART, director of the Federal Housing Finance
Agency

CALLUM MCCARTHY, chairman of the Financial Services Authority
(United Kingdom)

KEVIN WARSH, governor of the Federal Reserve Board

INTERNATIONAL LEADERS

ALISTAIR DARLING, chancellor of the Exchequer of the United
Kingdom

HU JINTAO, president of the People's Republic of China

MERVYN KING, governor of the Bank of England

ALEXEI KUDRIN, finance minister of Russia

CHRISTINE LAGARDE, finance minister of France

ANGELA MERKEL, chancellor of Germany

VLADIMIR PUTIN, prime minister of Russia

NICOLAS SARKOZY, president of France

JEAN-CLAUDE TRICHET, president of the European Central Bank

WANG QISHAN, vice premier of the State Council of the People's
Republic of China

WU YI, vice premier of the State Council of the People's Republic
of China

ZHOU XIAOCHUAN, governor of the central bank of the People's
Republic of China

PRESIDENTIAL CANDIDATES
AND THEIR RUNNING MATES

SEN. JOSEPH BIDEN, JR. (D-Delaware), vice presidential candidate for
the Democratic Party; later elected 47th vice president of the
United States

SEN. JOHN MCCAIN (R-Arizona), presidential candidate for the
Republican Party

SEN. BARACK OBAMA (D-Illinois), presidential candidate for the
Democratic Party; later elected 44th president of the United
States

GOV. SARAH PALIN (R-Alaska), vice presidential candidate for the
Republican Party

TREASURY DEPARTMENT

Michele Davis, assistant secretary for public affairs and director of policy planning

Kevin Fromer, assistant secretary for legislative affairs

Robert Hoyt, general counsel

Dan Jester, contractor

Neel Kashkari, assistant secretary for international economics and development and interim assistant secretary for financial stability

James Lambright, chief investment officer of TARP

Clay Lowery, acting undersecretary for international affairs

Jeb Mason, deputy assistant secretary for business affairs

David McCormick, undersecretary for international affairs

David Nason, assistant secretary for financial institutions

Jeremiah Norton, deputy assistant secretary for financial institutions policy

Karthik Ramanathan, director of the Office of Debt Management

Anthony Ryan, assistant secretary for financial markets

Steven Shafran, senior adviser to the secretary of the Treasury

Robert Steel, undersecretary for domestic finance; later president and CEO of Wachovia

Phillip Swagel, assistant secretary for economic policy

James Wilkinson, chief of staff

Kendrick Wilson, contractor

WHITE HOUSE

Joshua Bolten, chief of staff

George W. Bush, 43rd president of the United States

Richard Cheney, 46th vice president of the United States

Edward Gillespie, counselor to the president

STEPHEN HADLEY, national security adviser

KEITH HENNESSEY, assistant to the president for economic policy; later director of the National Economic Council

JOEL KAPLAN, deputy chief of staff for policy

EDWARD LAZEAR, chairman of the Council of Economic Advisers

DANIEL MEYER, assistant to the president for legislative affairs

Author's Note

The pace of events during the financial crisis of 2008 was truly breathtaking. In this book, I have done my best to describe my actions and the thinking behind them during that time, and to convey the breakneck speed at which events were happening all around us.

I believe the most important part of this story is the way Ben Bernanke, Tim Geithner, and I worked as a team through the worst financial crisis since the Great Depression. There can't be many other examples of economic leaders managing a crisis who had as much trust in one another as we did. Our partnership proved to be an enormous asset during an incredibly difficult period. But at the same time, this is my story, and as hard as I have tried to reflect the contributions made by everyone involved, it is primarily about my work and that of my talented and dedicated team at Treasury.

I have been blessed with a good memory, so I have almost never needed to take notes. I don't use e-mail. I rarely take papers to meetings. I frustrated my Treasury staff by seldom using briefing memos. Much of my work was done on the phone, but there is no official record of many of the calls. My phone log has inaccuracies and omissions. To write this book, I called on the memories of many of the people who were with me during these events. Still, given the high degree of stress during this time and the extraordinary number of problems I was juggling in a single day, and often in a single hour, I am sure there are many details I will never recall.

I'm a candid person by nature and I've attempted to give the unbridled truth. I call it the way I see it.

In Washington, congressional and executive branch leaders are underappreciated for their work ethic and for the talents they apply to difficult jobs. As a result, this book has many heroes.

I've also tried to tell this story so that it could be readily understood by readers of widely varying degrees of financial expertise. That said, I am sure it is overly simplified in some places and too complex in others. Throughout the narrative, I cite changes in stock prices and credit default swap rates, not because those numbers matter in and of themselves, but because they are the most effective way to represent the plummeting confidence and rising sense of crisis in our financial markets and our economy during this period.

I now have heightened respect for anyone who has ever written a book. Even with a great deal of help from others, I have found the process to be most challenging.

There is no question that these were extraordinary and tumultuous times. Here is my story.

On the Brink

CHAPTER 1

Thursday, September 4, 2008

Do they know it's coming, Hank?" President Bush asked me.

"Mr. President," I said, "we're going to move quickly and take them by surprise. The first sound they'll hear is their heads hitting the floor."

It was Thursday morning, September 4, 2008, and we were in the Oval Office of the White House discussing the fate of Fannie Mae and Freddie Mac, the troubled housing finance giants. For the good of the country, I had proposed that we seize control of the companies, fire their bosses, and prepare to provide up to $100 billion of capital support for each. If we did not act immediately, Fannie and Freddie would, I feared, take down the financial system, and the global economy, with them.

I'm a straightforward person. I like to be direct with people. But I knew that we had to ambush Fannie and Freddie. We could give them no room to maneuver. We couldn't very well go to Daniel Mudd at Fannie Mae or Richard Syron at Freddie Mac and say:

"Here's our idea for how to save you. Why don't we just take you over and throw you out of your jobs, and do it in a way that protects the taxpayer to the disadvantage of your shareholders?" The news would leak, and they'd fight. They'd go to their many powerful friends on Capitol Hill or to the courts, and the resulting delays would cause panic in the markets. We'd trigger the very disaster we were trying to avoid.

I had come alone to the White House from an 8:00 a.m. meeting at Treasury with Ben Bernanke, the chairman of the Federal Reserve Board, who shared my concerns, and Jim Lockhart, head of the Federal Housing Finance Agency (FHFA), the main regulator for Fannie and Freddie. Many of our staffers had been up all night—we had all been putting in 18-hour days during the summer and through the preceding Labor Day holiday weekend—to hammer out the language and documents that would allow us to make the move. We weren't quite there yet, but it was time to get the president's official approval. We wanted to place Fannie and Freddie into conservatorship over the weekend and make sure that everything was wrapped up before the Asian markets opened Sunday night.

The mood was somber as I laid out our plans to the president and his top advisers, who included White House chief of staff Josh Bolten; deputy chief of staff Joel Kaplan; Ed Lazear, chairman of the Council of Economic Advisers; Keith Hennessey, director of the National Economic Council (NEC); and Jim Nussle, director of the Office of Management and Budget. The night before, Alaska governor Sarah Palin had electrified the Republican National Convention in St. Paul, Minnesota, with her speech accepting the nomination as the party's vice presidential candidate, but there was no mention of that in the Oval Office. St. Paul might as well have been on another planet.

The president and his advisers were well informed of the seriousness of the situation. Less than two weeks before, I had gotten on a secure videoconference line in the West Wing to brief the president at his ranch in Crawford, Texas, and explained my thinking. Like him, I am a firm believer in free markets, and I certainly hadn't come to Washington planning to do anything to inject the government into the private sector. But Fannie and Freddie were congressionally chartered companies that already relied heavily on implicit government support, and in August, along with Bernanke, I'd come to the conclusion that taking them over was the best way to avert a meltdown, keep mortgage financing available, stabilize markets, and protect the taxpayer. The president had agreed.

It is hard to exaggerate how central Fannie and Freddie were to U.S. markets. Between them they owned or guaranteed more than $5 trillion in residential mortgages and mortgage-backed securities—about half of all those in the country. To finance operations, they were among the biggest issuers of debt in the world: a total of about $1.7 trillion for the pair. They were in the markets constantly, borrowing more than $20 billion a week at times.

But investors were losing faith in them—for good reason. Combined, they already had $5.5 billion in net losses for the year to date. Their common share prices had plunged—to $7.32 for Fannie the day before from $66 one year earlier. The previous month, Standard & Poor's, the rating agency, had twice downgraded the preferred stock of both companies. Investors were shying away from their auctions, raising the cost of their borrowings and making existing debt holders increasingly nervous. By the end of August, neither could raise equity capital from private investors or in the public markets.

Moreover, the financial system was increasingly shaky. Commercial and investment bank stocks were under pressure, and we were nervously monitoring the health of several ailing institutions, including Wachovia Corporation, Washington Mutual, and Lehman Brothers. We had seen what happened in March when Bear Stearns's counterparties—the other banks and investment houses that lent it money or bought its securities—abruptly turned away. We had survived that, but the collapse of Fannie and Freddie would be catastrophic. Seemingly everyone in the world—little banks, big banks, foreign central banks, money market funds—owned their paper or was a counterparty. Investors would lose tens of billions; foreigners would lose confidence in the U.S. It might cause a run on the dollar.

The president, in suit coat and tie as always, was all business, engaged and focused on our tactics. He leaned forward in his blue-and-yellow-striped armchair. I sat in the armchair to his right; the others were crowded on facing sofas.

I told the president we planned to summon the top management of Fannie and Freddie to meet with Bernanke, Lockhart, and me the following afternoon. We'd lay out our decision and then present it to their boards on Saturday: we would put $100 billion of capital behind each, with hundreds of billions of dollars more available beyond that, and assure both companies of ample credit lines from the government. Obviously we preferred that they voluntarily acquiesce. But if they did not, we would seize them.

I explained that we had teams of lawyers, bank examiners, computer specialists, and others on standby, ready to roll into the companies' offices and secure their premises, trading floors, books and records, and so forth. We had already picked replacement chief executives. David Moffett, a former chief financial officer from U.S. Bancorp, one of the few nearly pristine big banks in the country, was on board for Freddie Mac. For Fannie Mae we'd selected former TIAA-CREF chief executive and chairman Herb Allison. (He was vacationing in the Caribbean, and when I reached him later and twisted his arm to come to Washington the next day, he'd initially protested: "Hank, I'm in my flip-flops. I don't even have a suit down here." But he'd agreed to come.)

White House staff had been shocked when we first suggested conservatorship for Fannie and Freddie, which had the reputation of being the toughest street fighters in Washington. But they liked the boldness of the idea, as did the president. He had a deep disdain for entities like Fannie and Freddie, which he saw as part of a permanent Washington elite, detached from the heartland, with former government officials and lobbyists cycling through their ranks endlessly while the companies minted money, thanks, in effect, to a federal entitlement.

The president wanted to know what I thought the longer-term model for Fannie and Freddie ought to be. I was keen to avoid any existential debate on the two companies that might bog down in partisan politics on the Hill, where Fannie and Freddie had ardent friends and enemies.

"Mr. President," I replied, "I don't think we want to get into that publicly right now. No one can argue that their models aren't seriously flawed and pose a systemic risk, but the last thing we want to start right now is a holy war."

"What do you suggest?"

"I'll describe this as a time-out and defer structure until later. I'll just tell everybody that we're going to do this to stabilize them and the capital markets and to put the U.S.A. behind their credit to make sure there's mortgage finance available in this country."

"I agree," the president said. "I wouldn't propose a new model now, either. But we'll need to do it at the right time, and we have to make clear that what we are doing now is transitory, because otherwise it looks like nationalization."

I said that I had come to believe that what made most sense longer-term was some sort of dramatically scaled-down structure where the extent of government support was clear and the companies functioned like utilities. The current model, where profits went to shareholders but losses had to be absorbed by the taxpayer, did not make sense.

The president rose to signal the meeting was over. "It will sure be interesting to see if they run to Congress," he said.

I left the White House and walked back to Treasury, where we had to script what we would say to the two mortgage agencies the following day. We wanted to be sure we had the strongest case possible in the event they chose to fight. But even now, at the 11th hour, we still had concerns that FHFA had not effectively documented the severity of Fannie's and Freddie's capital shortfall and the case for immediate conservatorship.

The cooperation among the federal agencies had generally been superb, but although Treasury, the Fed, and the Office of the Comptroller of the Currency (OCC) agreed, FHFA had been balky all along. That was a big problem because only FHFA had the statutory power to put Fannie and Freddie into conservatorship. We had to convince its people that this was the right thing to do, while making sure to let them feel they were still in charge.

I had spent much of August working with Lockhart, a friend of the president's since their prep school days. Jim understood the gravity of the situation, but his people, who had said recently that Fannie and Freddie were adequately capitalized, feared for their reputations. The president himself wouldn't intervene because it was inappropriate for him to talk with a regulator, though he was sure Lockhart would come through in the end. In any event, I invoked the president's name repeatedly.

"Jim," I'd say, "you don't want to trigger a meltdown and ruin your friend's presidency, do you?"

The day before I'd gone to the White House, I spoke with Lockhart by phone at least four times: at 9:45 a.m., 3:45 p.m., 4:30 p.m., and then again later that night. "Jim, it has to be this weekend. We've got to know," I insisted.

Part of FHFA's reluctance had to do with history. It had only come into existence in July, as part of hard-won reform legislation. FHFA and its predecessor, the Office of Federal Housing Enterprise Oversight, which Lockhart had also led, were weak regulators, underresourced and outmatched by the companies they were meant to oversee, and constrained by a narrow view of their charters and authorities. FHFA's people were conditioned by their history to judge Fannie and Freddie by their statutory capital requirements, not, as we did, by the much greater amounts of capital that were necessary to satisfy the market. They relied on the companies' own analyses because they lacked the resources and ability to make independent evaluations as the Fed and OCC could. FHFA preferred to take the agencies to task for regulatory infractions and seek consent orders to force change. That approach wasn't nearly enough and would have taken time, which we did not have.

Complicating matters, FHFA had recently given the two companies clean bills of health based on their compliance with those weak statutory capital requirements. Lockhart was concerned— and Bob Hoyt, Treasury's general counsel, agreed—that it would be suicide if we attempted to take control of Fannie and Freddie and they went to court only to have it emerge that the FHFA had said, in effect, that there were no problems.

We had been working hard to convince FHFA to take a much more realistic view of the capital problems and had sent in teams of Fed and OCC examiners to help them understand and itemize the problems down to the last dollar. The Fed and the OCC saw a huge capital hole in Fannie and Freddie; we needed to get FHFA examiners to see the hole.

Lockhart had been skillfully working to get his examiners to come up with language they could live with. But on Thursday they still had not done enough to document the capital problems. We sent in more help. Sheila Bair, chairman of the Federal Deposit Insurance Corporation, which had ample experience in closing banks, agreed to send me her best person to help write a case.

Finally, Lockhart managed to get his examiners to sign off on what we needed. Either Jim had worn those examiners down or they had come to realize that immediate conservatorship was the best way for them to resolve this dangerous situation with their reputations intact.

Thursday evening, Jim put in calls to the CEOs of Fannie and Freddie, summoning them to a meeting Friday afternoon that Ben and I would attend at FHFA's headquarters on G Street. (Jim didn't speak directly to Mudd until Friday morning.) We arranged for the first meeting to start just before 4:00 p.m. so that the market would be closed by the time it ended. We decided to lead with Fannie Mae, figuring they were more likely to be contentious.

The companies obviously knew something was up, and it didn't take long for me to start getting blowback. Dan Mudd called me on Friday morning and got straight to the point.

"Hank," he asked, "what's going on? We've done all you asked. We've been cooperative. What's this about?"

"Dan," I said, "if I could tell you, I wouldn't be calling the meeting."

We'd been operating in secrecy and had managed to avoid any leaks for several weeks, which may be a record for Washington. To keep everyone in the dark, we resorted to a little cloak-and-dagger that afternoon. I drove to FHFA with Kevin Fromer, my assistant secretary for legislative affairs, and Jim Wilkinson, my chief of staff, and instead of hopping out at the curb, we went straight into the building's parking garage to avoid being seen. Unfortunately, Ben Bernanke walked in the front door and was spotted by a reporter for the *Wall Street Journal*, who posted word on the paper's website.

We met the rest of our teams on the fourth floor. FHFA's offices were a contrast to those at the Fed and Treasury, which are grand and spacious, with lots of marble, high ceilings, and walls lined with elegant paintings. FHFA's offices were drab and cramped, the floors clad in thin office carpet.

As planned, we arrived a few minutes early, and as soon as I saw Lockhart I pulled him aside to buck him up. He was ready but shaky. This was a big step for him.

Our first meeting was with Fannie in a conference room adjacent to Jim's office. We'd asked both CEOs to bring their lead directors. Fannie chairman Stephen Ashley and general counsel Beth Wilkinson accompanied Mudd. He also brought the company's outside counsel, H. Rodgin Cohen, chairman of Sullivan & Cromwell and a noted bank lawyer, who'd flown down hastily from New York.

Between our group from Treasury, the Fed's team, Lockhart's people, and Fannie's executives, there must have been about a dozen people in the glass-walled conference room, spread around the main table and arrayed along the walls.

Lockhart went first. He took Fannie Mae through a long, detailed presentation, citing one regulatory infraction after another. Most didn't amount to much, frankly; they were more like parking tickets in the scheme of things. He was a little nervous and hesitant, but he brought his speech around to the key point: his examiners had concluded there was a capital deficiency, the company was operating in an unsafe and unsound manner, and FHFA had decided to put it into conservatorship. He said that we all hoped they would agree to do this voluntarily; if not, we would seize control. We had already selected a new CEO and had teams ready to move in.

As he spoke I watched the Fannie Mae delegation. They were furious. Mudd was alternately scowling or sneering. Once he put his head between his hands and shook it. In truth, I felt a good bit of sympathy for him. He had been dealt a tough hand. Fannie could be arrogant, even pompous, but Mudd had become CEO after a messy accounting scandal and had been reasonably cooperative as he tried to clean things up.

I followed Lockhart and laid out my argument as simply as I could. Jim, I said, had described a serious capital deficiency. I agreed with his analysis, but added that although I'd been authorized by Congress to do so, I had decided that I was not prepared to put any capital into Fannie in its current form. I told them that I felt Fannie Mae had done a better job than Freddie Mac; they had raised $7.4 billion earlier in the year, while Freddie had delayed and had a bigger capital hole. Now, however, neither could raise any private money. The markets simply did not differentiate between Fannie and Freddie. We would not, either. I recommended conservatorship and said that Mudd would have to go. Only under those conditions would we be prepared to put in capital.

"If you acquiesce," I concluded, "I will make clear to all I am not blaming management. You didn't create the business model you have, and it's flawed. You didn't create the regulatory model, and it is equally flawed."

I left unspoken what I would say publicly if they didn't acquiesce.

Ben Bernanke followed and made a very strong speech. He said he was very supportive of the proposed actions. Because of the capital deficiency, the safety and soundness of Fannie Mae was at risk, and that in turn imperiled the stability of the financial system. It was in the best interests of the country to do this, he concluded.

Though stunned and angry, the Fannie team was quick to raise issues. Mudd clearly thought Fannie was being treated with great injustice. He and his team were eager to put space between their company and Freddie, and the truth was they had done a better job. But I said that for investors it was a distinction without a difference—investors in both companies were looking to their congressional charters and implicit guarantees from the United States of America. The market perceived them as indistinguishable. And that was it. The Fannie executives asked how much equity capital we planned to put in. How would we structure it? We wouldn't say. We weren't eager to give many details at all, because we didn't want to read about it in the press.

"Dan's too gracious a man to raise this," said Beth Wilkinson. "But we're a unified management team. How come he is the only one being fired, and why are you replacing him?"

"I don't think you can do something this drastic and not change the CEO," I replied. "Beyond that, frankly, I want to do as little as possible to change management."

"Our board will want to take a close look at this," Mudd said, attempting to push back.

Richard Alexander, the managing partner for Arnold & Porter, FHFA's outside counsel, replied: "I need you to understand that when these gentlemen"—he meant Lockhart, Bernanke, and me—"come to your board meeting tomorrow, it's not to have a dialogue."

"Okay," Rodge Cohen said, and it was clear he understood the game was over.

After the meeting, I made a few quick calls to key legislators. I had learned much, none of it good, since going to Congress in July for unprecedented emergency authorities to stabilize Fannie and Freddie. I had said then that if legislators gave me a big enough weapon—a "bazooka" was what I specifically requested—it was likely I wouldn't have to use it. But I had not known of the extent of the companies' problems then. After I had learned of the capital hole, I had been unable to speak about it publicly, so conservatorship would come as a shock, as would the level of taxpayer support. I was also very concerned that Congress might be angered that I had turned temporary authority to invest in Fannie and Freddie, which would expire at year-end 2009, into what effectively was a permanent guarantee on all their debt.

First up were Barney Frank, chairman of the House Committee on Financial Services, and Chris Dodd, his counterpart on the Senate Banking Committee. Barney was scary-smart, ready with a quip, and usually a pleasure to work with. He was energetic, a skilled and pragmatic legislator whose main interest was in doing what he believed was best for the country. He bargained hard but stuck to his word. Dodd was more of a challenge. We'd worked together on Fannie and Freddie reform, but he had been distracted by his unsuccessful campaign for the Democratic presidential nomination and seemed exhausted afterward. Though personable and knowledgeable, he was not as consistent or predictable as Barney, and his job was more difficult because it was much harder to get things done in the Senate. He and his staff had a close relationship with Fannie, so I knew that if they decided to fight, they would go to him.

As it turned out, the calls went well. I explained that what we were doing was driven by necessity, not ideology; we had to pre-empt a market panic. I knew their initially supportive reactions might change—after they understood all the facts and had gauged the public reaction. But we were off to a good start.

Then I went into the meeting with Freddie. Dick Syron had brought his outside counsel, along with a few of his directors, including Geoff Boisi, an old colleague from my Goldman Sachs days.

We ran through the same script with Freddie, and the difference was clear: Where Mudd had been seething, Syron was relaxed, seemingly relieved. He had appeared frustrated and exhausted as he managed the company, and he looked like he'd been hoping for this to happen. He was ready to do his duty—like the man handed a revolver and told, "Go ahead and do it for the regiment."

He and his people mostly had procedural issues to raise. Would it be all right for directors to phone in or would they have to come in person? How would the news be communicated to their employees?

As we had with Fannie Mae, we swore everyone in the room to silence. (Nonetheless the news leaked almost immediately.) When the meeting broke up, I made some more calls to the Hill and to the White House, where I gave Josh Bolten a heads-up. I spoke with, among others, New York senator Chuck Schumer; Alabama senator Richard Shelby, the ranking Republican on the Senate Banking Committee; and Alabama representative Spencer Bachus, the ranking Republican on the House Committee on Financial Services.

I went home exhausted, had a quick dinner with my wife, Wendy, and went to bed at 9:30 p.m. (I'm an "early to bed, early to rise" fellow. I simply need my eight hours of sleep. I wish it weren't the case, but it is.)

At 10:30 p.m. the home phone rang, and I picked it up. My first thought, which I dreaded, was that maybe someone was calling to tell me Fannie was going to fight. Instead I heard the voice of Senator Barack Obama, the Democratic nominee for president.

"Hank," he began, "you've got to be the only guy in the country who's working as hard as I am."

He was calling from someplace on the road. He had learned about the moves we'd made and wanted to talk about what it meant. I didn't know him very well at all. At my last official function as Goldman Sachs CEO before moving to Washington, I'd invited him to speak to our partners at a meeting we'd held in Chicago. The other main speaker at that event had been Berkshire Hathaway CEO Warren Buffett.

I would, in fact, get to know Obama better over the course of the fall, speaking to him frequently, sometimes several times a day,

about the crisis. I was impressed with him. He was always well informed, well briefed, and self-confident. He could talk about the
issues I was dealing with in an intelligent way.

That night he wanted to hear everything we'd done and how
and why. I took the senator through our thinking and our tactics.
He was quick to grasp why we thought the two agencies were so
critical to stabilizing the markets and keeping low-cost mortgage
financing available. He appreciated our desire to protect the taxpayers as well.

"Bailouts like this are very unpopular," he pointed out.

I replied that it wasn't a bailout in any real sense. Common and
preferred shareholders alike were being wiped out, and we had
replaced the CEOs.

"That sounds like strong medicine," Obama said. He was glad
we were replacing the CEOs and asked about whether there had
been any golden parachutes.

I told him we would take care of that, and he shifted the conversation to discuss the broader issues for the capital markets and
the economy. He wanted to hear my views on how we'd gotten to
this point, and how serious the problems were.

"It's serious," I said, "and it's going to get worse."

In all, we were on the phone that night for perhaps 30 minutes.
Arizona senator John McCain's selection of Sarah Palin as his running mate had energized the Republican base, and McCain was
surging in the polls, but at least overtly there didn't seem to be
"politics" or maneuvering in Obama's approach to me. Throughout the crisis, he played it straight. He genuinely seemed to want
to do the right thing. He wanted to avoid doing anything publicly—
or privately—that would damage our efforts to stabilize the markets and the economy.

But of course, there's always politics at play: the day after the election Obama abruptly stopped talking to me.

When I woke the next morning, word of our plan to take control of Fannie and Freddie was bannered in all the major newspapers. Then, when I got to the office, I told my staff about my conversation with Obama, and they got a bit panicky. Since some Republicans considered me to be a closet Democrat, my staff had misgivings about any action on my part that might be construed as favoring Obama. So we figured I had better put in a call to McCain to even things up.

I connected with the Republican candidate late in the morning. I had a cordial relationship with John, but we were not particularly close and had never discussed economic issues—our most in-depth conversations had concerned climate change. But that day McCain was ebullient and friendly. The Palin selection had clearly revitalized him, and he began by saying he wanted to introduce me to his running mate, whom he put on the phone with us.

McCain had little more to say as I described the actions we had taken and why, but Governor Palin immediately made her presence felt. Right away she started calling me Hank. Now, everyone calls me Hank. My assistant calls me Hank. Everyone on my staff, from top to bottom, calls me Hank. It's what I like. But for some reason, the way she said it over the phone like that, even though we'd never met, rubbed me the wrong way.

I'm also not sure she grasped the full dimensions of the situation I had sketched out—or so some of her comments made me think. But she grasped the politics pretty quickly.

"Hank," she asked, "did any of their executives get golden para-chutes? Did you fire all the people you need to? Hank, can we claw back any of their compensation?"

From that call I went into a noon meeting that lasted perhaps an hour with the board of directors of Freddie Mac. In the afternoon, around 3:00 p.m., it was Fannie Mae's turn. To avoid publicity, we switched from FHFA headquarters to a ground-floor conference room at the Federal Housing Finance Board offices, a few blocks from Lafayette Square.

Lockhart, Bernanke, and I followed the same script from the previous afternoon: Jim led off explaining that we had decided on conservatorship, citing capital inadequacy and his list of infractions. I laid out our terms, and Ben followed with his description of the catastrophe that would occur if we did not take these actions.

Going into the weekend, there had been some trepidation among our team that the two government-sponsored enterprises (GSEs), especially Fannie, would resist. But after all my years as a Goldman Sachs banker I knew boards, and I felt sure that they would heed our call. They had fiduciary duties to their shareholders, so they would want us to make the strongest case we could. We emphasized that if the government didn't put them into conservatorship, the companies would face insolvency and their shareholders would be worse off. I also knew that having these arguments made directly to them by their companies' regulator, the secretary of the Treasury, and the chairman of the Federal Reserve Board would carry immense weight.

Just like the initial meetings the day before, the session with the Freddie board went much easier than the one with its sister institution. Fannie's directors, like its management, wanted to differentiate their company from Freddie, but we made clear we could do no such thing.

I made a round of phone calls Saturday and Sunday to congressional leaders, as well as to senior financial industry executives, outlining our actions and the importance of stabilizing Fannie and Freddie. Just about everyone was supportive, even congratulatory, although I do remember Chris Dodd being a little put out when I talked to him a second time, on Sunday.

"Whatever happened to your bazooka, Hank?" he asked.

I explained that I had never thought I'd have to use the emergency powers Congress had given me in July, but given the state of affairs at the GSEs, I'd had no choice. Still, I knew I would have to spend some time with Chris to make him feel more comfortable.

After the Fannie board meeting, I received a call I'd been expecting most of the day. Word had gotten out that I'd talked to Palin, so I'd been thinking, *Joe Biden's bound to call, too.* And, sure enough, he did. The predictability of it gave me my one good laugh of the day, but the Democratic vice presidential candidate was on top of the issue; he understood the nature of the problem we faced and supported our strong actions.

Sunday morning at 11:00, Jim Lockhart and I officially unveiled the Fannie Mae and Freddie Mac rescue with a statement to the press. I described four key steps we were taking: FHFA would place the companies into conservatorship; the government would provide up to $100 billion to each company to backstop any capital shortfalls; Treasury would establish a new secured lending credit facility for Fannie and Freddie and would begin a temporary program to buy mortgage-backed securities they guaranteed, to boost the housing market.

I wanted to cut through all the complex finance and get to the heart of our actions and what they meant for Americans and their families. The GSEs were so big and so interwoven into the fabric of the financial system that a failure of either would mean grave distress throughout the world.

"This turmoil," I said, "would directly and negatively impact household wealth: from family budgets, to home values, to savings for college and retirement. A failure would affect the ability of Americans to get home loans, auto loans, and other consumer credit and business finance. And a failure would be harmful to economic growth and job creation."

It would also have major international financial ramifications.

Among the many financial leaders I spoke to that day were my old friends Zhou Xiaochuan, the head of the central bank of China, and Wang Qishan, vice premier in charge of China's financial and economic affairs. It was important to relay what was going on to the Chinese, who owned a vast quantity of U.S. securities, including hundreds of billions of dollars of GSE debt. They had trusted our assurances and held on to this paper at a crucial time in a shaky market. Fortunately, I knew both men well, and we had been able to speak frankly to one another throughout the crisis.

"I always said we'd live up to our obligations," I reminded Wang. "We take them seriously."

"You're doing everything you know how to," Wang said, adding that the Chinese would continue to hold their positions. He congratulated me on our moves but struck a cautious note: "I know you think this may end all of your problems, but it may not be over yet."

Still, that Sunday afternoon in my office, placing calls all around the world, I couldn't help but feel a bit relieved. We had just pulled off perhaps the biggest financial rescue in history. Fannie and Freddie had not been able to stop us, Congress was supportive, and the market looked sure to accept our moves.

I was alone, looking out the tall windows of my office, which faced south toward the National Mall. I was not naïve. I knew there were plenty of danger spots in the financial system and in the economy, but I felt a burden lift off of me as I looked out on the Washington Monument. I had come to Washington to make a difference, and we had, I thought, just saved the country—and the world—from financial catastrophe.

The next day, Lehman Brothers began to collapse.

CHAPTER 2

Sunday, May 28, 2006

I come from a line of strong women—smart, independent, plain-spoken women. When my mother learned that President Bush was going to nominate me to be Treasury secretary and that I had agreed to take the job, she didn't mince words.

"You started with Nixon and you're going to end with Bush?" she moaned. "Why would you do such a thing?"

It was the Sunday of Memorial Day weekend in 2006. My mother and I were in the kitchen of my boyhood home in Barrington, Illinois. My wife, Wendy, and I owned a home just down a shared driveway and we had flown in for the weekend to think things through—and to tell my mother.

The president was set to announce his intent to nominate me on Tuesday. I was scheduled to return to New York later that day to talk to the Goldman Sachs board and to meet with Lloyd Blankfein, my successor as CEO, on Memorial Day. That morning I had made the mistake of telling a good friend in church my news, but

I forgot to tell her that I hadn't yet told my mother. By the time I walked up to Mom's house, she was in tears.

"You're going to do what you're going to do," she said. "But I hope you don't get confirmed."

It was just after noon, and Mom was sitting in a wooden chair at the table in the breakfast room, staring through the window at a beautiful white oak in her sunlit yard. I couldn't remember the last time I had seen her cry. Her harsh criticism was also a first—usually she was a loyal, adoring mother who supported my decisions unstintingly.

My mother's feelings marked a dramatic shift from my youth. Staunch Republicans, she and my father had been delighted when, in my first job after business school, I went to work at the Pentagon and later in Richard Nixon's White House. But after Watergate, and as she got older—and especially after my dad passed away in 1995—my mother had become a lot more liberal, particularly in her views about women's and environmental issues. Republicans irritated her on the subject of abortion. She began to support various Democratic candidates, hated the war in Iraq, and was very anti–George W. Bush.

She wasn't alone in my family. Wendy, a college classmate and supporter of Hillary Clinton's, vehemently opposed my taking the job, as did our son, Merritt. Only our daughter, Amanda, the most liberal member of the family, understood and supported my decision.

"Mom, I've been asked to serve my country," I said, doing my best to calm her down. "And that's what I am going to do."

"Well," she replied, unconsoled, "you'll be jumping onto a sinking ship."

I returned to New York on an afternoon flight. Wendy stayed behind to comfort my mom, then flew back a couple of days later. She remembers standing in front of a television monitor in O'Hare airport and watching in anguish as the president announced my appointment in the Rose Garden, with me by his side.

My mother did not take calls for 24 hours. Then, on Wednesday, when the press was filled with largely favorable coverage, Mom finally started answering the phone. It helped that the callers weren't saying, "How could your idiot son do this?" They were calling to congratulate her.

My mother inherited her grit and determination from her own mother, Kathryn Schmidt, who graduated from Wellesley College in 1914 and supported her family through the Depression with a catering business. She died when I was just six months old.

My mom, Marianna Gallauer, followed her to Wellesley, graduating in 1944. An athletic woman, she has remained active throughout her life—in community matters and in sports. She continued to downhill-ski at age 86 and, during baseball season, she drives herself into Chicago to watch the Cubs play at Wrigley Field.

She and my father, Henry Merritt Paulson, were married in 1944. I am the oldest of three children, followed by my brother and best friend, Dick, who is two years younger and worked as a bond salesman at Lehman Brothers before moving to Barclays. My sister, Kay, who is five years younger, is a residential real estate broker in Colorado.

My father also came from the Midwest. His mother, Rosina Merritt, grew up on a Wisconsin farm, a descendant of Wesley Merritt, the Civil War general and onetime superintendent of West Point. After receiving a master's degree in psychology from New York's Columbia University, she returned to Wisconsin to teach. My grandfather Henry Paulson attended school only through the eighth grade, but this son of a Norwegian immigrant farmer was a driven, self-taught man. He founded and ran Henry Paulson &

Company, a successful wholesale watch supply and repair business in Chicago that, at its height, supported a prosperous lifestyle: my grandparents lived in Evanston, outside of Chicago, and had a modest winter home in Palm Beach, Florida.

My dad wanted to be a farmer. He loved the outdoors, the land, and the wildlife, birds in particular. I inherited from him my interest in birds of prey. After graduating from Principia College in southern Illinois, Dad persuaded my grandfather to buy land in Stuart, Florida, and started a ranch with Brahma bulls down there just after World War II. My mom hated it. I was born in 1946 in Palm Beach while my parents were living on that ranch.

That year, during the severe postwar economic downturn, my grandfather's company fell on hard times. My father had to sell the ranch for next to nothing and return to Illinois to help his father manage a dying business. We lived in a small garage apartment in Winnetka for a few years before moving to a 75-acre farm in Barrington, a small town of some 3,500 people 40 or so miles from downtown Chicago. It was about as far as you could get from the city back then and still commute comfortably.

We always had horses, hogs, cows, sheep, and chickens, not to mention my pet raccoon and crow. I spent a lot of time doing chores—milking cows, mucking out stalls, baling hay. We churned cream for butter, drank milk from our cows. We put up food for the winter, butchering the chickens, hogs, and sheep. Mom froze vegetables from the garden.

My father had a fierce work ethic; he was industrious and thrifty. From the time I was very young, I understood that you didn't lie around in bed in the morning. You didn't stay in the shower for more than a couple of minutes. You got up; you worked; you were useful.

At one point, when I was nine or ten years old and the family was barely scraping by, Dad decided he'd cut our hair himself and mail-ordered a pair of clippers. He did such a bad job that he left bare patches on our scalps, then he filled in the bald spots with pencil and said no one would notice. It took several haircuts until Dad became proficient. These traumatized my brother, but I was largely indifferent to my physical appearance and to what I wore—a lack of fashion sense that I have not outgrown.

Real happiness, my father liked to say, came not from anything that was given to you, or that was easy to get. It came from striving to accomplish things and then accomplishing them. You had to do things right. If you left grass tufts sticking up when you mowed the lawn, you had to do it again.

But my father wasn't all work and no play. He helped set up an extensive network of riding trails in the village, convincing farmers in the neighborhood to put up gates on their fields to let us go through on our horses. My parents took up skiing when they thought that my brother and sister and I might have an interest in it. I lived for the outdoors—and especially for fishing. My parents indulged this passion by taking us on wilderness canoe trips with difficult portages through Canada's Quetico Provincial Park, just above Ely, Minnesota. (Not that this meant extravagance: my father once told me proudly that we spent less on our annual two-week trip than it would have cost to live at home.) Wendy joined us the summer before we were married, and later we brought our kids along on the canoe trips with Mom and Dad.

In 1958, just before I started seventh grade, my parents decided we were land rich but cash poor, so they sold the farm and moved us to a smaller place a little farther out of town. On our 15 acres, we had a barn, seven horses, and a big vegetable garden, but no more livestock. We had to buy our chickens and beef and milk in the supermarket like everyone else, though we still ate the vegetables that we grew.

I went to local town schools and then Barrington High. As a boy,

I was very goal oriented. It's what Wendy calls my gold-star mentality. I no sooner became a Boy Scout than I made up my mind to become an Eagle Scout, which I did, at 14. I switched my focus to school and excelled in football, wrestling, and my studies.

The idea of heading east to college came from my mom, who wanted me to go to Amherst. Its students wore coats and ties back then. Dartmouth College seemed uncouth to her, but I was recruited to play football there.

I loved Dartmouth. I made good friends on and off the football team—and my professors challenged me. I majored in English because I loved literature, and though I didn't like economics, I took several courses in it, as well as lots of math and some physics.

I did well in football, despite my size: I was a six-foot-two-inch, 198-pound offensive lineman, often outweighed by 50 or more pounds by opposing tackles. Our coach, Bob Blackman, was a superb teacher who trained many other coaches. We won the Lambert trophy as the top Division 1-A team in the East in 1965 not because we had the finest athletes but because we were the best coached. As a senior I won the award for outstanding lineman in New England.

During two of the summers I was at Dartmouth, I worked at a Christian Science camp in Buena Vista, Colorado, called Adventure Unlimited. We climbed in the mountains, took float trips down the Arkansas River, and rode horses—I couldn't have been happier. It was also terrific preparation for the future. The first year I was a camp counselor and the next year a unit leader, responsible for the oldest boys, up to 17 and 18 years old, as well as counselors who were older than I. It was a chance to manage and to lead.

Christian Science has always been a big influence on me. It is a religion based on a loving God, not a fearsome one. An authentic confidence comes out of this. You understand that you have great capacity to accomplish good that comes from God. Humility is at the core of the religion. As the evangelist John writes: "I can of mine own self do nothing."

Christian Science is known to the public mostly for one aspect, physical healing, especially as an alternative to modern medicine and its drugs. There is, in fact, no prohibition against medical treatment. But I am comfortable relying on prayer because it has proven to be consistently effective for physical healing, for dealing with challenges in my career, and for spiritual growth.

In my senior year, several weeks before graduation, I met Wendy Judge, a junior at Wellesley, on a blind date set up by a friend. I was immature and behaved badly. We went to a Boston Pops concert, and she was not impressed when I folded my program into a paper airplane and sailed it off the balcony at Arthur Fiedler, the conductor. Wendy asked to be taken home early, and I thought I'd never hear from her again. But she called me up later and invited my roommate and me to come down for Tree Day, a Wellesley celebration of spring. So I had reason to think there was hope.

I graduated from Dartmouth in 1968, in the midst of the Vietnam War. As a member of the Naval ROTC program, I spent the summer before Harvard Business School on the campus of Purdue University in West Lafayette, Indiana. It was a strange place for the Naval ROTC—surrounded by cornfields with no water in sight.

Wendy and I started dating regularly my first fall at Harvard Business School. I did well enough there without studying too hard, and I spent much of my time at Wellesley. I was 22 and she was 21, awfully young, but we'd come to know each other very well. She was engaging and athletic, determined and competitive. We shared similar values and interests. Her dad was a Marine colonel, and she was on scholarship. A Phi Beta Kappa English major who loved the outdoors, she wore secondhand clothes, rowed stroke on the crew team, and was an excellent squash player. She earned all her expense money delivering linens and newspapers, and working as a tutor and a night watchman. She was extraordinarily trustworthy and knew her mind.

Wendy and Hillary Rodham Clinton were in the same class. They were friendly from student activities: Wendy served as senior class president, while Hillary was president of the student government. They stayed in touch over the years, and Wendy hosted one of the first fund-raisers in New York City for Hillary's Senate campaign in 2000.

My earliest exposure to official Washington came between my first and second years at Harvard Business School. Like all Naval ROTC cadets, I was meant to go on a sea cruise in the summer. Wendy was going to spend the summer after her graduation teaching sailing and swimming in Quantico, Virginia. I was very much in love and wanted to be near her, so I cold-called the office of the secretary of the Navy and ended up talking to a captain named Stansfield Turner, who later became CIA director under President Jimmy Carter. I proposed doing a study on the issue of the ROTC on Ivy League campuses. At the time antiwar protesters were burning down ROTC headquarters at schools across America. Turner agreed, and my sea cruise turned into a berth at the Pentagon. My big achievement that summer was proposing to Wendy and getting married eight weeks later, before beginning my second year of business school. I moved quickly even then!

I finished Harvard the following spring, and we moved to Washington, where I started my first job, also at the Pentagon. I worked for a unit called the Analysis Group, a small team that undertook special projects for an assistant secretary of Defense. It was quite a team. I worked with John Spratt, now chairman of the House Committee on the Budget, and Walt Minnick, who would be elected to the House from Idaho in 2008. Bill George, who later ran Medtronic, preceded us; Stephen Hadley, President Bush's national security adviser, followed.

One project—ironic when you consider my tenure at Treasury—involved analyzing the controversial loan guarantee for Lockheed Corporation, the big defense contractor, which had run into trouble developing the L-1011 TriStar commercial jet. John Spratt and I were working directly for deputy Defense secretary David Packard, the legendary co-founder of technology pioneer Hewlett-Packard. Driving to work one day, I was so focused on my first presentation for him that I ran out of gas on the George Washington Parkway. I left my car beside the road and hitched a ride to the Pentagon, only to discover that I'd left my suit coat at home. Spratt scrambled to borrow something that fit me. When I finally got my opportunity to brief Packard about Lockheed, he responded as I would today—with great impatience. He took off his glasses, looked out the window, and twirled them, while I went on and on. He didn't say anything. Wendy would say I still haven't learned the lesson. I like others to be brief, but brevity is not one of my virtues.

Packard left Defense in December 1971. Not long after, I landed a spot at the White House on the Domestic Council, which was headed by John Ehrlichman. I joined in April 1972. It was an extraordinary time. The Vietnam War was winding down, but the country remained polarized. The economy was under great strain—Nixon had taken the U.S. off the gold standard the previous year.

I hit the ground running, working on a variety of matters such as tax policy, minority and small-business issues, and the minimum wage. I worked directly for a smart lawyer named Lew Engman, who was a great mentor. When he went off to run the Federal Trade Commission after the 1972 election, I took his place—a big promotion.

In early 1973, I became liaison to the Treasury Department, which was then run by George Shultz. Then the effects of Watergate crashed down on us. I had worked well with Ehrlichman. He was an impressive, dedicated person who cared deeply about policy issues. He gave me good advice, too. I remember him telling me that it was important not only to do the right things, but also to be perceived to be doing them.

Ehrlichman warned me off certain people in the White House, particularly Chuck Colson, the president's special counsel.

"Nixon is a very complex guy," Ehrlichman explained before the 1972 election. "He's got a liberal side to him. That's Len Garment. He's got an intellectual side and that's Henry Kissinger." But, he went on, Nixon was also paranoid. "He's never had an election that was easy. He thinks the presidency was stolen from him by the Kennedys in 1960, and that in '68, if the campaign had lasted a couple more days, he would have lost. So he does not want to go into this election without a derringer strapped to his ankle. And that derringer is Chuck Colson."

I ended up, of course, being disappointed in Ehrlichman, who served time in prison for perjury, conspiracy, and obstruction of justice; Colson was convicted of obstruction of justice. Seeing men who were one day on top of the world and in jail the next taught me an enduring life lesson: never be awed by title or position. Later, I would frequently caution young professionals never to do something they believed was wrong just because a boss had ordered it.

I didn't spend a lot of time with Nixon, but I got along fine with him when I did. He liked athletes and enjoyed working with young people. I was not smooth, and I occasionally interrupted him out of eagerness to get my point in, but he didn't take offense.

When I was getting ready to leave my post in December 1973, I was called in to see the president. I went into the Oval Office, and Nixon and I had a brief chat. I'd had this idea to improve the quality of education by replacing property taxes in inner-city and blighted neighborhoods with a value-added tax, essentially a national sales tax, and using the proceeds to fund a voucher system. "Let me tell you about this VAT," Nixon said. "I liked the idea, but the reason I didn't go along with it is because the liberals will say it's regressive, which it is, but if they ever got their hands on it, they'd love it so much they'd never let it go, because it raises so much money so painlessly it would fund all these Great Society programs."

The repercussions of Watergate had given me plenty of time to look for a job. I chose Goldman Sachs because I wanted to work in the Midwest, and investment banking would give me the chance to work on a number of different projects at once. Goldman had a strong Chicago presence, and I was impressed by its people: Jim Gorter, the senior partner in Chicago, and Bob Rubin and Steve Friedman, who were young partners in New York. My time in government had taught me that whom you work with is as important as what you do.

Goldman wasn't on top of the heap then. It was not the leading underwriter or merger adviser that it would become; in fact, it was doing few deals. I spent a year training in New York before being placed in the so-called investment banking services unit: we were a group of generalists who learned all areas of finance and managed client relationships.

After that year, Wendy and I moved to Barrington, and we bought five of my father's 15 acres from him. Then we each borrowed from our parents to build the house we still call home today. It's a rustic house, nestled at the edge of a woodland on a hill looking out over a grassland. I cut the path for the driveway with a chain saw, built the retaining walls, and split most of the boulders for our stone fireplace. Wendy, who is mechanically inclined, installed the central vacuum system and built a large play area for the children.

Maybe it was because I was already balding and looked older than my 28 years that Goldman had me calling on clients early in my career, which was unusual. My experience in the White House interacting with Cabinet secretaries and the president gave me the confidence to deal directly with the chief executives of companies. Gorter, who ran Goldman's Midwest business, was very helpful. He told me that if I were patient and always put the client first, I'd come out ahead in the long run.

He was right, but it was very difficult, and I felt a lot of stress. Before, it had been enough to be smart and work hard—success would follow. Now I also had to convince other people to trust me, and every potential client was already someone else's. But I worked hard and built a big stable of Midwestern clients. I had to fight doggedly for each one. For example, Sara Lee, then known as Consolidated Foods, was a longtime Morgan Stanley client, but I called on the company with one idea after another, building our relationship through small transactions. Eventually we worked on more significant things. Along the way, I became close to the CEO, John Bryan, an extraordinary man whom I admired as an executive, as well as for his values: he had an active philanthropic life away from the office, and he became a friend and mentor to me. When Goldman went public, I convinced him to join our board of directors.

There are different ways to build relationships. It helps to socialize, but I liked to sell substance. I had a very direct approach that clients needed time to get used to. I wanted people to feel they'd learned something from me each time we met. I advised my clients on all kinds of things that, strictly speaking, had nothing to do with investment banking: from help with business strategies to advice on foreign competition and even insights on the quality of their executives. It was the beginning of the era of hostile takeovers and leveraged buyouts, and we advised many companies in the 1980s on how to defend themselves from unwanted overtures.

Long hours at the office can cause problems at home, and this was a period of great stress in my marriage. I'd come home too tired to want to do much with the children when they were very young. We couldn't afford to finish our bedroom, so we were living in an open loft, with the kids in rooms right next to us. I sometimes locked myself in the bathroom with *Sports Illustrated* to relax in quiet. Wendy made it clear I had to help out and get home earlier to give the kids baths, read a story, and put them to bed.

With Gorter's support, I began a pattern where I'd leave the office at 4:30 p.m., run for the 4:42 p.m. train, and be home at 5:25 p.m. After supper, I'd read to the kids. I had them trained so I could zip through a bedtime story very quickly. One night Wendy came in and urged, "Slow down and read with expression." I tried, but as soon as I did, both kids started crying: "No, no! Read like a daddy, not like a mommy." Once they were asleep, I'd get on the phone and start talking to clients, who'd say, "Good Lord, you're still in the office working?"

When I tell this story about work-life balance, people say: "Paulson, you SOB, you worked people harder than anybody at Goldman Sachs." Fair enough. But I always told folks at Goldman: It's not your boss's job to figure out your life. You spend so much time planning your work schedule and your career, you need to make that kind of effort to manage your private life, too. Learn how to say no. Remember, you are not going to get ahead, in any case, being a grunt.

These days, Amanda is the Midwestern bureau chief for the *Christian Science Monitor* in Chicago, and she and her husband, Josh, have two children. Merritt owns and runs the Portland Beavers Triple-A baseball team and the Portland Timbers soccer team. He and his wife, Heather, have a daughter.

Over the years I developed an interest in management. When Gorter moved up to run investment banking for Goldman, he prodded me to take over the Midwestern region. I chaired a couple of strategic planning committees, and in 1990, when John Weinberg retired as head of the firm, his successors, Steve Friedman and Bob Rubin, picked me to run investment banking with Bob Hurst and Mike Overlock. I was also asked to put together a strategy for growing our private-equity business and to oversee it. We had also decided to expand in Asia, and my New York colleagues said to me: "Chicago is closer to Asia than New York. Why don't you take that?"

I welcomed the challenge. Asia, and China in particular, was on the verge of the incredible boom we have seen in recent years, but we did almost nothing on the mainland then. My first meeting with China's senior leaders came in 1992, when Tung Chee-hwa, who was then running his own company and later became chief executive of the Hong Kong Special Administrative Region, took me to meet President Jiang Zemin. We were talking about economic reform, and Jiang told me that he had been reading about the U.S. economy, ticking off the names of companies he knew, like General Electric, Boeing, and IBM. Then he looked me right in the eye and said, "Assets equal liabilities plus equity."

I'm not sure that our country's leaders could have summed up a balance sheet as succinctly as this born-and-bred Communist. I flew back and told Rubin and Friedman that there was a huge opportunity in China and that I thought we should expand aggressively. From having virtually no presence there at all in 1992, we went to having perhaps 1,500 people in the country when I left Goldman in 2006. In that time I made about 70 trips to China.

The effort paid off in many ways—including some I couldn't have imagined before. It made Goldman the leading banking adviser in the world's fastest-growing economy, and it gave me a range of close relationships and contacts with the most senior Chinese leaders. These would help us enormously when I was at Treasury, especially during the financial crisis. Because of the high-profile nature of the work—generally privatizations of state-owned companies—I got very involved in our early efforts. These deals required a terrific amount of strategic and technical work as we prepared China's often bloated and creaky state-run companies for the demands of Western investors, who expected world-class business operations and sound corporate governance. The Chinese, for their part, were eager to adopt the best practices from the West.

During this time Goldman was growing rapidly all over the world and prospering handsomely. But we also had two big scares that made me reexamine my views on risk. Both episodes led me to take a greater role in the management of the firm.

The first came in 1994, when Goldman had a very difficult year, with big trading problems. The firm lost more than a hundred million dollars every month for a number of months. Our capital structure was also a big problem. When partners left, they took half of their money and left the rest in the firm, earning interest on it. That year, spooked by the trading losses, far more partners than usual decided to leave and "go limited," putting our capital under great strain. As long as we could keep the partners, the firm's viability was never in question. Even though the size of our balance sheet had grown dramatically, Goldman's leadership had always understood that if you were relying on wholesale funding, like an investment bank does, you had better have great amounts of excess liquidity—in layman's terms, more than enough cash on hand at all times to pay off any immediate demands from creditors.

Complicating matters, Steve Friedman, a mentor and friend who had been running the firm alone—Bob Rubin had joined the Clinton administration—decided to retire in September because of concerns about his health. Jon Corzine was named chairman, with me as vice chairman and chief operating officer. Out of our near disaster, we set up new oversight committees and installed far better systems, processes, and controls for managing risk.

The next scare came in 1998. That spring the partners voted to become a public company. A number of investment banks were making big bets on Russia, which defaulted. As these firms lost money, they raced to raise cash. They couldn't sell their Russian holdings, which had become worthless, so they started selling other investments, like mortgage securities, which drove down their value.

Even if you had a conservatively managed mortgage business, as Goldman did, you lost heavily. The markets began to seize up, and securities that had been very liquid suddenly became illiquid. The biggest victim of this was the hedge fund Long-Term Capital Management, whose failure, it was feared, might lead to a broad collapse of the markets. The investment banking industry, prodded by the Federal Reserve, banded together to bail out LTCM, but the pain was broader. I remember watching some of our competitors struggling for survival because they had relied on short-term funding that they couldn't roll over. Goldman made money—I think we ended up earning 12 percent on capital for the year—but we were hemorrhaging for a month or two, and it was frightening. We had to postpone our initial public offering, which had been scheduled for the fall.

Meantime, tension was growing between Jon Corzine and me. I had been named co-chairman and co-CEO that June, and, frankly, the pairing was never right. The structure wouldn't work for a public company, and I concluded I could not continue to work with Jon as co-CEO. I secured the support of our management committee, and in early January 1999, Corzine's friend and protégé John Thain, then our CFO, went to talk with him. Then I followed and told Jon that he would need to step aside.

"Hank," I remember him saying, "I underestimated you. I didn't know you were such a tough guy."

But it wasn't about being tough. It was about what I thought was the right thing for Goldman. Corzine stepped down immediately as CEO and left in May 1999, when Goldman went public, ending 130 years of partnership.

Like many Goldman executives, I worried about what it would mean to the culture and ethos of the firm to be a public company. We worked hard to maintain the cohesiveness and the frankness of the old partnership culture. I was determined to properly align my interests with those of our shareholders. During my final three years as CEO, my bonus was paid entirely in stock. With the exception of charitable giving (including donations to our family foundation), I decided that as long as I remained CEO, I would not sell a single share of the stock I had received in exchange for my partnership interest when we went public, nor would I sell those shares I received for my annual compensation. This emulated the pre-public Goldman Sachs, whose leaders were long-term owners with the vast majority of their net worth invested in the firm.

Those first years were trying ones. We had to contend with the end of the dot-com boom and the subsequent recession, the effects of the 9/11 terror attacks, and the onset of a bear market for stocks. But I think it fair to say that by any measure, we were successful. In the seven years between May 1999 and May 2006, just before I left, the number of Goldman employees (including affiliates) grew from nearly 15,000 to about 24,000. Net earnings of $5.6 billion for 2005 were more than double the pro forma net earnings of $2.6 billion of 1999.

Success notwithstanding, the financial industry had plenty of problems, and we had our share. Much of Wall Street, including Goldman Sachs, got tarred with the scandal over tainted securities research that came to light in 2002. I was concerned about such lapses in judgment, particularly at Goldman Sachs. I knew we could all do better, and I began to speak out.

I soon earned a bit of a reputation as a crusader or at least as a moralist. I wasn't a wild-eyed reformer, and I had never wanted a microphone. For me the issue was simple: in business, as in life, we should do not just what is legal but what is right. I hadn't heard anybody state this obvious point, which was what I tried to do when I gave a well-covered speech at the National Press Club in June 2002.

"In my lifetime, American business has never been under such scrutiny," I said. "And to be blunt, much of it is deserved."

I was later told that my speech was helpful in passing the Sarbanes-Oxley legislation. These reforms were enacted after a rash of corporate and accounting scandals, most notoriously the collapse of Enron, and created tougher standards for public accounting firms and the management and boards of public companies.

Every now and then I'd chide my colleagues about the dangers of the ostentatious lifestyles I saw among Goldman bankers. I'd get in front of the partners—I was never scripted—and say things like: "You have got to remember something. No one likes investment bankers. You make your life more difficult when you build a 15,000-square-foot house." Of course I also recognized that for some of our people, the desire to make money was what kept them working so hard and kept Goldman Sachs doing well.

I guess it's fair to say that the excesses of investment bankers were just an extreme example of conspicuous consumption in a disposable age. Wendy groused about this all the time—people buying things they didn't need, then casually throwing those things away. Wendy is an avid environmentalist: she carries trash off airplanes to recycle it. She still wears clothes from the early '70s and uses pots and pans that came from my parents' basement. We even use the same toaster oven we've had since we got married 40 years ago. Why wouldn't we? It works perfectly well.

Wendy and I share a love of natural landscapes and wildlife, which has led to a strong interest in conservation. We have been active in philanthropic activities, devoted to the stewardship of our natural heritage both here in the United States and globally. For me this has meant serving as chairman of the board of the Nature Conservancy, co-chairman of the Asia Pacific Council of the Nature Conservancy (where, among other initiatives, we worked to establish parks in the Yunnan Province of China), and chairman of the board of the Peregrine Fund, which is dedicated to protecting birds of prey around the world.

By the spring of 2006, Goldman Sachs was enjoying record levels of activity and income, its shares were at an all-time high, and I was not looking to make any change in my life when the possibility of my going to Treasury started being discussed. There were rumors that Treasury Secretary John Snow would be leaving, and one Sunday morning I woke to see a *New York Times* article with a picture of me and the American flag, suggesting that I would be the next Treasury secretary.

Not long after that, I got a call from Josh Bolten, President Bush's new chief of staff and a former Goldman executive, to gauge my interest in the job. Goldman was clicking, and I wasn't eager to leave. I told Josh I couldn't see doing it, and I used Wendy as an excuse: she did not want to go to Washington, and she was a supporter of Hillary Clinton's. I also wasn't sure what I'd be able to accomplish at the end of a second term.

Josh was persistent. He knew that I had been invited to an upcoming lunch on April 20 at the White House in honor of Chinese president Hu Jintao, and he invited me to meet with President

Bush then. "The president normally only meets with people when they want to accept," Josh explained. "But he'd like to visit with you privately in his residence the night before the lunch."

"Fine," I said. "I'll be there."

A day or so before I was scheduled to go down to Washington, John Rogers, my chief of staff at Goldman, asked me whether I was planning to accept the post.

"Probably not. I can't think of what he could say to persuade me," I said.

"You shouldn't meet with him, then," said John, who was wise in the ways of Washington. "You don't tell the president no like that."

I called Josh immediately and explained that I was not going to see the president after all because I had decided against taking the job.

Wendy and I flew to Washington for the Hu Jintao lunch, and I met beforehand with Zhou Xiaochuan, the Chinese central bank governor, at the headquarters of the International Monetary Fund. He asked to see me alone, and we went off to a room where no one could listen in and where there were no note takers.

"I think you should become Treasury secretary," he said.

"I'm not going to do it," I said, without going into the details. I was surprised at how well informed he was.

"I think you'll be sorry," Zhou replied. "I am someone who's spent my life in government. You are a public-spirited person, and I think there's much you could accomplish in the world right now."

The lunch at the White House was an impressive gathering. Still, I felt the president was cool with me when I saw him, as was Vice President Dick Cheney, with whom I'd had a good relationship. Someone in the receiving line who was well plugged into the administration said to me, "Hank, you'd have been a great Treasury secretary. And you know there may not be a chance for another

Republican for years. Do you know what you're doing turning this down?"

When the lunch was over, Wendy and I walked onto the White House grounds by the entrance to the Treasury. It was a gorgeous day, the magnolias and cherry blossoms in full bloom set dramatically against a crisp blue sky.

I felt awful.

I don't hide my emotions well, and Wendy could see I was distressed. She said: "Pea"—which is what she likes to call me—"I hope you didn't turn this down because of me. You know if it was really important to you, I would have agreed."

At the time, she thought that was a throwaway line.

"No," I said, "I didn't."

Shortly after, I went down to the Yucatán for a Nature Conservancy meeting, and I was in agony wondering whether I'd made a mistake. Almost everyone I'd consulted had advised against it. They would say: "You're the head of Goldman Sachs. You're the man; why go to Washington? The president has just two and a half years left. Look how unpopular he is. The Republicans are about to lose Congress. What can you possibly get done?"

And yet part of me knew I owed much to my country, and it troubled me to say no to the president when he was asking for help. My good friend John Bryan reminded me that "there are no dress rehearsals in life. Do you really want to be 75 and telling people 'I *could have been* Treasury secretary'?"

I called Rogers and said, "John, I can't believe I've done this."

He said, "Well, you may get another chance. They may come back."

And they did. I was in Germany on business in May, when Josh called again, and I agreed to meet him in D.C. on my way out to the West Coast for a Microsoft conference. We talked in a private suite at the Willard Hotel about what could be accomplished in the remaining years of the administration. We talked about what it was like to work with the president and about pressing policy matters like the need for entitlement reforms, as well as other areas where he thought I might be helpful, such as with Iran and cracking down on terror financing.

I turned to a number of people for advice. Jim Baker, the former secretary of Treasury and State, who had recommended me to the president and urged me to accept the position, said that I should ask to be the primary adviser and spokesman for all domestic and international economic issues. "That," as he put it, "really covers everything."

I was still struggling to decide. My epiphany came while I was flying out to the Microsoft meeting. As I thought through my decision, I recognized that it was simply fear that was causing me such anxiety. Fear of failure, fear of the unknown: the uncertainty of working with a group of people I had never worked with before and managing people I had never managed before.

Once I understood this, I pushed back hard against the fear. I wasn't going to give in to that. I prayed for the humility to do something not out of a sense of ego, but out of the fundamental understanding that one's job in life is to express the good that comes from God. I always believed you should run toward problems and challenges; it was what I told the kids in camp when I was a counselor, and I now told myself that again. Fear of failure is ultimately selfish; it reflects a preoccupation with self and overlooks the fact that one's strength and abilities come from the divine Mind.

I arranged to go back to Washington to see Josh again. As we sat in front of the fireplace in his office, beneath a portrait of Abraham Lincoln, I laid out my "asks." In addition to being the administration's primary economic adviser and spokesman, I wanted to be able to replace political appointees and bring in my own team, and to have regular access to the president, on a par with the secretaries of Defense and State. I asked to chair the economic policy lunch held at the White House. Josh rang up Al Hubbard, the National Economic Council (NEC) director, at his home in Indianapolis to be sure he was all right with this, and he was.

After Josh and I worked out these details, I went up to see the president in the residence. I found George Bush to be personable, direct, and very engaged. He was relaxed, having come in from a bike ride that morning, and had his feet up. We talked about a number of issues: how important it would be to address entitlements, and that perhaps having the Treasury secretary as opposed to the president lead this effort might help win support from both sides of the aisle. We talked about using financial sanctions to make a difference with Iran and North Korea. At the end of the hour-long meeting, I told him that I planned to accept.

From there, things went into overdrive. An announcement had to be made before the news leaked. I flew out to Barrington for the weekend to spend some time with Wendy, who was in despair over the impending loss of our privacy as we were fed into the Washington meat grinder, and to tell Mom the news. Then I returned to New York and called Lloyd Blankfein, summoning him back from a weekend with his family to discuss the developments. I asked Lindsay Valdeon, my trusted assistant at Goldman Sachs, to make the move to Washington with me, and she agreed.

I then called the board members and all 17 executives on the management committee to tell them, and asked Lloyd and John Rogers to fly with me to Washington for the ceremony.

Afterward, we flew out to Chicago for a previously scheduled partners' meeting. I woke up the next morning, and I was on the front page of every newspaper. It took my breath away. Even though the coverage was positive, it was unnerving.

The Senate voted to confirm me before the Fourth of July recess. There was only one hurdle remaining—my mother. I was concerned about what she might say when she met the president. She promised me that she would be on her best behavior.

I was sworn in on July 10, 2006. The ceremony took place in the Treasury Building's Cash Room, an extraordinary space that was designed in the 1860s to look like an Italian palazzo. It has marble floors and marble-clad walls that soar to an ornate gold-edged ceiling from which massive bronze chandeliers hang. Until it was closed for security reasons in the 1970s, the room had been open to the public: government checks could be cashed there and Treasury bonds purchased. My oath of office was administered by Supreme Court Chief Justice John Roberts with President Bush—and my mother—in attendance.

My mother suffered when Hillary Clinton lost in the 2008 Democratic primaries to Barack Obama; she wants to live to see a woman become president and the Cubs win the World Series. And she voted for Obama. Given the chance again, she probably still would not have voted for George W. Bush in 2000 or 2004. But after watching the way he worked with me, and having heard me report back to her about one issue after another, I can tell you this: she looks at the president a lot differently today than she did when I first went to Washington. So do Wendy, Merritt, and Amanda.

CHAPTER 3

Thursday, August 17, 2006

In August 2006, President Bush gathered his economic team at Camp David. The presidential retreat is a beautiful wooded spot with rustic lodges and mulched paths one and a half hours by car from Washington, in western Maryland's Catoctin Mountain Park. It had been five weeks since I had been sworn in as secretary of the Treasury, and I was still feeling my way as an outsider in a close-knit administration.

The economic outlook was strong. Stocks were trading just below their near-record highs of May. The dollar had shown some weakness, particularly against the euro, but overall the U.S. economy was humming—the gross domestic product had risen by nearly 5 percent in the first quarter and by just below 3 percent in the second quarter.

Nonetheless I felt uneasy. On the macro front, the U.S. was conducting two wars, the expenses from Hurricanes Katrina, Rita, and Wilma were mounting, and our entitlement spending kept growing even as the budget deficits shrank. This odd situation was ultimately the result of global financial imbalances that had made policy makers nervous for years. To support unprecedented consumer spending and to make up for its low savings rate, the U.S. was borrowing too much from abroad, while export-driven countries—notably China, other Asian nations, and the oil producers—were shipping capital to us and inadvertently fueling our spendthrift ways. Their recycled dollars enriched Wall Street and inflated tax receipts in the short run but undermined long-term stability and, among other things, exacerbated income inequality in America. How long could this situation last?

My number one concern was the likelihood of a financial crisis. The markets rarely went many years without a severe disruption, and credit had been so easy for so long that people were not braced for a systemic shock. We had not had a major financial blowup since 1998.

We arrived at Camp David late Thursday morning, August 17, ate lunch, and spent the afternoon hiking. That evening, Wendy, ever the athlete, defeated all comers, including me, in the bowling tournament. Though the retreat is well known for the foreign dignitaries who have stayed there, the atmosphere is quite casual. On Josh Bolten's recommendation I had even bought a pair of khaki pants—at the time, I just had dress slacks and jeans.

In the morning, I went for a brisk run, accompanied by the loud singing of Carolina wrens and, high up in the canopy, migrating warblers. I came across Wendy and First Lady Laura Bush, trailed by a Secret Service detail, heading off to do their birding. I was on my way to see a more exotic species of Washington animal.

After breakfast, the president's economic team gathered in a large wood-paneled conference room in Laurel, as the main lodge is known (all of Camp David's buildings are named for trees). Ed

Lazear, chairman of the Council of Economic Advisers, led off with a discussion of wages and later talked about pro-growth tax initiatives. Rob Portman, the former congressman then serving as the head of the Office of Management and Budget, dissected budget matters, while Al Hubbard, then director of the National Economic Council, and his deputy director, Keith Hennessey, took us through entitlement issues.

The president's operating style was on full display. He kept the atmosphere shirt-sleeve informal but brisk and businesslike, moving purposefully through the agenda with a minimum of small talk. Some people have claimed that as president, George W. Bush lacked curiosity and discouraged dissent. Nothing could be further from my experience. He encouraged debate and discussion and picked up on the issues quickly. He asked questions and didn't let explanations pass if they weren't clear.

I focused on crisis prevention. I explained that we needed to be prepared to deal with everything from terror attacks and natural disasters to oil price shocks, the collapse of a major bank, or a sharp drop in the value of the dollar.

"If you look at recent history, there is a disturbance in the capital markets every four to eight years," I said, ticking off the savings and loan crisis in the late '80s and early '90s, the bond market blowup of 1994, and the crisis that began in Asia in 1997 and continued with Russia's default on its debt in 1998. I was convinced we were due for another disruption.

I detailed the big increase in the size of unregulated pools of capital such as hedge funds and private-equity funds, as well as the exponential growth of unregulated over-the-counter (OTC) derivatives like credit default swaps (CDS).

"All of this," I concluded, "has allowed an enormous amount of leverage—and risk—to creep into the financial system."

"How did this happen?" the president asked.

It was a humbling question for someone from the financial sector to be asked—after all, we were the ones responsible. I was also keenly aware of the president's heart-of-the-country disdain for Wall Street and its perceived arrogance and excesses. But it was evident that the administration had not focused on these areas before, so I gave a quick primer on hedging; how and why it was done.

"Airlines," I explained, "might want to hedge against rising fuel costs by buying futures to lock in today's prices for future needs. Or an exporter like Mexico might agree to sell oil in the future at today's levels if it thinks the price is going down."

I explained how on Wall Street, if you had a big inventory of bonds, you could hedge yourself by buying credit derivatives, which were relatively new instruments designed to pay out should the bonds they insured default or be downgraded by a rating agency. My explanation involved considerable and complex detail, and the president listened carefully. He might not have had my technical knowledge of finance, but he had a Harvard MBA and a good natural feel for markets.

"How much of this activity is just speculation?" he wanted to know.

It was a good question, and one I had been asking myself. Credit derivatives, credit default swaps in particular, had increasingly alarmed me over the past couple of years. The basic concept was sound and useful. But the devil was in the details—and the details were murky. No one knew how much insurance was written on any credit in this private, over-the-counter market. Settling trades had become a worrying mess: in some cases, backlogs ran to months.

Tim Geithner, president of the Federal Reserve Bank of New York, shared my concern and had pressed Wall Street firms hard to clean up their act while I was at Goldman. I had loaned him Gerry

Corrigan, a Goldman managing director and risk expert who had been a no-nonsense predecessor of Tim's at the New York Fed. Gerry led a study, released in 2005, calling for major changes in back-office processes, among other things. Progress had been made, but the lack of transparency of these CDS contracts, coupled with their startling growth rate, unnerved me.

"We can't predict when the next crisis will come," I said. "But we need to be prepared."

In response to a question of the president's, I said it was impossible to know what might trigger a big disruption. Using the analogy of a forest fire, I said it mattered less how the blaze started than it did to be prepared to contain it—and then put it out.

I was right to be on my guard, but I misread the cause, and the scale, of the coming disaster. Notably absent from my presentation was any mention of problems in housing or mortgages.

I left the mountain retreat confident that I would have a good relationship with my new boss. Wendy shared my conviction, despite her initial reservations about my accepting the job. I later learned that the president had also been apprehensive about how Wendy and I would fit in, given her fund-raising for Hillary Clinton, my ties to Wall Street, and our fervent support of environmental causes. He, too, came away encouraged and increasingly comfortable with us. In fact, we would be among the few non-family members invited to join the president and First Lady for the last weekend they spent at Camp David, in January 2009.

My first months were busy and productive. Treasury would no longer take a back seat in administration policy making, waiting for the White House to tell it what to do. Shaping my senior team, I kept Bob Kimmitt as deputy but changed his role. Typically, deputy secretaries run the day-to-day operations of Cabinet departments, but as a longtime CEO, I intended to do that myself. I'd use Bob, who knew Washington cold and had wide experience in diplomacy and foreign affairs, to complement me in those areas. Bob would bring us expertise, sound advice, and a steady hand as the crisis came on. I was also fortunate to inherit a talented undersecretary for terrorism and financial intelligence, Stuart Levey, with whom I worked to cut Iran off from the global financial system.

The first outside addition to my team was Jim Wilkinson, former senior adviser to Secretary of State Condoleezza Rice and a brilliant outside-the-box thinker, as my chief of staff. Then I recruited Bob Steel as undersecretary for domestic finance; a longtime colleague and friend, he had been a vice chairman of Goldman Sachs and left in early 2004, after a 28-year career. It was an absolutely critical appointment given my forebodings and his intimate knowledge of capital markets.

There was plenty to do. Treasury needed desperately to be modernized. Its technology infrastructure was woefully antiquated. For one critical computer system, we depended on a 1970s mainframe. In another instance, an extraordinary civil servant named Fred Adams had been calculating the interest rates on trillions of dollars in Treasury debt by hand nearly every day for 30 years, including holidays. And he was ready to retire!

To save money, one of my predecessors had closed the Markets Room, so we lacked the ability to monitor independently and in real time what was happening on Wall Street and around the world. I quickly built a new one on the second floor, with help from Tim Geithner, who loaned us staffers from the New York Fed's own top-notch team. The Markets Room was my first stop many mornings. During the crisis I came to dread the appearance at my door of New York Fed markets liaison Matt Rutherford, who was on loan to Treasury and would come to deliver market updates. It almost never meant good news.

I'm a hands-on manager, and I tried to establish a tone and style that ran counter to the formality of most governmental organizations. I insisted on being called Hank, not the customary Mr. Secretary. I returned phone calls quickly and made a point of getting out of the office to see people. Typically, the Treasury secretary had not spent much time with the heads of the various Treasury agencies and bureaus—from the Bureau of the Public Debt to the Bureau of Engraving and Printing—which account for nearly all of the department's 110,000 employees. But I believed that face-to-face communications would help us avoid mistakes and improve morale. This would prove helpful later when I would need to work closely with people like John Dugan, the comptroller of the currency, whose office oversaw national banks and who reported to me on policy and budget matters. When the crisis struck, I knew I could rely on John's calmness and sharp judgment.

To my mind, Treasury secretary is perhaps the best job in the Cabinet: the role embraces both domestic and international matters, and most of the important issues of the country are either economic in nature or have a major economic component. But the Treasury secretary has much less power than the average man or woman in the street might think.

Treasury itself is primarily a policy-making institution, charged with advising the president on economic and financial matters, promoting a strong economy, and overseeing agencies critical to the financial system, including the Internal Revenue Service and the U.S. Mint. But Treasury has very limited spending authority, and the law prohibits the secretary from interfering with the specific actions of regulators like the Office of the Comptroller of the Currency and the Office of Thrift Supervision, even though they are nominally part of the department. Tax-enforcement matters at the IRS are also off-limits. Depression-era legislation allows the president and the Treasury secretary to invoke emergency regulatory powers, but these are limited to banks in the Federal Reserve

System and do not extend to institutions like the investment banks or hedge funds that play a major role in today's financial system.

The power of the Treasury secretary stems from the responsibilities the president delegates to him, his convening power, and his ability to persuade and influence other Cabinet members, independent regulators, foreign finance ministers, and heads of the Bretton Woods institutions like the World Bank or the International Monetary Fund.

I came to Washington determined to make the most of my position. The first order of business was to restore credibility to Treasury by building a strong relationship with President Bush and making clear that I was his top economic adviser. It also helped to make clear to the president that although I would always speak my mind behind closed doors, there would never be any daylight between us publicly.

I chose to define my role broadly. I held regular meetings with Tim Geithner and Federal Reserve Board chairman Ben Bernanke, knowing that in a crisis we would have to work together smoothly. I also tried to develop my relationship with Congress. I had come to Washington with no close contacts on the Hill, but the way I saw it, I now had 535 clients with whom I needed to build relationships, regardless of their party affiliations. I was fortunate to inherit an outstanding assistant secretary for legislative affairs in Kevin Fromer, who had great judgment and a knack for getting things done. I don't like briefing memos, and Kevin could tell me what I needed to know in two minutes as we rushed from one meeting to the next on the Hill. Afterward, he didn't shy from telling me what I could have done better. We made a good team.

On August 2, I'd met for the first time with the President's Working Group on Financial Markets (PWG), in the large conference room across the hall from my office. Led by the secretary of the Treasury, the PWG included the chairs of the Federal Reserve Board, the Securities and Exchange Commission (SEC), and the Commodity Futures Trading Commission. It had been formed after the 1987 market crash to make policy recommendations but had functioned more or less ceremonially. What little preparatory work was done was handled at a very junior staff level. The agencies were competitive and didn't share information with one another. Meetings were brief, with no staff presentation, and held on an ad hoc basis.

I decided to change that. I added Tim Geithner to our group of principals, reasoning that the New York Fed would be at the forefront of fighting any crisis. I also asked John Dugan to attend the meetings, because the OCC played a major role as a regulator of the largest banks. I was determined to form a cohesive group with close working relationships—it would be critical to how we performed in a crisis.

We scheduled meetings every four to six weeks and put these on the calendar a year in advance. Before long we were clicking, sharing information and developing substantive agendas. Meetings ran three hours and were well organized, with detailed presentations, including a memorable one by the New York Fed on how various financial institutions were managing risk.

Early on we focused on the issues of over-the-counter derivatives and leverage in the system. We homed in on hedge funds. As of February 2006, the SEC had begun requiring them to register as investment advisers, subjecting some to regulatory scrutiny for the first time (others had already volunteered to be regulated). Then in June a federal appeals court had overturned that rule.

The PWG focused on auditing the relationship between the hedge funds and the regulated institutions that, among other services, financed them. In February 2007 we would release a report calling for greater transparency from hedge funds and recommending they follow a set of best-practice management and investing principles. A year later we proposed that the biggest funds, which posed a risk to the system, be required to have a federal charter or license.

In preparation for the PWG meetings, Treasury staff, under the direction of Tony Ryan, assistant secretary for financial markets, studied scenarios that included the failure of a major bank, the blowup of an investment bank, and a spike in oil prices. They had originally planned to conduct tabletop exercises on the failure of a government-sponsored enterprise like Fannie Mae and the collapse of the dollar, but decided against doing so for fear that word might leak to the press, leading the public to believe we thought these scenarios imminent.

When I accepted the job at Treasury, I told President Bush that I wanted to help manage our economic relationship with China. To be successful, we needed to involve the key policy makers of both countries, and I knew I could assist the administration, given my years of experience in China. Launched in September 2006, the Strategic Economic Dialogue (SED) brought together the most senior leaders of both countries to focus on long-term economic matters such as economic imbalances, trade, investment, finance, energy, and the environment. I led the U.S. side, while the feisty vice premier Wu Yi (followed in 2008 by the very able Wang Qishan) represented China.

The SED's success is one of the achievements I am most proud of, and I am delighted to see it continued by the Obama administration. By focusing on our bilateral strategic relationship, the SED kept our dealings with the Chinese on an even keel through a wave of food- and product-safety scares. And when the financial crisis erupted, the relationships we had built and strengthened with Chinese officials helped us to maintain confidence in our system. That was crucial, given China's vast holdings of U.S. debt.

Though I took an expansive view of my position, I took care not to run roughshod over other Cabinet secretaries' turf. I well remember Steve Hadley, the president's national security adviser, cautioning me that I needed to be properly deferential to Condoleezza Rice. "Her first concern," he said, "will be that you can't have two secretaries of State, one for economics and one for everything else."

When I told Condi about my ideas for the SED, I made the case that a strong economic relationship would help her in her foreign policy leadership role. I made clear to her, "There's one secretary of State. That's you. I just want to coordinate and work with you, and help you achieve what you want to achieve."

Condi and I hit it off from the start. I'd met her when she was the provost at Stanford University and I was CEO at Goldman Sachs. Former secretary of State and Treasury George Shultz, who was at Stanford's Hoover Institution, had called me and asked if I would meet with her. She was an expert on Russia and was interested in working for Goldman. Now, I hadn't seen the Russian financial crisis coming—none of us had—so I thought she might be a great asset. But she decided instead to join George W. Bush's campaign.

Condi and I had lunch my second day at Treasury. She knew the president very well, and she gave me great advice on how to relate to him, suggesting that I make sure to spend time alone with him. Condi is smarter and more articulate than I am. I'm no diplomat and I'm terrible on protocol—where to stand and that sort of thing—but I do know how to get things done. More than once she had to tell me, "Remember, you're number two in protocol, right after the secretary of State. Walk out right behind me."

In the early days, with Condi watching out for me, I was fine. But when she wasn't, problems sometimes arose. In 2007, President Bush hosted the nation's governors at a conference in Washington at the White House. Condi was unavailable, so Wendy and I were supposed to sit beside George and Laura Bush during the after-dinner entertainment in the East Wing. We got to talking with

California governor Arnold Schwarzenegger about environmental issues, and when the time came to sit down, Wendy and I took seats in the back of the room, leaving two empty chairs next to the president and First Lady. Finally, Bob Gates, the Defense secretary, moved over and took one of the vacant seats. Everybody was laughing, especially my Cabinet colleagues. As we walked out after the event, the president said to me, "Paulson, do you want to be a governor?"

But that wasn't my worst faux pas. President Bush hated it when cell phones went off in meetings. In January 2007, I was in the Oval Office for a meeting with José Manuel Barroso, the president of the European Commission. As dictated by protocol, I sat on the couch to the left of the president, beside Condi. My phone, I thought, was turned off.

We were all listening intently as the two leaders engaged in a pleasant discussion, when my cell phone began to ring. I jumped like I'd been stabbed with a hot stick. I patted myself down, looking first in my suit coat where I always kept the phone, but I couldn't find it. In my desperation I stood up and checked under the couch cushions in case it had fallen down there—no luck. It just kept ringing, while my mortification level rose. Finally, Condi figured out where it was. She pointed to my right pants pocket, and I turned it off as quickly as I could.

"Paulson," the president ribbed me later, "that's a three bagger: in the Oval Office; with a visiting head of state; and you couldn't find it." I never let it happen again.

I wish I could say that the offending phone call concerned a critical Treasury matter, but in fact it was from my son, who had called to talk about the Chicago Bulls.

No one has ever accused me of being too smooth. I come at people aggressively and tell them how I think a problem should be solved. I listen to anybody with a good idea, then I make sure that the best solution is adopted. While this approach worked well for me in business, I found that decision making is much more complex and difficult in Washington, particularly on Capitol Hill.

No matter what the problem, large or small, there is no such thing as a quick solution when you deal with Congress. Frankly, you cannot get important and difficult change unless there's a crisis, and that makes heading off a crisis quite challenging.

Working effectively with lawmakers is a big part of the job of a Treasury secretary, and although I knew it would be frustrating, I underestimated just how frustrating it would be.

We had some early successes in the international arena, staving off potentially harmful anti-China protectionist legislation and getting a bill that clarified the process for foreign investment in the U.S. But we stalled on a number of domestic initiatives, including the administration's attempts to reform Social Security and Medicare.

Fannie Mae and Freddie Mac, the mortgage giants, presented another difficult legislative challenge. When I first arrived in Washington, I was living out of my suitcase at the St. Regis Hotel at 16th and K Streets. Washington summers are hot and humid, but I enjoyed running around the National Mall, past the monuments and museums, weaving my way through the throngs of tourists. One day in late June 2006, I had just returned to the hotel from a run, dripping wet, when Emil Henry, Treasury assistant secretary for financial institutions, and his deputy, David Nason, showed up at my room to brief me on the two GSEs.

I was no expert on the subject. But the administration and the Fed had warned for years about the dangers these companies posed, and it didn't take a genius to see that something had to be done.

As I sat there dripping in my soggy running gear, Emil and David explained how Fannie and Freddie were odd constructs. Though they had public shareholders, they were chartered by

Congress to stabilize the U.S. mortgage markets and promote affordable housing. Neither lent directly to homebuyers. Instead, they essentially sold insurance, guaranteeing timely payment on mortgages that were packaged into securities and sold by banks to investors. Their charters exempted them from state or local taxes and gave them emergency lines of credit with Treasury. These ties led investors all over the world to believe that securities issued by Fannie and Freddie were backed by the full faith and credit of the U.S. That was not true, and the Clinton and Bush administrations had both said as much, but many investors chose to believe otherwise.

In this murkiness, Fannie and Freddie had prospered. They made money two ways: by charging fees for the guarantees they wrote, and by buying and holding large portfolios of mortgage securities and pocketing the difference—or, in bankers' talk, the "spread"—between the interest they collected on those securities and their cost of funds. The implicit government backing they enjoyed meant that they paid incredibly low rates on their debt—just above the Treasury's own.

The companies also got a break on capital. Congress required them to keep only a low level of reserves: minimum capital equal to 0.45 percent of their off-balance-sheet obligations plus 2.5 percent of their portfolio assets, which largely consisted of mortgage-backed securities. Their regulator had temporarily required them to maintain an additional 30 percent surplus, but that still left the GSEs undercapitalized compared with commercial banks of comparable size. Together the companies owned or guaranteed roughly half of all residential mortgages in the U.S.—a stunning $4.4 trillion worth at the time.

Oversight was weak. They had dual regulators: the Department of Housing and Urban Development oversaw their housing mission, while the Office of Federal Housing Enterprise Oversight

(OFHEO), an overmatched HUD offshoot, created in 1992, kept watch on their finances.

In short, Fannie and Freddie were disasters waiting to happen. They were extreme examples of a broader problem that was soon to become all too evident—very big financial institutions with too much leverage and lax regulation.

But change was hard to come by. The GSEs wielded incredible power on the Hill thanks in no small part to their long history of employing—and enriching—Washington insiders as they cycled in and out of government. After accounting scandals had forced both GSEs to restate years of earnings, their CEOs were booted, and House and Senate efforts at reform broke down in a dispute over how to manage the size and composition of the GSEs' portfolios. These had been expanding rapidly and moving into dicier assets—exposing Fannie and Freddie to greater risk.

Answering one of my many questions, Nason pointed out a simple fact: "Two-thirds of their revenue comes from their portfolios, and one-third comes from the securitization business."

I didn't need to hear much more than that. "That's why this is next to impossible to get done," I said. Their boards had a fiduciary duty to resist giving up two-thirds of their profit, and they would.

The administration, I concluded, had to be more flexible to accomplish any meaningful reform. My idea was to work off a bill that had passed the House the previous year by a three-to-one margin. It would have established a new entity, the Federal Housing Finance Agency, and given it powers, equal to those of banking regulators, to oversee Fannie's and Freddie's portfolios.

This House bill had passed with bipartisan support, and I was convinced we could negotiate tougher standards. The White House, however, had opposed it. Convinced that Fannie and Freddie were simply too powerful for their regulator to control, it wanted Congress to write clear statutes limiting the investment portfolios. The administration's thinking was aligned with a Republican-backed Senate bill, which authorized a more powerful regulator and capped the GSEs' portfolios. But once the November midterm elections gave the Democrats control of both chambers, the need for flexibility became clear.

Fortunately, I had been forging relationships on both sides of the aisle. One was with longtime Democratic congressman Barney Frank of Massachusetts. With his gravelly voice and pugnacious demeanor, Barney is famous not only inside the Beltway but, for wildly different reasons, to fans of *The O'Reilly Factor* and *Saturday Night Live*. Barney's a showman with a quick, impromptu wit. But he's also a pragmatic, disciplined, completely honorable politician: he never once violated a confidence of mine. Secure in his seat, he pushes for what he thinks is right. To get things done, he's willing to deal, to take half a loaf.

Right from the start, he indicated that he was willing to work with me on GSE reform, hashing out the issues of portfolio limits and regulation. Even as we made progress, I ran into opposition inside the administration, leading to one of the worst meetings I would ever have at the White House.

On November 21, David Nason and I met in the Roosevelt Room with HUD secretary Alphonso Jackson and a large group of White House staff that included NEC director Al Hubbard, White House counsel Harriet Miers, and deputy chief of staff Karl Rove. Across the hall from the Oval Office, the Roosevelt Room serves as a daily meeting room for White House staff. With a false skylight and no windows, it's designed for serious business, and this meeting was no exception.

I explained my position that we should be willing to negotiate on the GSEs, then we went around the table to get people's opinions. Hubbard declined to declare himself, but everybody else was dead set against my approach. I was used to dissent and debate, but I couldn't remember the last time everyone in the room had opposed me on an issue. I found this frustrating in the extreme. They were right on principle, but if we didn't compromise, there would be no reform.

My response, more or less, was a bit petulant: "I know better than all of you on this. I'm going to send a memo to the president."

I drafted my memo and sent it around. Rove protested that it was disrespectful of the administration's no-compromise position, and he offered to help me rewrite it over Thanksgiving weekend. I swallowed my pride and accepted. In any event, Rove made clear that I would get my way.

"You're going to win this because the president will not want to undercut his new Treasury secretary," he said quietly.

A few days later, on the Sunday after Thanksgiving, I attended a meeting with President Bush in his residence. At the end, he took me aside, handed the memo back to me, and said simply, "Hank, that's why I brought you here. You go do it."

We didn't get a bill passed in the lame-duck session, but Barney made good on his promise to honor the agreements we'd reached after the new Congress came in the following year. By the end of our negotiations in late May, we had pushed a far-from-perfect bill through the House. But our efforts went nowhere in the Senate. The new Banking Committee chairman, Chris Dodd, was running for president so for all practical purposes, the important committee business was put on hold, and the Senate did nothing on the GSEs.

I don't have a lot of patience for people who came out of the woodwork after we put Fannie and Freddie into conservatorship and declared: "Here's what I said before: I saw it coming." Anyone can make a speech pointing out a problem, but the way you solve that problem is by working hard, hacking it out, and, frankly, eating a little dirt.

I came to Washington determined to compromise when necessary to make change happen. But that is not the culture of our capital. It would take until July 2008 to get meaningful GSE reforms passed. By then it was almost too late.

Chapter 4

Thursday, August 9, 2007

The crisis in the financial markets that I had anticipated arrived in force on August 9, 2007. It came from an area we hadn't expected—housing—and the damage it caused was much deeper and much longer lasting than any of us could have imagined.

I was in my car on my way to the Federal Reserve when I got a call shortly after 7:00 a.m. from Clay Lowery, the acting undersecretary for international affairs, who told me that the European markets were in turmoil. Earlier that morning, continental time, BNP Paribas, France's biggest bank, had halted redemptions on three investment funds that held mortgage-backed bonds, citing a "complete evaporation of liquidity" that had made it impossible to value "certain assets fairly regardless of their quality or credit rating."

The action was disturbing, but it came with news that was even more alarming: Europe's credit markets had tightened dramatically, as banks hesitated to lend to one another. In response, the European Central Bank (ECB) had announced that it would make as much money available as European banks needed at its official rate of 4 percent. Euro-zone overnight borrowing rates, which normally tracked the official rate, had reached 4.7 percent. Within a couple of hours of its announcement, the ECB would reveal that 49 banks had borrowed a stunning total of 94.8 billion euros, or $130 billion. That was more than the central bank had lent after the 9/11 attacks.

I sped on to my scheduled breakfast with Ben Bernanke. I was eager to see him—we'd skipped the previous week's breakfast since I had only just returned from China. Before I'd come to Washington, I'd hardly known Ben, but I liked him immediately, and soon after I settled in at Treasury, he and I began to meet for breakfast every week. It was such an established routine, and I'm enough of a creature of habit, that when I arrived at the Fed I could count on seeing, already set out for me, a bowl of oatmeal along with glasses of orange juice, ice water, and Diet Coke.

In the year I'd been in government, Ben and I had developed a special bond. Though we shared some common interests, such as a love of baseball, our relationship was 95 percent business. What made it special was our complete candor—laying all the cards on the table, determining where we had differences, and talking very directly about them. I kept Ben abreast of what I saw happening, passing along to him any market color I picked up from my conversations with senior bankers in the U.S. and around the world, including difficulties we'd begun to see in July with funding based on the London Interbank Offered Rate (LIBOR).

By law, the Federal Reserve operates independently of the Treasury Department. Though we took care to observe this separation, Ben, Tim Geithner, and I developed a spirit of teamwork that allowed us to talk continually throughout the oncoming crisis without compromising the Fed's independence.

Ben was always willing to cooperate and a pleasure to work with.

He is, easily, one of the most brilliant people I've ever known, astonishingly articulate in his spoken word and in his writing. I read carefully his speeches—on a wide range of subjects, from income inequality to globalization. And he was kind enough to look over some of my speeches before I gave them. He explained complex issues clearly; a chat with him was like a graduate school seminar.

Ben shared my concern with the developments in Europe. We agreed to keep our staffs in close contact, while I would talk directly to bankers and relay to Ben what they thought of the problem. That morning the Fed loaned $24 billion to banks via the New York Fed; on Friday it followed with an additional $38 billion even as the ECB lent out another 61 billion euros, or $83.4 billion.

When I returned to my office, I found Treasury on full alert. Bob Steel, the undersecretary for domestic finance, briefed me on the markets and possible responses. Keith Hennessey phoned from the White House to find out what was going on. I immediately started making calls to see how Wall Street was responding: Dick Fuld at Lehman, Stan O'Neal at Merrill Lynch, Steve Schwarzman at Blackstone, and Lloyd Blankfein at Goldman Sachs. All these CEOs were on edge. I also called Tim Geithner and Chris Cox, chairman of the Securities and Exchange Commission.

Throughout the crisis, in fact, I would keep in constant touch with Wall Street CEOs, while Bob Steel and other members of my team talked with traders, investors, and bankers around the world. To know what was really going on, we had to get behind the numbers we monitored on Bloomberg screens. We knew, of course, that we were dealing with self-interested parties, but getting this practical market knowledge was absolutely essential.

Beginning that morning, we went into high gear. Bob Hoyt, our general counsel, asked his team in the legal department to begin examining the statutes and historical precedents to see what authorities the Treasury—or other agencies—might have to deal with market emergencies. Earlier in the summer I'd asked Bob Steel to begin developing solutions for our mortgage problems, though at the time we didn't realize how far-reaching those problems would become. Now I asked him to speed up his efforts. On Monday, after a long weekend of work, Bob and I would lay out the problem in detail to the president, agreeing to roll out a plan of action by Labor Day.

It was pretty clear from what I gleaned from my conversations that the market was in for a bad patch. That Friday, the Dow Jones Industrial Average, which had passed 14,000 for the first time in mid-July, fell nearly 400 points, its second-biggest one-day drop in five years. I could sense a big storm coming.

In retrospect, the crisis that struck in August 2007 had been building for years. Structural differences in the economies of the world had led to what analysts call "imbalances" that created massive and destabilizing cross-border capital flows. In short, we were living beyond our means—on borrowed money and borrowed time.

The dangers for the U.S. economy had been obscured by an unprecedented housing boom, fed in part by the low interest rates that helped us recover from the downturn that followed the bursting of the late-'90s technology bubble and the impact of the 9/11 attacks. The housing bubble was driven by a big increase in loans to less creditworthy, or subprime, borrowers that lifted homeownership rates to historic levels. By the time I took office in July 2006, fully 69 percent of U.S. households owned their own homes, up from 64 percent in 1994. Subprime loans had soared from 5 percent of total mortgage originations in 1994 to roughly 20 percent by July 2006.

Encouraging high rates of homeownership had long been a cornerstone of U.S. domestic policy—for Democrats and Republicans alike. Homeownership, it's commonly believed, helps families build wealth, stabilizes neighborhoods, creates jobs, and promotes economic growth.

But it's also essential to match the right person to the right house: people should have the means to pay for the homes they buy, and lenders should ensure that they do. As the boom turned into a bubble, this disciplined approach fell away. Far too many houses were bought with little or no money down, often for speculative purposes or on the hope that property values would keep rising. Far too many loans were made or entered into fraudulently. Predatory lenders and unscrupulous brokers pushed increasingly complex mortgages on unsuspecting buyers even as unqualified applicants lied to get homes they couldn't afford. Regulators failed to see, or stop, the worst excesses. All bubbles involve speculation, excessive borrowing and risk taking, negligence, a lack of transparency, and outright fraud, but few bubbles ever burst as spectacularly as this one would.

By the fourth quarter of 2006, the housing market was turning down. Delinquencies on U.S. subprime mortgages jumped, leading to a wave of foreclosures and big losses at subprime lenders. On February 7, 2007, London-based HSBC Holdings, the world's third-largest bank, announced that it was setting aside $10.6 billion to cover bad debts in U.S. subprime lending portfolios. The same day, New Century Financial Corporation, the second-biggest U.S. subprime lender, said it expected to show losses for fourth-quarter 2006. By April 2, 2007, it was bankrupt. Two weeks after that, Washington Mutual, the biggest savings and loan in the U.S., disclosed that 9.5 percent of its $217 billion loan portfolio consisted of subprime loans and that its 2007 first-quarter profits had dropped by 21 percent.

The housing market, especially in the subprime sector, was clearly in a sharp correction. But how widespread would the damage be? Bob Steel had organized a series of meetings across government agencies to get on top of the problem, scrutinizing housing starts, home sales, and foreclosure rates. Treasury and Fed economists concluded that the foreclosure problem would continue to get worse before peaking in 2008. Of perhaps 55 million mortgages totaling about $13 trillion, about 13 percent, or 7 million mortgages, accounting for perhaps $1.3 trillion, were subprime loans. In a worst-case scenario we thought perhaps a quarter, or roughly $300 billion, might go bad. Actual losses would be much less, after recoveries from sales of foreclosed homes. They would, unfortunately, cause great pain to those affected, but in a $14 trillion diverse and healthy economy, we thought we could probably weather the losses.

All of this led me in late April 2007 to say in a speech before the Committee of 100, a group promoting better Chinese-American relations, that subprime mortgage problems were "largely contained." I repeated that line of thinking publicly for another couple of months.

Today, of course, I could kick myself. We were just plain wrong. We had plenty of company: In mid-July, in testimony before Congress, Ben Bernanke cited estimates of subprime losses reaching $50 billion to $100 billion. (By early 2008 losses from subprime lending had reached an estimated $250 billion and counting.)

Why were we so off? We missed the dreadful quality of the most recent mortgages, and we believed the problem was largely confined to subprime loans. Default rates on subprime adjustable-rate mortgage loans (ARMs) from 2005 to 2007 were far higher than ever; ARMs made up half of subprime loans, or about 6.5 percent of all mortgages, but they accounted for 50 percent of all foreclosures. Even worse, the problems were coming far more quickly. In some cases, borrowers were missing their very first payments.

Homeowner behavior had also changed. More borrowers chose to do the previously unthinkable: they simply stopped paying when they found themselves "underwater," meaning the size of their loan exceeded the value of the home. This happened quickly in cases where there was little or no down payment and housing prices were falling sharply. These homebuyers had no skin in the game.

The housing decline would have been a problem in its own right. It might even have caused a recession—though I doubt one as deep or as long lasting as what we would experience later. But what we did not realize then, and later understood all too well, was how changes in the way mortgages were made and sold, combined with a reshaped financial system, had vastly amplified the potential damage to banks and nonbank financial companies. It placed these firms, the entire system, and ultimately all of us in grave danger.

These changes had taken place inside of a generation. Traditionally, U.S. savings and loan institutions and commercial banks had made mortgage loans and kept them on the books until they were paid off or matured. They closely monitored the credit risk of their portfolios, earning the spread between the income these loans produced and the cost of the generally short-term money used to fund them.

But this "originate to hold" approach began to change with the advent of securitization, a financing technique developed in 1970 by the U.S. Government National Mortgage Association that allowed lenders to combine individual mortgages into packages of loans and sell interests in the resulting securities. A new "originate to distribute" model allowed banks and specialized lenders to sell mortgage securities to a variety of different buyers, from other banks to institutional investors like pension funds.

Securitization took off in the 1980s, spreading to other assets, such as credit card receivables and auto loans. By the end of 2006, $6.6 trillion in residential and commercial mortgage-backed securities (MBS) were outstanding, up from $4.2 trillion at the end of 2002.

In theory, this was all to the good. Banks could make fees by packaging and selling their loans. If they still wanted mortgage exposure, they could hold on to their loans or buy the MBS of other originators and diversify their holdings geographically. Pension funds and other investors could buy securitized products tailored for the cash flow and risk characteristics they wanted. The distribution of the securities beyond U.S. banks to investors around the world acted as a buffer by spreading risks wider than the banking system.

But there was a dark side. The market became opaque as structured products grew increasingly complex and difficult to understand even for sophisticated investors. Collateralized debt obligations, or CDOs, were created to carve up mortgages and other debt instruments into increasingly exotic components, or tranches, with a wide variety of payment and risk characteristics. Before long, financial engineers were creating CDOs out of other CDOs—or CDOs-squared.

Lacking the ability of traditional lenders to examine the credit quality of the loans underlying these securities, investors relied on rating agencies—which employed statistical analyses rather than detailed studies of individual borrowers—to rate the structured products. Since investors typically wanted higher-rated securities, the structurers of CDOs sometimes turned to so-called monoline insurance companies, which would for a fee guarantee the creditworthiness of their products, many of which were loaded with subprime mortgages. Savvy investors seeking protection often bought credit default swaps on the CDOs and other mortgage-backed products they owned from deep-pocketed financial companies like American International Group (AIG).

As financial companies scrambled to feed the profit machine with mortgage-backed securities, lending standards deteriorated badly. The drive to make as many loans as possible, combined with the severing of the traditional prudential relationship between borrower and lender, would prove lethal. Questionable new loan products were peddled, from option adjustable-rate mortgages to no-income-no-job-no-assets (NINJA) loans. By the end of 2006, 20 percent of all new mortgages were subprime; by 2007, more than 50 percent of subprime loans were originated by mortgage brokers.

All of this was complicated by the rapidly growing levels of leverage in the financial system and by the efforts of many financial institutions to skirt regulatory capital constraints in their quest for profits. Excessive leverage was evident in nearly all quarters.

This leverage was hardly limited to mortgage-related securities. We were in the midst of a general credit bubble. Banks and investment banks were financing record-size leveraged buyouts on increasingly more lenient terms. "Covenant-lite" loans appeared, in which bankers eased restrictions in order to allow borrowers, like private-equity firms, increased flexibility on repayment.

Indeed, I recall a dinner at the New York Fed on June 26, 2007, that was attended by the heads of some of Wall Street's biggest banks. All were concerned with excessive risk taking in the markets and appalled by the erosion of underwriting standards. The bankers complained about all the covenant-lite loans and bridge loans they felt compelled by competitive pressure to make.

I remember Jamie Dimon, the JPMorgan chairman and CEO, saying that such loans, made mostly to private-equity firms, did not make sense, and that his bank wouldn't be making any more of them. Lloyd Blankfein said Goldman, too, would not enter into any such transactions. Steve Schwarzman, the CEO of Blackstone, a dominant private-equity firm, acknowledged he had been getting attractive terms and added that he wasn't in the business of turning down attractive money.

Chuck Prince, the Citigroup CEO, asked whether, given the

competitive pressures, there wasn't a role for regulators to tamp down some of the riskier practices. Basically, he asked: "Isn't there something you can do to order us not to take all of these risks?"

Not long after, I remember, Prince was quoted as saying, "As long as the music is playing, you've got to get up and dance."

It was, in retrospect, the end of an era. The music soon stopped. Two of the CEOs at that dinner—Prince and Jimmy Cayne of Bear Stearns—would be gone shortly, their institutions reeling.

Leverage works just great when times are good, but when they turn bad it magnifies losses in a hurry. Among the first to suffer when housing prices fell were a pair of multibillion-dollar hedge funds set up by Bear Stearns that had made leveraged investments in mortgage-related securities that subsequently went bad. By late July both funds had effectively shut down.

Bad news came fast, from within and outside the United States. Spooked investors began to shun certain kinds of mortgage-related paper, causing liquidity to dry up and putting pressure on invest-ment vehicles like the now-notorious structured investment vehi-cles, or SIVs. A number of banks administered SIVs to facilitate their origination of mortgages and other products while minimizing their capital requirements, since the SIV assets could be kept off the banks' balance sheets.

These entities borrowed heavily in short-term markets to buy typically longer-dated, highly rated structured debt securities— CDOs and the like. To fund these purchases, these SIVs typically issued commercial paper, short-term notes sold to investors out-side of the banking system. This paper was backed by the assets the SIVs held; although the SIVs were frequently set up as stand-alone entities and kept off banks' balance sheets, some maintained contingent lines of credit with banks to reassure buyers of their so-called asset-backed commercial paper, or ABCP.

Financing illiquid assets like real estate with short-term borrowings has long been a recipe for disaster, as the savings and loan crisis of the 1980s and early 1990s demonstrated. But by 2007, several dozen SIVs owned some $400 billion in assets, bought with funds that could disappear virtually overnight. And disappear these funds did—as investors refused to roll loans over even when they appeared fully collateralized. The banks like Citi that stood behind the SIVs now faced a huge potential drain on their capital at just the moment they had to contend with a liquidity crunch.

SIVs weren't the only issuers of asset-backed commercial paper. Other entities that invested in debt securities relied on that market—as did a number of specialized mortgage lenders, which lacked access to the retail deposits of their commercial bank rivals. They were all part of a shadow banking market that had grown quickly and out of the sight of regulators. By 2007, some $1.2 trillion in asset-backed commercial paper was outstanding.

These issuers had found willing buyers in pension funds, money market funds, and other institutional investors eager to pick up a little yield over, say, U.S. Treasuries on what they considered a perfectly safe investment. But after the Bear Stearns hedge funds blew up, and with mortgage securities being downgraded by the rating agencies, the assets backing up the ABCP no longer seemed so safe. Investors stopped buying, a disaster for investment funds that owned longer-term hard-to-sell securities.

IKB Deutsche Industriebank, a German lender that specialized in lending to midsize industrial firms, discovered this in late July 2007 when an SIV it ran was having difficulty rolling over its commercial paper. The German government stepped in and organized a bank-led 3.5 billion-euro ($4.8 billion) rescue. As we watched LIBOR-based funding tighten, we began to wonder if European banks were in as good a shape as they had been claiming.

Then on August 6, attention switched back to the U.S. when American Home Mortgage Investment Corporation, a midsize mortgage lender, filed for bankruptcy, unable to sell its commercial paper. The market was becoming increasingly unsettled. With mortgage-related paper plunging in value—the triple-A portion of the ABX index hit 45 percent of face value in late July—and, with no buyers for asset-backed commercial paper, the securitization business ground to a halt, even as banks began to shy away from lending to one another, driving LIBOR lending rates up.

Part of the problem was in the nature of these shadow banking markets: their lack of transparency made it impossible for investors to judge the value of what they were invested in, whether an SIV or a CDO or a CDO-squared. Perhaps only one-third of the $400 billion in SIV assets were mortgage-related, but investors had no way of knowing precisely what was owned by the SIV they were lending to or had purchased a piece of.

It was, as Bob Steel memorably described it, the financial version of mad cow disease: only a small portion of the available beef supply may be affected, but the infection is so deadly that consumers avoid all beef. Just so, investors shunned anything they thought might be infected with toxic mortgage paper. In practical terms this meant that very solid borrowers—from the Children's Hospital of Pittsburgh to the New Jersey Turnpike Authority—could see their normal funding sources evaporate.

Despite the actions of the ECB and the Fed, markets relentlessly tightened. By August 15, Countrywide Financial Corporation, the biggest U.S. mortgage originator, had run into trouble. It had funded its loans in an obscure market known as the repurchase, or repo, market, where it could essentially borrow on a secured basis. Suddenly its counterparties were shunning it. On the following day, it announced that it was drawing down on $11.5 billion in backup lines with banks, unnerving the market. A week later, Bank of America Corporation invested $2 billion in the company in return for convertible preferred shares potentially worth 16 percent of the company. (It would agree to buy Countrywide in January 2008.)

On August 17, the Fed responded to market difficulties by cutting its discount rate by half a percentage point, to 5.75 percent, citing downside risks to growth from tightening credit. The central bank announced a temporary change to allow banks to borrow for up to 30 days, versus its normal one-day term, until the Fed determined that market liquidity had improved.

Investors ran away from securities that made them nervous—driving the current yield of 30-day ABCP up to 6 percent (from 5.28 percent in mid-July)—and began to accumulate Treasury bonds and notes, long the safest securities on the planet. This classic flight-to-quality nearly resulted in a failed auction of four-week bills on August 21, when massive demand for government paper so muddied the price discovery process that, ironically, some dealers pulled back from bidding to avoid potential losses. As a result, there were barely enough bids to cover the auction, so yields shot up despite the strong real demand. Karthik Ramanathan, head of Treasury's Office of Debt Management, had to reassure global investors that the problems stemmed from too much demand, not too little. In the end, the Treasury auctioned off $32 billion in four-week bills at a discount rate of 4.75 percent, nearly 2 percentage points higher than the prior day's closing yield.

The next morning, Ben and I briefed Senate Banking Committee chair Chris Dodd on the markets. Dodd had interrupted his presidential campaign for what appeared to be a publicity event. I was new enough to Washington to be put off by this request, and I was also frustrated that GSE reform had been held up during the year.

Ben and I met with Dodd in his office at the Russell Senate Office Building, discussing the markets and the housing crisis. The affable Dodd was friendly but criticized me to reporters afterward, questioning whether I understood the importance of the subprime mortgage problem.

In fact, I was watching the mortgage market more closely than the senator realized. It was becoming increasingly clear that the housing problems had crossed into the financial system, producing the makings of a much more ominous crisis. The sooner the housing correction ran its course, the sooner the credit markets would also stabilize.

The president had encouraged me to put together a foreclosure initiative that we could launch before Congress returned after Labor Day. On August 31, I stood beside President Bush as he tasked me, along with Housing and Urban Development secretary Alphonso Jackson, to spearhead an effort to identify struggling homeowners and help them keep their primary residences. We began by announcing an expansion of a Federal Housing Administration program and a proposed tax change to make it easier to restructure mortgages.

The administration's goal was to minimize as much as possible the pain of foreclosure for Americans, without rewarding speculators or those who walked away from their obligations when their mortgages were underwater. We knew we couldn't stop all foreclosures—in an average year 600,000 homes were foreclosed on. But we sought to avoid what we called preventable foreclosures by helping those who wanted to stay put in their homes and who, with some loan modifications, had the basic financial ability to do so. In practice this meant working with homeowners who held subprime adjustable-rate mortgages and who could afford the low initial rate before the first reset kicked their monthly payments up to more than they could afford.

Complicating matters, we learned that many foreclosures occurred for the simple, if appalling, reason that borrowers frequently didn't communicate with their lenders. Indeed, after mortgage loans were made and securitized, the only communication borrowers had was with the mortgage servicers, the institutions that collected and processed the payments. Fearful of foreclosure, only 2 to 5 percent of delinquent borrowers, on average, responded to servicers' letters about their mortgages, and those who did had trouble reaching the right person to help them. The servicers were not prepared for the tidal wave of borrowers who needed to modify their loans.

In addition, the mechanics of securitization impeded speedy modifications: homeowners no longer dealt with a single lender. Their mortgages had been sliced and diced and sold to investors around the world, making the modification process much more difficult.

I asked special assistant Neel Kashkari to take on the foreclosure effort. He promptly set up a series of meetings that included lenders, subprime servicers, counseling agencies, and industry advocacy groups like the American Securitization Forum (ASF) and the Mortgage Bankers Association, with the goal of getting the parties to improve communication and coordinate their actions to avoid preventable foreclosures. I told my team that I didn't want to hear of a single family being foreclosed on if they could be saved with a modification.

On October 10, HUD and Treasury unveiled the result of Neel's efforts: the HOPE Now Alliance, created to reach out to struggling borrowers and encourage them to work with counselors and their mortgage servicers. This sounded simple, but it had never been tried before. Notably, the program would not require any government funding.

We felt a sense of urgency. As bad as things were, we knew they would get a lot worse. We calculated that about 1.8 million subprime ARMs would reset from 2008 to 2010.

To deal with this problem, Neel worked with the ASF and the big lenders on ways to speed up loan modifications. Surprisingly, the servicers contended that resets were not the critical issue. Rather, a good number of borrowers had other circumstances that drove them into foreclosure; many were overextended with other debts—auto loans or credit cards, for example. As Treasury's chief economist Phill Swagel looked into the loans, he saw that often the original underwriting was not the sole cause of foreclosures. As he would put it, "Too many borrowers were in the wrong house, not the wrong mortgage."

Still, resets remained a concern, and we pushed the industry for faster loan modifications. Given the volume of problem mortgages, lenders could no longer take a loan-by-loan approach; we needed a streamlined solution. FDIC chairman Sheila Bair, who deserves credit for identifying the foreclosure debacle early, had proposed freezing rates. Treasury worked with the HOPE Now Alliance and the ASF to come up with a workable plan, and on December 6, 2007, I announced that thanks to this effort, up to two-thirds of the subprime loans scheduled to reset in 2008 and 2009 would be eligible for fast-tracking into affordable refinanced or modified mortgages.

My announcement was part of a bigger presentation that day at the White House in which President Bush laid out a program that would freeze interest rates for five years for those people who had the basic means to stay in their homes. The president also explained our outreach program, but this did not go off without a hitch: When it came time to announce the counseling hotline, instead of saying, "1-888-995-HOPE," he said, "1-800-995-HOPE," which turned out to be the number of a Texas-based group that provided Christian homeschooling material.

Despite this inauspicious start, many people called the hotline and were able to get help and keep their homes. But after all of our concerns about resets, interest rates ended up not being an issue once the Fed began to cut rates. By the end of January 2008, the central bank had slashed the Fed funds rate to 3 percent from 5.25 percent in mid-August.

HOPE Now received criticism from all sides of the political spectrum. Conservatives didn't like the idea of bailing out homeowners, even though HOPE Now gave out no public money. Many Democrats and housing advocates complained that we weren't doing enough, but much of this (from lawmakers, anyway) was posturing—until late 2008, there was no congressional support to spend money to prevent foreclosures.

HOPE Now wasn't perfect, but I think it was an overall success. Government action was essential because even a few foreclosures could blight an entire community, depressing the property values of homeowners who were current on their payments, destroying jobs, and setting off a downward spiral. The program helped a great many homeowners get loan modifications or refinance into fixed-rate mortgages—almost 700,000 in just the last three months of 2008 alone, more than half of them subprime borrowers. The Alliance grew to include servicers that handled 90 percent of subprime mortgages.

But the hard fact was that we could not help people with larger financial issues—those who had lost their jobs, for example. And as the credit crisis continued, I became concerned that a slowdown in consumer lending could lead to full-fledged recession. After investors stopped buying asset-backed commercial paper in the wake of August's credit meltdown, it was harder for people to get all kinds of loans—credit cards or loans for cars and college. The banks, forced to put on their balance sheets loans previously financed by asset-backed commercial paper, suddenly became stingy with new credits.

Throughout the fall of 2007, the markets remained tight and unpredictable. In mid-September, British mortgage lender Northern Rock sought emergency support from the Bank of England, sparking a run on deposits. Coincidentally, I had scheduled a trip to France and the U.K. just a couple of days later, flying first to Paris on September 16 to meet with President Nicolas Sarkozy and his finance minister, Christine Lagarde. I noted how the French leader took a political approach to the financial markets. In his view, political leaders needed to take decisive action to revive public confidence—and he wanted to scapegoat the rating agencies.

I disagreed. "The rating agencies have made a lot of mistakes," I told him. "But it's hard to say that all of this should be blamed on them."

Still, I had to give Sarkozy credit: he understood the growing public resentment and the need for government to take aggressive actions to satisfy it. And the rating agencies did need to be reformed.

Overall, I found the French president to be engaging, with a biting sense of humor. He joked with me about the many Goldman Sachs leaders who had worked for the government. Perhaps he should look for a job at Goldman in a few years, he said. I can only wonder what he might think today.

I had become more worried over the summer about the dangers posed by the hidden leverage of major U.S. banks. Though entities like SIVs ostensibly operated off balance sheets, the banks frequently remained connected to them through, among other things, backup lines of credit. Starved for funding, the SIVs would have to turn to their sponsoring banks for help or liquidate their holdings at bargain prices, devastating a wide range of market participants.

I asked Bob Steel, Tony Ryan, and Karthik Ramanathan to figure out a private-sector solution. They presented me with a plan for what we would dub the Master Liquidity Enhancement Conduit, or MLEC. (Because this was a mouthful, the press ended up calling it the Super SIV.)

The idea was simple. Private-sector banks would set up an investment fund to buy the high-rated but illiquid assets from the SIVs. With the explicit backing of the biggest banks, and Treasury's encouragement, the MLEC would be able to finance itself by issuing commercial paper. With secure financing to hold securities longer-term, it would avert panic selling, help set more rational prices in the market, allow existing SIVs to wind down in orderly fashion, and restore liquidity to the short-term market. We just needed to get everyone on board.

Industry leaders had a mixed response to the plan. Finally, on October 15, 2007, a month after the first meeting, JPMorgan, Bank of America, and Citi announced that they and other banks would put in upward of $75 billion to fund MLEC, but the announcement met with skepticism in the press. Critics predicted that the industry would never go along with the plan, and in the end, they were right. Banks dealt with the problem assets themselves by taking them onto their balance sheets or selling them.

The bad news mounted. Bank after bank announced multi-billion-dollar write-downs, losses, or drastically shrunken profits as they reported wretched results for the third quarter and made dire forecasts for the fourth. In the U.S., Merrill Lynch was the first big bank to be rocked. On October 24, it announced the biggest quarterly loss in its history—$2.3 billion—and CEO Stan O'Neal resigned less than a week later. Then Citi blew up. In early November, it announced it faced a possible $11 billion in write-downs on top of $5.9 billion it had taken the previous month, and Chuck Prince was out. (By year-end, John Thain had replaced O'Neal, and Vikram Pandit had been chosen to succeed Prince.)

The next day, November 5, Fitch Ratings said it was reviewing the financial strength of triple-A-rated monoline insurers. This raised the prospect of a wave of downgrades on the more than $2 trillion worth of securities they insured, many of them mortgage backed. Banks would be obligated to take losses as they wrote down the value of the assets on which these insurance guarantees were no longer reliable. With traders betting that the Fed would further slash interest rates, the U.S. dollar slid, and the euro and pound hit new highs.

From the onset of the crisis, I had leaned on the banks to raise capital to fortify themselves in a difficult period, and many of them took my advice, issuing stock and seeking overseas investors. In October, Bear Stearns reached an agreement with Citic Securities, the state-owned Chinese investment company, in which each firm would invest $1 billion in the other. This would give Citic a 6 percent stake in Bear, with an option to buy 3.9 percent more. In December, Morgan Stanley sold a 9.9 percent stake to state-owned China Investment Corporation for $5 billion, and Merrill Lynch announced that it would sell a $4.4 billion stake, along with an option to buy another $600 million in stock, to Singapore's state-run Temasek Holdings.

But not everyone was pulling in their horns. In October, Lehman and Bank of America committed a whopping $17.1 billion of debt and $4.6 billion of bridge equity to finance the acquisition of the Archstone-Smith Trust, a nationwide owner and manager of residential apartment buildings.

Even as this frothy deal closed, the economy as a whole was coming under increasing stress. Energy costs skyrocketed, with a barrel of oil approaching the $100 mark, and consumer confidence declined along with new-home sales and housing prices. The United States, long the engine of worldwide economic growth, was running out of steam. Volatility wracked the markets: between November 1 and November 7, the Dow dropped 362 points one day, rose 117 points five days later, then plunged 361 points the day after that, partly because of the weak dollar. By mid-November the dollar had dropped 14 percent over the preceding year against the euro, to the $1.46 level.

Many people around the world blamed the U.S. for the crisis—specifically, Anglo-American-style capitalism. Federal Reserve chairman Ben Bernanke and I flew separately to the G-20 gathering in Cape Town, South Africa, that month with one intention: to buttress confidence in the United States. The timing was fortuitous. The G-20 was an increasingly important group because it included both developed economies and such emerging-markets powerhouses as China, India, and Brazil. We were able to reach out directly and reassure the representatives of these countries, which accounted for just under 75 percent of global gross domestic product (GDP).

At the meeting Ben and I took pains to reassure our fellow finance ministers and central bankers of our commitment to a strong U.S. economy and currency. At the same time, we tried to make clear that the main problem was not the dollar but the financial system in general—under strain from the rapid global deleveraging and the threat it posed to our economy. We emphasized how focused we were on that problem.

Before I left Cape Town, I was fortunate to have a private breakfast in my hotel room with China's central bank governor, Zhou Xiaochuan, a charming, straightforward old friend and committed reformer. Our group was staying at a beautiful resort, Hôtel Le Vendôme, outside of Cape Town, and my room overlooked the sea and a golf course, where I'd stolen a few moments to go birding the previous day. At one point, Zhou and I stepped out on the balcony to take in the splendor of a South African summer morning.

I had been pressing the Chinese to move ahead with the liberalization of their financial markets by opening them more to foreign competition, but now Zhou told me that with the U.S. markets in disarray, China was not prepared to give us the capital markets opening we wanted. Zhou did tell me he was confident there would be progress in other important areas.

Not long after the G-20 meeting, I went to Beijing for the Third China-U.S. Strategic Economic Dialogue, and my deputy chief of staff, Taiya Smith, and I met with my Chinese counterpart, Vice Premier Wu Yi, ahead of the formal sessions. After months of negotiations with the Chinese, Taiya had arranged this special meeting so I could make one last push for raising the equity caps that limited the percentage of ownership that foreigners could hold in Chinese financial institutions. The Chinese had been under pressure from the U.S. and other countries to no longer maintain an artificially weak currency that prevented market forces from helping China rebalance its economy, which was overly reliant on cheap exports. Popular opinion attributed China's large trade imbalances and huge capital reserves to its currency policy, but this was only part of the story. The bigger factor, in my view, was the lack of savings by Americans, which translated into our massive levels of imports and overreliance on foreign capital flows. And because the Chinese managed their currency to move in sync with the dollar, other trading partners, particularly Canada and European countries, had begun to complain about swelling imbalances. I explained, as I often had, that a currency that reflected market reality was a key to China's continued economic reform and progress. It would alleviate mounting inflationary pressure in China, spurring the development of its domestic market and reducing its dependence on exports.

Wu Yi looked at me directly and said she could do nothing to change the equity caps at that point. However, she quickly followed up by saying that my arguments on the currency were more persuasive.

She said no more on the subject, but I knew that I would not be going home to Washington empty-handed. We had made great progress on food and product safety and on an effort to combat illegal logging. But most important, over the next six months I watched the yuan, which was trading at 7.43 to the dollar in December, strengthen to about 6.81 by mid-July. China's sudden flexibility not only benefited that country but would help forestall protectionist sentiment in the U.S. Congress.

On the financial side, however, the bad news piled up day by day. In mid-November, Bank of America and Legg Mason said they would spend hundreds of millions of dollars to prop up their faltering money market funds, which had gotten burned buying debt from SIVs. Although the public considered money market funds among the safest investments, some funds had loaded up on asset-backed commercial paper in hopes of raising returns.

Meantime, the credit markets relentlessly tightened as banks grew increasingly reluctant to lend to one another. One key measure of the confidence banks had in one another, the LIBOR-OIS spread—which measures the rate they charge each other for funds—had begun to widen dramatically. Traditionally this rate had stood at about 10 basis points, or 0.10 percent. The spread jumped to 40 basis points on August 9, and climbed to 95.4 basis points in mid-September, before easing to just under 43 basis points on October 31. But then the markets sharply tightened, anticipating big losses at major banks, which would force them to sell assets to increase their liquidity. By the end of November, the LIBOR-OIS spread had topped 100 basis points.

Faced with spiking interbank lending rates, the Fed on November 15 pumped $47.25 billion in temporary reserves into the banking system—its biggest such injection since 9/11. The Fed continued to take extraordinary steps in December to ease liquidity in the markets. On the 11th it cut both the discount rate and Fed funds rate by 25 basis points, to 4.75 percent and 4.25 percent, respectively. On the 12th it announced that it had established $24 billion in "swap lines" with the European Central Bank and the

Swiss National Bank to increase the supply of dollars to overseas credit markets.

The following day the Fed unveiled the Term Auction Facility (TAF), which was designed to lend funds to depository institutions for terms of between 28 and 84 days against a wide range of collateral. Launched in conjunction with similar programs undertaken by central banks of other countries, TAF was created to give banks an alternative to the Fed discount window, whose use had long carried a stigma; banks feared that if they borrowed directly from the Fed, their creditors and clients would assume that they were in trouble.

The first TAF, on December 17, 2007, auctioned $20 billion in 28-day credit; the second, three days later, provided an additional $20 billion in 35-day credit. Banks hungrily lapped up the funds, and on December 21 the Fed said it would continue the auctions as long as necessary.

While helpful to the financial system, such measures could not halt the broader economy's ongoing slide. When the White House first began to consider a tax stimulus, right after Thanksgiving, I hated the idea. For me, a stimulus program was the equivalent of dropping money out of the sky—a highly scattershot and short-term solution. But by mid-December 2007 it was clear that the economy had hit a brick wall.

I'm no economist, but I'm good at talking to people and figuring out what's happening. After speaking with a variety of business executives, I knew that the problems from financial services had spilled over into the broader economy. In mid-December, after I'd returned from China, I traveled around the country to promote HOPE Now. I talked with local officials, large and small businesses, and citizens in places hard-hit by foreclosures, including Orlando, Florida; Kansas City, Missouri; and Stockton, California. I called Josh Bolten from the road and told him to tell the president that the economy had slowed down very noticeably. Clearly, we needed to do something, for economic—and political—reasons.

On January 2, 2008, I met with the president, and he asked me to consult with Congress, investors, and business leaders so we could make a decision when he returned from an eight-day overseas trip. I'd had enough conversations with the president to know that he was prepared to move quickly and in a bipartisan way as long as the program was designed to have an immediate impact, which almost certainly meant transfer payments to those with low incomes. This was a touchy point for Republicans, but the president was not an ideologue: he wanted to see quick results.

During the first half of January, I made a number of outreach calls to both Republicans and Democrats on the Hill, consistently arguing that each side needed to compromise to create a program that would be timely, temporary, and simple, yet big enough to make a difference. The legislation, I stressed, shouldn't be used to further the longer-term policy goals of either party. The Republicans were reluctantly willing to go along with a stimulus plan if we didn't add things like increased unemployment insurance, but Democratic leaders believed that we had to address needs that could only be handled through traditional programs like unemployment insurance and food stamps. Still, I thought we could hold the line; House Speaker Nancy Pelosi wanted a deal badly enough to control the most liberal members of her caucus.

On Friday, January 18, President Bush called for a spending package of 1 percent of GDP, or about $150 billion, designed to give the economy a "shot in the arm" with one-time tax rebates and tax breaks to encourage businesses to buy equipment. I gave interviews all day to reinforce the president's decision. The weekend and following week, I knew, would be filled with negotiations with lawmakers.

On the following Tuesday I went to Nancy Pelosi's conference room to meet with the Speaker, Senate Majority Leader Harry Reid, Senate Minority Leader Mitch McConnell, House Majority Leader Steny Hoyer, and House Minority Leader John Boehner. Reid and McConnell agreed to let the House take the lead on the stimulus, and Pelosi—clearly hungry for a bipartisan achievement after a slow first year as Speaker—worked her tail off. She dropped demands for unemployment and food stamp benefits in exchange for tax rebates for virtually everyone, regardless of whether they paid income tax or not.

The combination of slumping financial markets and the growing macroeconomic concerns gave us a powerful impetus. Economic conditions had become so worrisome that the Fed, on January 22, slashed the Fed funds rate by 75 basis points, to 3.5 percent, in a rare move made between scheduled Federal Open Market Committee meetings. (On January 30, it would cut the funds rate by another 50 basis points at its regular meeting.)

On January 24—just two days after I first went to the Hill—Pelosi, Boehner, and I announced a tentative agreement for a $150 billion stimulus plan centering on $100 billion in tax rebates for an estimated 117 million American families. Depending on income level, the stimulus would give as much as $1,200 to certain households, with an additional $300 for each child.

Because the stimulus was a bipartisan effort, I had to swallow a few things I didn't like, including an increase in Fannie and Freddie's loan limit for high-cost areas, to $729,750 from $417,000. Nonetheless, the stimulus represented a huge political and legislative accomplishment, and President Bush signed it into law on February 13, after a remarkably quick two-week passage through the House and the Senate. And the Internal Revenue Service and Treasury's Financial Management Service did something that initially seemed impossible: they got all the rebate checks out by July. Some were sent out as early as late April, despite the crunch of tax season.

I hoped the stimulus would solve many of the economic problems. We believed we were looking at a V-shaped recession and assumed that the economy would bottom out in the middle of 2008.

The market difficulties had a decidedly global cast. At the G-7's fall meeting in Washington, I had begun questioning the strength of European banks; they used a more liberal accounting method than U.S. banks, one that in my opinion covered up weaknesses. In January 2008, a group of Treasury officials, including Acting Undersecretary for International Affairs Clay Lowery, traveled to Europe to get a better handle on what was happening in its financial sector. After visiting a number of countries, including the U.K., France, Switzerland, and Germany, they concluded that Treasury's suspicions were correct: European banking was weaker than officials were letting on.

On February 17, just a few days after President Bush signed the stimulus bill, U.K. chancellor of the Exchequer Alistair Darling announced that the British government would nationalize Northern Rock. The credit crisis had pushed the big mortgage lender to the brink of failure.

In the U.S., the markets continued to slip, troubled by oil prices, a weakening dollar, and ongoing concerns about credit. Over the week of March 3–7, the Dow lost almost 373 points, ending at 11,894—far below the 14,000 of the preceding October. That Thursday I traveled to California for a round of appearances in the San Francisco Bay Area, including a speech on March 7 at the Stanford Institute for Economic Policy Research. My talk centered on the U.S. housing situation, and I outlined our continuing efforts with HOPE Now and fast-track modifications, pointing out that more than 1 million mortgages, 680,000 of them subprime, had been reworked. In the question-and-answer period that followed, I fielded a query about whether I would consider guaranteeing mortgage-backed bonds issued by Freddie and Fannie. I sidestepped this, saying that the institutions needed reform and a strong regulator.

My audience included former Treasury secretary Larry Summers, who told me before the speech that he'd been looking into the GSEs. "This is a huge problem," he said. Working off public numbers, he had done some analysis that led him to believe they were likely to need a lot of capital. "They are a disaster waiting to happen," he said.

While I shared Larry's concerns about the GSEs, in my mind the monoline insurers presented a more immediate problem. They had become the latest segment of finance hurt by the spiraling credit crisis, and their troubles imperiled a vast range of debt.

Fitch Ratings had downgraded Ambac Financial Group, the second-largest bond insurer, to AA in January. The move raised concerns that rival rating agencies would follow suit, causing other insurers to lose their high ratings. That meant that the paper they insured faced downgrades, including the low-risk debt that local governments issued to pay for their operations. Forced to pay more to borrow, U.S. cities might have to reduce services and postpone needed projects.

The monoline troubles had spilled over into yet another market sector—that of auction-rate notes, which were longer-term, variable-rate securities whose interest rates were set at periodic auctions. The market was sizable—slightly more than $300 billion—and was used chiefly by municipalities and other public bodies to raise debt, as well as by closed-end mutual funds, which issued preferred equity.

The vast majority of the auction-rate notes had bond insurance or some other form of credit enhancement. But with the monolines shaky, investors shunned the auction-rate market, which completely froze in February, as hundreds of auctions failed for lack of buyers. The brokerage firms that sold the securities had typically stepped in to buy them when demand lagged. But faced with their own problems they were no longer doing so.

Although the monolines did not have a federal-level regulator, I had asked Tony Ryan and Bob Steel to look for ways to be helpful to Eric Dinallo, the superintendent of insurance for New York State, who regulated most of the big monolines and had begun work on a rescue plan. New York governor Eliot Spitzer also got involved, testifying on the insurers' troubles before a House Financial Services subcommittee on February 14.

I knew the governor from his days as New York State attorney general, and he called me on February 19 and 20 to discuss potential solutions. I saw him at the Gridiron Club's annual dinner, held at the Renaissance Washington DC Hotel on March 8.

This good-natured roast of the capital's political elite drew more than 600 people, including Condi Rice and a number of other Cabinet members. President Bush supplemented his white tie and tails with a cowboy hat and sang a song about "the brown, brown grass of home" to mark his last Gridiron dinner as president.

Wendy and I were glad to have a chance to chat with Eliot, whom Wendy knew from her environmental work, when he came up to the dais to speak to us. He was friendly and relaxed, and he looked like a million bucks as he talked to me about the monolines and thanked me for Bob Steel's help.

Looking back now, I realize that Spitzer must have known that he would be named within days as the customer of a call-girl service, and that his world would come crashing down. But that night he looked like he didn't have a care in the world.

CHAPTER 5

Thursday, March 13, 2008

I can't remember many speeches I looked forward to less than the one I was scheduled to deliver Thursday morning, March 13, at the National Press Club.

My purpose was to announce the results of a study of the financial crisis by the President's Working Group and to unveil policy recommendations affecting areas ranging from mortgage origination and securitization to credit rating agencies and over-the-counter derivatives like credit default swaps. We had worked hard on these proposals since August, coordinating closely with the Financial Stability Forum in Basel, which planned to release its response in April at the upcoming G-7 Finance Ministers meeting.

But our timing was dreadful. It seemed premature to suggest steps to avoid a future crisis with no end in sight to this one. As much as I wanted to cancel the speech, I felt that if I did, the market would have smelled blood.

I hurried through my brief remarks, preoccupied and impatient to get back to the office. It had been a rough week. The markets had taken a sharp turn for the worse, as sinking home prices continued to pull down the value of mortgage securities, triggering more losses and widespread margin calls. Financial stocks were staggering, while CDS spreads—the cost to insure the investment banks' bonds against default or downgrade—hit new highs. Banks were reluctant to lend to one another. The previous weekend there had been a banking conference in Basel, and Tim Geithner had told me that European officials were worried that the crisis was worsening. It was an unsettling confirmation of conversations I had had with a number of European bankers.

The firm under the most intense pressure was Bear Stearns. Between Monday, March 3, and Monday, March 10, its shares had fallen from $77.32 to $62.30, while the cost to insure $10 million of its bonds had nearly doubled from $316,000 to $619,000. Other investment banks also felt the heat. The next-smallest firm, Lehman Brothers, which was also heavily overweighted in mortgages and real estate, had seen the price of CDS on its bonds jump from $228,000 to $398,000 in the same time. A year before, CDS rates on both banks had been a fraction of that—about $35,000.

On the Tuesday before my speech, the Fed had unveiled one of its strongest measures yet, the Term Securities Lending Facility (TSLF). This program was designed to lend as much as $200 billion in Treasury securities to banks, taking federal agency debt and triple-A mortgage-backed securities as collateral. The banks could then use the Treasuries to secure financing. Crucially, the Fed extended the length of the loans from one day to 28 days and made the program available not just to commercial banks but to all primary government dealers—including the major investment banks that underwrote Treasury debt issues.

I was pleased with the Fed's decision, which let banks and investment banks borrow against securities no one wanted to buy. And I had hoped that this bold action would calm the markets. But just the opposite happened. It was an indication of the markets' jitters that some took the move as a confirmation of their worst fears: things must be very serious indeed for the Fed to take such unprecedented action.

On Wednesday, most of America found itself temporarily diverted from the markets' tremors when Eliot Spitzer announced he was resigning as New York's governor following a two-day riot of news coverage after he was named as a client of a prostitution ring. I know many on the Street took pleasure in his troubles, but I just felt shock and sadness. The Gridiron dinner where he had seemed so carefree just days before seemed an eternity ago.

I was too preoccupied to dwell on Spitzer's misfortunes. Not only did I have to prepare my own speech, but I'd also been advising President Bush on an upcoming address of his own. It was scheduled for Friday at the Economic Club in New York. The president hoped to reassure the country with a firm statement on the administration's resolve. We were agreed on just about everything except for one key point. I advised him to avoid saying that there would be "no bailouts."

The president said, "We're not going to do a bailout, are we?"

I told him I wasn't predicting one and it was the last thing in the world I wanted.

But, I added, "Mr. President, the fact is, the whole system is so fragile we don't know what we might have to do if a financial institution is about to go down."

When I stood at the podium at 10:00 a.m. that Thursday at the National Press Club, I knew only too well that the current system, weakened by excessive leverage and the housing collapse, would not be able to withstand a major shock.

To a room full of restless reporters I sketched the causes of the crisis. We all knew the trigger had been poor subprime lending, but I noted that this had been part of a much broader erosion of standards throughout corporate and consumer credit markets. Years of benign economic conditions and abundant liquidity had led investors to reach for yield; market participants and regulators had become complacent about all types of risks.

Among a raft of recommendations to better manage risk and to discourage excessive complexity, we called for enhanced oversight of mortgage originators by federal and state authorities, including nationwide licensing standards for mortgage brokers. We recommended reforming the credit rating process, especially for structured products. We called for greater disclosure by issuers of mortgage-backed securities regarding the due diligence they performed on underlying assets. And we suggested a wide range of improvements in the over-the-counter derivatives markets.

I finished and hurried back to the Treasury Building. I had hardly gotten inside my office when Bob Steel rushed in. Bob's the consummate professional and is almost always upbeat. But that day he looked grim.

"I spent some time with Rodge Cohen this morning," he said, mentioning the prominent bank lawyer advising Bear Stearns. "Bear is having liquidity problems. We're trying to learn more."

Before Bob had finished, I knew Bear Stearns was dead. Once word got out about liquidity problems, Bear's clients would pull their money and funding would evaporate. My years on Wall Street had taught me this brutal truth: when financial institutions die, they die fast.

"This will be over within days," I said.

I swallowed hard and braced myself. Whatever we did we would have to do quickly.

———

The crisis seemed to have arrived suddenly, but Bear Stearns's plight was not a surprise. It was the smallest of the big five investment banks, after Goldman Sachs, Morgan Stanley, Merrill Lynch, and Lehman Brothers. And while Bear hadn't posted the massive losses of some of its rivals, its huge exposure to bonds and mortgages made it vulnerable. Bear had found itself in increasingly difficult straits since the previous summer, when, in one of the first signs of the impending crisis, it had been forced to shut down two hedge funds heavily invested in collateralized debt obligations.

For all that, I also knew Bear as a scrappy firm that liked to do things its own way: alone on Wall Street it had refused to help rescue Long-Term Capital Management in 1998. Bear's people were survivors. They had always seemed to find a way out of trouble.

For months, Steel and I had been pushing Bear, and many other investment banks and commercial banks, to raise capital and to improve their liquidity positions. Some, including Merrill Lynch and Morgan Stanley, had raised billions from big investors such as foreign governments' sovereign wealth funds. Bear had talked with several parties but had only managed to make an agreement with China's Citic Securities under which each would invest $1 billion in the other. The deal was not the answer to Bear's needs and in any case hadn't yet closed.

Investment banks were more vulnerable to market pressures than commercial banks. For most of this country's history, there had been no practical differences between them. But the Crash of 1929 changed that. Congress passed a series of reforms to protect bank depositors and investors by controlling speculation and curbing conflicts of interest. The Glass-Steagall Banking Act of 1933 prohibited depository institutions from engaging in what was seen as the risky business of underwriting securities. For many years, commercial banks, viewed as more conservative, took deposits and made loans, while investment banks, their more adventurous cousins, concentrated on underwriting, selling, and trading securities. But over time the dividing lines blurred, until in 1999 Congress allowed each side to jump fully into the other's businesses. This gave rise to a wave of mergers that created the giant financial services companies that dominated the landscape in 2008.

But regulation had not kept pace with these changes. Oversight bodies were too fragmented and lacked adequate powers and authorities. That was one reason Treasury was working hard to complete our blueprint for a new regulatory structure.

Commercial banks enjoyed a greater safety net than investment banks did: When in trouble, commercial banks could turn to the Federal Reserve as their lender of last resort. If that failed, the government could step in, take the bank over, and put it in receivership. Seizing control of the bank's assets, and standing behind its obligations, the FDIC could carefully wind down the bank, or sell it, to protect the financial system.

Though the more highly leveraged investment banks were regulated by the SEC and followed stricter accounting standards than the commercial banks did, the government had no power to intervene if one failed—even if that failure posed a systemic threat. The Fed had no facility through which investment banks could borrow, and the SEC was not a lender and did not inspire market confidence. In a world of large, global, intertwined financial institutions, the failure of one investment house, like Bear Stearns, could wreak havoc.

As soon as Bob Steel left my office that Thursday morning, I made a flurry of calls, beginning with the White House. Then I phoned a very concerned Tim Geithner, who assured me he was all over Bear. He asked if I had talked with SEC chairman Chris Cox.

I tracked Chris down in Atlanta. Though Bear's name had been tarnished, Cox thought it had a good business and would make a perfect acquisition candidate, and that it ought to be able to find a buyer within 30 days. He'd spoken with Bear's CEO, Alan Schwartz, who said he had unencumbered collateral—all he needed was for someone to loan against it.

President Bush soon called, and I explained the Bear Stearns situation and the consequences I saw for the markets, and the broader economy, if Bear failed. The president quickly grasped the seriousness of the problem and asked if there was a buyer for the stricken firm. I told him I didn't yet know, but that we were thinking through all our options.

"This is the real thing," I summed up. "We're in danger of having a firm go down. We're going to have to go into overdrive."

Later that afternoon, Steel caught up with me and we agreed that he should go ahead and fly to New York for his daughter's 21st birthday dinner. He could work from there and we might need him in the city, anyway. It was a stroke of luck that Bob went. He arrived at 6:00 p.m. or so and then found himself so caught on calls with officials at the New York Fed, the SEC, and Bear that he spent two hours on the phone in a conference room at the Westchester County Airport. He barely made it to his daughter's party for dessert.

By the time I got home I was filled with foreboding. It was Thursday night, so the new *Sports Illustrated* had arrived. Wendy always left it for me on our bed, and I was flipping through the pages, trying to unwind, when the phone rang. It was Bob calling in from the airport in Westchester; he told me the situation was bad and that I would be hooked into a conference call around 8:00 p.m. with Ben Bernanke, Chris Cox, Tim Geithner, and key members of their staffs.

It had been an ugly day for Bear Stearns. Lenders and prime brokerage customers were fleeing so quickly that the company had told the SEC that without a solution, it would file for bankruptcy in the morning. We had limited options. A Bear bankruptcy could cause a domino effect, with other troubled banks unable to meet their obligations and failing. But it was unclear what we could do to stop that disaster. This was a dangerous situation and there weren't any obvious answers.

We discussed taking preventive measures. The Fed was exploring options for flooding the market with liquidity, or, as Tim said, "putting foam on the runway." But with conditions as fragile as they were, I questioned whether there was much we could do to stabilize the markets if Bear went down suddenly.

We agreed to confer again first thing in the morning. Tim said, "We'll have our teams working all night." His staff would drill down on what a Bear failure might mean to the infrastructure—the markets for secured loans, derivatives, and such that constituted the unseen but vital plumbing of finance. It would be the first of many nights during the crisis when teams at the Fed—or Treasury—would work through the night against excruciating deadlines to try to save the system.

I couldn't sleep. I was hot and agitated. I tossed and turned. I couldn't stop thinking about the consequences of a Bear failure. I worried about the soundness of balance sheets, the lack of transparency in the CDS market, and the interconnectedness among institutions that lent each other billions each day and how easily the system could unravel if they got spooked. My mind raced through dire scenarios.

All financial institutions depended on borrowed money—and on the confidence of their lenders. If lenders got nervous about a bank's ability to pay, they could refuse to lend or demand more collateral for their loans. If everyone did that at once, the financial system would shut down and there would be no credit available for companies or consumers. Economic activity would contract, even collapse.

In recent years banks had borrowed more than ever—without increasing their capital enough. Much of the borrowing to support this increase in leverage was done in the market for repurchase agreements, or repos, where banks sold securities to counterparties for cash and agreed to buy them back later at the same price, plus interest.

While many commercial banks had big pools of federally insured retail deposits to rely on for part of their funding, the investment banks were more heavily dependent on this kind of financing. Dealers used repos to finance their positions in Treasuries, federal agency debt, and mortgage-backed securities, among other things. Financial institutions could arrange the repos directly with one another or through a third-party intermediary, which acted as administrator and custodian of the securities being loaned. Two banks, JPMorgan and Bank of New York Mellon, dominated this triparty repo business.

The market had become enormous—with perhaps $2.75 trillion outstanding in just the triparty repo market at its peak. Most of this money was lent overnight. That meant giant balance sheets filled with all kinds of complex, often illiquid assets were poised on the back of funding that could be pulled at a moment's notice.

This hadn't seemed like a problem to most bankers during the good times that we'd enjoyed until the previous year. Repos were considered safe. Technically purchase and sale transactions, they acted just like secured loans. That is to say, repos were considered safe until the times turned tough and market participants lost faith in the collateral or in the creditworthiness of their counterparties— or both. Secured or not, no one wanted to deal with a firm they feared might disappear the next day. But deciding not to deal with a firm could turn that fear into a self-fulfilling prophecy.

A Bear Stearns failure wouldn't just hurt the owners of its shares and its bonds. Bear had hundreds, maybe thousands, of counterparties—firms that lent it money or with which it traded stocks, bonds, mortgages, and other securities. These firms—other banks and brokerage houses, insurance companies, mutual funds, hedge funds, the pension funds of states, cities, and big companies—all in turn had myriad counterparties of their own. If Bear fell, all these counterparties would be scrambling to collect their loans and collateral. To meet demands for payment, first Bear and then other firms would be forced to sell whatever they could, in any market they could—driving prices down, causing more losses, and triggering more margin and collateral calls.

The firms that had already started to pull their money from Bear were simply trying to get out first. That was how bank runs started these days.

Investment banks understood that if any questions arose about their ability to pay, creditors would flee at wildfire speed. This is why a bank's liquidity was so critical. At Goldman we had absolutely obsessed over our liquidity position. We didn't define it just in the traditional sense as the amount of cash on hand plus unencumbered assets that could be sold quickly. We asked how much money, under the most adverse conditions, could disappear on any given day; if everyone who could legally request their money back did so, how short would we be and could we meet our obligations? To be on the safe side, we kept a lockbox at the Bank of New York filled with bonds that we never invested or lent out. When I was CEO at Goldman, we had amassed $60 billion in these cash reserves alone. Knowing we had that cushion helped me fall asleep at night.

Bear had started the week out with something like $18 billion in cash on hand. It now had closer to $2 billion. It couldn't possibly meet demands for withdrawals. And in the morning, when the markets opened, no counterparties were going to lend to Bear: they'd all be pulling their money out. This would be bad news indeed, not just for Bear Stearns, but for every institution dealing with them.

No wonder I slept no more than a couple of hours that night. I had never had trouble before, but this night was the beginning of a prolonged bout of sleeplessness that would haunt me throughout the crisis, and particularly after September. On tough days, I would fall asleep exhausted around 9:30 p.m. or 10:00 p.m., then wake up several hours later and lie awake for much of the rest of the night. Sometimes I did my clearest thinking during these hours, occasionally getting up to write things down. By the time the newspapers were delivered at 6:00 a.m., I would have already been up for an hour or two, often turning on cable TV to check on overseas markets.

Friday, March 14, 2008

On Friday morning I had just shaved and was about to get in the shower when the phone rang. It was Bob Steel telling me that a conference call would start around 5:00 a.m. Still wearing the boxer shorts and T-shirt I slept in, I jogged up to the third-floor study of our house so I wouldn't wake Wendy. On the line were Tim Geithner, Ben Bernanke, Kevin Warsh, and Don Kohn from the Fed; Tony Ryan and Bob Steel from Treasury; and Erik Sirri from the SEC. We waited at first for Chris Cox, who was standing by in his office but never came on because of a communications mix-up. For a few minutes, we plugged in Jamie Dimon, CEO of JPMorgan, Bear's clearing bank. He painted a dark picture, emphasizing that a Bear Stearns failure would be disastrous for the markets, and that the key was to get Bear to the weekend.

Once Jamie got off, Tim reviewed a creative way he and his team had devised to buy time. The Fed would lend money to JPMorgan, which in turn would lend the money to the beleaguered brokerage firm. To make this work, the Fed's loan would have to be non-recourse: it would be backed by collateral from Bear, but neither JPMorgan nor Bear would be liable for repayment.

By law the Federal Reserve can lend against assets only when the loan is secured to its satisfaction, meaning in practical terms that there is a minimal chance of the Fed's losing money. But if this loan could not be repaid, for whatever reason, and the Fed had to sell the collateral for less than the value of the loan, the central bank would incur a loss. It would be a bold, unprecedented action for the Fed to make such a deal.

So Ben threw in a crucial caveat: "I'm prepared to go ahead here only if Treasury is supportive and prepared to protect us from any losses."

To be honest, I wasn't sure what, if any, legal authority Treasury might have had to indemnify the Federal Reserve, but I was determined to make it to the weekend. The repo markets would open shortly—around 7:30 a.m.—and I wasn't about to drag in a lot of lawyers and debate any legal fine points now.

"I'm prepared to do anything," I said. "If there's any chance of avoiding this failure, we need to take it."

First, though, I had to get off the line and speak with President Bush to confirm that he would sign off on the plan. Yes, he said, we had his support. But now he had to scramble. That day he not only had the speech in New York at the Economic Club but also a meeting with the editorial board of the *Wall Street Journal*, which was renowned for its free-market views and its opposition to government interference in the economy.

I told him not to worry; Steel was on top of the Bear situation in New York and could meet him on his arrival. I reiterated, with a touch of black humor: "Mr. President, you can take out that line in your speech about 'no bailouts.'"

The president reworked his speech, and when he flew to New York, Steel was waiting at the Wall Street Heliport. He hopped in the presidential limousine and briefed the president on the way to Midtown, bringing him up to date on Bear.

I got back on the conference call to say we had the president's backing. Afterward Tim and I spoke privately. We were rushing this rescue through very fast. The Board of Governors of the Federal Reserve had not yet formally approved the loan, and we had not yet put out an announcement. But the market was about to open, so we needed to move rapidly.

We asked ourselves again what would happen if Bear failed. Back in 1990, the junk bond giant Drexel Burnham Lambert had collapsed without taking the markets down, but they had not been as fragile then, nor had institutions been as entwined. Counterparties had been more easily identified. Perhaps if Bear had been a one-off situation, we would have let it go down. But we realized that Bear's failure would call into question the fate of the other financial institutions that might share Bear's predicament. The market would look for the next wounded deer, then the next, and the whole system would be at serious risk.

I talked to Tim probably two dozen times between Friday and Sunday. We made a good team. Tim brought to the crisis a keen analytical mind and a great sense of calm, of deliberative process and control. He had great stamina and a welcome sense of humor. But although we were relying on the Fed's powers to deal with Bear Stearns, it was uncharted water for him, and he relied on my market knowledge and my familiarity with Wall Street. Tim knew I understood the thought processes and the strengths and weaknesses of the Wall Street CEOs. I understood how to deal with boards of directors and shareholders. I knew how extraordinarily difficult it was to buy a company over a weekend with no time for due diligence. I also knew what it felt like to be afraid of losing your company, because I'd had that fear in 1994 at Goldman Sachs, when big trading losses had caused many spooked partners to withdraw their capital.

Tim had already explained the government's plan to Bear CEO Alan Schwartz, but he was worried that Alan hadn't completely grasped the consequences. The government didn't put taxpayer money at risk without expecting something in return—in this case, essentially, control.

"Let's make sure he understands, Hank," I remember Tim saying. "You need to speak to him with force and clarity so he hears it from you and not just me."

When I reached Alan, he sounded rattled, but it was clear that he was doing his best. I had great sympathy for him. He was a good investment banker and a highly regarded adviser to companies who had been thrust into a terrible situation that did not play to his strengths. When I called, he'd been meeting with his board, which was a fractious group.

"Alan," I said, "you're in the government's hands now. Bankruptcy is the only other option."

"Tim said the same thing to me," he said. "I was nervous because when you called I thought maybe the rules were changing. Don't worry. I got the message."

Just before 9:00 a.m., JPMorgan announced that it would join with the Fed to lend to Bear Stearns for an initial period of up to 28 days. The release did not specify how much money would be lent.

I almost never let myself be scripted. I work best by writing down a few bullet points and two or three key phrases to use. Still, in a conference call soon afterward with the CEOs of all the major banks, I knew I had to be careful—I couldn't order these bankers to do anything. But I had to make clear that if they pulled their credit lines from Bear, the investment bank wouldn't survive the day. I told them that I understood they all had fiduciary responsibilities, but that this was an extraordinary situation and the government had taken unprecedented action.

"Your regulators have worked together to come up with a solution. We ask you to act in a responsible manner," I said. "All of us here are thinking about the system. Our goal is to keep Bear operating and making payments."

The group asked a lot of questions about the Fed's emergency backstop. Tim and I let Jamie Dimon answer most of these. The bankers were nervous but obviously relieved, which gave me some comfort that Bear would make it through the day.

Initially, Bear shares rallied, but it didn't take long for the market to weaken. During the morning, Bear's stock plunged nearly in half, to below $30. The broader markets fell sharply, too, with the Dow Jones Industrial Average off nearly 300 points. For the day, the dollar hit a then-record low of $1.56 against the euro, while gold soared to a new high of $1,009 an ounce.

Despite the backing of JPMorgan and the Fed, doubts remained about Bear's ability to survive. Its accounts continued to flee, draining its reserves further. We needed to get a deal done by Sunday night, before the Asian markets opened and the bank run went global.

That afternoon during a meeting on our housing initiatives, I asked Neel Kashkari if he was going to be around during the weekend, because we might need help on Bear. Neel said: "I have to imagine I'd be more useful to you in New York than sitting next to you in D.C."

I agreed, but before he took off I said, "I am sending you to do

something you are totally unqualified to do, but you're all I've got."
I could always rib Neel because he was talented and self-confident.

He laughed. "Thanks, I guess."

I called Jamie Dimon at 4:30 p.m. and told him we needed to get the deal done by the end of the weekend. Self-assured, charismatic, and quick-witted, Jamie had the ability to walk the line between being a tough businessman and knowing when to rein in his competitive instincts for the good of the financial system. He had the confidence of his board, which allowed him to make decisions quickly and stand by them. He said his team would move as fast as possible, but he knew better than to give me any guarantees.

President Bush had returned to Washington after his speech in New York and wanted an immediate briefing on Bear Stearns. When was JPMorgan going to buy the company? he asked. I told him I didn't know, but I emphasized that something had to happen over the weekend or we would be in trouble.

In New York, Tim Geithner was growing increasingly concerned. After talking with Schwartz, he suspected that the Bear CEO didn't realize that the day's events had so compromised his firm that the timetable had to be accelerated. Schwartz, he said, was still operating under the illusion that he had a month to sell the company.

Tim suggested that he and I call Schwartz. "I think it will have a bigger impact if we do it together," he said. We reached him at about 6:30 p.m. and told him we had to act faster.

"Why don't we have more time?" Alan asked.

"Because your business isn't going to hold together," I explained. "It will evaporate. There will be nothing left to lend against if you don't have a deal by the end of the weekend."

After that difficult call, Tim and I agreed there was nothing else we could do that night. We agreed to talk in the morning.

That evening Wendy and I went to the National Geographic Society to see *The Lord God Bird*, a terrific documentary on the ivory-billed woodpecker, a bird so spectacular it made people say *Lord God!* Normally, I would have enjoyed this immensely, but I was preoccupied with Bear Stearns. Every time one of our friends from the environmental community came over, I would look right through them. Wendy got really upset with me.

"I understand that you're under pressure," she said, "but that's no excuse for not being courteous to people."

"I am being courteous to everyone," I protested.

"You aren't saying anything to them except 'Hi.'"

I apologized, adding, "I'm worried about the world falling apart!"

Saturday, March 15, 2008

I woke up Saturday after another restless night, anxious about the need to find a solution for Bear Stearns that weekend. The first call I received was from Lloyd Blankfein, my successor as Goldman Sachs CEO. It was as unnerving as it was unexpected. It was the first, and only, time Lloyd called me at home while I was at Treasury. Lloyd went over the market situation with me, providing a typically analytical and extraordinarily comprehensive overview, but I could hear the fear in his voice. His conclusion was apocalyptic.

The market expected a Bear rescue. If there wasn't one, all hell would break loose, starting in Asia Sunday night and racing through London and New York Monday. It wasn't difficult to imagine a record 1,000-point drop in the Dow.

I talked to Tim Geithner shortly after, and we reviewed our plan for the day. We needed a buyer for Bear, and we agreed that JPMorgan was far and away our best candidate. We decided to speak with Jamie Dimon and Alan Schwartz throughout the day to press them to make sure their boards were actively engaged and getting the information they needed to conclude a deal by Sunday afternoon.

Under normal circumstances, I would have preferred to find multiple potential bidders to at least create the semblance of competition. But I didn't believe there was another buyer for Bear Stearns anywhere in the world—and certainly not one that could get a deal done in 36 hours. Nonetheless, we considered every possibility we could.

Tim asked about Chris Flowers, the private-equity investor who had expressed interest in Bear Stearns. I'd known Chris for years. He'd been in charge of financial institutions' banking at Goldman before striking out on his own. But I knew he didn't have the balance sheet necessary to do a deal, and I told Tim it would be a waste of time to deal with Flowers. Seth Waugh, the North American head of Deutsche Bank, had also expressed some interest. I said I'd call Joe Ackermann, the Deutsche Bank CEO, but added that based on many conversations I'd had with him over the last seven months, I doubted he'd have any real interest. Joe had enough problems of his own.

The Swiss-born Ackermann was one of the most direct men I knew, a relentless competitor who was unafraid to exploit the perceived weakness of his rivals. He happened to be walking down Madison Avenue in New York when I reached him on his cell phone. True to form, he answered me with breathtaking bluntness.

"Buy Bear Stearns? That's the last thing in the world I would do," he exclaimed. He added that he had no interest in financing Bear, either. He'd held his funding together so far and had been a good corporate citizen, but he couldn't continue. Then he asked me why Deutsche should do business with any U.S. investment bank.

This was not competitive zeal but fear speaking, and I was surprised by the level of worry I heard. I assured him that he didn't need to be concerned about the other U.S. investment banks and that we were dealing with Bear.

Shuttling between JPMorgan's and Bear's offices—across the street from each other—Neel Kashkari gave me updates on the big bank's due-diligence efforts. With me frequently patched in by phone, the teams labored in New York to push a deal along. I also talked to people in the industry to keep them in line. Lehman CEO Dick Fuld called me back from an airport in India, where he was on a business trip. Worried about his own firm, he asked if the situation was serious enough that he should come home.

"I sure wouldn't be overseas right now," I told him.

He asked if I could get him flyover rights from Russia. I explained that I didn't have that kind of power, but emphasized that he should return.

All Saturday when Tim and I spoke to Jamie Dimon, the JPMorgan CEO would say things like: "We're making progress. We're optimistic, but there's a lot of work." It was nerve-wracking not to have an alternative. Finally, late in the day, we had an encouraging conversation with Jamie, during which it sounded as though he were going to do the deal—he just needed to work out a few more things with his board.

We left it with Jamie that he would continue to work with his directors. If there was a problem, he would get back to Tim first thing in the morning. Otherwise, we would talk a little later on Sunday. I slept well for the first time in days.

Sunday, March 16, 2008

The next morning I was booked on several Sunday talk shows to answer questions about the rescue. I spoke to Tim first thing. Neither of us had heard a word from Jamie, which was good news. I left for the TV studios around 7:30 a.m., making a mental note not to say a word about the negotiations and to stick to my carefully prepared talking points. I taped ABC's *This Week* first. The host, George Stephanopoulos, zeroed in on what was on the public's mind, asking whether we weren't using taxpayer dollars to bail out Wall Street.

"We're very aware of moral hazard," I said, adding, "My primary concern is the stability of our financial system."

"Are there other banks in a situation similar to Bear Stearns's right now?" he wanted to know. "Is this just the beginning?"

"Well, our financial institutions, our banks and investment banks, are very strong," I stressed. "Our markets are resilient, they're flexible. I'm quite confident we're going to work our way through this situation."

And I was. In retrospect, as concerned as I was about the markets, I had no idea of what was coming in just a few months. Right then, however, I was optimistic that Jamie was on board, that we could settle the Bear Stearns problem and calm things down. But what I didn't realize as I went from one show to another—after *This Week*, I was interviewed by Wolf Blitzer at CNN and Chris Wallace at Fox News—was that the situation had taken a turn for the worse. Neel had called Brookly McLaughlin, my deputy press secretary, with bad news. Brookly, who had accompanied me to the shows, wanted me to stay focused on the interviews, so it wasn't until I was headed home, after 10:00 a.m., that she told me that there was a problem and asked me to contact Neel. He said JPMorgan wasn't willing to proceed. I called Tim.

"It's too much of a stretch for them," Tim said.

JPMorgan thought Bear was too big and was particularly concerned with the firm's mortgage portfolio. I was disappointed but not shocked. It was a bit unrealistic to believe that with no competition we could get JPMorgan to buy Bear Stearns over a weekend in the midst of a credit crisis. And Tim had already pushed Jamie to no avail.

We discussed how we could put some pressure on Jamie. We agreed that the best course would probably be to find a way to enable JPMorgan to buy Bear with some help from the Fed.

So I called Jamie and told him we needed him to buy Bear. And, as always, he was straightforward and said that it would be impossible.

"What's changed?" I pressed. "Why aren't you interested now?"

"We've concluded it's just too big. And we've already got plenty of mortgages ourselves," he said. "I'm sorry. We can't get there."

"Then we need to figure out under what terms you would do this," I said, changing tack. "Is there something we can work out where the Fed helps you get this deal done?"

Jamie's tone changed. "I'll see what I can do," he said, promising to get back to us quickly.

I called Tim back, and we vowed to provide as little government assistance as possible for JPMorgan to acquire Bear. But we would have to find some way to eat what got left behind.

I set myself up on my living room couch with a pad of paper and a can of Diet Coke. Our house is perched on an incline with a small stream at its base. Looking out through the sliding doors into a thicket of trees, bare and forlorn in March, I worked the phones, talking with Tim and Neel constantly. Together Tim and I would check in with Jamie and others. We needed to get this deal done.

Jamie soon said he was willing to buy Bear, but there were several big issues to resolve. JPMorgan didn't want any of Bear's mortgage portfolio, which was on the investment bank's books for about $35 billion. The question wasn't quality so much as size. The bank had reasons to keep its powder dry; we knew that it had an interest in acquiring Washington Mutual, which was looking to shore up its capital. So it was pretty clear that JPMorgan wasn't going to buy Bear without government help for the mortgage assets.

The Fed eventually concluded that it could assist in the deal by financing a special purpose vehicle that would hold and manage those assets of Bear's that JPMorgan didn't want. The loan to this entity would be nonrecourse, which brought back Friday morning's dilemma: the Fed could find itself facing losses, and it would want indemnification. I had our legal team, led by general counsel Bob Hoyt, looking into exactly what we could do. The Fed had brought in BlackRock, a fixed-income investment specialist, to examine the mortgage portfolio, which JPMorgan wanted priced as of the previous Friday.

We kept an open conference line linking Washington, the New York Fed, and JPMorgan. I got hold of Neel in a JPMorgan conference room and asked him to step out and call me privately.

"Neel," I said, "your job is to protect us. These guys will be incentivized to dump all sorts of crap on us. You need to make sure that doesn't happen. Make sure we know what we are getting."

Because the Fed could only take dollar-denominated assets, the pool shrank, and when we were somewhere in the $30 billion range, we had the outlines of a deal. Still, no price had been determined for Bear Stearns's shares. Tim told me JPMorgan was considering offering $4 or $5 per share, but that sounded like too much to me, and Tim agreed. Bear was dead unless the government stepped in. How could the firm come to us, say they would fail without government help, and then have any sort of payday for its shareholders? With Tim's encouragement, I called Jamie, who put me on the speakerphone.

"I understand you're talking $4 or $5 per share," I said. "But the alternative for this company is bankruptcy. How do you get so high?"

"They should get zero, but I don't know how you get a deal done if you do that," he said.

"Of course, you've got to pay them something to get them to vote," I said. "It would have to be at least $1 or $2."

I stressed that the decision on price was JPMorgan's. It wasn't my place to dictate terms. And I knew that whatever deal was announced, there was a good chance it would need ultimately to be increased because the required shareholder vote would give Bear leverage. But better to start from a lower price.

JPMorgan decided to offer $2 a share.

Meantime, as we raced to save Bear, we saw an opportunity to take a positive step with Fannie Mae and Freddie Mac. The market's weakness ultimately stemmed from housing troubles, and they were right in the center of that. A negative *Barron's* cover story the previous weekend had hit them hard.

Why not use the crisis to our advantage? Tim and I believed some positive news from Fannie and Freddie might help the market. I called Bob Steel and asked him to arrange a conference call with the GSEs and their regulator, OFHEO, to nail down an agreement he had been working on. Steel, on the fly, rounded up Fannie Mae CEO Dan Mudd, Freddie Mac CEO Richard Syron, and OFHEO chief Jim Lockhart, and we jumped on a conference call for about half an hour beginning at 3:00 p.m.

Fannie and Freddie were operating under a consent order temporarily requiring 30 percent more capital than mandated by federal statute. They were pressing to have this surcharge removed early. To get them to raise more capital—which we felt they sorely needed—Steel and Lockhart had for weeks been pushing a deal: for every $1.50 to $2 of new capital the GSEs raised, OFHEO would reduce the surcharge by $1.

I had no time to waste, so I began the call by saying we were expecting to get a deal done on Bear Stearns and that we wanted an agreement from the GSEs to help calm the market. Steel had done his work well, and we quickly hammered out an agreement that, we estimated, would lead each firm to raise at least $6 billion. We calculated that this, in turn, would translate into $200 billion in much-needed financing for the sagging mortgage market. We agreed to make the announcement as soon as possible. (It was made on March 19.)

After this, Tim and I spoke with Jamie to review the terms before he went to his board for approval. The deal featured a $2-a-share offer from JPMorgan and a $30 billion loan from the New York Fed secured by Bear's mortgage pool. We all knew that the complexity of the deal—from its structure and legal documentation down to the specifics of how the mortgage portfolio would be managed— meant that all the details could not be nailed down formally before Asia opened. We would have to announce a deal on the basis of a "verbal handshake" that required trust and sophistication on both sides. And we could only have done that with a CEO like Jamie Dimon, who was technically proficient, deeply self-assured, and had the support of his board.

The short call was over by 3:40 p.m., and Jamie went off to talk to his directors.

I got on a call with the president and Joel Kaplan to give them a heads-up on our progress.

"Hank," the president asked, "have you got it done?"

"Almost, sir," I said. "We still need to get board approval from both companies."

I explained the $30 billion loan and how the Fed wanted indemnification against loss from the Treasury, adding that the Fed would essentially own the mortgages.

"Can we say we are going to get our money back?"

"We might, but that will depend upon the market."

"Then we can't promise it. A lot of folks aren't going to like this. You'll have to explain why it was necessary."

"That won't be easy," I said.

"You'll be able to do it. You've got credibility."

While I was speaking, Wendy motioned to me. She had answered our other line and was saying: "Neel needs to talk with you urgently."

After finishing with the president's call, I got on with Neel, who had Bob Hoyt patched through to me.

"We can't do this," Bob said. He quickly explained that the Anti-Deficiency Act barred Treasury from spending money without a specific congressional allocation, which we didn't have. Hence, we couldn't commit to indemnifying the Fed against losses.

"My God," I said. "I just told the president we have a deal."

I immediately alerted Tim that I had just learned of a problem.

He was surprised and angry. "Hank, you've made a commitment. You need to find some way to meet it."

I called Hoyt back. "Come up with something," I told him.

Bob is a great lawyer and a can-do guy. Before coming to me he had spent hours trying out a couple of imaginative, outside-the-box theories and had run them by the Department of Justice. The lawyers concluded that their ideas wouldn't survive the third question at a congressional oversight hearing.

Finally, when Tim understood that we didn't have the power to do any more, we figured out a compromise. The Fed's $30 billion loan was based on a provision in the law that gave it the authority, under what is called "exigent circumstances," to make a loan—even to an investment bank like Bear Stearns—provided it was "secured to the satisfaction of the Federal Reserve bank." Over the course of the afternoon, BlackRock's CEO, Larry Fink, had assured Tim and me that his firm had done enough work on the mortgages to provide the Fed with a letter attesting that its loan was adequately secured, meaning the risk of loss was minimal. So what the Fed really needed from the executive branch was political—not legal—protection.

Since Treasury couldn't formally indemnify the Fed, we agreed that I would write a letter to Tim commending and supporting the Fed's actions. I would also acknowledge that if the Fed did take a loss, it would mean that the Fed would have fewer profits to give to the Treasury. In that sense the burden of the loss would be on the taxpayer, not the Fed.

I called this our "all money is green" letter. It was an indirect way of getting the Fed the cover it needed for taking an action that should—and would—have been taken by Treasury if we had had the fiscal authority to do so. Hoyt started drafting the letter immediately. As it turned out, we were still hashing out the details a week later.

We had heard back from Jamie just before 4:00 p.m. that the JPMorgan board had approved the deal. Now we had to wait to hear from Bear, and I admit I was nervous. Even as our earlier call with Jamie had wound down, I had begun to worry about the Bear Stearns board. What if they decided to be difficult? If they threatened to choose bankruptcy over JPMorgan's deal, as irrational as this might appear, they would have leverage over us. Though I thought this unlikely, I became anxious as the minutes ticked by without an answer from Bear. Finally, at 6:00 p.m., the Bear board approved the deal.

The *Wall Street Journal* broke the story of the Bear Stearns–JPMorgan deal online Sunday evening. JPMorgan would buy Bear for $2 per share, or a total of $236 million (it had been valued at its peak, in January 2007, at about $20 billion). If a shareholder vote failed to approve the transaction, the deal would have to be put to a revote by the shareholders within 28 days—a process that could go on for up to six months. This revote measure was intended to give the market certainty that the deal would ultimately close even if the Bear shareholders balked at the $2 a share. As part of the deal, the Federal Reserve Board would provide a $30 billion loan to a stand-alone entity named Maiden Lane LLC that would buy Bear's mortgage assets and manage them.

The Fed board also approved a Primary Dealer Credit Facility (PDCF), which opened the discount window to investment banks for the first time since the Great Depression. We had been discussing this over the weekend, and it was a critical move. We hoped that the market would be comforted by the perception that the investment banks had come under the Fed umbrella.

That night we convened another call with financial industry CEOs. Jamie Dimon led off the call by saying, "All of your trading positions with Bear Stearns are now with JPMorgan Chase."

This was a crucial element to the deal. JPMorgan would guarantee Bear's trading book—meaning it would stand behind any of its transactions—until the deal closed. This was exactly the assurance the markets needed to keep doing business with Bear.

Tim spoke, and then I addressed the group. I noted that the Fed had taken strong actions to stabilize the system and asked for their help and leadership. "You need to work together and support each other," I remember saying. "We expect you to act responsibly and avoid behavior that will undermine market confidence."

"What happens if the shareholders don't vote for it [the deal], but we're still acting responsibly, like you ask?" Citigroup CEO Vikram Pandit asked. "Is the government going to indemnify us?"

It was exactly the right question, but neither Jamie Dimon nor, for that matter, any of the rest of us were in a mood to hear it.

"What happens to Citigroup if this institution goes down?" Jamie snapped. "I've stepped up to do this. Why are you asking these questions?"

With JPMorgan on board, Bear's liquidity—and solvency—were no longer at issue. Asia sold off Sunday night, but the London and New York markets held steady on Monday.

Nonetheless, despite Joe Ackermann's blunt warning to me on Saturday, I had underestimated the recent loss of confidence in U.S. investment banks, particularly in Europe. I had asked David McCormick, the undersecretary for international affairs, to brief the staffs of the finance ministries in Europe on the Bear rescue and the strong U.S. response. But on Monday night, David asked me to make the calls because, he said, the Europeans were so scared. On Tuesday I spoke with several of my European counterparts—Alistair Darling from the U.K., Christine Lagarde from France, Peer Steinbrück from Germany—to explain our actions and to ask for their support.

It was quite an eye-opener. I frankly had been disappointed at the negative attitudes of some of the European banks, and I had hoped my counterparts would encourage their banks to be more constructive. I could now see there was no way they would do that. They were understandably shocked by Bear.

And of course, the deal was hugely controversial in the U.S. Although plenty of commentators thought it was a brilliant, bold stroke that saved the system, there were just as many who thought it outrageous, a clear case of moral hazard come home to roost. They thought we should have let Bear fail. Among the prominent members of this camp was Senator Richard Shelby, who said the action set a "bad precedent."

To be fair, I could see my critics' arguments. In principle, I was no more inclined than they were to put taxpayer money at risk to rescue a bank that had gotten itself in a jam. But my market experience had led me to conclude—and rightly so, I continue to believe—that the risks to the system were too great. I am convinced we did the best we could with what we had. It's fair to say we underestimated the speed with which the Bear Stearns crisis arrived, but we realized pretty quickly the limitations on our statutory powers and authorities to deal with the trouble that came our way. In the next week we redoubled our efforts to finish our work on the new regulatory blueprint that we were planning to unveil at the end of the month.

But the debate about the rescue was beside the point. For all the headlines and noise, we didn't actually have a finished deal. We had announced a transaction that the market initially wouldn't accept because it wanted certainty and wanted it quickly.

However, in the end, it still came down to price. Many Bear Stearns shareholders—and employees owned about one-third of the company—were incensed at what they saw as a lowball offer. After all, shares had traded for almost $173 in January 2007, and shareholders had lost billions of dollars. I felt sympathy for them, and I could understand their anger. On the other hand, the only reason the company had any value at all was because the government had stepped in and saved it.

By and large, traders in the marketplace, and many commentators in the financial press, agreed that the price was too low. On Monday, Bear shares traded at $4.81—more than twice JPMorgan's $2 offer—in expectation that JPMorgan would have to offer more to be sure to close the deal.

This created real uncertainty, which wasn't good for anyone. Not for Bear, not for JPMorgan, and not for the markets, which were settling down. The Dow jumped 420 points on Tuesday, and credit insurance rates on financial companies fell away sharply: Bear's CDS dropped from 772 basis points on Friday to 391 basis points on Tuesday, while those on Lehman fell from 451 basis points to 310 basis points and Morgan Stanley from 338 basis points to 226 basis points. We certainly didn't want to return to the previous week's tumultuousness.

JPMorgan understandably wanted to get the deal closed as soon as possible. As long as there was uncertainty, clients would continue to leave Bear Stearns, reducing the value of the acquisition. Why would a prime brokerage account or any other account want to stay when they could do business with any other bank or investment bank in the world?

Toward the end of the week, the deal looked like it was in danger of breaking apart. After talking to Alan Schwartz on Friday, March 21, Jamie was concerned that Bear could shop for another buyer and leave JPMorgan on the hook. Worried what might happen if shareholders did turn down his offer, Jamie wanted to be sure he could lock in enough votes to assure acceptance.

On Friday afternoon, I had a conference call with Tim Geithner, Bob Steel, Neel Kashkari, and Bob Hoyt in my office. We were on edge. We knew that the deal was far from certain, but we had no choice but to complete it.

The key was to deliver certainty. JPMorgan could raise its offer, but the bank and the market needed to be sure that at a higher price, Bear shareholders couldn't hold up the deal in an attempt to get even more.

Sweetening the deal to lock in shareholder approval made sense, but it gave me another idea. "We should also try to get more for the government," I said to Tim.

He agreed and pointed out that we had some leverage we could use. "They can't change the deal unless we let them," Tim said. "Our commitment is based upon the whole deal."

"Maybe we can now get JPMorgan to take all the mortgages without government support," I suggested.

But neither Tim nor I could get Jamie to agree. However, he did accept that with the Bear shareholders getting a higher price and JPMorgan's shares up on news of the acquisition, the government deserved a better deal, too.

The question now was how to improve the U.S.'s position. There was a whole lot of discussion and turning in circles about whether we should try to share in the upside—by taking an interest in the mortgage assets so that if they were sold above their appraised value, we could participate in the gains. But in the end it was clear to everyone that negotiating downside protection for the taxpayer was the more prudent course. So JPMorgan agreed to take the first $1 billion loss on the Bear portfolio.

Meantime, the lawyers on both sides had restructured the deal to give JPMorgan the certainty it needed and Bear shareholders a boost in price. As part of the agreement, JPMorgan would exchange some of its shares for newly issued Bear Stearns stock that would give JPMorgan just under 40 percent of Bear's shares. This arrangement came close to locking up the transaction.

The key to the share exchange was price. By Sunday, JPMorgan was ready to offer Bear stockholders $10 a share to close the deal. When I heard that Tim had signed off on $8 to $10, I wanted to go back and say, "Don't go above eight."

But Ben Bernanke said, "Why do you care, Hank? What's the difference between $8 and $10? We need certainty on this deal."

I realized that he was right. Even though it was an unseemly precedent to reward the shareholders of a firm that had been bailed out by the government, I knew that getting a deal done was critical. Bear had continued to deteriorate in the past week and had the capacity to threaten the entire financial system. So I called Jamie Dimon and gave him my blessing. Bear's shareholders would vote on May 29 to approve, overwhelmingly, the $10-a-share offer.

———

I've read through old newspaper reports and recently published books about the Bear weekend. None of them quite captures our race against time or how fortunate we were to have JPMorgan emerge as a buyer that agreed to preserve Bear's economic value by guaranteeing its trading obligations until the deal closed. We knew we needed to sell the company because the government had no power to put in capital to ensure the solvency of an investment bank. Because we had only one buyer and little time for due diligence, we had little negotiating leverage. Throughout the process, the market was determined to call our bluff. Clients and counterparties were going to leave; Bear was going to disintegrate if we didn't act. And even though many people thought Jamie Dimon had gotten a great deal, the Bear transaction remained very shaky to the end.

We learned a lot doing Bear Stearns, and what we learned scared us.

CHAPTER 6

Late March 2008

For the first few days after the Bear Stearns rescue, the markets calmed. Share prices firmed up, while credit default swap spreads on the investment banks eased. Some at Treasury, and in the market, thought that after seven long months, we had finally reached a turning point, just as the industry intervention in Long-Term Capital Management had marked the beginning of the end of 1998's troubles.

But I remained wary. Bear Stearns's failure had called into question not only the business models but also the very viability of the other investment banks. This uncertainty was unfair for those firms that, after adjusting for accounting differences, had stronger capital positions and better balance sheets than many commercial banks. But these doubts threatened the stability of the market, and we needed to do something about the situation.

The Fed's opening of its discount window to the primary dealers on March 17 had been a big boost. Because of its potential exposure, the Fed, working jointly with the SEC, began to put examiners on-site. This was a critical move. Investors who had lost confidence in the SEC as the investment banks' regulator would be reassured to see them under the Fed umbrella.

The regulators' initial analyses showed that Merrill Lynch and Lehman Brothers had the most work to do to build larger liquidity cushions. Merrill suffered from its share of well-publicized mortgage-related problems, but the firm was diversified and had by far the best retail brokerage business in the U.S., along with a strong brand name and a global franchise. I believed they would be able to find a buyer if they had to. Having worked with John Thain when he was Goldman's president and COO, I was optimistic that he would get a handle on Merrill's risk exposure and take care of its balance sheet. If anyone understood risk, it was John.

Lehman was another matter. I was frankly skeptical about its business mix and its ability to attract a buyer or strategic investor. It had the same profile of sky-high leverage and inadequate liquidity, combined with heavy exposure to real estate and mortgages, that had helped bring down Bear Stearns. Founded in 1850, Lehman had a venerable name but a rocky recent history. Dissension had torn it apart before it was sold to American Express in 1984. A decade later it was spun off in an initial public offering. Dick Fuld, as CEO, had done a remarkable job of rebuilding it. But in many ways, Lehman was really only a 14-year-old firm, with Dick as its founder. I liked Dick Fuld. He was direct and personable, a strong leader who inspired and demanded loyalty, but like many "founders," his ego was entwined with the firm's. Any criticism of Lehman was a criticism of Dick Fuld.

As Treasury secretary, I often turned to Dick for his market insights. A former bond trader, he was shrewd, willing to share information, and very responsive. I could tell that Bear's demise had shaken Dick. How far he was willing to go to protect his firm was another question.

For some time, I had been encouraging a number of commercial and investment banks to recognize their losses, raise equity, and strengthen their liquidity positions. I said that I had never, over the course of my career, seen a financial CEO who had gotten into trouble by having too much capital.

I emphasized this point to Fuld in late March. He maintained he had enough capital but knew he needed to restore confidence in Lehman. Shortly after, Dick called to say that he was thinking of approaching General Electric CEO Jeff Immelt and Berkshire Hathaway CEO Warren Buffett as possible investors. Dick said he served on the New York Fed board with Immelt and could tell that the GE chief liked and respected him. And he thought Berkshire Hathaway would be a good owner. I told Dick that GE was unlikely to be interested but that calling Warren Buffett was worth a try.

A few days later, on March 28, I was lying on my couch at home, watching ESPN on my birthday, when the phone rang. Dick was calling to say he had talked to Buffett. He wanted me to call Warren and put in a good word. I declined, but Dick persisted. Buffett, he said, was waiting for my call.

It was a measure of my concern for Lehman that I decided to see just how interested Warren was. I picked up the phone and called him at his office in Omaha. I considered Warren a friend, and I trusted his wisdom and invariably sound advice. On this call, however, I had to be careful about what I said. I pointed out that I wasn't Lehman's regulator and didn't know any more than he did about the firm's financial condition—but I did know that the light was focused on Lehman as the weakest link, and that an investment by Warren Buffett would send a strong signal to the credit markets.

"I recognize that," Buffett said. "I've got their 10-K, and I'm sitting here reading it."

Truth is, he didn't sound very interested at all.

I learned later that Fuld had wanted Buffett to buy preferred stock at terms the Omaha investor considered unattractive.

The following week, Lehman raised $4 billion in convertible preferred shares, insisting it was raising the capital not because it needed to, but to end any questions about the strength of its balance sheet. Investors greeted the action heartily: Lehman's shares rose 18 percent, to above $44, and its credit default spreads dropped sharply, to 238 basis points from 294 basis points.

It was April 1—April Fools' Day.

Bear Stearns's failure in March had highlighted many of the flaws in the regulatory structure of the U.S. financial system. Over the years, banks, investment banks, savings institutions, and insurance companies, to name just some of the many kinds of financial companies active in our markets, had all gotten into one another's businesses. The products they designed and sold had become infinitely more complex, and big financial institutions had become inextricably intertwined, stitched tightly together by complex credit arrangements.

The regulatory structure, organized around traditional business lines, had not begun to keep up with the evolution of the markets. As a result, the country had a patchwork system of state and federal supervisors dating back 75 years. This might have been fine for the world of the Great Depression, but it had led to counterproductive competition among regulators, wasteful duplication in some areas, and gaping holes in others.

I had aimed my sights at this cumbersome and inefficient arrangement from my first days in office. In March 2007, at a U.S. Capital Markets Competitiveness Conference at Washington's Georgetown University, participants from a wide spectrum of the markets had agreed that our outmoded regulatory structure could not handle the needs of the modern financial system. Over the following year, Treasury staff, under the direction of David Nason, with strong support from Bob Steel, had devised a comprehensive plan for sweeping changes, meeting with a wide variety of experts and soliciting public comment. On March 31, 2008, we unveiled the final product, called the Blueprint for a Modernized Financial Regulatory System, to a standing-room-only crowd of about 200. There must have been 50 reporters there amid the marble and chandeliers of the 19th-century Cash Room.

Calling for the modernization of our financial regulatory system, I emphasized, however, that no major regulatory changes should be enacted while the financial system was under strain. I hoped the Blueprint would start a discussion that would move the reform process ahead. And I stressed that our proposals were meant to fashion a new regulatory structure, not new regulations—though we clearly needed some.

"We should and can have a structure that is designed for the world we live in, one that is more flexible, one that can better adapt to change, one that will allow us to more effectively deal with inevitable market disruptions, and one that will better protect investors and consumers," I said.

Long-term, we proposed creating three new regulators. One, a business conduct regulator, would focus solely on consumer protection. A second, "prudential" regulator would oversee the safety and soundness of financial firms operating with explicit government guarantees or support, such as banks, which offer deposit insurance; for this role we envisioned an expanded Office of the Comptroller of the Currency. The third regulator would be given broad powers and authorities to deal with any situation that posed a threat to our financial stability. The Federal Reserve could eventually serve as this macrostability regulator.

Until this ultimate structure was in place, the Blueprint recommended significant shorter-term steps that included merging the Securities and Exchange Commission with the Commodity Futures Trading Commission; eliminating the federal thrift charter and combining the Office of Thrift Supervision with the Office of the Comptroller of the Currency; creating stricter uniform standards for mortgage lenders; enhancing oversight of payment and settlement systems; and regulating insurance at the federal level.

Though our team worked closely with other agencies in crafting the Blueprint, we had run into some disagreements with the Federal Reserve. It wanted to retain its role as a bank regulator, particularly its umbrella supervision over bank holding companies; without this it felt it couldn't effectively oversee systemically important firms. We saw no reason to highlight our differences. We all agreed that it would not be wise for the Fed to relinquish these responsibilities in the short run because it was the bank regulator with the most credibility—and resources. Ben Bernanke supported the Fed's taking on the new macro responsibilities from the beginning. But he and Tim Geithner wanted to be sure, and rightly so, that we gave the Fed the necessary authorities and access to information to do the thankless job of super-regulator. (I was pleased to see that the Obama administration, in its program of reforms, echoed the Blueprint's call for a macrostability regulator.)

The Blueprint did not focus much on government-sponsored enterprises like Fannie Mae and Freddie Mac. We did note that a separate regulator for the GSEs should be considered, and we also recommended that they fall under the purview of the Fed as market stability overseer.

Meantime, I was determined to push forward on the reform of the two mortgage giants. As credit dried up, their combined share of new mortgage activity had grown from 46 percent before the crisis to 76 percent. We needed them to provide low-cost mortgage funds to support the housing market. Hence the importance of their March 19 announcement that they would be making up to $200 billion in new funds available to the markets, in conjunction with planned new capital raising.

By April it was clear that the downturn would be long, and not just in the U.S.—mortgage activity in the U.K., for example, had ground to a near halt. Oil prices continued to rise, the dollar stumbled, and the press was filled with stories of food shortages, and riots, in several countries.

I traveled to Beijing to meet with Wang Qishan, who had replaced Wu Yi as vice premier, to set the table for the next round of the Strategic Economic Dialogue. I had known and worked with Wang, whom I considered a trusted friend, for 15 years. A former mayor of Beijing, with an appetite for bold action and a sly sense of humor, he had guided his country out of the SARS crisis and led the preparation for the 2008 Olympic Games. Though we spent considerable time discussing the vital issues of rising energy prices and the environment, which were to be the focus of our upcoming June meeting, Wang was most interested in the problems in the U.S. capital markets. I was candid about our difficulties but mindful that China was one of the top holders of U.S. debt, including hundreds of billions of GSE debt. I stressed that we understood our responsibilities.

In truth, U.S. markets were weakening again. Banks continued their efforts to raise capital, even as they suffered more big losses. On April 8, Washington Mutual said it would raise $7 billion to cover subprime losses, including a $2 billion infusion from the Texas private-equity group TPG. On April 14, Wachovia Corporation announced plans to raise $7 billion. Merrill Lynch reported first-quarter losses of $1.96 billion on $4.5 billion in write-downs, mostly from subprime mortgages, while Citigroup recorded a $5.1 billion loss, owing to a $12 billion write-down on subprime mortgage loans and other risky assets.

A somber mood prevailed when the G-7 held its ministerial meeting in Washington on April 11. That day, the Dow plunged 257 points, after General Electric's first-quarter earnings came in lower than expected. Talk of oil prices, which were topping $110 a barrel on their way to a July high of nearly $150, dominated the meeting, but the state of the capital markets was very much on the ministers' minds.

There was a great deal of discussion about mark-to-market, or fair-value accounting. European bankers, led by Deutsche Bank CEO Joe Ackermann, had cited this as a major source of their problems, and a number of my counterparts were understandably looking for a quick fix. Many favored a more flexible approach, but I staunchly defended fair-value accounting, in which assets and liabilities are recorded on balance sheets at current-market prices rather than at their historical values. I maintained that it was better to confront your problems head-on and know where you stood. Frankly, I believed the European banks had been slower than our own to confront their problems partly because of these differences in accounting practices. But I sensed that my European colleagues were increasingly aware of the seriousness of the banking problem.

The G-7 meeting featured an "outreach dinner" in the Treasury's Cash Room for financial CEOs. Most of the major institutions were represented: the guest list included John Mack of Morgan Stanley, John Thain of Merrill Lynch, Dick Fuld, Citigroup chairman Win Bischoff, JPMorgan CEO Jamie Dimon, and Deutsche's Ackermann.

The mood was dark. A few of the bankers thought we were nearing the end of the crisis, but most thought it would get worse. I went around the table and called on people, asking how we had gotten to where we were.

"Greed, leverage, and lax investor standards," I remember John

Mack saying. "We took conditions for granted, and we as an industry lost discipline."

"Investment managers now know what we don't know," noted
Herb Allison, the TIAA-CREF CEO, in what was his last day on the
job. "We used to think we knew a lot more about these assets, but
we've been burned, and until we see large-scale transparency in
assets, we're not going to buy."

Mervyn King, governor of the Bank of England, took a look at
the big picture, questioning whether we had allowed the financial
sector to become too big a part of our economies.

"You are all bright people, but you failed. Risk management
is hard," he said to the assembly. "So the lesson is, we can't let
you get as big as you were and do the damage that you've done
or get as complex as you were—because you can't manage the
risk element."

The bankers complained bitterly about hedge funds, which
they felt were shorting their stocks and manipulating credit default
swaps and, in the CEOs' minds, all but trying to force some institutions under. Almost every one of them wanted to regulate the
funds, and no one wanted that more than Dick Fuld, whose face
reddened with anger as he asserted, "These guys are killing us."

As we left the dinner, Dave McCormick, who served as the main
liaison to the G-7 and other countries' finance ministries, told me,
"Dick Fuld is really worked up."

I told Dave I wasn't surprised. Lehman was in a precarious position. "If they fail, we are all in deep trouble," I said. "Maybe we can
figure out how to sell them."

Congress had recessed for two weeks in the second half of March,
and lawmakers got an earful from constituents who were worried
about the ongoing housing woes and the weakening economy—
and were in some cases resentful about what they perceived as the

government bailout of Wall Street. The House and the Senate pushed ahead with housing legislation, which included a constellation of plans for foreclosure mitigation, affordable housing, and bankruptcy relief. Democrats, led by Chris Dodd and Barney Frank, pushed HOPE for Homeowners, a Federal Housing Administration program to provide guarantees to refinance mortgages for subprime borrowers at risk of losing their homes.

Republican lawmakers, particularly in the House, lambasted many of these proposals as bailouts of deadbeats and speculators. And the White House threatened a veto because of its displeasure with bankruptcy modifications of mortgages and a proposal to distribute $4 billion in Community Development Block Grants to state and local governments to buy foreclosed properties. I myself had real doubts about the efficacy of many of the proposals—we calculated that HOPE for Homeowners would aid 50,000 borrowers at most.

But GOP senators had returned from the spring recess more in a mood for compromise. On April 10 the Senate voted 84 to 12 in favor of a $24 billion bill of tax cuts and credits designed to boost the housing market.

On April 15, Bob Steel, Neel Kashkari, Treasury chief economist Phill Swagel, and I met with Ben Bernanke and some of his aides at the Fed to review a contingency plan that Neel and Phill had been working on for some time. Termed the "Break the Glass" Bank Recapitalization Plan, after the fire axes kept ready in glass cases until needed, the paper laid out the pros and cons of a series of options for dealing with the crisis.

Among its main options, the government would get permission from lawmakers to buy up to $500 billion in illiquid mortgage-backed securities from banks, freeing up their balance sheets and encouraging lending. Other moves included having the government guarantee or insure mortgage-backed assets to make them more appealing to investors, and having the FHA refinance individual mortgages on a massive scale. "Break the Glass" also laid out the possibility of taking equity stakes in banks to strengthen their capital bases—though not as a first resort.

"Break the Glass" was the intellectual forerunner of the Troubled Assets Relief Program (TARP) we would present to Congress in September. In April, however, the state of the markets was not yet so dire, nor was Congress anywhere near ready to consider granting us such powers.

Later that afternoon, the longtime block to GSE reform broke. At my urging, Chris Dodd had called a meeting with Richard Shelby and the chief executives of Fannie Mae and Freddie Mac. We gathered in Dodd's offices at the Russell Senate Office Building, in a small room that was unusually warm and intimate for an office on the Hill. Wood-paneled, with red curtains and carpet, it was decorated with memorabilia from Dodd's long political career, including photos of his father, Thomas J. Dodd, who had also served as a U.S. senator from Connecticut. It was a strangely homey setting for a meeting between some of the fiercest opponents on the GSE issue.

Although Dodd, like many leading Democrats, was sympathetic to Fannie and Freddie, Shelby had long wanted to put them under stricter supervision; in 2005 he had backed an unsuccessful bill that would have drastically reined in their portfolios.

Fannie's chief, Dan Mudd, the son of famed CBS News correspondent Roger Mudd, had grown up in Washington and had spent much of his career working at GE Capital, the finance unit of GE. Unlike many who rode the Washington gravy train, he knew how to run a real business and had been recruited to clean up Fannie after the accounting scandal of 2004. Since then, he had built a strong, loyal team.

Freddie Mac's CEO, Dick Syron, a former CEO of the Boston Fed and the American Stock Exchange, faced a more difficult situation. He had a problematic board, and I wasn't convinced he could deliver on what he promised.

By the time we sat down together, it was clear that the two CEOs recognized that something needed to be done. But the key was Shelby, who had finally decided that it was time to act.

Before we went in, my legislative aide, Kevin Fromer, reminded me, "This is Dodd's meeting, so let Dodd run it." He knew I had a tendency to jump in and take over.

But after a few pleasantries, Dodd turned to me. I made clear that Fannie and Freddie were critically important to helping us get through this crisis; that we needed to restore confidence in them; that reform required a new, stronger regulator; and that it was crucial for them to raise capital. Mudd noted that Fannie planned to raise $6 billion; Syron was noncommittal.

We'd come with a list of crucial unresolved issues, and at Shelby's prompting I asked David Nason to run through them. They concerned the new regulator's increased jurisdiction over the portfolio, including the power to force divestitures, its ability to set and temporarily increase capital requirements without congressional approval, and its oversight of new GSE business activities. Other issues included increasing conforming loan limits for high-cost areas and setting up an affordable housing fund.

"Well," Shelby said, "those are the key items."

Shelby is a formidable talent, a crafty legislator, and an astute questioner. But, frankly, I never clicked with him. He was a true conservative. I don't think he ever really trusted me, because I came from Wall Street, and he hated the Bear Stearns rescue. This was the rare time in the two and a half years I was in D.C. where I saw him do much more than sidestep an issue or point out the problems with someone else's proposal.

But here Shelby took charge, and I saw the Alabama senator at his best.

"I liked our bill," I remember him saying. "But I know I can't get everything I want."

Shelby was now ready to move. For him, the big issues were how to deal with the sizes of the portfolios and new product approval. Treasury cared mostly about systemic risk and safety and soundness matters, while Dodd—like Barney Frank—wanted bigger loan limits and an affordable housing fund.

"Are you going to work with us?" Shelby asked Mudd and Syron. "Do you guys really want to get this done?"

Under Shelby's no-nonsense gaze, they said yes, and I left the Russell Building feeling very optimistic and determined to draft the language that would help fix Fannie and Freddie.

It wouldn't be a moment too soon.

In early May, Fannie announced a first-quarter loss of $2.2 billion—its third straight quarterly loss—cut its common stock dividend, and announced plans to raise $6 billion through an equity offering. Eight days later, Freddie announced its first-quarter results—a loss of $151 million—along with plans to raise $5.5 billion in new core capital in the near future.

On May 6, Treasury officials met with a group of large mortgage lenders to speed up loan modifications for qualified homeowners facing foreclosure. That same day, the White House issued a statement outlining its opposition to the housing stimulus bill working its way through the House. Officially known as H.R. 3221, this ungainly and complicated piece of legislation had begun life as an energy bill in 2007, before turning into a housing vehicle in February. It contained a hodgepodge of provisions that were expensive and likely to be ineffective. The administration considered the bill burdensome, prescriptive, and risky to taxpayers. The legislation addressed GSE reform, but the White House was concerned about the other measures. I was convinced we could work with Barney Frank to fashion an acceptable compromise.

On the Senate side, our summit meeting with Dodd and Shelby

was paying dividends. After considerable wrangling, they ushered the Federal Housing Finance Regulatory Reform Act of 2008 through the Senate Banking Committee on May 20. It provided for a strong new GSE regulator, the Federal Housing Finance Agency, with the authority to set standards for minimum capital levels and sound portfolio management.

After Bear Stearns, it would not have been unusual for the regulators involved to have resorted to turf building and finger pointing. That's too often the way in Washington. But we knew how important it was that we continue to act in a united way. We were focused on increasing market confidence in the remaining four investment banks by encouraging them to take tangible steps to strengthen their balance sheets and their liquidity management.

The Primary Dealer Credit Facility (PDCF) allowed the Fed to conduct on-site examinations of institutions regulated by the SEC. I had dispatched a Treasury team led by David Nason to visit the investment banks to find out how the process was working. They met with the firms' CFOs, treasurers, and lawyers, and found that the arrangement was working fine—Lehman was the most pleased to have the Fed on-site.

But there was a considerable amount of tension and borderline mistrust between the agencies. Chris Cox was open and cooperative, but some SEC staff were understandably uneasy that their agency could be overshadowed by the Fed on the regulation of securities firms. I had a lot of confidence in the New York Fed, because it had been proactive and creative in dealing with Bear and consistently tried to get ahead of the curve.

I believed it vitally important for the regulators to work together. Ben Bernanke and Chris Cox agreed. They weren't interested in turf wars. They cared, as I did, about market stability and wanted the Fed inside the firms to protect that.

Traditional protocol would have left the agencies to sort out their issues, but I took the initiative in mid-May to convene a meeting with Ben, Tim Geithner, Chris Cox, Bob Steel, and David Nason. The SEC and the Fed agreed to draft a memo of understanding that would set ground rules to coordinate on-site examinations and to improve information sharing between the agencies. We also discussed how long the PDCF should run. It was a temporary program, created under Federal Reserve emergency authority, and was scheduled to expire in September. I supported Ben and Tim's view that the facility should be extended.

It would have been easy to leave many technical and legal issues for the regulators to work out, but the policy and greater economy implications were too great for Treasury to sit on the sidelines.

Even as we worked on these regulatory matters, the heat was rising under Lehman Brothers. In April a New York hedge fund manager named David Einhorn had announced that he was shorting Lehman. Then, on May 21, at an investment conference in New York, he raised the ante, questioning Lehman's accounting of its troubled assets, including mortgage securities. He insisted that the bank had vastly overvalued these assets and had underreported its problems in the first quarter. With his frequent television appearances and negative public comments, Einhorn seemed to be leading a crusade against Lehman.

Almost on cue, the firm's health took a turn for the worse. On June 9, the bank released earnings for the second quarter a week early, reporting a preliminary loss of $2.8 billion, owing to writedowns in its mortgage portfolio. Lehman also said it had raised $6 billion in new capital—$4 billion in common stock and $2 billion in mandatory convertible preferred shares. But the damage was done. The shares had tumbled from $39.56 the day of Einhorn's speech to $29.48.

I had been constantly in touch with Dick Fuld. (My call log

would show nearly 50 discussions with him between Bear Stearns's failure and Lehman's collapse six months later, and my staff probably was on at least as many calls.) He asked me what I thought of his president and his chief financial officer. How would the market react if he replaced them? I said I didn't know, but there was a chance the market would see that as a desperate act. On June 12, he fired longtime friend Joseph Gregory, who was president and chief operating officer, and demoted Erin Callan, his chief financial officer. Herbert (Bart) McDade, a senior member of Dick's team and the company's former global head of equities, replaced Gregory, while co–chief administrative officer Ian Lowitt succeeded Callan. Lehman shares touched a new year low of $22.70. They would end June at $19.81.

All year, Dick had been struggling to come to grips with the erosion of confidence in his firm. Yet even though he was on full alert, he remained overly optimistic. He would insist Lehman didn't need capital and then reluctantly raise it, hoping to calm the market. Finally, after the second-quarter numbers went public, he admitted that he needed to find a buyer or a strategic investor by September, when new results would be released.

"What are your third-quarter earnings going to be like?" I asked.

"Not good."

Yet even in their efforts to find that buyer or investor, Dick and his people found it hard, I think, to price the firm attractively enough. When I talked with him about possible buyers, I pointed out—and Dick agreed—that Bank of America was the most logical candidate. Not only did BofA lack a strong investment banking business, but CEO Ken Lewis had great confidence in his own ability to buy and assimilate things. He had bought Countrywide and Chicago's LaSalle Bank in the last year. He was in a buying mood. Dick had his lawyer, Rodge Cohen, call Lewis, and Lewis had Gregory Curl, BofA's head of global corporate development and planning, look at Lehman's books. But after Curl and his team had done their work, BofA decided not to pursue a deal.

My conversations with Dick were becoming very frustrating. Although I pressed him to accept reality and to operate with a greater sense of urgency, I was beginning to suspect that despite my blunt style, I wasn't getting through.

With Lehman looking shakier, I asked my senior adviser, Steve Shafran, to begin contingency planning with the Fed and SEC for a possible failure. Steve, a brilliant 48-year-old former Goldman Sachs banker who had retired from the firm in 2000, was an expert financial engineer. A widower who had moved to Washington to raise his four children, he had offered to help me on a part-time basis. As the crisis unfolded, Steve would work around the clock as a go-to problem solver.

While Bob Hoyt and his people combed through Treasury history to see what authorities we might use if Lehman failed, Treasury, the Fed, and the SEC worked to assess potential damages and devise ways to minimize these. They identified four areas of risk that had to be controlled in any collapse: Lehman's securities portfolio, its unsecured creditors, its triparty repo book, and its derivatives positions. The team managed to hammer out some possible protocols over the course of three months.

The SEC would want to be sure it could ring-fence the broker-dealer and ensure that all customers got back their collateral; the Fed might be able to step in and take over the triparty repo obligations of Lehman, which were secured. But figuring out what to do with the derivatives book proved elusive. There were no silver bullets, and I worried that the team wasn't doing enough. Wasn't there something else we could try, I'd ask, some legal authority we could invoke?

But there was none. The financial world had changed—with investment banks and hedge funds playing increasingly critical roles—but our powers and authorities had not kept up. To avoid damaging the system, we needed the ability to wind down a failing nonbank outside of bankruptcy, a court process designed to resolve creditor claims equitably rather than to reduce systemic risks. I raised the issue publicly for the first time at a speech in Washington in June. And I followed that up with a July 2 speech in London.

Shafran's team briefly worked on crafting legislation to give the secretary of the Treasury wind-down powers. Barney Frank was supportive but cautioned us against trying to push legislation that was so complex substantively and politically. We concluded there was no way we could get what we needed passed with the congressional summer recess on the way and presidential elections in November. We knew it wasn't going to be easy to work with the inadequate authorities we had, but we also knew that aggressively making the case for new authorities might itself precipitate Lehman's failure. Instead, Barney encouraged the Fed and Treasury to interpret our existing powers broadly to protect the system, saying: "If you do so, I'm not going to raise legal issues."

Meantime, the housing and GSE reform legislation continued to move much slower than expected. Initially, we'd thought it would be done by the July 4 recess, but that deadline had slipped away as Republicans dug in against homeowner bailouts, placing much of the burden for passage on the Democrats.

While Congress dithered, the markets got jittery. I was at a meeting of finance ministers from the Americas and the Caribbean in Cancún, Mexico, on June 23, when I heard that Freddie Mac shares had dropped below $20. That was off more than $10 since they'd announced plans to raise capital in March. I'd been hoping all along that the GSEs would be able to raise capital. Fannie had done so in May and June, raising $7.4 billion in common and preferred stock. But Freddie had not done anything. Now they would not be able to access the market, and we did not have the legislation we needed to protect them or the taxpayers.

I put in a call to Barney Frank to find out the progress of the bill, but I couldn't reach him. I had just gone into the lavatory in the hotel where the finance ministers were meeting, when Barney returned my call.

"Barney," I said, "you're getting me in a men's room in Mexico!"

"Don't drink the water," he replied without losing a beat. Barney then told me he was committed to GSE reform and optimistic about getting our legislation.

On June 28 I went on a five-day trip to meet with political leaders, finance ministers, and central bankers in Russia, Germany, and the U.K. After seeing Russia's finance minister, Alexei Kudrin, a voice of reason and a straight-shooting reformer, I had meetings scheduled with Prime Minister Vladimir Putin and President Dmitry Medvedev.

Once I arrived at the White House, as the Russian government building is called, an official tried to usher me into the conference room where Putin and I were to meet. There was a long table, and at the end of the room a gallery with the press and TV cameras. It was clear that the Russians intended to make me sit there and cool my heels in front of the U.S. and Russian press until the great man arrived. But my chief of staff, Jim Wilkinson, had other ideas.

"Whoa!" he exclaimed. "We're not going to let the U.S. secretary of the Treasury be a political prop for Putin."

So we remained in the hall, and we waited and waited, concerned that we wouldn't make our next meeting, with Medvedev at the Kremlin. Putin was, I imagine, flexing his muscles, showing that he was more important than the new president.

Finally, the prime minister arrived, and we walked into the meeting room together. We had agreed to exchange brief opening statements, then dismiss the media and begin our meeting. But instead Putin launched into a soliloquy on the U.S. financial crisis. With oil prices at record highs, the Russians were feeling their oats. I spoke about the work we had been doing with Kudrin on sovereign wealth funds, and Putin responded, "We don't have a sovereign wealth fund. But we are ready [to create one], especially if you want us to."

Frankly, this was too good a political opportunity for Putin to pass up. In 1998 it was a humiliating Russian default that started the global financial crisis. And now he was temporarily able to point to a reversal of fortunes.

Our private session was much more productive, like all such Putin meetings: he was direct and a bit combative, which made it fun. He never took offense, and we could spar back and forth. We discussed the U.S. economic situation, then went four rounds on Iran. I talked about the Russian banks living up to the United Nations sanctions, and he pushed back hard, saying, "They're our neighbors, and we have to live with them. We don't want a nuclear weapon in Iran, and I've talked to the president many times about this, but sanctioning them is not the way to do it."

The talk turned to the World Trade Organization, a sore subject for Putin. He basically said, "We've made many concessions, and if we don't get admission to the WTO, we're going to pull back the concessions we made. I have Russian companies telling me that we have gone too far to open up to foreign competition. So this is going to get done soon, or we're going to start pulling things back."

After the long wait for Putin, we barely made the meeting with Medvedev, who was a couple of miles away in the Kremlin. Once more I had to endure some public gloating about the U.S. financial crisis, though he was more moderate and polite in front of the cameras than Putin. Behind closed doors Medvedev was very engaged, and as he peppered me with questions, he revealed a good understanding of markets. I was surprised not to be asked about Fannie Mae and Freddie Mac, because Kudrin had told me to be ready to talk about the GSEs, and Putin himself had raised the subject in 2007 with President Bush. I was soon to learn, though, that the Russians had been doing a lot of thinking about our GSEs' securities.

Shortly after I returned from my trip, on Monday, July 7, the Federal Reserve and the SEC announced that they had finally signed a memo of understanding. The next day, speaking at an FDIC-sponsored forum on mortgage lending in Arlington, Virginia, Ben Bernanke signaled that the Fed was considering extending into 2009 the duration of the Primary Dealer Credit Facility and the Term Securities Lending Facility, its lending programs for primary government dealers.

But there was more bad news than good. The same day the Fed and the SEC announced their agreement, a report came out of Lehman Brothers, of all places, speculating that Fannie and Freddie might need as much as $75 billion in additional capital. It set off an investor stampede. Freddie's stock dropped almost 18 percent, to $11.91, on July 7, while Fannie's shares fell more than 16 percent, to $15.74. Both stocks rebounded somewhat the next day, as a result of assurances from their regulator, the Office of Federal Housing Enterprise Oversight, but they plunged again on July 9. I made two public statements myself that week in support of the GSEs. Each time, the market steadied for a while then resumed its downward tilt. Short sellers were becoming active. The press and investors in the U.S. and around the world were losing confidence in Fannie's and Freddie's viability. The GSEs went to the market almost as often as the U.S. government, with funding needs in the tens of billions of dollars every month. We couldn't afford a failed auction of their securities.

Investment banks were sinking, too, and Lehman was hit hardest. Its shares dropped 31 percent that week, while its credit default swaps ballooned out to 360 basis points on Friday from 286 basis points on Monday.

I'd hoped that a combination of capital raising and reform would be enough to shore up the GSEs. Fannie had raised some equity, but Freddie had missed the opportunity, and Congress still had not acted on the proposed reforms. Now, we would need much more. For the first time, I seriously considered going to Congress for emergency powers on the GSEs. Before, with Democrats and Republicans at war, it had been impossible to get relatively modest things done without a crisis.

But now we had one—and we needed to act swiftly. I made a series of calls to alert key Hill leaders to the worsening situation and let them know, without being too specific, that we might need more authorities in the bill. Next, I needed to explain the urgency of this situation to the president and to request his permission to formally approach Congress. I knew he was always at work by about 6:45 a.m., so Friday morning I called Josh Bolten and asked to see President Bush. I walked over just after 7:00 a.m. and joined the president in the Oval Office, where I ran through my concerns about the capital markets, the vulnerability of Lehman, and the need to move on the GSEs. Later that morning, the president was to meet with his economic team at the Department of Energy to discuss oil prices, which hit a peak of $147.27 that day. I arranged to ride over with Josh and the president in his limo. I asked the president to publicly affirm the importance of the GSEs after his meeting.

"We're probably going to have to take emergency action," I said. "But you can help calm the markets in the meantime."

The president understood the gravity of the moment. After the meeting, he called in the press, as was the custom, and made a point of emphasizing how important Fannie and Freddie were. I also gave a statement, noting that we were focused on supporting Fannie and Freddie "in their current form." I hoped to calm market fears of a government takeover that would wipe out shareholders.

Later we had lunch in the president's private dining room, adjacent to the Oval Office, with Vice President Cheney and Josh. I had come to ask for the authority to deal with Fannie and Freddie, but the first words out of my mouth were "I don't believe there's a buyer for Lehman."

I mentioned that I'd spoken with former Fed chairman Alan Greenspan, who believed we should get authority to wind Lehman down, in case of failure.

Then I laid out the case for acting quickly on the GSEs, requesting permission to ask Congress for power to, among other things, invest in the mortgage giants. I didn't provide a lot of details, because we were still debating what we would need. The president said it was unthinkable to let Fannie and Freddie fail—they would take down the capital markets and the dollar, and hurt the U.S. around the world. Although he disliked everything the GSEs represented, he understood that we needed them to provide housing finance or we weren't going to get through the crisis. The first order of business, he said, was "save their ass."

July 11 turned out to be a day for the books. The president and the Treasury secretary's reassuring words about the GSEs failed to soothe the markets—Fannie's shares fell 22 percent, to $10.25, while Freddie's dropped 3.1 percent, to $7.75. Then, late in the afternoon, the Office of Thrift Supervision seized the teetering IndyMac Federal Bank, with more than $32 billion in assets, and turned it over to the FDIC. It was to that point the third-biggest bank failure in U.S. history.

The news reports of that day showed the first scenes of depositors lined up in the hot sun outside the failed thrift's headquarters in Pasadena, California, desperate for their money. The government guaranteed deposits up to $100,000, but these citizens had lost faith in the system. This all-too-eerie reprise of the haunting images of the Great Depression was the last thing anyone needed just then.

1963: Preparing to embark on a canoe trip in Ely, Minnesota. Left to right: My cousin Lisann; me; my mother, Marianna; my sister, Kay; my brother, Dick; and my father, Merritt.

As All-Ivy, All-East Dartmouth College tackle.
Dartmouth archives

1969: With Wendy during my first year of Harvard Business School.
Brooks Zug

1973: Banding a peregrine falcon at Assateague Island National Seashore with
F. Prescott Ward. *Wendy Paulson*

At home in Barrington, Illinois. Left to right: Wendy, me, Merritt, and Amanda. Merritt is holding one of several raccoons we raised.

April 2002: The family at Little St. Simons Island, Georgia. Left to right: Merritt, me, Wendy, and Amanda. *Clark Judge*

November 2002: As co-chairman of the Asia-Pacific Council of the Nature Conservancy, with Wendy, in Yunnan Province in China, working to establish national parks.
Amanda Paulson

May 4, 1999: Trading begins at the New York Stock Exchange as the Goldman Sachs IPO ends the firm's 130 years as a private company. Front row, left to right: Co-president and co-COO John Thain, board member and former senior partner Steve Friedman, NYSE CEO Dick Grasso, and me. Behind, left to right: Co–general counsel Esta Stecher, CFO David Viniar, partner and head of financial institutions group Chris Cole, treasurer Dan Jester, and co-president and co-COO John Thornton. *Mike Segar/Reuters*

July 10, 2006: Chief Justice John Roberts swearing me in as 74th U.S. secretary of the Treasury in the Cash Room, with President George W. Bush and Wendy. *Chris Taylor, Treasury Department*

December 2006: Meeting at the Great Hall of the People in Beijing with Chinese president Hu Jintao (second from right) and vice premier Wu Yi (far right), my first counterpart for the Strategic Economic Dialogue, and U.S. ambassador Clark Randt, Jr. (far left). *Ng Han Guan/Associated Press*

With senior adviser
Steve Shafran.
Chris Taylor,
Treasury Department

Meeting of the
Financial Stability
Oversight Board
in the large
conference room
at Treasury.
Chris Taylor,
Treasury Department

January 25, 2008: Negotiating the economic stimulus package with Speaker of the House
Nancy Pelosi and House Minority Leader John Boehner, late into the night at the Capitol.
Brendan Smialowski for The New York Times/Redux

April 3, 2008: Testifying before the Senate Banking Committee about Bear Stearns. Left to right: Fed chairman Ben Bernanke, SEC commissioner Chris Cox, Treasury undersecretary for domestic finance Bob Steel, and New York Fed president Tim Geithner. *Susan Walsh/Associated Press*

June 8, 2008: Chinese vice premier Wang Qishan, my second Strategic Economic Dialogue counterpart, and me signing the 10-Year Framework on Energy and the Environment at the Naval Academy in Annapolis. Left to right, standing: Carlos Gutierrez, secretary of Commerce; Elaine Chao, secretary of Labor; Taiya Smith, my deputy chief of staff; and Mike Leavitt, secretary of Health and Human Services. *Chris Taylor, Treasury Department*

September 7, 2008: Federal Housing Finance Agency director Jim Lockhart and me signing the $100 billion keepwell agreement for both Fannie Mae and Freddie Mac, effectively guaranteeing the debt of both agencies after placing them into conservatorship. With Treasury's Dan Jester. *Courtesy of Dan Jester*

September 18, 2008, 9:30 a.m.: Some of the Treasury participants on a conference call with me and the Fed and the SEC. Left to right, standing: Jim Wilkinson, Michele Davis, Neel Kashkari, Bob Hoyt, and Kevin Fromer. *Chris Taylor, Treasury Department*

September 18, 2008: Discussing the TARP capital program with (left to right) Treasury's Dan Jester, Jeremiah Norton, and David Nason. *Chris Taylor, Treasury Department*

September 18, 2008, 7:00 p.m.: Meeting in Nancy Pelosi's office to request TARP authority. Left to right: Rep. Barney Frank, Ben Bernanke, me, Chris Cox, Sen. Chris Dodd, Sen. Richard Shelby, Rep. Spencer Bachus, Sen. Jon Kyl, Senate Majority Whip Dick Durbin, Senate Majority Leader Harry Reid, Nancy Pelosi, John Boehner, and House Majority Leader Steny Hoyer. *Molly Riley/Reuters*

September 23, 2008: Testifying before the Senate Banking Committee seeking TARP authority. Left to right: Me, Ben Bernanke, Chris Cox, and Jim Lockhart. *Kevin Lamarque/Reuters*

September 25, 2008, 3:40 p.m.: Pre-meeting with Republican leadership before meeting with presidential candidates Barack Obama and John McCain and congressional leaders of both parties. Sitting, left to right: President Bush, Senate Minority Leader Mitch McConnell, me, Kevin Fromer, Keith Hennessey, Ed Lazear, Joel Kaplan, Ed Gillespie, Dana Perino, Josh Bolten, Dan Meyer, John Boehner, and Vice President Dick Cheney. Standing, left to right: Barry Jackson and a White House staffer. *Eric Draper, Courtesy of the George W. Bush Presidential Library*

September 25, 2008, 4:00 p.m.: Bicameral, bipartisan meeting with the presidential candidates, the president, and the vice president to discuss the economic crisis. Left to right: Richard Shelby, Josh Bolten, Vice President Cheney, me, Spencer Bachus, Barney Frank, Steny Hoyer, Republican presidential candidate Sen. John McCain, John Boehner, Nancy Pelosi, President Bush, Harry Reid, Mitch McConnell, and Democratic presidential candidate Sen. Barack Obama. *Pablo Martinez Monsivais/Associated Press*

Sunday, September 28, 2008, 12:30 a.m.: Press conference in National Statuary Hall announcing the successful conclusion to TARP negotiations. Left to right: Nancy Pelosi, Sen. Judd Gregg, Spencer Bachus, Chris Dodd, me, House Minority Whip Roy Blunt, and Harry Reid. *Lauren Victoria Burke/Associated Press*

October 3, 2008: President Bush visits Treasury's Markets Room after Congress passes the TARP legislation. Left to right: Matt Rutherford, President Bush, Megan Leary, Tim Dulaney, and Michael Pedroni (shaking hands). *Eric Draper, Courtesy of the George W. Bush Presidential Library*

October 10, 2008: Finance ministers and central bank governors of many nations gather on the steps of the Treasury Department after agreeing to a set of coordinated policy efforts to stabilize the global financial system.

Front row, left to right: Canada's finance minister James Flaherty, France's finance minister Christine Lagarde, Germany's minister of finance Peer Steinbrück, me, Italy's finance minister Giulio Tremonti, Japan's finance minister Shoichi Nakagawa, Britain's chancellor of the Exchequer Alistair Darling, and Eurogroup's president Jean-Claude Juncker. Back row, left to right: Bank of Canada governor Mark Carney, Bank of France governor Christian Noyer, president of Germany's Bundesbank Axel Weber, Ben Bernanke, Italy's central bank governor Mario Draghi, Japan's central bank governor Masaaki Shirakawa, Bank of England governor Mervyn King, president of the European Central Bank Jean-Claude Trichet, International Monetary Fund managing director Dominique Strauss-Kahn, and World Bank president Robert Zoellick. *Chris Taylor, Treasury Department*

⏱ Calendar

Start Time	End Time	Category	Description
13 6:00 AM	6:55 AM		COLUMBUS DAY -- FEDERAL HOLIDAY
6:55 AM	7:10 AM		Arrive White House
7:10 AM	7:45 AM		Meeting with the President, Oval Office, White House
7:50 AM	8:10 AM		Call to Tim Geithner, left word
8:10 AM	8:20 AM		Call to Tim Geithner
8:30 AM	9:10 AM		Meeting with Commerce Secretary Carlos Gutierrez, Claire Buchan, Sean Reilly, Chris Padilla, Richard Wagoner of GM, Ray Young, Executive Vice President and Chief Financial Officer, Erskine Bowles, President, University of North Carolina, John Bryan, Retired Chairman and Chief Executive Officer of Sara Lee Corporation, Secretary's Office with Jim and Phill Swagel
9:10 AM	9:15 AM		Call from FED Chairman Ben Bernanke
9:15 AM	9:30 AM		Call from Speaker Nancy Pelosi
9:30 AM	10:00 AM		Meeting with Reverend Jesse Jackson and Group, Secretary's Large Conference Room
10:00 AM	11:00 AM		Meeting with FED Chairman Bernanke, Tim Geithner, Sheila Bair, John Dugan, Joel Kaplan, Dave Nason, Jeremiah Norton, Dan Jester, Bob Hoyt, Michele Davis, Neel Kashkari, Kevin Fromer, Phill Swagel, Dave McCormick, Secretary's Large Conference Room
11:00 AM	11:25 AM		Drop by Ken's Meeting with Bill Powers, Pacific Investment Management Co. (PIMCO)
11:25 AM	11:30 AM		Call to Joel Kaplan
11:30 AM	12:00 PM		Conference Call with Financial Stability Oversight Board, Secretary's Office
12:20 PM	12:30 PM		Call to FED Chairman Bernanke
1:30 PM	1:55 PM		Meeting with Kevin Fromer, Secretary's Office
2:15 PM	3:00 PM		Principals Briefing for CEO Meeting with FED Chairman Bernanke, Tim Geithner, Sheila Bair, John Dugan, Joel Kaplan, Secretary's Office
3:00 PM	4:10 PM		Meeting with CEOs of Financial Institutions, Vikram Pandit, Citigroup, Jamie Dimon, JP Morgan, Richard Kovacevich, Wells Fargo, John Thain, Merrill Lynch, John Mack, Morgan Stanley, Lloyd Blankfein, Goldman Sachs, Robert Kelly, Bank of New York, Ronald Logue, State Street Bank, FED Chairman Bernanke and FDIC Chairwoman Sheila Bair, large conference room
4:20 PM	4:30 PM		Call to Senator Chris Dodd
4:30 PM	4:40 PM		Call to Senator John McCain, left word
4:40 PM	4:50 PM		Call to Congressman Spencer Bachus
5:00 PM	5:10 PM		Call to Congressman Barney Frank
5:10 PM	5:20 PM		Call to Speaker Nancy Pelosi
5:55 PM	6:05 PM		Call to Senator Barack Obama
6:25 PM	6:30 PM		Call from Jeff Immelt, GE
6:30 PM	6:35 PM		Call to Congressman John Boehner
6:35 PM	6:40 PM		Meeting with CEOs of Financial Institutions -- Vikram Pandit, Citigroup, Jamie Dimon, JP Morgan, Richard Kovacevich, Wells Fargo, John Thain, Merrill Lynch, John Mack, Morgan Stanley, Lloyd Blankfein, Goldman Sachs, Robert Kelly, Bank of New York, Ronald Logue, State Street Bank, FED Chairman Bernanke, and FDIC Chairwoman Sheila Bair, large conference room
6:40 PM	6:50 PM		Call to Congressman Steny Hoyer
6:50 PM	7:00 PM		Call to Senator Max Baucus
7:10 PM	7:20 PM		Call to Congressman Roy Blunt
7:25 PM	7:30 PM		Call to Senator Mitch McConnell
7:30 PM	7:35 PM		Call to Senator Dick Durbin, left word
7:35 PM	7:40 PM		Call to Senator Charles Schumer
7:40 PM	7:50 PM		Call to Senator Harry Reid
9:15 PM	9:25 PM		Call to Senator John McCain

A page from my log, October 13, 2008, the day we urged the bank CEOs to accept equity capital from the government.

October 14, 2008: Announcing the TARP capital purchase program and the Federal Deposit Insurance Corporation's temporary liquidity guarantee program in Treasury's Cash Room. With, left to right, Ben Bernanke, FDIC chairman Sheila Bair, Tim Geithner, and Comptroller of the Currency John Dugan. *Hyungwon Kang/Reuters*

My trusted partners Tim Geithner (left) and Ben Bernanke. *Lucas Jackson/Reuters*

November 15, 2008: With President Bush at the G-20 summit on financial markets and the world economy, in Washington, D.C. Dan Price is in the background. *Eric Draper, Courtesy of the George W. Bush Presidential Library*

With Ben Bernanke. *Manuel Balce Ceneta/Associated Press*

Chapter 7

Saturday, July 12, 2008

We needed congressional action to contain the deteriorating situation at Fannie Mae and Freddie Mac, so on Saturday, July 12, I tried calling Chris Dodd and Nancy Pelosi, but I couldn't reach either of them during the day. Finally, Nancy returned my call from California at about 10:30 p.m. Normally, I'd have been fast asleep, but I was still up and working. When I told her we needed emergency powers to invest in the GSEs, she came right back at me, ready to start negotiating.

"This won't be easy," she said. "Will the president support our housing legislation?"

I told her I thought so. That is, with the exception of the block grants to state and local governments.

She rolled right past me. "We're going to get the block grants," she said.

That was a problem. House Republicans and the administration absolutely hated all of the Democrats' proposed housing legislation but most especially the block grants. Barney Frank had explained to me how important they were to him and his colleagues, but his foremost objective was to get HOPE for Homeowners and GSE reform through. He had indicated that if the president made clear he would not accept the grants, they would be removed from the bill.

"I've got this deal with Barney," I explained to Nancy. "If the president strongly objects to the grants, they're going to come out."

"Well, Barney didn't talk to me. I don't know how he can make deals like this without talking to me. I'm going to call him."

Worried that I'd said too much, I decided I had better get to Barney before Nancy could. I reached him in Boston on his cell, but I could barely make out what he was saying over peals of laughter and a host of chattering voices in the background.

"Barney, can you hear me?" I said.

"I hear you, Hank," he shouted, then paused, and with perfect timing quipped, "Can the president?"

I told him about my conversation with Nancy and that she hadn't known about our understanding.

"That was just between the two of us, Hank," he said, clearly annoyed. He said he would do his best, but that things had changed—given the dire circumstances, the threat of a presidential veto now seemed empty.

Block grants were just one of the political land mines we had to avoid. The weekend of July 12 and 13 was a blur of nonstop phone calls, meetings, and brainstorming: Ben Bernanke, Tim Geithner, and Chris Cox. Chuck Schumer, Barney Frank, John Boehner, and Spencer Bachus. Conference calls, one-on-one calls, still more meetings.

Though we did not have firsthand access to Fannie's and Freddie's financials, we knew we would need billions of taxpayer dollars to backstop the institutions from catastrophic failure and a strong regulator with powers to make subjective judgments about capital quality, just as other prudential regulators were able to do.

With this in mind, I had asked the Federal Reserve if it could provide discount-window funding for the GSEs. Ben Bernanke made clear that this was properly a fiscal matter, but indicated that the Fed Board of Governors would be willing to provide temporary support to the GSEs if I could assure them that Congress was likely to grant us the emergency legislation we would be seeking. I told him I would consult with congressional leaders and the GSEs and let him know for sure before his noon board meeting on Sunday.

I had very solid reasons for requesting additional powers: I was concerned that investors had lost faith in Fannie and Freddie. The mortgage giants had lost almost half of their value that week. This worried the debt holders, from U.S. pension funds to foreign governments, that held hundreds of billions of dollars of GSE paper, and raised red flags about the companies' ability to fund themselves in future auctions.

Nonetheless, we faced the catch-22 of crisis policy making. There was always the chance that by asking for these powers we would confirm just how fragile the GSEs were and spook investors. Then, if Congress failed to come through, the markets would implode. The stakes were enormous: more than $5 trillion in debt either guaranteed or issued by Fannie and Freddie. Every time spreads grew—that is to say, the yields of these securities increased relative to Treasuries—investors lost billions of dollars. It was not my job to protect private investors. But a collapse of the GSEs would have drastic consequences for the economy and the financial system.

Fannie and Freddie needed to be brought on board, quickly. Without their support, legislation would go nowhere. On Saturday I called Dan Mudd and Dick Syron to get their cooperation. Mudd, the Fannie Mae CEO, wanted to save his company and asked a lot of questions. Syron, though, was compliant; he was looking for a way out. He was on a short leash and had had a difficult time working with his board. But the next morning, when I spoke with them at his request, his directors were supportive.

Then I huddled with my team at Treasury to review our options and nail down our proposed legislation. We were in an awkward position. The GSEs and their regulator, the Office of Federal Housing Enterprise Oversight, had said that the companies were adequately capitalized for regulatory purposes, but the market was skeptical. To know for sure, we would need experienced bank examiners to comb through their books. But we did not have the power to send in examiners.

Instead, we needed to get standby authority to deal with a potential liquidity problem, such as a failed auction of debt, and the authority to make an equity investment, if necessary. We didn't want to put a dollar limit on this authority because that would imply that we had identified the size of the problem, which we had not. Having an unlimited capacity—we used the term *unspecified*—would be more reassuring to the markets. Asking for this was an extraordinary act—indeed, an unprecedented one—but my team agreed we had to try.

The difficulty came when I said that our powers should have no set expiration date. Fannie and Freddie guaranteed securities for up to 30 years, and I questioned whether temporary standby authorities would be enough to satisfy long-term investors. But after a tense conversation, Kevin Fromer and David Nason convinced me.

"Hank, if we're going to sell this on the Hill, it needs to be temporary," Kevin insisted.

We decided to ask for unlimited investment authority until the end of 2009, to give the incoming administration a year of protection.

From my calls, I knew there was a lack of enthusiasm on the Hill for what we wanted. At the same time, I had not gotten a single definitive *No way*. So on Sunday, July 13, I told Ben I thought we could get Congress to act. When the Federal Reserve Board met at noon, they agreed to provide a temporary backup to Fannie and Freddie through the New York Fed. Later that afternoon, I walked out onto the west steps of the Treasury Building, facing the White House and a group of reporters. The day had turned overcast. Storm clouds moved in, and the wind began to pick up as I spoke.

"Fannie Mae and Freddie Mac play a central role in our housing finance system and must continue to do so in their current form as shareholder-owned companies," I said, emphasizing that their "continued strength is important to maintaining confidence and stability in our financial system and our financial markets."

I announced that President Bush had authorized me to work with Congress on a plan for immediate action, and that after consulting with other officials and congressional leaders, I would ask lawmakers for temporary authority to increase the GSEs' $2.25 billion line of credit with Treasury and allow us to buy equity in the GSEs if we deemed it necessary.

We would also seek to give the Federal Reserve a role as a consultative regulator. Doing so, I knew, would give the Fed access to all financial information available to the GSEs' new regulator, the soon-to-be-created Federal Housing Finance Agency, as well as a role in setting capital requirements. Crucially, the FHFA would have more flexibility to make judgments about capital adequacy and the power to place the GSEs in receivership. I had no sooner finished speaking than a downpour erupted.

I had been unable to reach Senator Dodd over the weekend. On Monday I heard he was scheduling a hearing for the following day, and I was mildly offended that he had not discussed this with me first. At that point, I considered congressional hearings to be a waste of time. I'd never seen any piece of legislation get done there, never saw any compromise get worked out at a hearing. I only saw politicians making statements meant to be seen back home.

"This is a crisis," I told Dodd on the phone. "How are we going to resolve this in a hearing? All we'll do is spook the markets."

"Trust me, Hank. We're going to use the hearings to build support and to build market confidence."

It turned out we were both correct. There was no way something this big could have passed the Senate without a hearing. But the hearing sure didn't help the markets.

The response on the Hill to our proposed legislation ranged from skeptical to hostile. The GSEs had plenty of friends in Congress. Many lawmakers didn't believe we needed new powers, while others didn't like putting the government behind those agencies. The tax committees objected because our request for unlimited authority to purchase securities and buy equity would require the federal debt limit to be waived; that had to be worked out with House Ways and Means chairman Charlie Rangel.

Richard Shelby's and Barney Frank's people assured us that they wouldn't let the GSEs fail, but the battle lines were drawn. Dodd wanted more foreclosure relief, and House Democrats were adamant about the block grants.

Even as they teetered, the GSEs still had remarkable influence. We wanted to buy equity on the open market if need be, but the GSEs persuaded Dodd to write the language in such a way that we had to get their consent first.

Before the Tuesday morning Senate Banking Committee hearing, Kevin Fromer and Michele Davis, assistant secretary for public affairs and director of policy planning, pounded me about what I should say—and, even more important, what I should not say. They agreed that I was right to emphasize the importance of GSEs to the availability and cost of mortgage financing and to helping homeowners stay in their homes or purchase new ones. "But Hank," Michele said, "you can't say that the GSEs are 'orders of magnitude' more important than HOPE for Homeowners." Angry Republicans opposed to HOPE for Homeowners might conclude the president and I would accept anything to get emergency legislation and GSE reform. I left for the Hill determined to bite my tongue.

Before the Senate Banking Committee, Ben Bernanke and I stressed the need to strengthen the weak housing market. I maintained that the bigger and broader our powers, the less likely we would be to use them and the less it would cost taxpayers.

"If you want to make sure it's used, make it small enough and it'll be a self-fulfilling prophecy," I said. Then I uttered the words that would come back to haunt me within a matter of months: "If you've got a squirt gun in your pocket, you may have to take it out. If you've got a bazooka, and people know you've got it, you may not have to take it out. By having something that is unspecified, it will increase confidence, and by increasing confidence it will greatly reduce the likelihood it will ever be used."

Kentucky Republican Jim Bunning was far from convinced, declaring that "the Fed's purchase of Bear Stearns' assets was amateur socialism compared to this." He asserted that "every time we propose and do something, it always gets used. And you want an unlimited amount used."

I had walked into the hearing hoping to reassure investors. But contentious comments by a few senators and the skeptical tone of most of the others had a big impact. By day's end, Fannie's shares plunged 27 percent, to $7.07; Freddie's sank 26 percent, to $5.26.

I spent the next day, Wednesday, July 16, in a grinding marathon of meetings and phone calls. In the afternoon, I met with GOP congressional leaders—Senators Mitch McConnell of Kentucky and Jon Kyl of Arizona, and Representatives John

Boehner of Ohio and Roy Blunt of Missouri—in the Oval Office with the president and vice president.

It was an extraordinary meeting. These were the administration's best friends on the Hill. They, and much of the White House staff, opposed the Democrats' foreclosure legislation for philosophical reasons. And with elections approaching, they were alert to the rising sentiment among taxpayers against helping delinquent homeowners. But the president understood the seriousness of the GSE emergency, and after they aired their complaints, he said firmly, "We've got to get this done."

It was a tremendous act of political courage. It was as if, in the last days of his administration, the president were suddenly switching sides, supporting Democrats and opposing Republicans on matters that went against the basic principles of his administration. But he was determined to do what was best for the country.

Boehner summed up the strangeness of the moment when he said: "I'm prepared to say something supportive about the urgency of moving a bill; I just won't vote for it."

Later I met with the entire House Republican Conference in a basement room at the Capitol. The meeting—my first with the group since becoming Treasury secretary—had been set up to let members blow off steam, but that didn't make it any more pleasant. That crowded room of angry House Republicans was a preview of what I would later see with the Troubled Assets Relief Program.

One member after another walked up to the microphones. They were irate about both the GSE situation and the proposed foreclosure legislation, and they were understandably upset that the bill's affordable housing fund could funnel money to anti-GOP activist groups like the Association of Community Organizations for Reform Now (ACORN). I must have listened to eight or ten speeches about that. Over and over I explained how critical the capital markets were to the economy, how important the GSEs were to housing, how we were getting real reform that was going to make a difference.

That caucus meeting showed me just how difficult this legislation was for the House Republicans to stomach. Even if the block grants had not been in the language, a lot of these Republicans wouldn't have voted for the bill. It was going to take the Democrats to get it passed, which was why Nancy Pelosi could demand the block grants as her pound of flesh.

I went straight from that meeting to the Russell Senate Office Building, where I sat down with Chris Dodd, Richard Shelby, and Spencer Bachus. The issue before us was how to move the legislation.

Although we were in one of Dodd's offices, the main player was Shelby, who hammered me on specifics: "You haven't told us how much equity you would put in. You haven't told us whether you're going to use this liquidity support. You're asking for an unlimited amount of money, and you haven't told us how you are going to use it. I'm trying to get there, but I've never seen anything like this. Convince me again."

Shelby was right. Even though we said we never intended to use it, we were asking for an unprecedented blank check—and Congress was understandably wary of signing one over to us. In fact, I don't know if any executive branch agency had ever before been given the authority to lend to or invest in an enterprise in an unlimited amount. All I could do was argue that the extraordinary and unpredictable nature of the situation warranted the authority in this case.

The day had drained me, but that evening there was a dinner at the White House in honor of Major League Baseball. Hall of Fame players, lawmakers, and administration officials all mingled in the elegant East Room, with its bohemian glass chandeliers, parquet floors, and grand piano.

I reveled in the guest list, which included former Chicago Cubs second baseman Ryne Sandberg. My table included Hall of Fame Baltimore Orioles third baseman Brooks Robinson, but my wife's table was even more noteworthy. The White House had chosen to seat Wendy next to Senator Bunning, the Hall of Fame pitcher, who had jumped all over me at the Banking Committee hearing the day before.

I showed Wendy the place card. "Someone's got to be making a joke here," I said.

But as it turned out, the senator could not have been more gracious to my wife. He and I even chatted a little bit after dinner. He told me that his differences with me weren't personal, and I complimented him on his baseball prowess.

The next morning I was back working the phones. I conferred with John Spratt, who led the House Budget Committee, and Ways and Means chair Charlie Rangel about how we could make the legislation work fiscally. Their committees were reluctant to exempt the new authorities from the debt ceiling, which meant no blank check for Treasury. But with help from Rangel and Spratt we were able to raise the debt ceiling by $800 billion concurrent with our legislation—giving us a great deal of headroom.

Later I had an important call with Shelby—at least 20 minutes, a long time for me and a near eternity for him. When I hung up, I told Kevin Fromer, "I'm sure I've got him."

"What did you do?" he asked.

"I took your advice," I said.

Kevin had repeatedly told me that Shelby was worried that we would go easy on the GSEs and just prop them up, regardless of their problems. As I recounted to Kevin, "I told him, 'You don't know me, Senator. If I find a problem, I'm going to deal with it. I'm a tough guy.'"

I needed to go back and forth with Dodd and Frank to resolve a number of issues, one of which was absolutely critical. Dodd was resisting our demand to make the Fed a consultative regulator. With Barney's help, Dodd reluctantly agreed to this, but only until December 31, 2009, when the temporary authorities expired.

On July 23 the Housing and Economic Recovery Act (HERA) passed the House, 272 to 152. Three days later the Senate approved the bill, 72 to 13.

It was, as Shelby and others had said, an unprecedented accomplishment. The legislation gave us broad discretion to provide financial support to the GSEs as we saw fit. The terms and conditions of the support were left almost entirely to the discretion of the Treasury secretary, giving us ample flexibility to structure investments and loans in any way that made sense. The legislation did not impose any limitations on the amount of that support, except that it would not be exempt from the debt ceiling and that we would need the GSEs to approve any equity investment we made in them. All told, it was perhaps the most expansive power to commit funds ever given to a Treasury secretary.

I didn't seek this power for its own sake, of course, but because we faced a national emergency. I hoped that we would never have to use our new authorities.

With all the attention on the GSEs, I still kept an eye on Lehman's travails, speaking regularly with Dick Fuld about his options. The best of these was to sell his firm, and Bank of America was the most likely buyer. BofA had taken a look at the firm and passed the month before, but I thought I'd see if anything had changed. So on one of my calls with Dick, I suggested that he give the Charlotte-based bank another try and that he not use an intermediary but instead personally approach its CEO, Ken Lewis.

"Ken respects people who are direct," I remember telling him. "You won't be able to look at yourself in the mirror unless you have gone the extra mile here."

Dick made the call and met with Lewis in late July. He called me with an enthusiastic report.

"Ken really liked me," he said. "We have a lot in common—we're both guys with a chip on our shoulder. He's going to take a hard look at it."

But nothing came of their subsequent meeting.

Meanwhile, there was no grand signing ceremony for HERA. The president wasn't enthused—nor, frankly, was I—with the many provisions we had to accept, and he believed that a ceremony would upset House Republicans. To assuage them, he made a point of saying he was reluctant to sign the bill and was only doing so on the Treasury secretary's strong recommendation.

So, after weeks of speeches, meetings, behind-the-scenes negotiations, and sleepless nights for me and my staff, HERA was finally signed shortly after 7:00 a.m. on July 30 in the Oval Office, before a tiny group of administration officials, including Housing and Urban Development secretary Steve Preston, and Federal Housing Administration commissioner Brian Montgomery, Jim Lockhart, David Nason, and me.

"I want to thank all the congressmen here," the president joked, but he wasn't taking a potshot at the absent Republicans. On the contrary, he so empathized with their frustrations that he had not invited anyone from Congress to attend.

With HERA in place, we launched an immediate analysis of the true financial condition of Fannie and Freddie. The Fed and the Office of the Comptroller of the Currency sent in examiners, and Treasury set out to hire an adviser to conduct a full review of the GSEs' financial positions and capital strength, and to develop alternatives for addressing the situation.

We selected Morgan Stanley, whose CEO, John Mack, offered to provide a team for free. You might think that hiring advisers for free would be simple, but nothing is simple in Washington. We had no time for a normal bidding process, so we had to use what's known as a limited competition. Then there was the conflict-of-interest issue: any firm we picked would be boxed out of doing business with the GSEs for an extended period of time and would have to work without legal indemnification. Merrill Lynch and Citigroup also offered to work for free, but only Mack was willing to accept the whole unattractive package. He also offered us an extraordinary team that included two of his top people, Vice Chairman Bob Scully and financial institutions chief Ruth Porat.

John had been one of my fiercest competitors when I was at Goldman, but he became one of my biggest allies when I was at Treasury. He understood that fixing the GSEs was critical to easing the credit crisis and to softening the economic blow of the housing decline.

In mid-summer I had lost a key member of my team when Bob Steel left to take over as CEO and president of Wachovia. Then David Nason, who had been planning to leave for a while—first, after his heroic efforts on the Blueprint for regulatory reform, then after his even more important work in getting HERA passed—finally made his break, though he would return before long at a critical time.

I'd had a hard time attracting Treasury people who had experience with Wall Street deal making. Now, with no time to lose, I reached out to two all-stars, Ken Wilson and Dan Jester. Neither was looking to come to Washington, but I had worked closely with both at Goldman Sachs. I trusted their expertise and judgment, and believed I could persuade them to join me.

When I called Ken in July, I knew the move would require a sacrifice on his part. I decided to reduce the likelihood of a turndown by having President Bush call his old friend and Harvard

Business School classmate personally. It worked: Ken began working full-time at Treasury on August 4.

Dan had been a banker in the financial institutions group, then Goldman's deputy CFO and a key member of the risk committee, before retiring in the spring of 2005. The following year I had asked him to join Treasury as an assistant secretary, but he hadn't wanted to uproot his family from their new home in Austin, Texas. This time I impressed on him the nature of our emergency, and he signed on immediately, even though it meant leaving his family behind for six months. Unflappable and brilliant, with strong analytical and financial engineering skills, he quickly won the confidence of the Treasury team as he dug into the GSEs' finances.

Ken, who had been a chairman of the financial institutions group at Goldman, also worked on the GSEs, and, equally important, I asked him to be the point of contact for Dick Fuld. With Lehman desperate for a solution, there could have been no better confidant than Ken, who probably knew more people and had better relationships in financial services than anybody in the business.

Dick regularly discussed his problems with Ken, as well as the conversations he was having with investors about possible transactions. At the time, Lehman was talking with, among others, the state-owned Korea Development Bank (KDB) and China's Citic Securities. (Later I would learn that Lehman's CEO had approached a stunning range of possible partners, from Deutsche Bank and Morgan Stanley to British giant HSBC, Middle Eastern sovereign wealth funds, and AIG, which soon would find itself in desperate straits.)

Unfortunately, word of Dick's search for possible investors popped up in the press, lending Lehman an air of desperation and eroding confidence in the firm. Ken did his best to impart a need for pragmatism. But it was clear to Ken and me that Dick was looking for an unrealistic price.

HERA failed to boost the market's faith in Fannie and Freddie. Their abysmal second-quarter earnings announcements made matters worse. On August 6, Freddie reported that it had lost $821 million in the period; two days later, Fannie followed with a $2.3 billion loss, forecasting "significant" credit-related expenses in 2009.

We worked to shore up confidence. In mid-July I had told Dave McCormick to reach out to international investors, approaching finance ministers and central bankers. "Make sure they understand what we're doing," I instructed him. "Make sure that to the extent we can say it that the U.S. government is standing behind Fannie Mae and Freddie Mac."

From the moment the GSEs' problems hit the news, Treasury had been getting nervous calls from officials of foreign countries that were invested heavily with Fannie and Freddie. These calls ratcheted up after the legislation. Foreign investors held more than $1 trillion of the debt issued or guaranteed by the GSEs, with big shares held in Japan, China, and Russia. To them, if we let Fannie or Freddie fail and their investments got wiped out, that would be no different from expropriation. They had bought these securities in the belief that the GSEs were backed by the U.S. government. They wanted to know if the U.S. would stand behind this implicit guarantee—and what this would imply for other U.S. obligations, such as Treasury bonds.

I flew to China for the Olympics on August 7. Officially it was a family trip, and Wendy and I were accompanied by our children and their families. Even though it was a vacation, I had a number of meetings scheduled with Chinese officials, and I worried about Fannie and Freddie the whole time I was in Beijing.

Wendy had planned our free time down to the minute. In the mornings we got up early and explored Beijing's stunning parks and historical sites, including the Summer Palace and the Forbidden City. (One day we practiced tai chi with a grand master.) Security at the Great Wall was high because an American couple had been stabbed at a Beijing tourist attraction just after the games started. At one point, exploring a guard tower with a low ceiling, I hit my head. Now, I've got a hard head, but I don't suffer in silence, and I screamed in pain. Chinese officials were beside themselves when they saw the U.S. Treasury secretary gushing blood. But afterward, a number of China's leaders made a point of apologizing to me, tongue in cheek, for not having built higher-ceilinged guard towers.

Between the sightseeing and the Olympic Games, my family had a great time. At 14 months, with blond hair and blue eyes, my granddaughter, Willa, was very cute, and many Chinese wanted to hold her and take her picture. At the Olympic events, they invariably handed her a little Chinese flag, which made me a bit uncomfortable. The last thing I needed in the newspapers back home was a picture of my granddaughter on my lap waving a Chinese flag. So whenever she was handed one, I would pass Willa off to another family member or take the flag away—carefully, because I didn't want her to start crying.

I was delighted to see swimmer Michael Phelps in action and to witness U.S. gymnast Nastia Liukin winning the individual allaround gold. But those who knew me well could sense my anxiety. NBC broadcaster Tom Brokaw spotted it when he interviewed me outside the Olympic stadium on a range of issues, from U.S.-China relations to Fannie and Freddie. I ended up leaving my cell phone, suit, and shirt on the NBC set; we had to go back and collect them. Tom, a longtime friend, told me afterward that he could tell I was deeply preoccupied, my mind far away, because of the heavy burden I was carrying.

It didn't help that my calls home needed to be cryptic. Communications in China weren't secure, and I didn't want any news to leak out about how bad things were going with the GSEs. On the contrary, I was doing my best, in private meetings and dinners, to assure the Chinese that everything would be all right.

What I learned in Beijing, however, left me less than reassured myself: Russian officials had made a top-level approach to the Chinese suggesting that together they might sell big chunks of their GSE holdings to force the U.S. to use its emergency authorities to prop up these companies. The Chinese had declined to go along with the disruptive scheme, but the report was deeply troubling—heavy selling could create a sudden loss of confidence in the GSEs and shake the capital markets. I waited till I was back home and in a secure environment to inform the president.

When I returned to Washington on Friday, August 15, I was preoccupied with the GSEs and Lehman Brothers. The GSEs were such a huge, obvious problem that I knew we would somehow take care of them, but Lehman presented another level of potential trouble. Without wind-down powers, we could be forced to stand by as the firm failed and the entire financial system felt the shock.

One of my first calls was with Dick Fuld, who was entertaining any number of ideas to raise capital, including a plan to package problem commercial real estate into a separate company and spin it off to shareholders. Lehman needed to raise capital for this so-called Spinco, but was having trouble attracting any from the private sector. Dick asked Tim Geithner and me if the government would invest in Spinco. We each said no—several times. The government had no authority to do so.

The GSEs' situation had grown increasingly dire. On August 11, Standard & Poor's had cut its preferred stock ratings for Freddie and Fannie, and the weekend I returned from China a piece titled "The Endgame Nears for Fannie and Freddie" appeared in *Barron's*. The lengthy article laid out the poor prospects for the two GSEs and predicted a government takeover that would wipe out holders of common shares. The market reacted violently on Monday, driving the stocks to nearly 18-year lows.

The story was pretty accurate. While I was away, Fannie's and Freddie's books had been analyzed by the Fed; the OCC; our adviser, Morgan Stanley; and BlackRock, the New York money manager that had a long-term relationship with Freddie. They agreed that the organizations were sorely undercapitalized. And the quality of their capital was suspect: some of it consisted of intangible items, such as deferred taxes, that would not have been counted to the same degree as capital by financial institutions overseen by the banking regulators. What's more, the GSEs had not adequately written down the value of guarantees provided by private mortgage insurers that had been downgraded by the rating agencies. Each of the companies looked to have true, economic capital holes amounting to tens of billions of dollars. (By November 2009, Fannie and Freddie would eat through all of their capital, and the government would be forced to inject more than $110 billion.)

We'd been prepared for bad news, but the extent of the problems was startling. We'd had no specific information when we'd pushed for extraordinary powers in July. Now, I told Josh Bolten that in all likelihood we would have to use our newly granted authorities.

We had evaluated such options as having the government backstop a private capital raising by the GSEs. But we'd become convinced that private capital would be impossible to raise unless we could clarify the GSEs' future status or structure, which we could not. And there was no practical way to invest in them in their current form because any government investment needed to be approved by the GSEs. They had a fiduciary duty to protect their shareholders, but our duty was to protect the taxpayer.

I concluded that the only solution was to get FHFA to put the GSEs into receivership. I knew this would be a shock to Fannie and Freddie, to their investors, to Congress, and even to their regulator. I also knew we needed the support of the Fed. If we acted alone, some might believe that this was a Bush administration vendetta against Fannie and Freddie.

The situation was awkward for me. I'm a man of my word, and

I had told Congress in July we did not intend to use the bazooka. But there was no alternative. I also knew we needed to keep our intentions confidential or Fannie and Freddie would run to their many friends on the Hill and possibly hinder us.

On August 19 I met privately with Ben Bernanke at the Fed. He was as concerned as I was, although he had been expecting Treasury to make an equity investment. But after I laid out the case for taking control of Fannie and Freddie and putting them in receivership, he offered his support on the spot. His staff would help document the capital hole in the GSEs. This was critically important because I wanted the Fed to attest to a capital deficiency in a letter.

"We're with you 100 percent," Ben told me.

Two days later, on August 21, I had lunch in my private dining room with Jim Lockhart, who headed the new FHFA, created by HERA to oversee Fannie and Freddie. Though outgoing and affable, Lockhart had a terrible relationship with the GSEs and their boards, after having pushed them hard to clean up their accounting problems. Because of his close ties to the White House, he was viewed as a megaphone for the administration.

I pressed him on the need for receivership, but he repeatedly told me that this would be difficult to do quickly because FHFA's most recent semiannual regulatory exams had not cited capital shortfalls. He was scheduled to leave the next day for vacation in Nantucket, but I urged him to stay in Washington and work on our plan. He called me back to tell me he had canceled his vacation and that he would work through the weekend and let me know on Monday if receivership was feasible.

With that, we needed outside advice to guide us through the intricacies of the law and the corporate governance issues involved. Anticipating this, Ken Wilson had already contacted Wachtell, Lipton, Rosen & Katz, a New York firm, and Bob Hoyt signed them up on Friday, August 22. This was another example of exemplary citizenship during the crisis. Just as Morgan Stanley had done, Wachtell, thanks to Ed Herlihy, the co-chairman of their executive committee, agreed to represent us for free and with no indemnification.

We hired them at 3:00 p.m. By the next morning they had torn through the GSEs' debt and preferred stock documents, and concluded that going the receivership route would be perilous for a number of practical and technical reasons. That approach would be terribly disruptive to the GSEs' businesses and extremely difficult to implement successfully in a short time frame, especially without the active involvement and cooperation of the GSEs' management in the planning stages. It would also have posed risks of court challenges and the early termination of the GSEs' valuable derivatives contracts. Receivership, which is used to liquidate companies, might trigger consequences every bit as bad as those we were trying to avoid, Wachtell said. By contrast, conservatorship was more like a Chapter 11 bankruptcy, where companies kept their current forms; it would provide a stable time-out for the GSEs to avoid defaulting on their debts and could be accomplished quickly.

We were in a race against time. The markets were fragile, and we knew that September was going to be even rockier. Lehman was going to announce a dreadful loss, and Washington Mutual and Wachovia both appeared headed for trouble. We needed to take care of Fannie and Freddie before then or we would have a real problem.

Initially, we had hoped to act by Labor Day. But we had to build a case for conservatorship, prepare to run the GSEs, and devise financing arrangements that would reassure bondholders and the market. There just wasn't enough time, even as teams from Treasury, the Fed, FHFA, and other agencies worked around the clock.

Then on Monday, August 25, I received a disturbing report about FHFA. It turned out that the previous Friday, when Lockhart had told me he was on board for conservatorship, his people had sent the GSEs draft letters reviewing their second-quarter financial statements and concluding that the companies were at least adequately capitalized and in fact exceeded their regulatory capital requirements.

The drafts had included a special reminder that the FHFA had discretionary authority to downgrade that assessment. Even so, for FHFA to reverse and say now Fannie and Freddie had capital holes big enough to justify conservatorship gave the agency pause. Jim had quite a challenge on his hands: his agency had been renamed with the HERA legislation, but it still had the same people and same approach as it had had a month earlier. Only FHFA had the legal power to put the GSEs under, and I was worried about its backsliding.

I arranged to have Lockhart meet with Bernanke and me at Treasury so the two of us could offer him our support and encouragement. I said I understood that looked at narrowly, FHFA's people might see conservatorship as an indication they hadn't been sufficiently vigilant earlier, but Fannie's and Freddie's problems could not be swept under a rug, and a bold action would put FHFA on the right side of history. I stressed repeatedly that the GSEs needed capital, and I would not put taxpayer money in them in their current form. Any Treasury investment would be conditioned on conservatorship.

There was no time to waste. That day Freddie sold $2 billion of short-term notes at their worst spreads ever. I called Josh Bolten and said, flatly, there was no good alternative to conservatorship.

The next morning I went to the Situation Room on the ground floor of the West Wing of the White House, with its secure communications equipment, to talk to the president, who was at his ranch in Crawford, Texas. There were several video screens on the far wall of this windowless room, and one displayed the president, who was relaxed and wearing a sports shirt. Once the national security briefing was through, I posted the president. I told him straightaway that I was worried about Lehman. It was looking for a solution to its problems, and we had been trying to help, but it didn't look like any investor was stepping up. We would do what we could, but there was a chance it would go down.

I then took the president quickly through our thinking on the GSEs. As always, he wanted to know what our long-term plan was, because he did not like the underlying structure that had produced profits for shareholders and losses for the taxpayers—and had led to all the problems. I said I thought that when the crisis was over they ought to be downsized, have their missions shrunk, and be recast as utilities, but felt we needed to defer that discussion until well after we had bolstered them financially and markets were stable. The president was completely supportive. He said, as he would frequently: "It won't always look good, but we are going to do what we need to do to save the economy."

Through the week the examiners from the Fed and the OCC continued to scrutinize the books of the GSEs, while trying to bring their FHFA counterparts up to speed. Meantime, our teams at Treasury worked double-time to refine our plans. Ken Wilson was running an informal employment agency, drawing on his extensive contacts to line up replacement CEOs and nonexecutive chairs for both Fannie and Freddie.

Just about everyone lived at the Treasury for the three days of the Labor Day weekend. We didn't know it then, of course, but it was a preview of how we would spend most of the fall, with senior and junior staffers alike surrendering their weekends, weeknights, and just about any trace of a personal life to try to solve problems that kept getting bigger than we had anticipated. All that weekend, we met, broke out into separate teams, reconvened, and ran frequent conference calls.

Ben proved again to be an incredible stand-up guy. He did not miss a meeting the entire weekend—and there were many. He was there to do what he thought was right for the country, even if some at the Fed worried he was getting too involved. Fed vice chairman Don Kohn and governor Kevin Warsh also joined our deliberations, along with the Board's general counsel, Scott Alvarez. Jim Lockhart was present with his senior staff and Rich Alexander, FHFA's outside legal counsel from Arnold & Porter, whose work was invaluable in preparing the legal case. Morgan Stanley was onsite, with lawyers from Wachtell plugged in from New York.

It was gratifying to see how everyone cooperated. When I asked for help, FDIC chairman Sheila Bair sent over her most experienced professional, Art Murton. Crucially, no one leaked any word of what we were up to. Everyone understood the stakes.

We reviewed all of our alternatives in a thorough and systematic way. My staff wanted to be sure we had an airtight case for conservatorship, given the GSEs' reputation as the toughest street fighters in town. I was less worried about the details than my colleagues were: I didn't think they completely recognized the awesome power of government and what it would mean for Ben and me to sit across from the boards of Fannie Mae and Freddie Mac and tell them what we thought was necessary for them to do.

Bob Scully of Morgan Stanley and Dan Jester had come up with the idea of using a version of a keepwell agreement, which is a contract between a parent company and a subsidiary in which the parent guarantees that it will provide necessary financing for the subsidiary. It was an inspired idea: Treasury's authority was good for 18 months, and guaranteeing debt for 18 months wasn't going to do much for investors in long-term debt. The keepwell, which became known as the Preferred Stock Purchase Agreement, allowed us to maintain a positive net worth at the companies no matter how much they lost long into the future. By entering into that agreement before December 31, 2009 (when our temporary authority expired), we would be acting within our authority, while providing investors the necessary long-term assurances. As losses were realized in the future, we could dip into the keepwell and increase the amount of financial support by purchasing preferred shares.

We had to decide how big to make the keepwells. We wanted a big number to send a message, and the only constraint was the debt ceiling, which had been increased by $800 billion. We initially set the size at $100 billion for each GSE. (The Obama administration would eventually increase the keepwells to $200 billion each as losses soared at the companies.)

It was crucial to win over FHFA's examiners because it would be next to impossible to put the GSEs into conservatorship without their support. They wanted to base their argument for doing so on Fannie's and Freddie's unsafe and unsound practices. But we knew, and the Fed and OCC agreed, that we couldn't take Fannie and Freddie down on a technicality—and besides, there were gross inadequacies in the quality and quantity of their capital.

A lot of work had to be done. Fed and OCC examiners scouring the portfolios had come up with estimates of embedded losses that were multiples of what the GSEs said they thought the losses were. The Fed and the OCC took FHFA through their models and assumptions, and finally persuaded Lockhart's people to change their minds.

The companies were struggling to solve their problems. Fannie was more diligent and more helpful. It had in fact raised $7.4 billion, while Freddie, despite its assurances, hadn't raised any equity. At one point, Fannie executives came in and gave a PowerPoint presentation, in which for the first time they made it clear they had no access to capital markets. Even so, their projections of losses were below what the examiners were coming up with.

Fannie's cheekiness was breathtaking. The essence of the presentation was: We're in deep trouble unless you do something to help us. But since we are clearly compliant with our regulatory capital requirements, you can't touch us other than to do what the statute allows you to do, which is inject capital on terms we agree to. Fannie even tried to make it seem that their plight was our fault, that our having gotten the bazooka had caused everyone to lose confidence in them. Hence, we should fix things on terms favorable to them.

But the problem wasn't the bazooka. It was that the market realized before the GSEs did that they were doomed. And Fannie was living in a world that the markets were declaring was dead and over.

As the Fannie team went through its slides, I said very little. I just sat there, and they thought I was being positive. Normally I'm the hammer: I challenge, I push to get the best possible result. Now I just looked on and nodded. As my staff said afterward, it was a classic example of people taking away the message they were looking for.

Right up to the end, Lockhart had quite a task trying to move his people to where he and we wanted them. They needed to be led to the conclusion they knew was right. Doing so would in effect overturn the work they'd done for years. But they were moving forward slowly. On September 1, FHFA wrote the GSEs to suspend the August 22 letter that had said their capital was adequate and informed them that the agency was conducting a new review of the adequacy of their reserves.

The clock was ticking. We would need a weekend with the markets closed to put the GSEs into conservatorship, but we were running out of weekends before Lehman was scheduled to report its second-quarter earnings, which were going to be disastrous.

By midweek FHFA had written up its semiannual review letters for Fannie and Freddie. These they sent on September 4 in draft form. They were tough letters, accompanied by affidavits from their examiners, that dissected capital and management deficiencies and noted all the corrections the companies had been asked to make and hadn't. Management was asked to share these with their boards.

Then Jim called the CEOs to say that he wanted to meet with them and that he would be joined by the chairman of the Fed and the Treasury secretary. They had to know something was wrong.

On Friday afternoon, September 5, we met with management of the companies; on Saturday, September 6, we met with their boards, which agreed to the takeover; and on Sunday, we announced that we had placed Fannie Mae and Freddie Mac into conservatorship. Asian markets rallied on the news.

The next day they opened for business with new CEOs: Herb Allison, former CEO of TIAA-CREF, at Fannie; and David Moffett, former chief financial officer of U.S. Bancorp, at Freddie. Treasury's administrative head, Peter McCarthy, organized a remarkably smooth transition. Common shareholders had lost nearly everything, but the government had protected debt holders and buttressed each entity with $100 billion in capital and generous credit lines. Fannie and Freddie would have to shrink their massive portfolios and would no longer be allowed to lobby the government.

Working nearly nonstop to stave off disaster for the crippled housing markets and U.S. economy, we had, within a few months, managed to force massive change at these troubled but powerful institutions that had stymied reformers for years.

I was concerned about explaining to Congress why we'd been forced to use our new authorities, and I also worried that I'd be criticized for turning temporary powers into a permanent guarantee. As it turned out, the bigger issue was that the government had been forced to "bail out" Fannie and Freddie, putting the taxpayers at risk. This was an indicator of things to come.

The GSE crisis left me dead tired. But my staff worked even harder, hammering out the details of this extraordinary government rescue. I told Josh Bolten that solving the GSE crisis was the hardest thing I had ever done.

I had no idea.

CHAPTER 8

Monday, September 8, 2008

I began Monday, September 8, with an early round of television interviews, part of my plan to spend much of the week reassuring taxpayers, the markets, and the institutions' employees that Fannie Mae and Freddie Mac had been stabilized. The initial reaction to our weekend moves to seize control of the two big mortgage companies had encouraged me. Asian and European markets had surged, and Japanese and Chinese central bankers had applauded. The U.S. government had essentially guaranteed the GSEs' debt, but I knew it would take time and a focused effort to communicate that clearly to all investors.

By 8:00 a.m. I'd talked to CNBC, CBS, and Bloomberg. I was careful to emphasize that Fannie's and Freddie's employees were not responsible for the housing decline or their companies' problems. "This was created by Congress a long time ago. It was a system that shouldn't have existed," I told CNBC's Steve Liesman.

When U.S. markets opened, Fannie's and Freddie's stocks fell like stones, as expected, but the Dow shot up 330 points at the start of trading. I had little time to exult, though, as the disaster that had loomed all summer began to unfold.

Ken Wilson came into my office to tell me that talks between Lehman Brothers and the Korea Development Bank were going nowhere. The week before, news leaks had prompted speculation that KDB would buy up to 25 percent of Lehman. But Ken, who was on the phone with Lehman CEO Dick Fuld every day—and had talked with him the night before—downplayed the possibility of a deal. Lehman shares were up at the opening, but if the talks failed they would plummet, just as the firm was about to announce a big third-quarter loss.

Lehman's plight wasn't the only troubling news. Late Monday morning, General Electric CEO Jeff Immelt called to tell me that his company was having problems selling commercial paper. This stunned me. Although GE's giant financial unit, GE Capital, had faltered along with the rest of the industry, the company as a whole was an American business icon—one of the few with a triple-A credit rating. If GE couldn't sell its paper, what did that mean for other U.S. companies?

Monday afternoon belonged to the GSEs. I gave interviews to the *Washington Post* and *Fortune* magazine and met with Chris Dodd, who was close to Fannie and Freddie, and had gotten upset with me over the weekend. I sat down with him and his staff at his office and explained our thinking, telling him that his leadership, and that of Barney Frank and Richard Shelby, had been critical to helping us avoid a disaster. He seemed much more comfortable after the meeting.

The market stayed strong through the day, with the Dow closing up 290 points, or 2.6 percent, at 11,511. But Lehman's shares dropped $2.05, to $14.15, while its credit default swaps edged up to a worrisome 328 basis points. And the markets still did not know that Lehman's talks with KDB were collapsing.

I had hoped that the GSE takeovers would give Lehman a bit of breathing room, but I was wrong.

Tuesday, September 9, 2008

I arrived at the office shortly after 6:00 a.m. and headed straight to the Markets Room. Lehman's shares were headed toward single digits, and its credit default swaps were under pressure. I went to Ken Wilson's office to get the latest on Dick Fuld. The KDB deal, Ken told me, was dead.

"Does he know how serious the problem is?" I asked.

"He's still clinging to the view that somehow or other the Fed has the power to inject capital," Ken answered.

I felt a wave of frustration. Tim Geithner and I had repeatedly told Dick that the government had no legal authority to inject capital in an investment bank. That was one reason I had been pushing him to find a buyer since Bear Stearns failed in March. Fuld had replaced Lehman's top management, laid off thousands of employees, and pitched restructuring ideas, but the firm's heavy exposure to mortgage-backed securities had discouraged suitors and left him unable to make a deal.

Ken had been telling Dick with increasing urgency that he needed to be ready to sell, but Dick did not want to consider any offer below $10 per share. Bear Stearns had gotten that, and he would accept nothing less for Lehman.

After I spoke with Ken, I had an important obligation to fulfill. I was scheduled to address Freddie Mac's employees. Many people at Treasury couldn't believe that I wanted to meet with a group that was sure to be angry with me. It was simple. I felt bad for them, and they deserved to hear straight from me where they stood. And I wanted them to know that our actions had not resulted from any fault of theirs.

David Moffett, the new CEO, and I stood on a stage in an auditorium at the company's headquarters in McLean, Virginia, facing hundreds of disheartened and confused Freddie Mac employees who wanted to hear about their futures and whether their shares would ever rebound. I knew that Freddie Mac stock had made up a big percentage of their net worth.

I was very direct. I told them that the odds were low that they would ever recapture the equity value that had been lost, but I emphasized that as long as they kept learning, honing their skills, and helping Freddie perform its vital function, their careers would likely remain intact. I couldn't say what Freddie's ultimate structure would be—that was for Congress and the next administration to decide—but I noted that the old business model was flawed and didn't work. It was a difficult meeting, but I was glad I went.

I returned to my office to find that once again all hell was breaking loose. Dow Jones Newswire was reporting that Lehman's talks with KDB had fallen through. The firm's shares were plunging and credit spreads widening—they would top 400 basis points by day's end. But I didn't need a Bloomberg terminal to tell me what was happening. Once more we had a big financial institution under assault, and no clear solution in sight. If Lehman didn't find a buyer soon, it would go down.

I couldn't help but think of all those Freddie Mac employees worried about their jobs and savings. We had staved off disaster with Bear Stearns and the GSEs, but the stakes just kept growing. Unlike in March, when Bear went down, the overall economy was now clearly hurting: unemployment had hit 6.1 percent in August, the highest level in five years, and we were clearly in a recession. The last thing we needed was a Lehman failure.

With these thoughts weighing on my mind, I met Commerce secretary Carlos Gutierrez for a scheduled lunch in the small conference room next to my office. I couldn't fully concentrate on our conversation. All I could think was, *What do we do about Lehman? There's got to be something—we've always managed to pull a rabbit out of the hat.*

Forty minutes into lunch, Christal West, my assistant, interrupted to tell me that Tim Geithner was on the line and needed to speak to me urgently. Maybe, I hoped, he had good news. But Tim was calling to say that the markets were very jittery, and that he did not see how Lehman could survive in its current form. He said he had already spoken with a shaken Fuld.

Thinking back to our experience with Bear Stearns, I wondered if Lehman would last long enough for us to pull an industry solution together over the weekend. I asked Tim, "Can we hold this situation together through the close on Friday?"

Tim said he thought we could do it. But the markets would need reassurance that we were working on a solution. They'd get that if it was clear that Lehman was looking for a buyer.

"I'll lean on Ken Lewis," I said. "Maybe at the right price BofA will be willing to do something."

Carlos and I finished lunch, and about an hour later I spoke to Fuld. The short sellers were all over him, and he sounded panicked. He wondered if he should release his earnings early and simultaneously announce his restructuring plan. I didn't know if these measures would be enough to appease investors, but I told Dick it was up to him to decide whether to try. I also said I would try to persuade Ken Lewis to acquire Lehman—even though Bank of America had looked at the firm twice over the summer and walked away both times. Dick agreed this was the best solution.

Ken had a love-hate relationship with Wall Street. The previous fall, announcing trading losses for BofA, he'd famously declared, "I've had all of the fun I can stand in investment banking at the moment." But he wanted to grow his bank through acquisitions and craved a business platform outside the U.S. I knew him as a man of few words, a tough negotiator who liked to do deals. With its big balance sheet and history of moving quickly, Bank of America would make an ideal buyer for Lehman.

Still, as much as I hoped that Lehman's bargain-basement stock price might entice Ken to take another look at the firm, I suspected from the start that he would be interested only if he could leave behind a large chunk of undesirable assets. What's more, neither Merrill Lynch nor Morgan Stanley was looking strong, and I suspected Ken might prefer to acquire one of them. Both had bigger investment banking businesses than Lehman, and both had retail franchises that Lewis wanted. In fact, I knew Ken had long coveted Merrill.

By Tuesday afternoon, the entire industry was beginning to understand the gravity of Lehman's situation. Few perceived this more keenly than Merrill CEO John Thain, who called me with his concerns. In the 29 years I'd known him—first as a young MIT graduate with a Harvard MBA, then as one of Goldman Sachs's rising stars, now as the self-confident CEO of Merrill Lynch—he had always been confident and analytical. But Merrill was generally considered to be the weakest bank after Lehman, and he could see the problem for the markets and his firm.

"Hank, I hope you're watching Lehman," he said. "If they go down, it won't be good for anybody."

John wanted to know how we planned to handle Lehman and how he could help. He had called me over the summer as Lehman had faltered, offering to play a role in any industry solution.

I thanked John for his offer, and after hanging up I called Ken

Lewis. He said he'd been watching the Lehman situation, and I told him that we wanted him to seriously consider buying the troubled firm. I pointed out that Lehman was a lot cheaper now. Could he take a closer look at it, as soon as possible?

"Hank," Ken told me, "we've looked at it a couple times before and determined that the risks were too great relative to what we might be getting."

Still, he said he might be willing to buy the firm if he could leave the commercial real estate assets behind in a Bear Stearns–type deal. I told him we couldn't put government money in but pressed him to get back to us with a decision as quickly as possible.

"This would be a big bite for us," he said.

He then raised another issue. BofA had bought Countrywide Financial, the troubled mortgage lender, in January for $4.1 billion, and had expected the Fed to give it some form of relief from regulatory capital requirements for having done the deal. Instead, the Federal Reserve Bank of Richmond, BofA's direct overseer, had been putting pressure on BofA to redo its capital plan and cut its dividend. Lewis wanted help getting his dispute with the Fed resolved.

On the face of it, the request was reasonable. How could BofA do a deal with Lehman and further strain its capital ratios without first clearing up this issue with the Fed? The solution, however, was out of my jurisdiction. I told Ken I would relay his concern to Tim and Ben Bernanke. I asked him to call Dick Fuld and start to do due diligence.

Next, Tim and I got on the phone with Dick. We had agreed that whenever possible we would speak to the Lehman CEO together. We wanted to be sure that he heard the same thing from both of us. I shared my reservations about Lewis's seriousness, but Dick was excited.

"The key is speed," he told us. "Can Lewis get his people here tonight? We're willing to work around the clock."

I called Ken and urged him to get a team together as soon as possible. We then convened a conference call with Chris Cox, Tim, Ben, and Treasury staff at 5:00 p.m. to deal with a possible Lehman bankruptcy.

Over the summer, the Treasury, the Fed, and the SEC had put a team together to deal with this contingency. We knew how disastrous it would be: a Lehman Chapter 11 would trigger a global shock. Tim and I stressed the urgency of the situation now.

"Lehman has been hanging like a dead weight in the market," I said. "Thank God we got to Fannie and Freddie before this."

We discussed ways to forestall a Lehman collapse. Tim suggested a reprise of the 1998 rescue of Long-Term Capital Management. Back then, a group of 14 Wall Street firms had banded together to craft a $3.6 billion package, receiving 90 percent of the imperiled hedge fund, which they proceeded to liquidate over time. To do something similar, I said, we would first have to get Lewis interested—no small thing—then allow him to buy what he wanted and convince an industry consortium to take on the remaining assets. John Thain had already declared himself willing to aid in a private-sector bailout, but we would need to persuade the other CEOs. This wouldn't be easy to pull off, with the entire financial industry under increasing pressure. Of course, the alternative, Lehman's demise, was far worse.

While I was on the conference call, Dick Fuld phoned me to report that he hadn't yet heard from Bank of America. I reassured him that we were doing everything we could, then I got hold of Ken Lewis and let him know that I had passed on the word about Countrywide.

"I've spoken with both Ben and Tim. They understand how important this is," I said, assuring him the issue could be resolved. At my urging, he agreed to send a team to Lehman right away.

A few minutes later, I heard back from Lewis. He said that he and

Fuld had spoken, and they were going to begin discussions. Dick called after that, excited, to say that Lewis's team was ready to go. Despite all the back-and-forth of that afternoon and evening—we logged nearly a dozen calls with Lewis or Fuld in three hours—I wasn't completely convinced of Lewis's seriousness. My doubts only grew when he called back one last time and once again pressed the point about his unhappiness over the Countrywide business. He wanted to be sure to get that matter resolved with the Fed.

I called Dick a little after 7:00 p.m. to reassure him that Lewis was still in the game. "We've got some things to work out," I said. "But he will be getting there."

That day the Dow had fallen 280 points, to 11,231, erasing Monday's gains. Lehman shares were down 45 percent, to $7.79, and its CDS had jumped by nearly 50 percent, to 475 basis points. And there was other worrisome news: investors concerned about AIG's exposure to mortgages had driven its stock down 19 percent, to $18.37.

But AIG was not my foremost concern that night as I lay sleepless, wondering how Lehman would manage to pull through to the weekend.

Three days was a long time.

Wednesday, September 10, 2008

I had barely gotten to my office early Wednesday morning when Dick Fuld called to let me know that BofA still hadn't shown up. It was just after 7:00 a.m.

"We haven't heard from them," Dick said, exasperated. "We missed a whole night."

"You haven't heard a thing?"

"Nothing," he said.

It was a bad start to a bad day. I assumed that the Fed still hadn't satisfied Ken Lewis on BofA's capital issue, so I followed up with Tim and Ben. Less than an hour later, Lehman pre-released its third-quarter results—a $3.9 billion loss, stemming from a $5.6 billion write-down on residential and commercial real estate. The firm also announced that it would sell a majority stake in its asset-management subsidiary, Neuberger Berman, and spin off between $25 billion and $30 billion of its commercial real estate portfolio.

Investors were having none of it. Lehman's shares fell in pre-market trading, while its CDS jumped to 577 basis points. The market smelled a corpse.

Even as I wondered whether Bank of America would come through, another possible partner for Lehman popped into view, taking me by surprise. Bob Steel—my former undersecretary for domestic finance, now CEO of Wachovia—called just before 8:00 a.m. to say that he'd spoken with Bob Diamond, the president of Barclays, the British bank. The two bankers knew each other from Steel's stint on Barclays's board a few years before.

Steel told me that Barclays was interested in Lehman. I admit I had to ask him if they were serious. The British bank had not previously demonstrated an ability to move fast or to consummate major strategic transactions. Barclays was still stinging from losing a takeover battle in 2007 for the Dutch bank ABN AMRO to the Royal Bank of Scotland. I also had some concerns about whether Barclays had the financial strength to do a Lehman deal.

Although I mentioned Barclays's potential interest in my discussions that day with Tim, Ben, Chris, and the group in New York, we were focused on Bank of America. Lewis had promised to get back to us by Thursday evening if there were no leaks. We understood that the Charlotte bank might well decide against buying Lehman or insist, despite my guidance to Lewis, that it would need financial support.

In my afternoon conference call with Tim and Treasury staffers, we again discussed how we could help Lehman. My team and I believed we should emphasize publicly that there could be no government money for a Lehman deal. To my mind, this was the only way to get the best price from a buyer, and the only way to prepare the industry to be fully ready for the likelihood that it would need to participate in any solution.

"We need to do everything we can to fashion a private-sector alternative," I told the group.

Tim agreed. He, too, favored an industry solution. But we both knew that if a Bear Stearns–style rescue was the only option, we would take it. As Tim put it, a Lehman failure would be more expensive for the taxpayers.

All of us were well aware that after Fannie and Freddie, the country, Congress, and both parties were fed up with bailouts. Obama and McCain, neck and neck in the national polls, each spoke out against them on the campaign trail. The previous day, in fact, McCain and Sarah Palin had published an op-ed in the *Wall Street Journal* entitled, "We'll Protect Taxpayers from More Bailouts." And just before our conference call had begun I'd spoken with Chris Dodd, who told me, "Fuld is a friend. Try to help, but don't bail Lehman out."

We discussed the worst-case scenario: no buyer for Lehman, no government authority to inject capital, and no legal authority to wind down a failing nonbanking financial institution. We knew a Lehman collapse would be a disaster. With roughly $600 billion in assets, the firm was bigger and even more interconnected than Bear Stearns. Under those circumstances, how could we stabilize the market?

After the conference call, Tim and I spoke privately, reviewing the situation: Neither of us had the authority to put money in the entity Lehman hoped to create to hive off its commercial real estate assets—unofficially known as Spinco. And clearly, the embedded losses were proving to be too big for Lehman to attract private capital. It was unlikely that a restructuring plan could help the firm now.

Just three days after the historic government takeover, the GSEs were already old news to the public. We hadn't taken our eyes off them, however. Mortgage rates had decreased, but they were still too high, given that the GSEs were now officially under the U.S.'s wing.

Meantime, I continued to reach out to unhappy GSE employees. Wednesday afternoon I met with Fannie Mae staff at their Wisconsin Avenue headquarters, just a little ways from the National Cathedral. I encountered an even tougher group than I had at Freddie's headquarters: they pushed back harder, upset about the losses on their shares, and worried about Fannie's long-term prospects. I answered their questions candidly, explaining how crucial their company would be to helping get the nation through this crisis, but the sight of their unhappy faces stayed with me after I left.

That evening, when I checked in with Ken Lewis, I learned that he had not yet sent a team to New York. He still hadn't resolved his issues with the Fed. But he assured me that BofA would be able to move quickly, given that they'd done due diligence on Lehman in the summer.

I called Tim to see when the Fed would clear up the problem with BofA. He assured me he would immediately work to find a solution.

Thursday, September 11, 2008

Early Thursday morning, not long after I arrived at my desk, Ken Wilson suggested I call Bob Diamond at Barclays. The British bank needed more encouragement. When I reached him, he confirmed that his bank was interested in acquiring Lehman.

"You'll need to move quickly," I told him. "I also want to let you know that we are unable to put public money in."

"I understand that."

I asked him if Barclays's board and its CEO, John Varley, were in agreement with him about a possible Lehman deal. British boards, I knew from experience, played a more active role in takeovers than did their counterparts in the U.S.

"They are," Bob said. "This is obviously a major undertaking."

I suggested that he talk further with Varley and his board, while I touched base with Tim Geithner, whom I immediately updated.

"Diamond is clearly interested," I said. "Barclays doesn't have much of a history of completing acquisitions, but I think we should move ahead here pretty aggressively."

We needed to act fast—and not just for Lehman's sake. Market worries were spilling over to other institutions. Shares of Washington Mutual, the troubled Seattle mortgage lender, were being battered. Tim and I agreed that, for the industry to be part of the solution, we needed to get all of Wall Street together quickly. I suggested that we set the meeting for Friday night, because we needed a deal by Sunday night. John Thain called later that morning to tell me that Merrill's stock was off significantly and its credit spreads were widening. He volunteered to participate in an industry solution for Lehman, and I told him that we planned to get a group together in New York over the weekend.

I stepped away from Lehman long enough to place more than 20 calls to members of Congress, briefing them on the GSEs and problems in the financial markets. They generally supported our action on the GSEs, but they gave me an earful about bailouts and—as Chris Dodd had done the previous day—warned me that they didn't want to see taxpayer money put into Lehman.

I touched base again with Bob Diamond, who confirmed that Barclays was serious and that Varley wanted to talk directly to me.

He noted that Barclays's board was keen not to be embarrassed, as they would be if word leaked out that they were an interested bidder and someone else did the deal.

"We're looking for an exclusive," I remember him saying. "If we get one, we can move very quickly."

"We can't give you an exclusive, and I don't believe Lehman Brothers can, either," I replied. Barclays hadn't asked for assistance in doing a deal, and because I assumed Ken Lewis would, I knew this would give the British bank a leg up. "I believe that if you move quickly, the odds are very high that you will be successful. I can assure you that the Fed and I will work together to make this happen."

I emphasized that because the government couldn't put money into the transaction, Barclays should focus on Lehman's troubled assets so we could discuss realistically how they could get a deal done. I recommended that he call Dick Fuld right away and arrange to get together.

Ken Lewis called a little after 5:00 p.m. He said that the capital issue had been more or less settled with the Fed; Ben Bernanke had assured him that the Fed would try to resolve the problem. But that was the extent of any good news.

"We took a hard look at Lehman Brothers, and there are a number of assets we're uncomfortable with," he said. "I'm sorry to tell you we won't be able to do this deal."

I wouldn't let him off the hook. "If you had help with the bad assets, would you be willing to proceed?"

"You said there would be no government money," he pointed out. "Have you changed your position?"

"No, we haven't. But I expect that if you made an acceptable offer, we could get others in the industry to help finance the part that you weren't going to take. It would be just like the LTCM consortium."

Lewis had watched the Fed assist JPMorgan in acquiring Bear Stearns, so it was only natural that he would try to get whatever help he could—from the government or the private sector. He agreed to put together a proposal and get back to me, and I said I would approach Wall Street firms to work something out. I told him we needed a deal finalized by Sunday, so I wanted his preliminary thoughts by Friday night.

Reports that buyers were circling Lehman helped prop up the market. The Dow had ended the day up nearly 165 points, at 11,434. Even WaMu gained, closing at a dismal $2.83, up from $2.32 the previous day, but its CDS had blown out to a breathtaking 2,838 basis points from 2,267. Lehman did not benefit from the market rally: its shares fell 42 percent, to $4.22. Merrill's shares dropped almost 17 percent, to $19.43, their lowest level in nearly a decade.

That night my team got on a conference call with the New York Fed, the Washington Fed, and the SEC. There must have been between 30 and 40 people on the line, all with one concern: getting Lehman to the weekend.

Tim took us through a quick review of the unsettled market. One New York Fed staffer noted that Lehman's funding was increasingly problematic. JPMorgan had renewed a week-old $5 billion collateral call that day. It felt like Bear Stearns all over again, with a critical difference: There were much bigger concerns about the losses in Lehman's balance sheet. Many were worried that all the bad news coming out would lead banks to begin to pull their funding. Lehman borrowed $230 billion overnight in the repo market—an extraordinary reliance on short-term funding that could be pulled at a moment's notice. Lehman could easily become the victim of a run triggered by a widespread loss of confidence. Chris Cox said that the SEC staff was making contingency plans for a Lehman bankruptcy.

I reminded the group that we had two potential buyers for Lehman. Bank of America was further along, but there was a significant amount of assets they were unwilling to take.

"I've heard from Lewis, and he wants to pass on this if there is no help, but I believe he'll come back with a proposal," I said. I added that Barclays seemed more interested in Lehman.

Then, realizing that I was speaking to a large group, I again emphasized that there would be no public assistance for a Lehman bailout and that we would be looking to the private sector to help the buyer complete the acquisition. My team at Treasury believed that we needed to publicly stress these two points, to prepare the industry for the likelihood it would have to help us. The New York Fed would be inviting Wall Street CEOs to a meeting, and we didn't want them to arrive thinking that we would be there waving a government checkbook. Even if by Sunday we had to resort to a government rescue, we needed on Friday to put as much pressure as possible on the private sector to help out.

On Thursday evening, Michele Davis told reporters off the record that there would be no government money for Lehman, hoping that our stance would become clear in Friday's papers. Michele wanted to lay the groundwork for what we all hoped would be a deal that would see Lehman bought that weekend.

Friday, September 12, 2008

I arrived at the office at 7:00 a.m., suitcase in hand, prepared to spend the weekend in New York. We had to get through one more trading day until then, and it was shaping up to be a brutal one. Lehman's credit spreads remained wide, while Merrill Lynch, WaMu, and AIG also were getting hammered.

Looking at the papers that morning, I realized that our communications strategy hadn't worked out as planned. Although a front-page story by David Cho, Heather Landy, and Neil Irwin in the *Washington Post* said, "The government is looking for an agreement that would not involve public money," I knew that few people on Wall Street paid attention to the Washington paper. Their more likely news sources, the *New York Times* and the *Wall Street Journal*, left the door open. So Michele quickly went to CNBC to reiterate that there would be no public money. At 9:15 a.m. CNBC's Steve Liesman reported that, according to a person familiar with my thinking, "there will be no government money in the resolution of this situation."

I had my Friday morning breakfast with Ben Bernanke in the small conference room just off my office. He was not going up to New York but would stay in close touch. I said I was hopeful but had serious doubts about both Bank of America and Barclays. But I didn't think any other institution had an interest or we would have heard about it.

Ben and I ran over our options for what to do if Lehman failed, but the tough fact was, we didn't have many. As I knew all too well, and as Ben reminded me, if Lehman filed for bankruptcy, we would lose control of the process, and we wouldn't have much flexibility to minimize market stress.

"We can only hope that if Lehman goes, the market will have had a lot of time to prepare for it," he said.

All morning I went back and forth with Tim and Ken Lewis, encouraging Ken to make an offer. Meantime, we were still waiting to hear back from Barclays. Tim expressed concern about my public stand on government aid: he said that if we ended up having to help a Lehman buyer, I would lose credibility. But I was willing to say "no government assistance" to help us get a deal. If we had to reverse ourselves over the weekend, so be it.

In the early afternoon, I received a call from Alistair Darling, the

U.K.'s chancellor of the Exchequer, with whom I had a good working relationship and who shared my views on the markets. I considered Alistair a straight shooter, and I gave him a candid update on Lehman.

"I understand one of your possible buyers is a British bank," I remember him saying. "I want you to know that we have some concern, because our banks are already under a lot of stress. We don't want them to become overextended and further weakened."

Afterward I commented to Jim Wilkinson that Alistair seemed to be telling me that the British didn't want their banks to catch the American disease. But because he couched this as a general concern, I didn't see his words as the red flag that in retrospect they appear to have been.

I left for New York shortly before 3:00 p.m., with Dan Jester, Jim Wilkinson, and Christal West in tow, amid a grim downshift in the markets. The Dow ticked down just 12 points, but Lehman shares had declined another 13.5 percent, to $3.65. AIG's shares dropped 31 percent for the day, ending at $12.14, and were off 46 percent for the week. I realized that I now had one more institution to put on our watch.

En route to the airport, I took a call from New York senator Chuck Schumer, who offered his views on Lehman. "We had better find a buyer who's not going to fire a lot of people," he said. "It would be better to have a domestic buyer than a foreign buyer."

I wondered if Fuld, who preferred BofA, had put Schumer up to this call, but there was no question that the senator cared deeply about his state. He pointedly told me that JPMorgan's purchase of Bear Stearns had cost New York jobs.

Tim had suggested I phone Ken Lewis to see just how serious he was. He felt, as I did, that Bank of America was drifting away. I spoke briefly with Lewis while I was on board the flight. He was trying to outline the rudiments of a proposal, but our connection was poor in the stormy weather, and I agreed to call back once we were on the ground.

I thought glumly of the challenge before us. This crisis was far greater than what we'd faced with LTCM, a decade before, almost to the day. And the circumstances were more ominous than when we saved Bear Stearns in March. The financial system, and the global economy, were in much weaker shape.

The plane touched down a little before 5:00 p.m., and I jumped into a waiting car, accompanied by Dan, Jim, and Christal. As we made our way slowly into Manhattan I got back on the phone with BofA. Lewis laid out a tentative but complex proposal. He said his people had figured that Lehman had a capital hole of about $20 billion. For BofA to buy the investment bank, it would have to leave behind $40 billion of assets. The North Carolina bank would split the first $2 billion in losses with the U.S., 49 percent to BofA and 51 percent to the government. The U.S. would have to absorb 100 percent of all other losses on the assets left behind. In return, as a modest sweetener, BofA would give the government warrants to buy its shares. I reminded him that there would be no government money but that we were bringing together a private-sector consortium, and we agreed to meet in New York to discuss the matter further.

Dan Jester followed up with a phone call to BofA's Greg Curl to get more details. I listened to snippets of the conversation and watched Dan's unenthusiastic reaction to what he was hearing. I had suspected that Lewis didn't really want to buy Lehman, but I had hoped that if he believed he could get some help, he might try to pick it up on the cheap.

When Dan hung up, he shook his head. BofA had only wanted to talk about Lehman's bad assets and the size of the valuation hole.

"It's a positive sign that they've come in with the outline of an offer," I told him. "But it sure doesn't sound like they really want this."

"They don't," Dan agreed. "But do we have anything better?"

As we slowly made our way through the heavy rain and traffic to the New York Fed's headquarters on Liberty Street in Lower Manhattan, I checked in with Tim. He said Barclays was having trouble getting access to all the information they wanted as quickly as they needed. I wasn't completely surprised; when I had first told Dick Fuld about Barclays's interest he had been hesitant—he clearly preferred BofA as a buyer.

Tim thought we should press Fuld on helping Barclays. We got hold of Dick and relayed our concern. We also outlined BofA's proposal. Dick said he didn't understand why BofA needed any assistance. He was still clinging to his belief in the value of his assets, but he was alone there, a point underscored by a subsequent conversation I had with Varley and Diamond. The Barclays executives were encouraging, but they had one important qualifier.

"We've been focusing on the most problematic assets, and we may need some help with the funding," Varley said.

He reported that he'd spoken with Barclays's board as well as the bank's regulator, the U.K.'s Financial Services Authority (FSA), and he believed a deal could be made.

Reassuring him again that we would not embarrass his bank, I told him we wanted his best bid right away. "Your team needs to work through the night doing due diligence," I said. "We need as much specificity as soon as possible."

Built in the decade before the Great Crash of 1929, the New York Federal Reserve is a Renaissance Revival fortress with iron-barred windows, hunkered amid the skyscrapers of Wall Street. Its 14 stories of offices sit atop what is said to be the biggest pile of gold in the world. I'd walked its corridors many times in my career, but never before with such a sense of urgency.

Tim had called the meeting for 6:00 p.m., but it didn't begin until closer to 7:00 p.m., because of the bad traffic. The weather, the delay, and the market conditions contributed to a gloomy atmosphere.

Tim, Chris, and I met upstairs on the 13th floor, where Tim had taken up temporary residence while the Fed's 10th-floor executive offices were being renovated. We quickly went through our order of presentation, then rode the elevator down to a first-floor conference room where the meeting was being held. We took our seats at a long table, where Wall Street's most prominent CEOs sat waiting for us. Among them were Jamie Dimon from JPMorgan, John Mack from Morgan Stanley, Lloyd Blankfein from Goldman Sachs, Vikram Pandit from Citigroup, John Thain from Merrill Lynch, Brady Dougan from Credit Suisse, and Robert Kelly from Bank of New York Mellon.

It was an extraordinary moment: These were the people who controlled Wall Street and global finance. They had fought for years, sometimes bitterly, to lead their institutions to the forefront of the business, and now they had gathered to save a rival—and their own skins.

Tim opened the meeting by noting the seriousness of the occasion and the fragility of the markets. He said it was crucial for everyone to work together to save Lehman and to find a way to contain the damage if that could not be done. A failure would be catastrophic, and we couldn't completely insulate the banks from the fallout. Tim had crafted his speech to get the CEOs focused, and when he handed the meeting over to me, I had their full attention.

I was straightforward: We all knew why we were there. Without their help, Lehman would not open for business on Monday, and the consequences for the markets—and for everyone sitting around the table—would be dire. I explained that we had two potential buyers for Lehman; with no one from Bank of America or Barclays in the room, it was clear to everyone who the potential buyers were.

I stressed that a Lehman sale was possible but not probable. The industry had to find its own solution. Both bids had capital holes whose sizes were still unclear. What was clear, however, was that there could be no government money involved in any rescue. I knew that unless I explicitly said this, some of them might think that Good Old Hank would come to the rescue.

After Chris Cox explained how the SEC had been planning to manage a bankruptcy, I concluded that we needed to work together to avert a Lehman failure—if we could fashion a deal—and to manage one if we couldn't.

Tim said the Fed was considering many options to make liquidity available to the markets. And to help prevent the market from tightening even more, he encouraged the CEOs not to keep pulling back from one another.

Immediately the questions flew: How much money did we expect the bankers to put in? Why should they risk their capital? What difference would saving Lehman make, given the problems wracking the entire industry?

All the attendees knew how fraught the market was and that its problems went way beyond Lehman. By now, everyone knew that AIG was in trouble. The insurance giant's problems had been all over the news that day. Apart from the dramatic plunge in its shares, Standard & Poor's had warned that it might downgrade the company's credit rating; this would force AIG to produce billions in additional collateral. Then what? What was the point of having the private sector weaken itself further to save Lehman if someone else was going to need help afterward?

But when Pandit asked if the group was also going to talk about AIG, Tim said simply: "Let's focus on Lehman."

Tim went on to outline a plan for three main groups to work through potential outcomes for Lehman. One group would plan ways to minimize the repercussions of what Tim called the "lights out" scenario of a Lehman bankruptcy, focusing on Lehman's vast skeins of derivatives, secured funding, and triparty repo transactions. A second set of firms would look into how the industry might buy all of Lehman with the intention of liquidating it over time—an approach similar to what Wall Street had done in the 1998 LTCM bailout. A third group of firms would examine how to finance the part of Lehman that a prospective buyer didn't want.

In the end, the meeting turned out to be much less contentious than I had feared. I could see that the CEOs weren't all convinced that they would solve anything by risking their own capital. No doubt, they also questioned the government's resolve in saying we wouldn't put any taxpayer money in. But it was also clear they had come to the meeting with a purpose: they were committed to working with us and wanted to find a solution that would avoid market chaos.

"Come back in the morning," Tim told the CEOs. "And be prepared to do something."

CHAPTER 9

Saturday, September 13, 2008

Early Saturday morning, Jim, Christal, and I, accompanied by my Secret Service detail, left the Waldorf-Astoria Hotel in Midtown Manhattan, climbed into a car, and sped down a deserted Park Avenue, arriving at the New York Fed just after 7:00 a.m. It was quiet in the gray light and early enough that the television crews had not yet set up. Though everything had been hush-hush the night before, the news of our meeting was all over the morning's papers. By the time Dan Jester arrived a few minutes later, reporters had begun to swarm outside the building.

We rode the elevator up to the 13th floor, where Tim Geithner had arranged for me to work in an office borrowed from his Information Technology department, just down the hall from his own suite. I went straight to work and called Ken Lewis, who reported that after closer inspection his people now believed that Lehman's assets were in even worse shape than they had thought the previous evening—when they had said they wanted to leave $40 billion behind. I wasn't surprised to hear Lewis put forward a new obstacle: it was increasingly obvious that he didn't really want to buy Lehman. Nonetheless, we arranged for his team to come over to brief me later that morning.

I joined Tim in his office for a conference call with Barclays at about 8:00 a.m. Bank chairman Marcus Agius and CEO John Varley were on the line from London, and Bob Diamond was at Barclays's Midtown Manhattan offices. Varley said they were working hard on a possible deal but needed to hear that Tim and I were serious. Barclays did not want to be used as a decoy. Varley said he had serious concerns about some of Lehman's assets and indicated that Barclays would need to leave $52 billion of them behind. In addition to the problematic commercial mortgages, the list of dubious holdings included undeveloped land and Chrysler bonds that hadn't been marked down.

I told Varley to focus on the biggest problems first—the assets he thought were going to be the most troubled—and tell us what he needed to take care of them. If Barclays gave us its best offer that day, we believed we could deliver a private-sector consortium that would fund whatever shortfall there was. Even as we spoke, I explained, the leaders of virtually the entire banking industry were assembling downstairs at the Fed. The Barclays bankers said they would keep working, and I ended the call encouraged that Lehman might have found its buyer.

We were scheduled to meet the Wall Street CEOs in the first-floor conference room at 9:00 a.m., but just before then Dick Fuld called. I briefed him on my unpromising conversation with Lewis and told him that it was more important than ever that he work with Barclays. He expressed great disappointment, bordering on disbelief, at BofA's findings. He wanted to know more, but I had to cut him off to get to the meeting.

Addressing the CEOs for the second time in 12 hours, I tried to be totally open. I knew I had to give them crucial information as soon as I received it so that we could all quickly make informed judgments. I told them that Barclays appeared to be the most likely buyer for Lehman. I added that we had a meeting scheduled with BofA for later that morning, but I didn't dwell on the prospects of a deal with the U.S. bank, and it must have been clear to the group that those talks weren't going anywhere. I emphasized that we couldn't do anything without their help.

"We're working hard on a transaction, and we need to know where you guys stand," I said. "If there's a capital hole, the government can't fill it. So how do we get this done?"

I can only imagine what was going through their minds. These were smart, tough businessmen, and they were in a difficult spot. We were asking them to rescue one competitor by helping to finance its sale to yet another competitor. But they had no idea of the true state of Lehman's books or how much they would have to cough up to support such a deal. Without this information, they were flying blind: they couldn't possibly predict the consequences of any course of action they chose. They knew how important it was to maintain a smoothly functioning market and how much we needed them to keep lending to one another if Lehman did go down. But their own institutions were all under grave pressure, and they had no idea what tests they might face in the days ahead—or whether they would be strong enough to survive this crisis.

As a group, the CEOs were nonetheless working hard to agree on a plan, but there was, understandably, some pushback. John Mack wanted to know why the government couldn't arrange another assisted transaction, like the Bear Stearns rescue.

Tim quickly dismissed the possibility. "It's not a feasible option," he said. "We need to put another plan in place." He made clear that the Fed could not lend against Lehman's dubious assets but asserted that it wasn't the government's place to dictate the terms of any deal.

The three groups that Tim had organized to examine Lehman scenarios had worked through the night and reported on their progress. Citi, Merrill Lynch, and Morgan Stanley had been looking into an LTCM-type rescue, but that approach faded quickly as an option because it was impractical to liquidate Lehman without incurring huge losses, given the poor quality of its assets.

The team looking into how the industry might assist an independent buyer had spawned a series of subgroups to, among other things, scour Lehman's books, identifying and valuing its toxic assets, and devise a deal structure that would allow an industry consortium to finance the purchase of, and absorb the losses on, those assets. Credit Suisse and Goldman Sachs led the way on valuing Lehman's dubious real estate (Goldman had taken a look at the portfolio on its own earlier in the week). Credit Suisse's Brady Dougan reported that private-equity assets carried by Lehman at $11 billion were worth around $10 billion, while real estate assets carried at $41 billion were more accurately valued at between $17 billion and $20 billion.

Brady's report wasn't a complete surprise, given the Street's doubts about Lehman's health, but it was shocking nevertheless. There was a more than $20 billion difference between what Lehman said its assets were worth and their true value. The CEOs were left wondering how their firms could fill a hole that size and what other bad assets—and losses—they would be asked to take.

With their background as major custodian banks, JPMorgan and Bank of New York Mellon had led the way on the "lights out" scenario. Noting the frailty of the market, and especially of the banks' funding sources, Bob Kelly of Bank of New York Mellon remarked: "We have to figure out how to organize ourselves and how to do something, because we're toast if we let this thing go," he said.

I reiterated the severity of the situation. "I'm just going to say bluntly that you need to help finance a competitor or deal with the reality of a Lehman failure," I told them.

"We must be responsible for our own balance sheet and now we're responsible for others'?" Blankfein asked. "If the market thinks we're responsible for other firms' assets, that ups the ante." The market, he believed, would now see all the investment banks as more vulnerable.

His observations had to trouble every free-marketer in the room. At what point were the interests of individual firms overridden by the needs of the many? It was the classic question of collective action. If the firms were forced to jointly support one failing institution, would they have to pony up aid for the next player to run into trouble? Where would it end? And what would the impact be on anyone's ability to discern the industry's true health? Potential investors assessing any bank's balance sheet would have to consider not only its assets and liabilities, but whether it had properly accounted for the risk that it might have to bail out any one of its competitors. Under the circumstances, how could the market accurately gauge the condition of any financial institution?

When we stepped out into the main lobby, I noticed that the Fed building was filling up quickly. Before long, it seemed as if everybody I knew from Wall Street was there—CFOs, chief risk officers, heads of investment banking, senior staff from financial institutions groups, and specialists on lending, real estate, and private equity. Dozens of bankers were working on foldout tables spread throughout the lobby, in rooms off the lobby, and in offices all over the building, trying to come up with a rescue plan. Barclays had set up shop four floors above; Lehman was on the sixth floor;

Bank of America was working at its New York offices. Each bank had a team of lawyers, and an unmistakable war-room atmosphere was evolving.

Tim and I decided we should meet individually with Jamie Dimon, Lloyd Blankfein, and John Thain. Jamie and Lloyd were the CEOs of the two strongest institutions and had been reducing their exposure to Lehman. We believed others would likely follow if they stepped up as leaders of a collaborative effort to save the stricken bank. John was a different matter entirely. Tim and I were concerned that if Lehman went down, his firm, which had the next-weakest balance sheet among investment banks, would be the next to go. We planned to ask him to find a buyer for Merrill Lynch.

Shortly before 11:00 a.m., Tim, Dan Jester, and I met in a 13th-floor conference room with Bank of America's deal team: CFO Joe Price, head of strategy Greg Curl, financial adviser Chris Flowers, and legal adviser Ed Herlihy. Price and Curl explained that after poring over Lehman's books, Bank of America now believed that to get a deal done it would need to unload between $65 billion and $70 billion worth of bad Lehman assets. BofA had identified, in addition to $33 billion of soured commercial mortgages and real estate, another $17 billion of residential mortgage-backed securities on Lehman's books that it considered to be problematic. In addition, its due-diligence team had also raised questions about other Lehman assets, including high-yield loans and asset-backed securities for loans on cars and mobile homes, as well as some private-equity holdings. The likely losses on all of those bad assets, they estimated, would wipe out Lehman's equity of $28.4 billion.

We asked if they would be willing to finance any of the assets they wanted to leave behind or take more losses. They said no.

To say the least, it was a disappointing session. Price and Curl weren't even working off paper—they simply sat back in their chairs, reeling off ranges of huge numbers that would require an enormous private-sector bailout. At another time it might have been a humorous charade, but we were desperate to find a solution. Still, I wasn't prepared to give up just yet, so I asked them if they would be available for a meeting or a call later to discuss in more detail what assets they wanted to leave behind. At a minimum I wanted to keep BofA warm as a bidder, because the presence of another buyer would help us negotiate more effectively with Barclays.

As everyone got up to leave, Chris Flowers motioned me aside and said, "Hank, can I tell you what a mess it is over at AIG?" He produced a piece of paper that he said showed AIG's day-by-day liquidity. Scribbling arrows and circles on the sheet to outline the problem, Flowers told me that according to AIG's own projections the company would run out of cash in about ten days.

"Is there a deal to be done?" I asked.

"They are totally incompetent," Flowers said. "I would only put money in if management was replaced."

I knew AIG was having problems—its shares had been pummeled all week—but I didn't expect this. In addition to its vast insurance operations, the company had written credit default swaps to insure obligations backed by mortgages. The housing market crash hurt AIG badly, and it had posted losses for the last three quarters. Bob Willumstad, who had shifted from chairman to CEO in June, was expected to announce a new strategy in late September.

I relayed Flowers's information to Tim, and we agreed to invite Willumstad over. He surprised me by saying Flowers shouldn't attend. "Flowers is the problem, not the solution," Willumstad said. I suspected that Chris was trying to buy pieces of AIG on the cheap, and I promised he would not be part of the meeting.

Tim and I met privately with Jamie Dimon. A number of CEOs had expressed concern to us that he was using the crisis to maneuver his bank into a stronger position. Indeed, some were convinced that he wanted to put them out of business entirely. We led off by raising these complaints. Jamie assured us that JPMorgan was behaving responsibly but pointed out that he ran a for-profit institution and had an obligation to his shareholders. I emphasized that we needed him to play a leadership role in averting a Lehman Brothers failure.

Then, because I respected his judgment, I pressed Jamie for his assessment of the situation. Did he think we had a chance of putting together an industry agreement to save Lehman? He said it would be difficult but possible. The European banks would have a tougher time getting a quick decision from their boards and regulators, but he felt they would probably come through, too. In the end, I felt reassured that I could count on Jamie's leadership.

Tim and I spoke to Lloyd in the afternoon. He was still questioning the idea of a private consortium, given the weakness of the industry.

"Do you think this makes sense?" he asked us. "What will you ask for next week when Merrill or Morgan Stanley goes?"

"Lloyd, we've got to try to stop this thing now," I said.

"Goldman will act responsibly," he replied. "We'll do our part, but this is asking a lot, and I'm not sure it makes sense."

Tim and I believed that both Lloyd and Jamie would ultimately support a private-sector consortium, and I was optimistic that the CEOs would come up with a plan. Now we had to make sure that Barclays was on board.

Tim and I returned to the first floor about 3:30 p.m., shortly after Lloyd left, and reconvened a group meeting with the CEOs. I assured them that Barclays seemed interested and aggressive. I didn't bother talking about BofA. It was obvious from the morning meeting that the Charlotte bank had lost interest. I asked the group to intensify its efforts and find a way to finance any assets Barclays might want to leave behind.

The CEOs were testy, but in what I felt was a productive way. They were being asked to risk billions of dollars. They had been getting due-diligence reports on the quality of Lehman's assets from their people, and they knew that to make the math work, they would have to make a loan secured by assets worth much less than their stated value. In other words, they would have to take a mark-to-market loss the moment a deal was completed. The question was: how much would they eventually get back?

Vikram Pandit asked why banks like Citi, which had retail-based funding sources, should have to put up as much as those that relied on wholesale funding. After all, it was the investment banks, which lacked consumer deposit bases and depended on the institutional money markets, that were in trouble.

"You've got as much wholesale funding as anybody here," Lloyd Blankfein shot back at Vikram. "And because you've got the Fed behind you, you're like a big utility."

As ever, Jamie Dimon zeroed in on specifics. "Barclays is going to buy all the assets they want and assume all the liabilities they want, but what liabilities are they going to leave behind?" he asked. "Are they going to take tax liabilities and shareholder litigation from prior years, or is that being left for the Street?"

Tim and I met one last time, for just a few minutes, with Curl and Price from Bank of America. But we made no progress. By the time we had our third call with Barclays that day, at 4:30 p.m., BofA was out of the picture. Everything now depended on the British bank.

Each time we had spoken on Saturday, our discussions had become more granular as Barclays focused on the quality of Lehman's assets and the due diligence they needed to perform. Earlier, Barclays had also mentioned that its regulator, the Financial Services Authority, wanted to be sure the British bank had an adequate capital plan in place to back the deal, an understandable requirement that we expected could be met.

Now Bob Diamond raised a new, troubling issue. Given the size of the transaction being contemplated, he said, it appeared that Barclays might be required, in accordance with its London listing requirements, to hold a shareholder vote to approve the merger. He said he hoped a vote wouldn't be needed, but if it was, would the Federal Reserve guarantee Lehman's massive trading book until the deal was approved? The vote could take 30 to 60 days.

Tim carefully replied that the Fed was unable to provide any such blanket guarantee. But if a vote proved to be necessary, Barclays should quickly come up with their best ideas on how to deal with it, and the Fed would examine its options.

Even as I strived to maintain industry backing for a Lehman deal, Merrill Lynch had been weighing on my mind. The weekend had bought the firm a little time, but I hated to think what would happen come Monday—especially if we couldn't save Lehman.

Around 5:00 p.m. John Thain, responding to my invitation, walked through the door of my 13th-floor office. He had never been good at hiding his emotions; now he looked somber and uneasy. Tim had to take a phone call, so I began the meeting alone.

By this point, I had begun to suspect that BofA had set its sights firmly on Merrill and the legions of retail stockbrokers that I knew Ken Lewis had long craved. But I wasn't positive that this was the case, and I felt the need to make sure John understood the seriousness of the situation: Merrill was in imminent danger and he needed to act.

As we talked about the lack of options for his firm, I could see that the full impact of the crisis had settled on John. Just as with Lehman, I stressed, the government had no powers to save Merrill. Under the circumstances, he should try to sell the firm. He said he was exploring his options and talking with Bank of America, Goldman Sachs, and Morgan Stanley. He asked what I thought about a merger between Merrill and Morgan Stanley. I told him it didn't make sense: there would be too much overlap, and the market wouldn't like it.

"I agree," John said.

We also discussed Bank of America. I told him that I believed that BofA was the only interested buyer with the capacity to purchase Merrill. Still, John's manner was somewhat evasive. I couldn't tell if he really wanted, or intended, to sell the firm. He himself may not have known at that point.

AIG's Bob Willumstad arrived at the New York Fed late in the day, accompanied by his financial and legal advisers. We sat down in a conference room on the 13th floor. Willumstad, a soft-spoken man who had once run Citi's global consumer group, was very candid, admitting that AIG had a multibillion-dollar liquidity problem stemming from losses in its derivatives business and an imminent credit rating downgrade. He now told us that without a big infusion of money, AIG estimated it would run out of cash as soon as the following week. He described efforts to raise $40 billion in liquidity by selling certain healthy insurance subsidiaries to private-equity investors and by using some unencumbered securities from its insurance subsidiaries as collateral. Doing so would require the approval of Eric Dinallo, the superintendent of insurance for New York State. Bob said that the New York regulators supported the plan, and he was optimistic that the problem would be resolved by the end of the weekend.

I knew that Willumstad had gone to Tim earlier to see if AIG could have access to the Fed's discount window in an emergency, and that Tim had said he couldn't loan to a nonbank like AIG. It gave me a chill to think of the potential impact of AIG's problems. The firm had tens of millions of life insurance customers and tens of billions of dollars of contracts guaranteeing 401(k)s and other retirement holdings of individuals. If any company defined systemic risk, it was AIG, with its $1 trillion balance sheet and massive derivatives business connecting it to hundreds of financial institutions, govern-ments, and companies around the world. Were the giant insurance company to go under, the process of unwinding its contracts alone would take years—and along the way, millions of people would be devastated financially.

The company's immediate difficulties stemmed from the fact that it had written huge amounts of credit default swap insurance on obligations backed by mortgages. Those contracts included triggers: if AIG got downgraded, it had to post additional collateral. AIG's collateral requirements also depended on the fair market value of the securities it insured, which was eroding with the de-clining housing market. In this Saturday meeting, Doug Braun-stein, AIG's financial adviser from JPMorgan, described AIG's books as aggressively marked.

"What do you mean by aggressively?" I asked.

"The opposite of conservatively," the veteran banker shot back quickly.

Not long afterward, I shared my concerns about Lehman with Josh Bolten at the White House. "This is one of the most difficult situations I could have imagined," I said. "There's a big difference between what Lehman assets were marked at and what the buyers are willing to pay."

Josh got an earful from me as I explained the other two balls we were juggling in New York. We had gone into the weekend to save Lehman Brothers, and now AIG was facing a liquidity crisis that had put it on the verge of bankruptcy, and we had become concerned enough about Merrill Lynch to urge John Thain to sell that firm.

Meantime, the CEOs and their teams were all working hard. It was an amazing scene, all these financial industry executives re-viewing spreadsheets, crunching numbers, trying to devise a so-lution. Rivals from different firms were working together. Senior traders sat at one set of tables, figuring out how to net out firms' exposures if Lehman went down. In another area, people studied Lehman's private-equity portfolio, trying to get a handle on the losses their firms would have to absorb if they lent money against it. It was inspiring to see all these fierce competitors trying to save a rival.

By evening the CEOs had agreed to support in principle a proposal under which Barclays would leave behind a pile of bad real estate and private-equity investments and wipe out Lehman's preferred and common shareholders. To make the deal work, Barclays wanted the consortium of Wall Street firms to agree to loan up to $37 billion to a special purpose vehicle that would hold the assets. These had been carried by Lehman at $52 billion, but after their analyses the firms estimated their value at closer to $27 billion to $30 billion. The firms stood to lose collectively up to $10 billion. Barclays was also going to contribute some of its own shares, which would reduce the loss to the firms. It would still cost them dearly, but Lehman would be saved.

I left the New York Fed before 9:00 p.m. optimistic about the prospects for a deal. The industry was doing its part to come up with funding, and I had reason to believe we would find a solution to Barclays's need for a shareholder vote.

Anticipating another sleep-deprived night, I arrived back at the hotel exhausted. I went into the bathroom of my room and pulled out a bottle of sleeping pills I'd been given in Washington. As a Christian Scientist, I don't take medication, but that night I desperately needed rest.

I stood under the harsh bathroom lights, staring at the small pill in the palm of my hand. Then I flushed it—and the contents of the entire bottle—down the toilet. I longed for a good night's rest. For that, I decided, I would rely on prayer, placing my trust in a Higher Power.

Sunday, September 14, 2008

I had gone to bed modestly optimistic about our chances of saving Lehman and hopeful that John Thain would find a partner for Merrill Lynch. I'd left Steve Shafran and Dan Jester behind, working at the New York Fed with Bob Diamond and the Barclays team to nail down their offer, and with the Wall Street consortium to structure the loan terms. When I spoke to Steve and Dan first thing Sunday morning, they'd barely had time to take a shower or shave, much less sleep. Reasonably confident that the Barclays bid was proceeding, they'd left the Fed at 4:00 a.m., when Diamond said he had to plug into a board meeting. They also reported that they had made good progress with the consortium on a preliminary term sheet for the loan that the Wall Street firms would need to provide for the Barclays deal.

Tim spoke with Diamond after the Barclays board meeting, at 7:15 a.m. New York time, and Bob warned him that Barclays was having problems with its regulators. Forty-five minutes later Chris and I joined Tim in his office to talk with Diamond and Varley, who told us that the FSA had declined to approve the deal. I could hear frustration, bordering on anger, in Diamond's voice. He and Varley indicated that they were surprised and embarrassed by this turn of events.

We were beside ourselves. This was the first time we were hearing that the FSA might not support the deal. Barclays had assured us that they were keeping the regulators posted on the transaction. Now they were saying that they didn't understand the FSA's stance. We told them we would contact the U.K. officials right away and get to the bottom of this.

Subsequently, Tim and Chris spoke separately with Callum Mc-Carthy, the FSA chairman. The British regulator, they learned, was not prepared to approve the merger, but at the same time, the FSA was careful to say it was not disapproving the merger, either. I recall both Tim and Chris saying that the FSA had raised concerns about the need for more due diligence, Barclays's plans to raise capital to fund the acquisition, and guaranteeing Lehman's trading book during the shareholder vote. All this added up to a delay, and delaying the deal was the same as killing it: we needed certainty today.

As I listened to Tim and Chris, I went over again in my head my Friday conversation with Alistair Darling, and it occurred to me that I had not caught his true meaning when he'd expressed concern about a British bank's buying Lehman. What I had taken as understandable caution should have been taken as a clear warning.

Tim spoke with Callum McCarthy again around 10:00 a.m. in an attempt to get the British to waive the listing requirement for a shareholder vote so that Barclays could go ahead and buy Lehman. But the FSA chief put the onus on Darling, saying that only the chancellor of the Exchequer had the authority to do that.

With Bank of America gone and Barclays now in limbo, we were running out of options—and time. Treasury had no authorities to invest capital, and no U.S. regulator had the power to seize Lehman and wind it down outside of very messy bankruptcy proceedings. And unlike with Bear Stearns, the Fed's hands were tied because we had no buyer.

Markets demand absolute certainty, and we had known all along that Lehman couldn't open for business on Monday unless it had lined up a major institution, like Barclays, to guarantee its trades. That had been the crucial element of the Bear Stearns rescue. Even after JPMorgan, backed by the Fed, had announced that it would lend to Bear Stearns on Friday, March 14, the investment bank had continued to disintegrate. A collapse was only avoided on Sunday when JPMorgan agreed to buy Bear and guarantee its trading obliga-

tions until the deal closed. That halted the ongoing flight of counterparties and clients, averting Bear's bankruptcy.

The Lehman situation differed from Bear's in another important
way. The Bear assets that JPMorgan left behind were clean enough
to secure sufficiently a $29 billion Fed loan. But an evaluation of
Lehman's assets had revealed a gaping hole in its balance sheet.
The Fed could not legally lend to fill a hole in Lehman's capital.
That was why we needed a buyer. And we hoped that the private
sector would assist the buyer by providing $37 billion in financing
that was exposed to $10 billion or so of expected losses from min-
ute one.

The Fed had no authority to guarantee an investment bank's
trading book, or for that matter any of its liabilities. And without an
acquirer with a big balance sheet to ensure solvency, a Fed liquidity
loan would not have been sufficient to hold Lehman together during a shareholder vote. Instead, the Fed would have been lending
into the same kind of run on Lehman that Bear suffered before
JPMorgan came through. In the 30 to 60 days that could elapse
before a shareholder vote, account balances would drain; huge
amounts of collateral would be pulled as trades were unwound
while hedge funds and other key customers fled; bank employees
would quit. And then, most likely, Barclays shareholders would vote
the deal down. The Fed would find itself in possession of an insol-
vent bank and out tens of billions of dollars.

I delivered the bad news to Josh Bolten, who had already spoken to the president about the possibility of a Lehman failure.

"You've got presidential approval to settle on a wind-down that
doesn't commit federal resources," Josh told me. "Anything else,
you should come back to the president and tell him what you're
planning."

Tim, Chris, and I were running late for our scheduled 10:00 a.m.
meeting with the CEOs downstairs. Believing we shouldn't sugar-

coat the situation, I told the bank chiefs we had run into some regulatory issues with Barclays but were committed to working through them.

The CEOs presented us with a term sheet for the deal. In the end, they had come much further than Tim and I thought they would. They had agreed to put up more than $30 billion to save their rival, and they had figured out how to spread the risk across the industry. If Barclays had committed to the deal, we would have had industry financing in place.

Tim asked the group to keep plowing ahead, but I imagine everyone suspected that the deal was in jeopardy.

At 11:00 a.m. I went back upstairs, and within half an hour I was on the phone with Alistair Darling, who wanted a report on Lehman. I told him that we were stunned to learn that the FSA was refusing to approve the Barclays transaction. I pointed out that we had run out of options for Lehman, because U.S. officials had no statutory ability to intervene.

He made it clear, without a hint of apology in his voice, that there was no way Barclays would buy Lehman. He offered no specifics other than to say that we were asking the British government to take on too big a risk, and he was not willing to have us unload our problem on the British taxpayer. Alistair's chief concern was the impact of a Lehman failure on the British financial system. He wanted to know what the U.S. would do once Lehman failed.

"We are very concerned over here," he said. "Lehman has a significant business in the U.K., and we have real concerns as to whether it is adequately capitalized."

The chancellor of the Exchequer was delivering a clear message: we would get no help from the British. Our last hope for Lehman was gone.

I hung up feeling deflated, and frustrated that we had wasted so much time with Barclays on a deal that could never have been done. I was frustrated, too, that unlike Barclays, the British were not simply asking directly that the Fed guarantee Lehman's trading book, even if the Fed lacked that power. Frankly, I was beginning to believe that the British were afraid that if they did push, the Fed would somehow find a way to guarantee it, leaving them one less excuse for not approving the deal.

I could only surmise that if Darling wasn't presenting any options or leaving any room to negotiate, it was because the British had their reasons for not wanting this deal done. In truth, I could understand their hesitation. The U.K.'s bank situation was more perilous than ours. Altogether, British banks' assets amounted to more than four times the size of the national GDP; total U.S. banking assets were about the same size as our GDP. Moreover, individual U.K. banks, including Barclays, had capital issues of their own. It was understandable that the country's officials might be reluctant to waive normal shareholder procedures for a deal that could have resulted in big losses to one of their largest institutions while carrying no risk for the U.S. government.

"Darling's not going to help," I told Tim. "It's over."

At that moment, I did not have time for regret, recriminations, or second-guessing. I could only think about the enormous challenge we faced.

I'd asked John Thain to come up to see me, and he arrived right after my conversation with Darling. I got to the point: "Have you done what I recommended and found a buyer?"

"Hank, I'm not thick," he responded, slightly irritated. "I heard you. I'm doing what I need to do."

John didn't mention Bank of America, but I did. By this point I assumed he was in serious negotiations to sell Merrill to the bank, and I said he should focus on doing that deal.

John's no actor, and I could tell he was deeply engaged in merger talks. I was relieved: with Lehman all but finished, I didn't want to see Merrill dragged down next.

I phoned my Treasury team in Washington to brief them on the unhappy developments with Lehman and warn them that the markets were going to get very choppy. I asked Kevin Fromer to get ready to talk to the appropriate staffs on the Hill, and I made sure that Michele Davis was prepared to deal with the press, which was expecting a big announcement on Lehman before the Asian markets opened.

All weekend Dick Fuld had been holed up at Lehman headquarters, making phone calls. Now I called him back.

"Dick, I feel terrible," I said. "We've come up with no options. The British government is not going to let Barclays go ahead. BofA isn't interested."

"This can't be happening," he said. "Hank, you have to figure something out!"

Fuld couldn't understand that the BofA deal was gone. It was impossible not to sympathize with him. After all, I had run a financial institution; he had been one of my peers. I couldn't help thinking what this would mean for the thousands of people who worked for Lehman Brothers, one of whom was my brother, Dick.

Fuld had also been calling Tim and Ben, but only I talked to him. Although I hadn't been directly involved in the discussions between Barclays and Lehman, I knew that he had been shunted aside and that Lehman president Bart McDade had taken over the negotiations.

We'd scheduled another meeting with the CEOs for 12:30 p.m., but once again we were running late, because Tim was back on the phone with Callum McCarthy, fighting to the end for a Barclays-Lehman deal. I stood beside him, watching him jot notes on a pad—calm and methodical as always, although he must have been as frustrated as I was. He was pressing McCarthy about his reasoning and asking if there was anything that could be done to speed the FSA's deliberations up or to get the deal done.

And then Tim hung up.

"I made no progress," he said simply. The FSA continued to be unwilling to say what it would take to approve the deal.

With that, we walked to the elevators. To reach the conference room, we had to wade through all the Wall Street executives milling around the first floor. It was like pushing through a crowd at a stadium. Everyone, it seemed, wanted to speak to us. They were working hard and were eager for an update, and I felt as though they were all scanning my face or Tim's to guess the verdict. I wish I could have been buoyed by their energy and effort, but I felt numb. The news I was about to deliver could only hurt them. Some of the crowd tried to follow us into the conference room, but we shut the door on them, limiting the meeting to the CEOs.

It was shortly before 1:00 p.m. when Tim, Chris, and I addressed the CEOs again. I was completely candid. Barclays had dropped out, and we had no buyer for Lehman. We were going to have to make the best of it.

"The British screwed us," I blurted out, more in frustration than anger.

I'm sure the FSA had very good reasons of their own for their stance, and it would have been more proper and responsible for me to have said we had been surprised and disappointed to learn of the U.K. regulator's decision, but I was caught up in the emotion of the moment.

"We're going to have to all work together to manage this," I went on. "We've got no buyer, and there's nothing to do about it."

Having been forewarned of this possibility at the morning's meeting, nobody seemed shocked by the bad news. They may even have felt momentary relief not to have to commit billions to an iffy rescue. But as the reality sunk in they became somber. And then they quickly began to come together, focusing on a single question: *How are we going to prepare for the markets' opening on Monday?*

Chris Cox talked a little about the process going forward. He said the SEC had been working for a long time on detailed plans for handling a Lehman bankruptcy.

As I made my way from the conference room, a number of executives rushed up to me for news. A contingent from Lehman crowded close to the doorway. Rodge Cohen, who was advising Lehman, approached me, accompanied by Bart McDade.

"Hank, what's happening?" he asked.

I gave them the bad news. "We had the banks ready to do the deal, but the British wouldn't approve it."

Rodge grabbed hold of me and said, "Hank, this is terrible."

I remember how he and McDade implored us to try something else. I could see the devastation in their faces as they took in the cold, stark reality: this was the end. They had scrambled all weekend, and I felt terrible for them, and particularly for McDade, a stand-up guy who had been thrust into an impossible job at the last possible minute.

Back in my temporary office on the 13th floor, a jolt of fear suddenly overcame me as I thought for a moment of what lay ahead of us. Lehman was as good as dead, and AIG's problems were spiraling out of control. With the U.S. sinking deeper into recession, the failure of a large financial institution would reverberate throughout the country—and far beyond our shores. I could see credit tightening, strapped companies slashing jobs, foreclosures rising ever faster: millions of Americans would lose their livelihoods and their homes. It would take years for us to dig ourselves out from under such a disaster.

All weekend I'd been wearing my crisis armor, but now I felt my guard slipping as I gave in to anxiety. I knew I had to call my wife, but I didn't want to do it from the landline in my office because other people were there. So I walked around the corner to a spot near some windows on the other side of the elevators and phoned Wendy, who had just returned from church. I told her about Lehman's unavoidable bankruptcy and the looming problems with AIG.

"What if the system collapses?" I asked her. "Everybody is looking to me, and I don't have the answer. I am really scared."

"You needn't be afraid," Wendy said. "Your job is to reflect God, Infinite Mind, and you can rely on Him."

I asked her to pray for me, and for the country, and to help me cope with this sudden onslaught of fear. She immediately quoted from the Second Book of Timothy, verse 1:7—"For God hath not given us the spirit of fear, but of power, and of love, and of a sound mind."

The verse was a favorite of both of ours. I found it comforting and felt my strength come back with this reassurance. With great gratitude, I was able to return to the business at hand. I called Josh Bolten and New York City mayor Michael Bloomberg to alert them that Lehman would file for bankruptcy that evening.

We had tried during the summer and more intensely in the last few days to be ready for this moment. Beginning right after I had informed the CEOs that Barclays was done, the Wall Street firms, under the guidance of Tim and the New York Fed, got down to work. Among other things, they divided the industry into teams to try to minimize the disruptions that were likely to occur the next day.

A group on the 13th floor worked through other issues. The Fed had decided it could and would lend directly to the Lehman broker-dealer arm to enable it to unwind its repo positions. (Over the next few days, it would lend as much as $60 billion for this purpose.) Separately, the International Swaps and Derivatives Association had agreed to sanction an extraordinary derivatives trading session. It began at 2:00 p.m., and though originally scheduled to run until 4:00 p.m., it would be extended another two hours. The aim was for the firms to unwind as much as they could, and to offset their exposure to Lehman, before the firm declared bankruptcy and threw the market into disarray.

With a company like Lehman that had operations across the globe, bankruptcy raised enormously complex issues. Which entities would file for bankruptcy, and which would not? Would the European and U.K. entities file before the New York holding company? The Federal Reserve and the SEC had to work these details out with Lehman in order to orchestrate the proper sequence of filings. Lehman's broker-dealer had to be open for business on Monday for the Fed to be able to backstop the unwinding of Lehman's giant repo book.

One of the biggest issues was that the firm did not appear to have taken seriously the possibility of having to file for bankruptcy until the last minute. A Lehman team, accompanied by their counsel Harvey Miller of Weil, Gotshal & Manges, would not arrive at the New York Fed to discuss bankruptcy options until early Sunday evening, and even then Lehman appeared to have no immediate intention of filing.

In the midst of all this, President Bush called me at about 3:30 p.m.

"Will we be able to explain why Lehman is different from Bear Stearns?" he asked.

"Yes, sir," I replied. "There was just no way to save Lehman. We couldn't find a buyer even with the other private firms' help. We will just have to try to manage this."

I had to add that Merrill, now in talks with BofA, was the next-weakest investment bank, and that AIG had a severe liquidity problem. I also told the president that in my opinion we might need to go to Congress to get expanded powers to deal with the crisis. The problems we had to contend with were coming at us fast and all at once. The case-by-case approach we had been using since Bear Stearns was no longer enough. President Bush—reassuring, as always—told me we would figure out how to work through the crisis. We agreed to meet the next day after I returned to Washington.

Even as we struggled with Lehman, AIG rushed to center stage. That afternoon, Chris Flowers called Dan Jester to say he'd made a proposal to AIG to acquire some of the company's most valuable subsidiaries. It sounded to me like Flowers was trying to take the company for next to nothing. At the same time, other private-equity firms were doing due diligence on various parts of AIG's operations. But Bob Willumstad had his own proposal for us.

A little before 5:00 p.m., Willumstad returned to the New York Fed with his advisers, and we again met in the conference room on the 13th floor. Willumstad delivered terrible news: The only proposal he had been able to generate from private-equity investors came from Flowers, and his board had rejected it as inadequate. Further, AIG had discovered another major problem: huge losses in its securities lending program. AIG had been lending out its high-grade bonds and receiving cash in return. It reinvested the cash in mortgage-backed securities, hoping to earn some extra income. As counterparties sought to unwind the deals to avoid exposure to AIG, the insurer faced the prospect of having to sell the illiquid mortgage-backed securities at big losses. It was clear that AIG's cash crunch would likely occur sometime within the week—sooner than we had been told Saturday morning.

But Willumstad had a new plan, in which the Fed would provide a $40 billion bridge loan, in addition to the $10 billion AIG would generate from unencumbered securities. The company would sell some of its insurance company subsidiaries and use the proceeds to pay back the loan.

It was unnerving. Tim and I knew that an AIG bankruptcy would be devastating, leading to the failure of many other institutions. In one day the company's shortfall had mushroomed to $50 billion. Tim said that the Fed was not prepared to lend to AIG and that the company should get a consortium of private lenders to make a bridge loan.

I joined Tim and Fed governor Kevin Warsh on a call with Ben, Fed vice chairman Don Kohn, and the rest of Ben's team in Washington. We reviewed the day's dreadful events. We were doing all we could, in Tim's phrase, to spread foam on the runway to cushion the coming crash of Lehman.

Among these measures, the Fed had expanded the range of collateral that brokers could pledge to receive loans via the Primary Dealer Credit Facility (PDCF) to include anything accepted in the triparty repo system—such as stocks and non-investment-grade bonds. The big worry was that in the wake of a Lehman failure repo lenders would shy away from investment banks and other financial firms heavily dependent on that kind of financing. By expanding the PDCF's eligible collateral, the Fed aimed to reassure repo lenders that if any investment bank counterparty ran into problems, it could get cash from the Fed for any collateral and use that to repay the triparty repo lender.

Separately, with encouragement from Tim and me, ten of the Wall Street firms had come together to create a $70 billion facility of their own that would provide emergency liquidity support for any of the participating banks that needed it.

After all these measures, though, we had run out of gas. None of us had any confidence that they would be sufficient. Some in the group asked if we should revisit the idea of putting public money into Lehman, but Tim said there was no authority to do that.

We were all frustrated to have worked so hard and come up empty. We knew that the consequences of the Lehman failure would be awful, but even so, we did not know what would face us in the morning—or in the days to come. I had a sense that the situation had gone beyond our ability to handle it on our own. I told Ben and Tim and the others on the call that the time had probably come to go to Congress for fiscal authorities to deal with the unfolding crisis. We had all wanted this for some time.

After the Fed call, I heard the only good news of the weekend: Bank of America was going to buy Merrill Lynch for $50 billion. Thain had managed to arrange a sale at $29 per share, a 70 percent premium over Merrill's market price. I was relieved: without this, I knew, Merrill would not have lasted the week.

We had planned to announce Lehman's bankruptcy at 4:00 p.m., four hours before Japan's markets opened, to allow as much time as possible for market participants to prepare themselves. The SEC was supposed to take the lead on this, but all afternoon I got reports from the Fed that the commission was moving slowly. Chris Cox had been in his office for hours working on a press release to assure Lehman's broker-dealer customers that they would be protected under SEC regulations. He was also supposed to discuss Lehman's planned course of action with the company's board of directors, but he had yet to do so.

Pressed by Tim and others, I finally walked into Chris's office around 7:15 p.m. and urged him to move quickly to execute the SEC's plan. "The Asia markets are opening!" I said. "You need to get your announcement out soon, and you can't do that unless you are coordinating with Lehman. It is essential that you call the company now."

Chris was waiting for Lehman to file for bankruptcy of its own volition. I understood that it was unusual and awkward for a regulator to push a private-sector firm to declare bankruptcy, but I stressed that he needed to do something to get the process moving for the good of the rest of the system. And although Chris wanted Tim and me to join him on the call, I said that as Lehman's regulator, he should make the call by himself.

Finally, sharing the line with Tom Baxter, the general counsel of the New York Fed, and other Fed and SEC staffers, Cox called Fuld shortly after 8:00 p.m. to reiterate that there would be no government rescue. Lehman had no alternative to bankruptcy. Fuld connected Cox to Lehman's board.

"I can't tell you what to do," Cox told them. "I can only tell you to make a quick decision."

As it was, Lehman did not file for bankruptcy until 1:45 a.m. Monday, well after the Asian markets had opened.

While Tim and I waited together for Chris to complete the call with Lehman, I phoned Michele Davis and told her that despite the good news on Merrill Lynch, I was expecting a tough week. As difficult as it was going to be to get fiscal authorities from Congress, we didn't have much choice, and it was going to take an all-out effort on the Hill. I told her I had alerted the president.

Kevin Fromer had been dealing with the legislative staffs, but I needed to brief the major congressional players and called Chuck Schumer, Barney Frank, Chris Dodd, and Spencer Bachus. "How are all of these free-market people going to feel about letting the markets work?" Barney asked me pointedly. But he clearly understood the ugly ramifications of these developments. He added that he was disappointed not to have heard from me earlier.

Before I left the New York Fed I met a final time with Tim. He had his work cut out for him, navigating the Lehman mess and trying to forestall an even worse one at AIG. Tim was still hoping to fashion a private-sector solution for the insurer. I agreed to have

Dan Jester stay in New York to help with AIG, and Jeremiah Norton, deputy assistant secretary for financial institutions policy, would fly up to relieve Steve Shafran. I would return to Washington the next morning, while Tim's team—with no time to rest after Lehman—tried to determine AIG's liquidity needs and develop a plan to raise money.

I got back to the Waldorf about 10:00 p.m. Shortly after I arrived, John Mack called me. I could tell that the Morgan Stanley CEO was on edge. In just one day, Wall Street had irrevocably changed: Lehman Brothers was headed for bankruptcy, and Merrill Lynch was about to be bought by Bank of America. Morgan Stanley had held up well so far, but with those two firms gone, John was deeply worried.

"Come tomorrow morning," he said, "the shorts will be on us with a vengeance."

CHAPTER 10

Monday, September 15, 2008

I woke up exhausted Monday morning after a few troubled hours of sleep, tormented by the increasing size of AIG's problems and John Mack's haunting words from the night before: with Lehman Brothers gone, Morgan Stanley could be next. From a window of my room in the Waldorf-Astoria, I watched as the still-quiet streets of Midtown Manhattan came slowly to life. It was just after 6:00 a.m. and not yet light, but I could see taxis dropping off passengers, trucks off-loading deliveries, workers hurrying to their offices to get a jump on the day.

Only a few hours before, just after midnight, Lehman Brothers had filed for bankruptcy, the biggest in U.S. history. I wondered if anyone out there on the streets could possibly imagine what was about to hit them.

President Bush called for an update shortly after 7:00 a.m., but I had nothing new to tell him. Lehman would have gone into administration by now in London, but the markets had not yet opened in New York. All I could offer were assurances that we would stay on top of the situation and keep him informed throughout the day. With luck, I told him, the system could withstand a Lehman failure, but if AIG went down, we faced real disaster. More than almost any financial firm I could think of, AIG was entwined in every part of the global system, touching businesses and consumers alike in many different and critical ways.

I stressed that I trusted Tim Geithner to do everything possible to come up with a private-sector solution, but AIG was in deep trouble, and I was not optimistic. Its shares had plunged 31 percent the previous Friday and, after the weekend's well-publicized problems, today was sure to be worse.

I called Chris Cox at 8:15 a.m. to urge him to get prepared to take action on short sellers. Before I left for the airport, I caught up with Tim. His news wasn't encouraging—AIG was already looking worse than last night. We agreed that I would get back to Washington as soon as possible and organize my team to deal with Congress and the broader crisis. He would oversee the steps being taken to manage the Lehman failure and, most important, press ahead with a private-sector rescue of AIG, which he hoped would be led by JPMorgan and Goldman Sachs.

I boarded my flight back to D.C. as the markets were just opening, so it wasn't until I landed at 10:30 a.m. and got back on the phone with Tim that I learned the day had begun in ugly fashion. In the first hour of trading, AIG shares had plunged nearly in half, to $6.65; the Dow was off 326 points, or 2.9 percent. In London, the FTSE 100 Index was down 183 points, or 3.4 percent.

Shortly after I'd gotten off with Tim, my friend and former Goldman colleague Ken Brody, now chairman of Taconic Capital Advisors, reached me.

"Hank, you made a big mistake," he said. "This market is too fragile to handle a Lehman Brothers bankruptcy. The system is on the verge of collapse, and Morgan Stanley could well be next."

I respected Ken's opinions tremendously, but this was the last call in the world I needed, coming on top of Tim's gloomy report. He assumed we had intentionally let Lehman go down and thought it might be good to acknowledge the mistake publicly. I told Ken that I was unbelievably frustrated but that we had had no choice. There had been no legal basis to bail out Lehman. Now we were doing everything we could to manage the situation.

Still, his assessment distressed me, and when I reached the office, I saw that the market was in full decline. Understandably, the prices of AIG (off by nearly 60 percent) and Lehman (down 95 percent) were in free fall, but Morgan Stanley and Goldman Sachs were also dropping fast. Their credit default swap rates had nearly doubled—to insure $10 million of debt now cost about $450,000 for Morgan Stanley and about $300,000 for Goldman. I could sense the start of a panic. Morgan Stanley's level approached where Lehman had been the previous Wednesday, and no one in the world— not a rational world, anyway—could have thought Morgan Stanley's business was in anywhere near as bad a shape as the now-bankrupt investment house.

It was the dismal beginning of the first day of what would be a thoroughly dismal week.

I hurried to the White House to update the president shortly after 1:00 p.m. and then went straight to the briefing room in the West Wing to hold a press conference. After a short statement, I took questions from four dozen or so journalists packed into the small, windowless room. They were all on edge.

In my answers, I attempted to put the crisis in perspective, noting its roots in the housing price collapse and pointing out that a more satisfying solution had been hindered by our archaic financial regulatory structure. "Moral hazard," I made clear, "is something I don't take lightly." But I drew a distinction between our actions in March with Bear Stearns and now with Lehman Brothers. I stressed that unlike with Bear, there had been no buyer for Lehman. For that reason, I said: "I never once considered it appropriate to put tax-payer money on the line in resolving Lehman Brothers." How could I? There was, in fact, no deal to put money into.

In retrospect, I've come to see that I ought to have been more careful with my words. Some interpreted them to mean that we were drawing a strict line in the sand about moral hazard, and that we just didn't care about a Lehman collapse or its consequences. Nothing could have been further from the truth. I had worked hard for months to ward off the nightmare we foresaw with Lehman. But few understood what we did—that the government had no authority to put in capital, and a Fed loan by itself wouldn't have prevented a bankruptcy.

I was in a painful bind that I all too frequently found myself in as a public official. Although it's my nature to be forthright, it was important to convey a sense of resolution and confidence to calm the markets and to help Americans make sense of things. Being direct and open with the media and general public can sometimes backfire. You might actually cause the very thing you hoped to avoid.

I did not want to suggest that we were powerless. I could not say, for example, that we did not have the statutory authority to save Lehman—even though it was true. Say that and it would be the end of Morgan Stanley, which was in far superior financial shape to Lehman but was already under an assault that would dramatically intensify in the coming days. Lose Morgan Stanley, and Goldman Sachs would be next in line—if they fell, the financial system might vaporize and with it, the economy.

By late afternoon I'd caught up with both presidential candidates. I was now in touch with Barack Obama almost daily, though less frequently with John McCain. My goal was to keep them from saying anything that might upset the markets—a task that would become more important, and more difficult, as the campaign heated up.

That afternoon, Obama asked insightful questions as I explained why we couldn't save Lehman and noted that the market was reacting worse than we'd feared. I also told him about the problems with AIG. As he did almost every time we talked, Obama asked if I'd spoken to McCain—perhaps it was to gauge what his opponent was thinking or to encourage me to keep McCain in line, so that on crucial economic points we presented a united front for the country's benefit.

McCain, who never asked me about Obama on our calls, kept his counsel while I updated him on the situation. He did suggest I speak to his running mate. "She's a quick study," he said admiringly. Still energized by the Sarah Palin nomination, the Republican ticket led in some of the polls, although that lead would disappear by the end of the week.

When I got in touch with the Alaska governor, she quickly showed her knack for focusing on the hot button. She asked me whether AIG's problems had to do with managerial incompetence, then got right to the point.

"Hank," she said, "the American people don't like bailouts."

"Neither do I, but an AIG failure would be a disaster for the American people," I replied.

In my view, we needed to be ready for anything. A little more than an hour before, the Dow Jones index had closed at a two-year low. It had fallen 504 points, or 4.4 percent—the worst one-day point decline since the markets reopened after 9/11. Even more ominously, the credit markets were deteriorating. The LIBOR-OIS spread, which had peaked at about 82 basis points during the Bear Stearns crisis, had jumped to more than 105 basis points, underscoring how little confidence the banks had in lending to one another. If I had any doubts that we were about to enter a new, ugly phase of the crisis, they were erased when General Electric CEO Jeff Immelt stopped by to see me a little before 6:00 p.m. We spoke privately in my office.

I'd known Jeff for years and admired the cool, unflappable demeanor he had displayed as CEO of the biggest, most prestigious company in America. Jeff was following up on a phone call from the week before when, just after the takeovers of Fannie Mae and Freddie Mac, he'd mentioned that GE was having problems in the commercial paper market. His report had alarmed me then. That market had been in distress since the onset of the credit crisis in August 2007. The worst of that had involved the asset-backed commercial paper market, which supported all those off-balance-sheet special investment vehicles filled with toxic collateralized debt obligations that banks had cooked up. I'd never expected to hear those troubles spreading like this to the corporate world, and certainly not to GE.

Commercial paper is essentially an IOU that is priced on the credit rating of the borrower and generally backstopped by a bank line of credit. It's usually issued for short periods of time—90 days or less. And it's often bought by money market funds looking for a safe place to get a higher rate of return than they would earn from short-term government bills. Companies use these borrowings to conduct their day-to-day business operations, financing their inventories and meeting their payrolls, among other things. If companies can't use the commercial paper market, they have to turn to banks (which in September 2008 were reluctant to lend). When their access to short-term financing is in question, companies have to curtail normal business operations.

Now here was Jeff telling me that GE was finding it very difficult to sell its commercial paper for any term longer than overnight.

The fact that the single-biggest issuer in this $1.8 trillion market was having trouble with its funding was startling.

If mighty GE was having trouble rolling its commercial paper over, so were hundreds of other industrial companies, from Coca-Cola to Procter & Gamble to Starbucks. If they all had to slash their inventories and cut back operations, we would see massive job cuts spreading throughout an already suffering economy.

"Jeff," I remember saying, "we have got to put out this fire."

Tuesday, September 16, 2008

Monday, September 15, had been grim. But on Tuesday, all hell broke loose.

Normally I left home by 5:45 a.m., went to my gym, and ran hard on the treadmill. Then I'd do some core exercises until 7:45 a.m. Fifteen minutes later I was in the office. (Those 90-second showers of my childhood sure helped me keep to this pace.)

That morning, sensing trouble, I skipped my workout, as I would for weeks, and went straight to the Markets Room, on the second floor of the Treasury Building, to get a quick fix from Matt Rutherford. What I learned was disturbing. Though the LIBOR-OIS spread had eased, financial institutions including Washington Mutual, Wachovia, and Morgan Stanley were under severe pressure. (The CDS of the venerable investment bank would soar from 497 basis points Monday to 728 basis points—a higher level than Lehman Brothers had traded at before its failure.)

I soon heard from Dan Jester and Jeremiah Norton, who were helping Tim out with AIG. I needed them in Washington, but Dan, in particular, had won Tim's confidence, and I had reluctantly agreed to let him stay at Tim's request. They gave me a discouraging update. The rating agencies had slashed the insurer's credit rating on Monday, forcing it to post additional collateral on its huge derivatives book. To my utter amazement and disgust, AIG's liquidity needs had mushroomed. On Sunday, the company was looking for $50 billion; now it would need an $85 billion loan commitment by the end of the day. A private-sector solution appeared very unlikely.

AIG's incompetence was stunning, but I didn't have time to be angry. I immediately called President Bush to tell him that the Fed might have to rescue AIG and would need his support. He told me to do what was necessary.

Tim Geithner called to tell me that he had talked with Ben Bernanke, who was amenable to asking the Fed board to make a bridge loan if the executive branch and I stood behind him. He said he thought $85 billion would be enough but stressed that we had to move quickly: the company needed $4 billion by the close of business Wednesday. Even this breathtaking assessment would prove optimistic. By late morning, we had learned AIG needed cash to avoid bankruptcy by day's end—the total would eventually reach $14 billion.

Tim, Ben, and I reviewed our options with great care in an hour-long conference call at 8:00 a.m. that included Fed vice chairman Don Kohn and governors Kevin Warsh and Elizabeth Duke. Whatever else happened, we could not let AIG go down.

Unlike with Lehman, the Fed felt it could make a loan to help AIG because we were dealing with a liquidity, not a capital, problem. The Fed believed that it could secure a loan with AIG's insurance subsidiaries, which could be sold off to repay any borrowing, and not run the risk of losing money. These subsidiaries were also more stable because of the strength of their businesses and their stand-alone credit ratings, which were separate from the AIG holding company's ratings and troubles. By contrast, prior to Lehman's failure, its customers had already begun to flee, causing the Fed to face the prospect of having to lend into a run. Moreover, the toxic quality of Lehman's assets would have guaranteed the Fed a loss, meaning the central bank could not legally make a loan.

We set a plan of action: Tim would figure out the details of the bridge loan, while I worked on finding a new CEO for the company. We had less than a day to do it—AIG's balances were draining by the second.

I asked Ken Wilson to drop everything and help. Within three hours he had pinpointed Ed Liddy, the retired CEO of Allstate and one of the savviest financial executives in the world. He reached Liddy in Chicago, then ran upstairs to my office to tell me to call him. I offered Ed the position of AIG chief on the spot. The job would be a thankless one, but I could think of no one else who had the ability and the grit to take it on.

On Tuesday morning, the consequences of Lehman's failure were becoming more and more apparent. I received an astounding call from Goldman CEO Lloyd Blankfein. He informed me that Lehman's U.K. bankruptcy administrator, Pricewaterhouse-Coopers, had frozen the firm's assets in the U.K., seizing its trading collateral and third-party collateral. This was a completely unexpected—and potentially devastating—jolt. In the U.S., customer accounts were strictly segregated, and were protected in a bankruptcy proceeding. But in the U.K., the bankruptcy administrator had lumped all the accounts together and frozen them, refusing to transfer collateral back to Lehman's creditors. This was particularly damaging to the London-based hedge funds that relied on Lehman as their prime broker, or principal source of financing.

Just about all the hedge funds in London and New York, whether or not they had any relationship with the bankrupt securities firm, became unnerved and leaped to a frightening conclusion: they should avoid doing business with any firm that could end up like Lehman. This was bad news for Morgan Stanley and Goldman, the leading prime brokers. Trading frequently and maintaining big balances, hedge funds were among their best, most profitable customers. Lloyd was afraid that if something wasn't done, Morgan Stanley would fail, as clients began to run and hedge funds pulled their prime brokerage accounts. And even though Goldman had plenty of liquidity and cash, it could be next.

"Hank, it is worse than any of us imagined," Lloyd said. If hedge funds couldn't count on the safety of their broker-dealer accounts, he went on, "no one will want to do business with us."

Hedge funds were just the tip of the iceberg. Liquidity was rapidly evaporating all over. When investors—pension funds, mutual funds, insurance companies, even central banks—couldn't withdraw their assets from Lehman accounts, it meant that in the interlinking daisy chain of the markets, they would be less able to meet the demands of their own counterparties. Suddenly everyone felt at risk and increasingly wary of dealing with any counterparty, no matter how sterling its reputation or how long a relationship one firm had had with another. The vast and crucial Treasury repurchase market, under duress since August 2007, began to shut down.

This was awful news. When institutional investors, for example, purchased securities like corporate bonds, they frequently hedged their positions by selling Treasuries. But if they did not have the Treasuries in their inventory, they used the repo market to borrow them from other investors.

With Lehman's failure, major institutional investors ceased lending securities for fear that their counterparties would fail and not return the securities as promised. Among the key investors now balking were reserve managers at some of the world's central banks, which had been earning extra income by lending part of their vast holdings of Treasuries overnight. Some small central banks had started pulling out of the repo market the week before as rumors had circulated about the imminent failure of Lehman;

by Monday, their bigger counterparts in Asia and Europe were doing the same.

In a classic "flight to quality," everyone wanted to get hold of Treasuries, the safest security in the world. In Tuesday's midday auction we received over $100 billion in orders for $31 billion in four-week bills. The rate on the bills was an astoundingly low 0.10 percent—a drop of 1.15 percentage points from the previous week. The consequences of this flight were enormous to global credit markets.

The sudden shortage of Treasury securities resulted in an unprecedented level of "fails to deliver," that is, investors who were unable to deliver securities they had previously borrowed. On September 12, the Friday before Lehman went down, these fails stood at $20 billion; one week later they would soar to $285 billion. By September 24 they would reach $1.7 trillion, before peaking at $2.3 trillion in early October—an extraordinary amount, never experienced before, and multiple times higher than any prior episode in history.

Major investors who desperately wanted Treasuries for safety or to hedge purchases of other securities could not purchase them because no investors were willing to lend securities from their portfolios. Major broker-dealers stopped selling Treasuries for fear that they would not be able to deliver the Treasury securities they sold. And without being able to hedge their positions with Treasuries, investors were reluctant to make any further purchases in other credit markets. The credit markets essentially were grinding to a halt.

Over the next couple of hours that morning, I must have made or taken a score of phone calls from senators and congressmen. These were short and to the point: we were doing our best to hold the system together; the bankruptcy of Lehman was regrettable, but there had been no buyer; AIG was a problem, and we were working hard on a solution.

Its impending failure was sending shock waves around the world. Peer Steinbrück, the German finance minister, called to say that it was unthinkable AIG could go down. Christine Lagarde, the French finance minister, echoed his view: everyone was exposed to AIG, and its failure would be catastrophic. "I assume you are going to do the right thing," she said to me. I told her what I had told Steinbrück—"I can't make any commitments"—but I assured her we were doing everything we could.

As I dealt with the phone calls, I learned that McCain had gone on NBC's *Today* show earlier and declared, "We cannot have the taxpayers bail out AIG or anybody else." I didn't want American taxpayers stuck with a bailout, either, but Ben, Tim, and I could see no other alternative, and I didn't want McCain—or Obama—to use populist language that would inflame the situation. So I called McCain to encourage him to be more careful in his choice of words.

"You should know that if this company were to go down, it would hurt many, many Americans," I explained. In addition to providing all kinds of insurance to millions of U.S. citizens, AIG was deeply involved in their retirements, selling annuities and guaranteeing the retirement income of millions of teachers and health-care workers. I asked him to refer to our actions as rescues or interventions, not bailouts. The next day McCain would temper his criticism, using some of my language, only to be criticized for flip-flopping.

By noon, European stocks had tumbled, the U.S. markets were starting to dip, and the news was about to get worse. Lehman's failure and AIG's escalating difficulties had begun to roil money market funds. Typically, these funds invested in government or quasi-government securities, but to produce higher yields for investors they had also become big buyers of commercial paper. All morning we heard reports that nervous investors were pulling their money out and accelerating the stampede into the Treasury market. The Reserve Primary Fund, the nation's first money market fund, had been particularly hard-hit because of substantial holdings of now-worthless Lehman paper.

Many Americans had grown accustomed to thinking that money market funds were as safe as their bank accounts. Money funds lacked deposit insurance but investors believed that they would always be able to withdraw their money on demand and get 100 percent of their principal back. The funds would maintain a net asset value (NAV) of at least 1.00, or $1 a share. No fund had dipped below that level—or, in industry parlance, "broken the buck"—since the bond market rout of 1994. Funds that broke the buck were as good as dead: investors would all withdraw their money.

In retrospect, I see that the industry's setup was too good to be true. The idea that you could earn more than what the federal government paid for overnight liquidity and still have overnight liquidity made absolutely no sense. It had worked for so long only because people didn't ask for their money. But when Lehman failed, people started to ask.

Around 1:00 p.m., Bill Osborn, the chairman of Northern Trust and a good friend from Chicago, called with a firsthand report. "I hate to bother you, Hank," he said. "But there is no liquidity in the markets. The commercial paper market is frozen."

Bill proceeded to tell me about problems he was having with his money market funds. Because the market for commercial paper had seized up, the funds were under real pressure from withdrawals, and he was looking for ways to avoid breaking the buck. He was working on a way the parent company could support the funds financially without taking the obligation on its balance sheet.

But this solution required accounting relief. He'd already called the SEC but wanted to let me know of the looming problem.

I told Bill that I was focused on AIG, but that the Fed was working on a number of liquidity programs to get people to start buying paper again.

"They can't come soon enough," he said. "I've never seen anything like this."

Nor had I. Begun as an alternative to banks for U.S. consumers, money funds had more than 30 million retail customers. In recent years, the business had become increasingly corporate—and global. Companies used the funds for their cash management needs, and money poured in from overseas investors—Singaporeans, British, and Chinese—eager to get a little more yield than on straight Treasuries.

This kind of money was "hot," likely to flee at the first sign of trouble, and I feared the start of a run on the $3.5 trillion industry, which provided so much critical short-term funding to U.S. companies. I immediately thought of my meeting with Jeff Immelt the day before, and his trouble selling commercial paper. I called Chris Cox, who told me that he was aware of the accounting issue; his accounting policy people were already working on it, but there was no obvious solution.

Tim, Ben, and I spoke throughout the day so Tim could keep us updated on the size of the AIG problem. We had a President's Working Group meeting set for 3:30 p.m. When I arrived at the Roosevelt Room, the president, the vice president, and my fellow members of the PWG, with the exception of Tim, were all there. I outlined AIG's dire situation, detailing the incompetence of its management and the need to prevent its collapse, given its worldwide financial products and the number of money market and pension funds that held its commercial paper.

"How did we get to this point?" the president asked in frustration.

He wanted to understand how we couldn't let a financial institution fail without inflicting widespread damage on the economy.

I explained that AIG differed from Lehman, because Lehman had issues with both capital and liquidity, whereas AIG just had a liquidity problem. The investment bank had been loaded with toxic assets worth far less than the value at which they were carried, creating a capital hole. Nervous counterparties had fled, draining liquidity.

In AIG's case the problem wasn't capital—at least we didn't think so at the time. The insurer held many toxic mortgages, but its most pressing problem was a derivatives portfolio that included a large amount of credit default swaps on residential mortgage CDOs. The decline in housing values, and now the cuts in AIG's ratings, required it to post more collateral. Suddenly, AIG owed money seemingly everywhere, and it was scrambling to come up with $85 billion on short notice.

"If we don't shore up AIG," I said, "we will likely lose several more financial institutions. Morgan Stanley, for one."

I noted that an AIG collapse would be much more devastating than the Lehman failure because of its size and the damage it would do to millions of individuals whose retirement accounts it insured. I added that I was worried about the flight I saw from money market funds and commercial paper. Chris Cox let us all know the Reserve Primary Fund had just broken the buck.

The president found it hard to believe that an insurance company could be so systemically important. I tried to explain that AIG was an unregulated holding company comprising many highly regulated insurance entities. Ben chimed in with a pointed description: "It's like a hedge fund sitting on top of an insurance company."

Ben said that under the Fed's plan, the government would lend AIG $85 billion, charging the company LIBOR plus 850 basis points, or about 11.5 percent at that time. The government would end up with 79.9 percent ownership, substantially diluting the existing equity, and would gradually liquidate the company to pay off the Fed's loan.

"Someday you guys are going to have to tell me how we ended up with a system like this and what we need to do to fix it," the president said, noting that we would have to put together a more consistent and comprehensive approach to the crisis.

I couldn't have agreed more. Sunday night, with Lehman about to file for bankruptcy, I had warned the president that we might have to ask Congress for broader powers to stabilize the financial system as a whole. Now, while still in firefighting mode as we dealt with the five-alarm emergency of AIG, I didn't raise the issue of going to Congress again. But I knew that when the time came, President Bush would support me.

The president was admirably stalwart. Even though the predominant mood at the time, both generally and on the Hill, was against bailouts, President Bush didn't care. His goal was to leave the country in as strong a financial position as possible for his successor. Skeptics may doubt me, but this is the truth: In any accurate recounting of the financial crisis, you won't find the president playing politics with these decisions—not one instance. He was genuinely trying to do his best for the country as he backed our AIG rescue plan.

"If we suffer political damage, so be it," he said.

Afterward I got confirmation of what Chris had said about the Reserve Fund. While we were with the president, the Reserve had announced that it would halt payment of redemptions for one week on its Primary Fund, a $63 billion money market fund that was caught with $785 million in Lehman short-term debt when the investment bank entered bankruptcy. On Monday, investors had flooded the company with requests for redemptions; by midafternoon Tuesday, $40 billion had been pulled. The fund had officially broken the buck, the first to do so since 1994, when the Denver-based U.S. Government Money Market Fund, which had invested heavily in adjustable-rate derivatives, fell to 96 cents.

The sense of panic was becoming more widespread. Dave McCormick and Ken Wilson came in to tell me that they had heard from their Wall Street sources that a number of Chinese banks were withdrawing large sums from the money market funds. They had also heard that the Chinese were pulling back on secured overnight lending and shortening the maturity of their holdings of Fannie and Freddie paper—all signs of their battening the hatches. I asked Dave to track down the Chinese rumors and report back to me as soon as possible.

While we were in the PWG meeting, Morgan Stanley released its third-quarter earnings, rushing them out a day early. Its reported $1.43 billion in profits were down 7.6 percent from a year earlier but better than expected. Not that it helped much: after briefly rallying, Morgan Stanley's shares fell 10.8 percent on the day, to $28.70, while its CDS rates ended at 728 basis points, after spiking to 880 basis points at one point. Goldman Sachs had released its earnings that morning: at $845 million, its net income was down 70.4 percent from the previous year.

Later I got an earful from John Mack, who said Morgan Stanley was in jeopardy. John was a strong leader, at once personable and tough. He was no whiner, but I could tell he was scared. What he had predicted Sunday night had come to pass: investors were losing confidence, and the short sellers were after his bank. His cash reserves were evaporating, and he was doing everything he could to hold things together.

"Hank," John said, "the SEC needs to act before the short sellers destroy Morgan Stanley."

Since Monday he had been calling senators, congressmen, the White House, and me, trying to persuade everyone to push the SEC to do something about abusive short selling. He wasn't alone. John Thain also called that afternoon to press about short selling. Shareholders had not yet approved Merrill's deal with Bank of America, and he was taking nothing for granted. But his immediate concern was Morgan Stanley. The failure of another major institution, he knew, would be devastating.

Ben and I had arranged to meet with congressional leaders that evening, but first Tim and I had to call AIG chief Bob Willumstad to confirm that the Fed was on track to make the loan—and to tell him that he was being replaced. He had been CEO for just three months; before that he had served as AIG chairman after a long financial services career that included retail banking at Citigroup. He was highly regarded for his acumen and integrity, but with AIG he had encountered more than he could handle—perhaps more than anyone could have handled. Through it all, Willumstad was an incredible gentleman, even calling Ken Wilson and voluntarily forfeiting the severance payments that were written into his management contract.

I next had to make arrangements to go to the Hill. In the afternoon, I'd run into resistance trying to get something scheduled. Before the PWG meeting I had spoken with Nancy Pelosi more than once, telling her that although the Fed hadn't made a final decision yet on the AIG loan, we probably would need to meet with congressional leaders to discuss it. I told her it was an emergency, but she'd replied: "This is difficult to schedule on short notice. Do we need to do it tonight?"

When I got back to my office from the White House, I tried Harry Reid. I'd always found the Senate majority leader to be a sincere, trustworthy, hardworking partner. The son of a Nevada miner, he had come up the hard way, and his modesty and earnestness appealed to me.

"We have a real problem with AIG," I told him. "The Fed is going to have to step in. I need you to get the leadership together." He agreed, and we scheduled a meeting for 6:30 p.m.

Before going to the Hill, I briefed Obama and McCain on AIG. In fact, I spoke to Obama twice before I went to the Capitol. If anything, I overcommunicated with both candidates because I understood that if either of them made AIG or any other part of the crisis into a campaign issue to win political popularity, we were dead. I told them the Fed had to take action and made the point that we were protecting taxpayers—not bailing out shareholders. Again I asked both of them not to characterize this as a bailout.

Ben and I rode to the Capitol separately for the meeting, which Harry Reid had convened in the Senate Rules Committee's conference room, a modest-size space devoid of tables or chairs, which left all of us standing. The Senate majority leader had gathered an important group to hear us out, including Chris Dodd; Judd Gregg, the ranking Republican on the Senate Budget Committee; and Barney Frank, who arrived late.

I led off by saying the government had decided to act to save the giant insurer, and that Treasury and the Fed were cooperating. Outwardly I was calm, but I could feel the effects of sheer physical exhaustion and the accumulated pressure of the last few days. Ben followed, speaking clearly and precisely. He laid out the terms of the two-year, $85 billion bridge loan we would be making.

There was an almost surreal quality to the meeting. The stunned lawmakers looked at us as if not quite believing what they were hearing. They had their share of questions but were broadly supportive.

John Boehner said we'd be crazy to let AIG fail. Reid put his head in his hands at the size of the loan, while Barney Frank asked, "Where did you find $85 billion?"

"We have $800 billion," Ben replied, referring to the balance sheet of the Federal Reserve.

Chris Dodd asked twice how the Fed had the authority to lend to an insurance company and seize control of it. Ben explained how Section 13(3) of the Federal Reserve Act allowed the central bank to take such actions under "unusual and exigent circumstances." It was the same provision the Fed had used to rescue Bear Stearns.

In the end, Reid said: "You've heard what people have had to say. But I want to be absolutely clear that Congress has not given you formal approval to take action. This is your responsibility and your decision."

As I left the meeting, accompanied by my Secret Service detail, I suddenly had to step away quickly from the group, out of sight. All my life, dating back to high school, I've occasionally had bouts of dry heaves when I am exhausted or sleep deprived. During the credit crisis, it must have happened six or eight times. That night, as I felt the nausea coming on, I ducked behind a pillar for a few seconds, in front of an American flag hanging from the ceiling. I was concerned that someone from the press might see me, but thankfully no one did.

At 9:00 p.m., the Fed announced that it would step in to save AIG. The company's board had approved a deal for a two-year, $85 billion loan that would be collateralized by AIG's assets, including the stock of its regulated subsidiaries, and would be repaid with the proceeds from the sale of the assets. Holding a 79.9 percent equity interest in AIG, the government retained the right to veto dividend payments to shareholders.

Wednesday, September 17, 2008

Tuesday was bad, but Wednesday was worse. Our intervention with AIG didn't calm the markets—if anything, it aggravated the situation.

I arrived at Treasury at 6:30 a.m. and went straight to the Markets Room. I saw that Morgan Stanley's situation had deteriorated even further. Its shares were plunging in premarket trading, while its CDS continued to climb. Shortly after 7:00 a.m. the president called. I told him the markets were being driven by fear and that the short sellers were now going after Morgan Stanley as if it were Lehman Brothers. I was very focused on the commercial paper market, where funding was drying up. We were being assailed on all sides.

"We've got a real problem," I said to the president. "It may be the time's come for us to go to Congress and get additional authorities."

"Don't you have enough with the Fed? You just bailed out AIG," he pointed out.

"No, sir, we may not."

After promising President Bush I'd stay in touch, I spoke with Dave McCormick, who confirmed the reports that the Chinese had been pulling back. He said he'd spoken with central bank governor Zhou Xiaochuan, who had emphasized that the moves had not been orchestrated by the government but had been made by midlevel bureaucrats and various financial institutions doing what they thought was the smart thing. The Chinese leadership, McCormick said, would be giving some guidance to these professionals not to pull back from the money markets or from secured lending. I told Dave to stay in constant touch with the Chinese officials and keep me posted.

Between 7:00 a.m. and 7:40 a.m., Ken Wilson called me three

times to brief me on the alarming calls he was getting: Bank of New York Mellon CEO Bob Kelly, BlackRock chief Larry Fink, and Northern Trust CEO Rick Waddell had all reported requests for billions in redemptions from their money market funds. The Reserve Primary Fund was bad enough, but if these institutions' funds broke the buck, we would have a full-scale panic as corporations, insurance companies, pension funds, and mom-and-pop customers all tried to withdraw their money at the same time.

Then Ken called me again: his computer screen showed that the demand for Treasuries had become so great the yield on three-month bills had entered negative territory. Investors were now paying for the safety of U.S. government securities. He said it was clear to him the wheels were coming off the financial system.

In the midst of the morning's gathering chaos, I spoke with Dick Fuld. He had been calling the office, and I felt I ought to talk to him. We hadn't spoken since the weekend. It was a very sad call.

"I see you bailed out AIG," I remember him saying. "Hank, what you need to do now is let the Fed come into Lehman Brothers. Have the government come in and guarantee it. Give me my company back. I can get all the people back. We will have Lehman Brothers again."

I remember talking with Tim Geithner a little later. I said, "I had a sad call from Dick Fuld." He replied, "He asked you to undo the bankruptcy, right?" I said, "Right." And he said, "Yes, very sad." He'd gotten a similar call from Dick. What made Dick's call and request even more poignant was the fact that it was known by then that Barclays was going to acquire the North American investment banking and capital markets businesses of Lehman out of bankruptcy.

I called Jamie Dimon to get his assessment of the market. I knew I could depend on JPMorgan's CEO to be cool, clinical, and right on the money. He wasn't reassuring. "The markets are frozen," he said.

I'd foreseen the previous Sunday that we would have to go to Congress for emergency powers and fiscal authorities to deal with the crisis. Kevin Fromer and I had discussed this on Monday and Tuesday, but I was leery about going to the Hill unless we could be sure of support there. Getting turned down by Congress on an urgent request of such magnitude could be calamitous. But the AIG rescue had failed to calm the markets, the panic was growing, and lawmakers were getting angry.

Early Wednesday morning, Kevin and I agreed that the problem was so big that Congress had to be part of the solution. I wasn't going to look for a statutory loophole that would let us commit massive amounts of public money; Congress would have to explicitly endorse our actions. And for the first time I believed Congress would likely give us what we needed. The extreme severity of the market conditions made it clear that no good alternative existed. And lawmakers were scheduled to leave town in nine days to campaign back home, so they had an incentive to act quickly. I relayed my thinking to Jim Wilkinson and Ken Wilson.

Around 8:30 a.m. I gathered my team in the large conference room. I told them we needed to figure out a way to get ahead of the markets and stabilize the system before other institutions went down. I told them Ben had made it clear that we couldn't rely on the Fed alone to solve the problem for us.

"This is our moment of truth," I said. "We've been dealing with one-off firefights, and we need to break the back of this crisis now."

I laid down two principles for my team to follow as we worked on solutions. First, any policies would have to be simple and easily understood by the markets. Second, our actions had to be decisive and overwhelming—I learned this lesson back in July during the Fannie and Freddie crisis.

With an eye toward managing the workload and spurring creativity, my team had already divided into groups to handle different aspects of the crisis. One team of Treasury staff, led by Steve Shafran, had begun working the previous evening with Fed staff in Washington and New York to develop solutions for the credit markets. A second group, headed by Neel Kashkari, would focus on ways to purchase the toxic assets clogging bank balance sheets. Dave McCormick and Ken Wilson would head a third team, working with the SEC on policy issues such as short selling.

I'd long since learned that you couldn't get anything done in Washington without a crisis. Well, this was an ongoing series of crises coming at us from all directions, all at once. At Goldman Sachs I had prided myself on my ability to handle many different issues simultaneously, but at Treasury I faced a different challenge. Each of the issues confronting me was enormously important—a wrong decision would hurt not just one client or one firm but the entire financial system and many millions of people in the U.S. and around the world.

Just after 1:00 p.m., John Mack called me in alarm. Morgan Stanley was under siege. Its shares had fallen below $20, and its CDS rates were way up—they were trading at around 800 basis points. To put that in perspective, Lehman had topped off at 707 basis points the Friday before—and it had gone belly-up. Short sellers were laying Mack's bank low. "We need some action," he said.

But John and his team weren't about to go down without a fight. He said Morgan Stanley was looking to raise capital from strategic investors, and that the Chinese were a strong possibility. China Investment Corporation, the country's sovereign wealth fund, already owned 9.9 percent of his firm.

"All the signals we get are that they'd like some reassurance and encouragement from you," Mack said.

He asked if I'd be willing to talk to my old friend Wang Qishan, China's vice premier in charge of economic and financial matters. I told John he could count on our support, and that Dave McCormick would follow up with him.

Shortly after that, Hillary Clinton called me on behalf of Mickey Kantor, who had served as Commerce secretary in the Clinton administration and now represented a group of Middle Eastern investors. These investors, Hillary said, wanted to buy AIG. "Maybe the government doesn't have to do anything," she said.

I explained to her that this was impossible unless the investors had a big balance sheet and the wherewithal to guarantee all of AIG's liabilities.

Her call stands out in my mind because it reflected the general sentiment about AIG—that it was a good company with many interested buyers. The market believed that its problem was liquidity, not capital.

When I finally had a few minutes to deal with the Morgan Stanley situation, I called Chris Cox to discuss market manipulation. The investment bank's falling stock price and widening CDS appeared to be driven by hedge funds and speculators. I wanted the SEC to investigate what looked to me to be predatory, collusive behavior as our banks were being attacked one by one.

Chris was considering various steps the SEC could take, including a temporary ban on short selling, but his board was divided. He wanted Tim, Ben, and me to support him on the need for a ban.

The short-selling debate was another of those issues where I found myself forced to do the opposite of what I had believed for my entire career. Short selling is a crucial element in price discovery and transparency—after all, David Einhorn, the hedge fund manager who shorted Lehman, had ultimately been proved right. I had long compared banning short selling to burning books, but now I recognized short selling as a big problem. I concluded that even though an outright ban would lead to all sorts of unintended consequences, it couldn't be worse than what we were experiencing just then. We needed to do something.

Wednesday afternoon I was cleared to fight all the fires we faced. I had sold my shares in Goldman Sachs and severed ties with the firm when I became Treasury secretary. I had also signed an ethics agreement that precluded me from being involved in any government transaction "particular to Goldman Sachs." With the two remaining investment banks on the edge, Tim Geithner argued that my role as Treasury secretary demanded that I get involved. We were in a national emergency, and I knew he was right. I obtained clearance from the White House counsel's office and the career designated agency ethics officer at Treasury.

We had set up a 3:00 p.m. call to review the progress of our three workstreams and to prepare for another long night of work. My office filled with people as we reviewed the state of play. The markets were in near chaos. Stocks were plunging—the Dow was on its way to a drop of 449 points, or 4.1 percent. The credit markets were locked up.

The turmoil was going global. Russia had suspended trading for an hour on Tuesday, and its stock market shut down again on Wednesday. Karthik Ramanathan was fielding panicky calls from central bank reserve managers begging us to improve liquidity in the Treasury market. Some even wanted Treasury to pay for securities that the banks' counterparties could not return.

At one point, Ben brought up the need to go to Congress. I couldn't have agreed more, but I was so preoccupied with the steps involved in getting emergency powers that I didn't respond. I was caught up in thinking of all that would have to be done, not least getting the White House on board. The president, I was sure, would support us, but we would need to get his press office, policy people, and legislative affairs staff involved in a course of action that we all knew was going to be very difficult and that some doubted could be successful. We needed to craft a winning strategy for the Hill and find a way to hold the financial system together while waiting for Congress to act.

We started to map out a comprehensive plan to deal with all the elements of the crisis that kept popping up. We had to tackle each problem as it arose and simultaneously devise a more far-reaching solution that we could present to the House and Senate.

The members of the three teams we'd set up earlier cranked away on their assignments: credit markets, asset purchases, policy. Periodically they would gather in my office to touch base and get direction, then they would go back to work for a few more hours. The credit markets team had been tasked with our most pressing issue: finding ways to add liquidity to the money markets and help the asset-backed commercial paper market before it pulled down companies like GE. Working with the SEC, the policy team investigated a wide range of issues: among them, whether regulators should reinstate the rule allowing short selling only on a stock's uptick and whether fair-value accounting rules should be adjusted regarding bank mergers. The team working on illiquid asset purchases hashed out three questions: what assets to buy, whom to buy them from, and how to buy them. As a starting point, we turned to Neel Kashkari and Phill Swagel's "Break the Glass" plan from the previous spring, which had outlined possibilities for recapitalizing the banks.

In our previous efforts with Congress—the 2008 stimulus bill and GSE reform—we'd had weeks to come up with plans and prep lawmakers. Now, facing a much more severe situation, we no longer had that luxury. Treasury staff worked straight through the night to Thursday morning. Most people broke for an hour around 5:00 a.m. or 6:00 a.m. to go home, shower, and change their clothes, then came straight back to the office. Others, like Neel Kashkari, showered in the gym at Treasury and slept in their offices. All learned to get by on little sleep and bad food.

Looking at my team's tired faces, I remembered the lectures I used to give at Goldman on the need to balance one's work and life. But back then I never foresaw a situation like this, with multiple crises demanding solutions, and the entire economy on the brink.

CHAPTER 11

Thursday, September 18, 2008

Early Thursday morning, members of my staff began to stream in and out of my office, briefing me, listening in on my phone calls. Weary but alert, most had worked through the night on one of the three crisis teams we had set up to look into policy issues, asset purchases, and credit markets. Another grinding day stretched out before us. The U.K. and Ireland were readying restrictions on short selling. Russia had suspended stock trading for a third straight day.

Just before 9:00 a.m. I took an unexpected call from Bob Scully, the Morgan Stanley vice chairman, who had played such a critical role in August in helping Treasury prepare to place Fannie Mae and Freddie Mac into conservatorship. A consummate banker, he had never spoken about his own firm during that period. But now he was calling to tell me that speculators and short sellers were not only driving Morgan Stanley's shares down but also undermining confidence in the investment bank. As nervous counterparties shied from the firm, its liquidity was declining rapidly. He didn't know what I could do, but he said he felt obliged to tell me, point-blank, that he was not sure Morgan Stanley was going to make it.

Coming from Bob, always calm and levelheaded, this was an alarming message. I alerted Tim Geithner and then called Chris Cox to urge him again to do something to end abusive short selling. I had been pressing Chris with increasing intensity since Monday. We'd spoken seven times Wednesday and would speak just as frequently Thursday on the subject. I implored him not to sit idly by while our financial system was destroyed by speculators. Any other time, I would have argued strongly against a ban, but my reasoning now was pragmatic: our short-selling rules hadn't been written for these conditions, and whatever we chose to do couldn't be worse than the panic we were now seeing. Chris worried about unintended consequences to the market.

"If you wait any longer," I said, "there won't be a market left to regulate."

Chris also faced opposition from within his own agency and from his fellow commissioners. He reiterated that he needed the clear public backing of Ben Bernanke, Tim, and me. Tim had concerns that a ban might inhibit risk taking and be destabilizing—the trading strategies of many highly leveraged hedge funds depended on shorting.

Not long after that, I spoke to the president, who had canceled a fund-raising trip to Alabama and Florida to focus on the financial emergency. He was joined by Deputy Chief of Staff Joel Kaplan. I told them that the crisis had reached the point where we were going to have to take dramatic actions, including going to Congress for sweeping fiscal authorities. The president seemed supportive but asked that I make sure to fully brief his whole team. It was essential that everyone in the executive branch work together, because we all knew it would be difficult to get Congress to act.

At 9:30 a.m. my staff and I got on a conference call with Tim, Ben, Chris, and their people. The Fed was working hard to ease liquidity pressures in global markets. At 3:00 a.m. New York time—8:00 a.m. in London—it had announced a dramatic $180 billion expansion of its swap lines, which made dollars available to other central banks for the needs of their commercial banks.

I was particularly worried about the money market funds. Treasury's Steve Shafran and his group, who had been working with the Fed people all night, had put together a list of ideas to improve liquidity. One idea would have had the Fed provide long-term financing to the investment banks in addition to the short-term money they already had access to. Another would have let the money funds borrow directly from the Fed.

"That won't stop a run," I said. If anything, a money fund borrowing from the Fed would be stigmatized and suffer even more withdrawals. "What would you do if you wanted to be more decisive than that?"

Steve threw out another suggestion: "Well, we could use the Exchange Stabilization Fund to guarantee the money market funds."

I slapped my desk. It was exactly what I was looking for—the strong step the situation required: something dramatic that would prevent an impending implosion of $3.5 trillion in money market funds.

"That's what I want to do," I told him. "Go make that happen."

Guaranteeing the money markets was an inspired idea; the problem was how to do it. Shafran's insight was crucial. Treasury had next to no funding power—with one exception. The Gold Reserve Act of 1934 had created the Exchange Stabilization Fund (ESF) to allow Treasury to intervene in the foreign exchange market to stabilize the dollar. The ESF had been used very selectively over the years, most controversially when President Bill Clinton tapped it in 1995 to extend up to $20 billion in loans to Mexico. Now money market funds were being hit by massive redemptions, some of them from skittish overseas investors. A collapse of the money fund industry could easily lead to a run on the dollar. If the president approved, we could use the ESF, which totaled about $50 billion, to fund the money market guarantee initially.

David Nason had put off his decision to leave Treasury to help us at this critical time, and I asked him to work with Steve. David had been at the SEC, and I knew that he had a long list of contacts in the money market industry as well as the technical expertise to design a temporary guarantee program. Even as they faced a rash of redemptions, money funds were choking on asset-backed commercial paper that they couldn't sell. Fed staffers were working on ways to purchase this paper from the money funds.

"Hank, are you willing to go to the Hill and get fiscal authority?" Bernanke asked.

"Ben, Ben, Ben," I interrupted, realizing I hadn't had time to update him on my just-concluded call with the president. "You and I will be going to the White House."

After the call, I asked my team to prepare a short presentation for the president. Joel Kaplan had wisely suggested that the most efficient way to brief the key White House staff was for them to sit in on our meetings at Treasury. By 1:30 p.m., Joel, Ed Lazear, Keith Hennessey, and Dan Meyer had come over to Treasury. They would spend many hours over the next few weeks with us, and I could tell they were taken aback by the atmosphere. There were probably 15 people in my office at all times, huddled in clusters and holding separate meetings, talking at a hundred miles an hour, as I sat at my desk in the center of the whirlwind. There was virtually a running conference call with Tim and Ben, with people getting off the line and getting back on. I'd be talking to someone else on my phone, always trying to speed things along.

Now the White House crew crowded into my office with Treasury staff for a scheduled call with Ben, Tim, and Chris. I did much of the talking.

"This is the economic equivalent of war," I said. "The market is ready to collapse."

We couldn't keep using duct tape and baling wire to try to hold the system together. This was a national crisis and both the executive and the legislative branches of government needed to be involved. Although I was determined to get new powers, I knew how hard it would be to win them and how difficult it would be to hold the system together while we were trying. We would have to choose carefully the authorities we requested, while honing our approach to Congress. It was Treasury's most crucial legislative undertaking since the Great Depression. The stakes were incalculably high: the cost of asking for powers and failing to get them might be bigger than not asking at all.

Chris raised the issue of a short-selling ban. Tim and Ben joined me in expressing support for a ban, which gave Chris the backing he needed to go to the rest of the commissioners for approval. We went through the need to guarantee the money market funds. I admitted that we still didn't know exactly how the program would work. The complexities were enough to make your head spin, but I was firm: "We've got to go with this."

Almost everyone liked the idea, but some were concerned that we were moving too fast. But frankly we had no choice but to fly by the seat of our pants, making it up as we went along. The alternative, waiting till we had figured out every angle, was untenable.

Before going to the White House, I called Ben and told him that the president was going to want to press him on the extent of his authorities, because the thought of being totally dependent on Congress was anathema to the administration. The president would want to know what the Fed could do if Congress didn't grant us the powers we needed. I encouraged Ben to think expansively. "If the market thinks Congress is our last line of defense, and they turn us down, it will be fatal," I said.

On my way to the White House, Nancy Pelosi called to ask about the market. She had wanted me to come up the following morning with Ben to brief the Democratic leadership. I related just how bad things were and told her we would have to go to the Hill that night to ask for emergency powers. She asked why it couldn't wait until the morning, and I replied it might be too late by then.

"We need legislation passed quickly," I said. "We need to send a strong signal to the market now."

The Speaker immediately pushed to put stimulus spending into any bill. "Nancy, we're racing to prevent a collapse of the financial markets," I told her. "This isn't the time for stimulus."

A large group gathered in the Roosevelt Room at 3:30 p.m. to meet with the president. Ben, Chris, and Fed governor Kevin Warsh were there, along with a hefty contingent of White House and Treasury staff. Joel Kaplan had warned the president ahead of time that Ben and I were on edge.

I began by telling the president that the Fed and Treasury were preparing to take some extraordinary steps and that we were going to need to get special powers from Congress.

"Mr. President, we are witnessing a financial panic," Ben put in. He vividly described what we were seeing in the markets, from the travails of commercial paper issuers to the difficulties in secured lending, and where this all might lead if we didn't find a way to stop its spread now.

"Is this the worst crisis since the Great Depression?" the president asked.

"Yes," Ben replied. "In terms of the financial system, we've not seen anything like this since the 1930s, and it could get worse."

Individuals and companies were in imminent danger, I told the president: "Money market funds are on the verge of breaking. Companies are taking drastic measures to preserve their finances— not just the big banks, but also companies like General Electric and Ford."

We had been dealing with these crises one at a time, on an ad hoc basis. But now we needed to take a more systematic approach before we bled to death. We all knew that the root cause lay in the housing market collapse that had clogged bank balance sheets with toxic mortgage assets that made them unwilling to lend. We were going to need to buy those bad assets where necessary, actions that required new powers from Congress and a massive appropriation of funds. In asking for this, we would be bailing out Wall Street. And that would look just plain bad to everyone from free-market devotees to populist demagogues. But not doing this would be disastrous for Main Street and ordinary citizens.

President Bush was very concerned about the money market funds and commercial paper markets because of how deeply they affected the average American's daily life. As he said, "You've got to protect the guy in Midland, Texas, who wants to take $10,000 out of his money market fund to buy something."

The president listened intently as we briefed him on the actions we planned to roll out: Treasury's money fund guarantees and the Fed's liquidity facility for asset-backed commercial paper. Although he had a genuine contempt for Wall Street and its minions, he did not let that stand in the way of what he thought had to be done. Just as he had swallowed hard to win Fannie and Freddie reform legislation in July, he now pushed his personal feelings aside.

"If we're in the midst of a financial meltdown, all I'm asking is whether it will work," President Bush said. He noted that we didn't have time to worry about politics. We had to figure out the right thing to do and let Congress know that it needed to act.

"Tell the Hill we're fixing to have a meltdown," he said. "We just need to tell them that this is our strategy and be firm."

I then asked Ben what the Fed could do if Congress refused to grant the powers we needed. I asked this because I knew that the president needed to hear the answer.

Ben insisted that, legally, there was nothing more that the Fed could do. The central bank had already strained its resources and pushed the limits of its powers. The situation called for fiscal policy, and Congress needed to make the judgment. President Bush pushed him, but he held firm.

"We are past the point of what the Fed and Treasury can do on their own," Ben said.

President Bush had never wavered in backing us, but that day he was exceptionally reassuring. He promised that his entire team would work with us to get congressional action as quickly as possible. After the meeting began to break up, he walked around the Roosevelt Room patting people on their shoulders.

"We're going to get through this," he told us. "We have to get through this."

I later learned that he took Michele Davis aside and said, "Tell Hank to calm down and get some sleep, because he's got to be well rested."

Leaving the meeting, I was more convinced than ever that we had to move fast on the money market guarantee. It was a step that we could take unilaterally. As soon as I returned to Treasury, I stopped by David Nason's office and told him I wanted the guarantee announced in the morning, even if it couldn't be finalized for weeks: we had to make clear right away what we were doing. I instructed David to work closely with Steve Shafran and make this his top priority.

The markets had gotten a badly needed shot of good news just before we went into the White House, when CNBC reported that Treasury was considering taking action to buy illiquid assets from the banks. The report also said that New York senator Chuck Schumer indicated that we would be announcing our plan later in the day. Stocks soared. In the last hour of trading, while we were in the White House, the Dow, down more than 200 points, surged 617 points to gain 410 points, or 3.9 percent, on the day.

Morgan Stanley's shares were particularly volatile, closing at $22.55, up 80 cents, after having fallen by as much as 46 percent during the day. But credit markets continued to weaken. Morgan Stanley's CDS were trading at 866 basis points, while its excess liquidity continued to drain away.

With Merrill Lynch seemingly secure in the arms of Bank of America, all eyes were on Morgan Stanley and Goldman Sachs. If either remaining investment bank failed, it would almost certainly bring down the other and touch off a worldwide run that would be catastrophic for the American people. And a failure was a very real possibility.

We had set a meeting with congressional leaders for 7:00 p.m., and as I rode up to the Hill, Ben called to review our strategy. I thought we were as well prepared as we could be. Ben would lay out the economic picture of what would happen if there were a systemic collapse. I would describe the powers we needed and provide some details. Kevin Fromer and I had agreed that we would need the authority to buy at least $500 billion of bad assets, but we didn't want to commit to a number yet.

We were to meet in Nancy Pelosi's conference room, adjacent to her office in the Capitol. Always smartly turned out, the Speaker of the House maintained an elegant, almost formal atmosphere, with fresh flowers and bowls of chocolates, that was quite removed from the rough-and-tumble of the floor. Once, when I walked in with a cup of Diet Coke, she'd said, "Oh, we don't use plastic cups," and an aide promptly handed me a very nice glass for my drink.

Ben and I conferred as we waited for the leaders to arrive. Chris Cox joined us. He was under heavy fire—at a campaign event earlier in the day, John McCain had said that if he were president, he would fire him. Soon the Hill's most powerful leadership figures came in, including Nancy Pelosi, John Boehner, Barney Frank, House Majority Leader Steny Hoyer, ranking Financial Services Committee member Spencer Bachus, and Democratic Caucus chairman Rahm Emanuel from the House; and the Senate's Harry Reid, Minority Leader Mitch McConnell, Majority Whip Dick Durbin, Chris Dodd, Richard Shelby, Chuck Schumer, and Democratic Conference secretary Senator Patty Murray.

We squeezed around the long table. I sat across from Nancy and Harry Reid, flanked by Ben and Chris. It was a long, tough meeting. Congress was about to break for recess in eight days, and no one was happy to be there. Ben described the severity of the crisis we faced, and I said that Treasury needed the money and powers to recapitalize the banks by buying toxic assets from their balance sheets.

Ben emphasized how the financial crisis could spill into the real economy. As stocks dropped perhaps a further 20 percent, General Motors would go bankrupt, and unemployment would rise—to 8 or 9 percent from the prevailing 6.1 percent—if we did nothing. It turned out to be a rather mild assessment of what would hit us (as I write, unemployment is now in double digits), but it was enough at the time to leave the members of Congress ashen-faced.

"It is a matter of days," Ben said, "before there is a meltdown in the global financial system."

The room erupted into questions. Everybody had an agenda to

push or an opinion to voice. Spencer Bachus asked why we didn't recapitalize banks by buying shares rather than assets. It was a good question, and I was glad he asked it, because it allowed me to emphasize my main point: the program wasn't meant as a sop for failing banks. We wanted financial institutions to sell illiquid assets so we could develop a market for them. This would encourage the free flow of capital for healthy banks, help them clean up their balance sheets, and break the logjam of credit.

Speaking for the Democrats, Barney Frank laid out provisions that he wanted to see in the bill, including pay restrictions for executives at the companies receiving government money. "If they sell, you're presumably doing them a service," he said. "They should be willing to have restrictions."

Though it didn't surprise me that Barney made this point, I pushed back hard. To my mind, restricting compensation meant putting a preemptive stigma on the program. And that is exactly what I didn't want to do. My priority was to get it off the ground fast so the system didn't collapse while we were still negotiating. Tim, Ben, and I wanted a program that encouraged maximum participation. Hundreds of perfectly sound banks across the country had toxic assets they'd be better off unloading—if only they could. We didn't want to discourage them from doing so, either by forcing their executives to take cuts in pay or by making it appear that participants, ipso facto, were all weak. They couldn't afford that perception in the marketplace.

I would continue to resist pressure on compensation restrictions for several days. I was as appalled as anyone at Wall Street's pay practices, particularly the flawed incentive structures, which we had tried to avoid at Goldman Sachs. When I was CEO, I did my best to align incentives with long-term performance. I knew compensation was too high industry-wide, but I couldn't change that. We needed to be competitive if we were going to have the best people.

By removing the CEOs at Fannie, Freddie, and AIG, the government had already demonstrated that we weren't going to reward failure, but in retrospect I was wrong not to have been more sensitive to the public outrage.

Understandably, the lawmakers pushed me to provide a dollar figure. But I was purposefully vague. "We don't have the number yet, and we want to work with you on this," I said. "It's got to be big enough to make a difference."

How big was "big," they wanted to know.

"We need to buy hundreds of billions of dollars of assets," I said. I knew better than to utter the word *trillion*. That would have caused cardiac arrest. "We need an announcement tonight to calm the market, and legislation next week," I said.

What would happen if we didn't get the authorities we sought, I was asked.

"May God help us all," I replied.

By the end of the meeting, everyone, with the notable exception of Shelby, was supportive to some degree. The tumult in the market had forced a rare bipartisan consensus. The leaders appeared to understand that something had to be done and that the only way to do this was to present a united front.

"This is a worldwide problem," Barney Frank said. "But we own it."

Chris Dodd told me that he wanted the administration to cooperate in drafting the legislation; he didn't want to be handed a fait accompli. The House and Senate needed to be able to sell any legislation we came up with, and the political calculus was tricky just weeks before an election. Averse to bailouts, voters would never grasp the pain of a meltdown unless they experienced it. As Barney put it: "No one will ever get reelected for avoiding a crisis." Nancy Pelosi noted: "We have to position this as a stimulus and relief for the American homeowner."

As we got ready to leave the nearly two-hour meeting, I was relieved at what soon became a public show of support and rather naïvely thought that legislation was going to be easier than I had first expected. But Harry Reid offered a more realistic assessment: "We can't act immediately," he said, noting that it usually took Congress weeks to get anything done.

Friday, September 19, 2008

I had been in my office for 15 minutes Friday morning when I received a call from an upset Sheila Bair, just after 7:00 a.m. We were scheduled to announce the money market fund guarantee in less than an hour, and in the rush we had not consulted with the FDIC chairman—or even notified her. She'd learned of our plans from press reports and was calling to complain. She said she knew I was under a lot of pressure, but it was outrageous that we had not checked with her first.

From the time I came to Treasury, in July 2006, I'd had a constructive relationship with Sheila, working closely with her on housing issues, about which she had many ideas. She had exceptionally good political instincts. We usually agreed on policy, but she tended to view the world through the prism of the FDIC—an understandable but at times narrow focus. Now she told me that our money market guarantee would hurt the banks.

"There are a lot of bank deposits that aren't insured," she said. "And they can now go to the money market funds."

Sheila had a good solution to prevent this from happening: insure only the customer balances that were in the money market funds on or before that day, September 19. I said that I liked her idea and that I would ask David Nason to work closely with her and her staff to implement it.

The truth is, we had to move quickly as the crisis mounted, and occasionally we stumbled. We grappled with this hard fact every time we worked on a new idea: often our fixes led to unattractive consequences. Whenever government came in—as with the guarantee program—we risked causing massive distortions in the markets. The risk of a misstep was greater the faster we had to move and the less time we had to think through every possible outcome. As a result, we had to be nimble, and flexible, enough to make midcourse corrections as needed.

The money market guarantee was an extraordinary improvisation on the part of Nason and Shafran. They had raced through the night to sketch its outlines and make the plan work. In time, funds participating in the guarantee would pay fees into a reserve that supplemented the ESF, which would not expend a single dollar on the program.

Treasury was operating so much on the fly that Nason drafted staff from the Terrorism Risk Insurance Program, which he oversaw, to help formulate the agreements and pricing schemes of the guarantee. It was announced on September 19, opened ten days later, and was, I believe, the single most powerful and important action taken to hold the system together before Congress acted. (The guarantee was intended to be a temporary program, and Congress has since ended it.)

Initially we worried about industry acceptance of the plan. Nason and Shafran had canvassed everyone from executives at Charles Schwab and Vanguard Group to the Investment Company Institute, the industry's trade association, and found that many were concerned about having to pay to insure what was already a low-margin product. But in the end we had virtually 100 percent market participation and collected over $1 billion in premiums.

That morning, the U.S. government unveiled a package of new programs to boost liquidity and calm the markets. The SEC issued an order prohibiting the short selling of 799 financial stocks for 10 business days (the order could be extended to 30 days). My efforts to round up Tim's and Ben's support had given Chris Cox the backing he needed, and after our meeting with Hill leaders the previous night, SEC commissioners had approved the ban in an emergency session. The announcement did not go off without a hitch, however. A number of major companies, including GE and Credit Suisse, had been omitted from the list, which Chris later had to expand.

At 8:30 a.m., the Federal Reserve unveiled its Asset-Backed Commercial Paper Money Market Fund Liquidity Facility, better known as AMLF. Under this program, the Fed would extend non-recourse loans to U.S. depository institutions and bank holding companies to finance their purchases of high-quality asset-backed commercial paper from money market mutual funds. In a separate action to boost liquidity, the Fed said it would buy short-term debt from Fannie Mae and Freddie Mac.

This raft of programs, coupled with news reports that we had gone up to the Hill to get new legislation, acted like a tonic to the markets. Led by financial shares, stocks rallied right from the opening. By 9:42 a.m., the Dow was already up 275 points, on its way to a full-day gain of 369 points. Morgan Stanley's shares jumped 33 percent in the first few minutes of trading.

As my staff labored on upcoming White House and congressional presentations, my phone pulled me every which way. Goldman CEO Lloyd Blankfein called to express his concern for Morgan Stanley and what its troubles might mean—for the market and for his firm. The market was losing confidence in investment banks, he said, and although Goldman had a strong balance sheet, counterparties and funding sources were scared.

"I've never rooted so hard for a competitor," he said. "If they go, we're next."

Dick Fuld also called, and although I didn't really have time to talk, I stayed on the line with him for 20 minutes. Like our conversation a few days earlier, I found it very sad. He was afraid he would spend years in court. He asked if I could please tell others how hard he had tried and what he'd done. I told him I knew that he'd made a big effort to save Lehman, but the crisis we faced was unprecedented. It was the last time I spoke with him.

The Treasury press office stayed busy that day. At 10:00 a.m., I issued a statement that explained our reasons for going to Congress—how illiquid assets were clogging the financial system and threatening Americans' personal savings and the entire economy. I said I would work with Congress over the weekend to get the legislation in place for the next week. And I took the opportunity to push for the regulatory reforms I had long advocated.

Forty-five minutes later Ben, Chris, and I stood in the White House Rose Garden with President Bush, who outlined the actions we were taking and announced that we had briefed Congress on the need for swift legislation granting the government authority to step in and buy troubled assets. "These measures will act as grease for the gears of our financial system, which were at risk of grinding to a halt," he said.

There was much still to be done. Treasury staff took the lead, representing the administration, in working with the House and Senate financial services committees to outline what would become the Troubled Assets Relief Program. I pushed our team to ask for the most expansive authorities, with as few limitations as possible, because I knew we had only one chance to get this from Congress.

In the afternoon, Kevin Fromer took me aside and said, "If you believe there is a possibility $500 billion won't be enough, we should request more."

"You're absolutely right," I said. I did want a bigger number, and

I knew the market would, too. But I didn't want to run the risk of asking for too much, then getting turned down. "What's the most you think we can get?"

"The public and Congress will hate $500 billion," he said. "It's already unthinkable. But I'm not sure they will hate $700 billion any more. If you get any higher, closer to a trillion, we will have a problem."

Our choice of the $700 billion figure wasn't just a political judgment. There was a market calculation as well: back of the envelope, we knew there were roughly $11 trillion of residential mortgages in the country, most of them good. We would need to buy only a small amount of them to provide transparency and energize the markets. And we believed that $700 billion was enough to make a difference.

Still, the $700 billion figure shocked many Americans—and Congress. Maybe my failure to anticipate this reaction showed how inured I was becoming to the extraordinary numbers associated with the prospect of an all-out financial meltdown. I was constantly being confronted by shocking figures. Friday, as the equity markets rallied, the credit markets remained tight, and investors' flight-to-quality kept demand unbelievably high for Treasuries. Fails to deliver rose to $285 billion that day, a jaw-dropping increase from $20 billion one week before.

We had raced the clock on Bear Stearns, then again on Fannie and Freddie, Lehman, and AIG. Now we were rushing to develop the outline of TARP, even as I feared we could lose four giant financial institutions—Washington Mutual, Wachovia, Morgan Stanley, and Goldman Sachs—in the next few days.

Congressional leaders had advised us not to present them with a finished document but to work with them, so we prepared a short, bare-bones proposal with open-ended language, knowing that members would add provisions that would make the legislation their own. At about 9:00 p.m. on Friday, Chris Dodd called to ask where our proposal was. "My staff's been waiting since 5:00 p.m.," he said, reminding us to be cooperative.

In the end, we cut the proposal down to three pages, and it turned out to be a three-page political mistake.

We asked for broad power to spend up to $700 billion to buy troubled assets, including both mortgages and mortgage-backed securities, under whatever terms and conditions we saw fit.

The assets would be priced using market mechanisms such as reverse auctions, in which sellers put out bids—not buyers, as is normally the case. Once purchased, they would be managed by private asset managers. The returns would go into Treasury's general fund, for the benefit of U.S. taxpayers.

Reflecting the urgency of the situation, our draft asked for Treasury to have the maximum discretion to retain agents to carry out the asset purchases, and for protection from lawsuits by private parties who might attempt to derail or delay the program. This freedom from judicial review we modeled in many respects after the Gold Reserve Act of 1934.

We were pilloried for the proposal—not least because it was so short, and hence appeared to some critics as if it had been done offhandedly. In fact, we'd kept it short to give Congress plenty of room to operate; April's "Break the Glass" review of policy options on which this outline was based was itself ten pages long. Making no provision for judicial review came across as overreaching, and that provision eventually went out the door. But nearly all of what we would ask for, and what would eventually form the basis of the legislation, was in those three pages.

Nonetheless, we could have managed our introduction of the TARP legislation more adroitly. At a minimum, we ought to have sent up the three pages as bullet points, rather than as draft legislation. We might have sent it up sooner: it went to the Hill at midnight, and waiting all day had put lawmakers, their staffs, and the media on pins and needles. And as Michele Davis later pointed out to me, we should have held a press conference that night to explain the language more clearly. We would have saved ourselves a lot of trouble had we emphasized that our proposal was an outline. But the entire staff was crunching to get the language right, and there was no time to consider niceties like news conferences. Later, of course, we would hold many such late-night press briefings.

Even with TARP sketched out, a temporary money market guarantee in place, and a short-selling ban in operation, I still couldn't breathe easily, because of the intense pressure on Morgan Stanley and Goldman Sachs. They were the top two investment banks in the world—not only for their prestige but also for the sheer size of their balance sheets, their trading books, and their exposures. Their counterparty risk was enormous, much bigger than Lehman's. And we unequivocally knew that the market could not tolerate another failure like that of Lehman.

Morgan Stanley was particularly beset. Friday's government actions had done wonders for its shares, which rose 21 percent to $27.21, and its credit default rates had fallen by more than a third. But its clients and counterparties had lost confidence; since Monday, hedge funds had been pulling their prime brokerage accounts, and other institutions were shying away from the firm. In one week the reserves available to the Morgan Stanley parent company had plunged from about $81 billion to $31 billion. We knew that if Morgan Stanley fell, the focus would turn to Goldman Sachs.

On Friday evening, around 6:30 p.m., John Mack called to update me. He was scrambling for a solution. He desperately needed a merger or a show of support from a strategic investor, but he had not gotten far with China Investment Corporation (CIC), Beijing's sovereign wealth fund, which he had thought might consider an additional equity investment in his firm.

"We're not making as much progress as I would like," he acknowledged. "The Chinese need to know that the U.S. government thinks it is important to find a solution."

"I'll talk to Wang Qishan," I assured him. I added that I was prepared to ask President Bush to say something to China's president, Hu Jintao, if it would be helpful and necessary.

After I got off the phone with John, I spoke with Ben and Tim to set our plan of attack for Saturday and Sunday. Deal talk dominated our conversation, as it would throughout the weekend. We believed that Wachovia and WaMu were on the edge of failing. They were plagued by piles of bad assets and had genuine solvency issues. By contrast, Morgan Stanley and Goldman Sachs were suffering from a lack of confidence. Morgan Stanley also faced a near-term liquidity crunch.

Morgan Stanley and Wachovia had discussed a merger earlier in the week. Morgan Stanley had concluded that it couldn't do one without enormous amounts of government assistance because of Wachovia's huge exposure, about $122 billion, to so-called option ARMs. Among the most toxic of loans, these adjustable-rate mortgages let borrowers choose from different payment methods; they frequently came with introductory teaser rates and often contained a feature by which the low mortgage payments caused the loan balance to grow.

Tim had had serious doubts as to whether a Morgan Stanley–Wachovia combination would be credible to the market. Both institutions were too wobbly, and these talks ended without Morgan Stanley's requesting or the Fed's offering assistance.

Spurred by the Federal Reserve, we discussed a range of ways to combine the investment banks with commercial banks. Our rationale was simple: confidence in the business model of investment banks had evaporated, so merging them with commercial banks would reassure the markets. In truth, I didn't like the idea of creating megabanks—they were too big and complex to manage effectively, and I believed that both Morgan Stanley and Goldman Sachs had better balance sheets than many of the commercial banks. But we had to find a way to reduce the likelihood of a failure of the investment banks—and the collapse of our financial system.

The Fed was also working on backup plans to enable Goldman and Morgan Stanley to become bank holding companies. This would bring them under the supervision of the Fed, which inspired more confidence in investors than the SEC. That, however, was Plan B, and we didn't believe it would be enough to save the two investment banks unless they could also raise capital from strategic investors. But in the ongoing market panic, both investment banks were having trouble finding credible partners.

Whatever we did, we felt that by Monday we had to give the market a signal that Morgan Stanley and Goldman Sachs weren't going to fail. The SEC's short-selling ban had bought them a grace period, but there was no time to waste.

Saturday, September 20, 2008

I arrived at the office at 9:15 a.m. Between the investment banks and the TARP legislation, I spent much of the day on the phone, taking multiple calls from, among others, both Barack Obama and John McCain.

Treasury and the White House held a midmorning conference call on legislative strategy. Our goal was to keep TARP as simple as possible while pressing for as broad a set of authorities as we could get. Treasury would lead the administration's effort, with Neel Kashkari, Bob Hoyt, and Kevin Fromer negotiating with legislative staff on the Hill. We also had to make sure our proposal worked for the White House and the Office of Management and Budget.

My mind was focused on the danger to the investment banks. Tim and I had spoken early that morning, and several times afterward. My style, when I'm on the phone and pressed for time, is to race through things, then say, "Okay, bye." If people don't know me, they'll find they're talking to an empty line. I wound up calling Tim repeatedly that morning because I kept hanging up too quickly.

I had several discouraging calls with John Mack that weekend. With his firm on the verge of going down, he was under great pressure. But John desperately hoped to avoid selling Morgan Stanley. By this point, he and I both doubted that he could make a deal with the Chinese, although I reassured him I would raise the issue directly with Vice Premier Wang Qishan that evening. John was more optimistic about finding a strategic investor in another Asian giant, Mitsubishi UFJ Financial Group, with whom he had begun talking. But I was skeptical that a Japanese bank could move quickly enough, given Morgan Stanley's situation.

"You need a solution by the end of this weekend," I reminded him.

"Hank, do you think I should sell Morgan Stanley?"

"The consequences of a Morgan Stanley failure are so great, John, I believe you should sell if you can."

During the afternoon I called the White House to update the president. He had been pleased by the market's rebound on Friday, which he took, along with Thursday's rally, as a positive sign. But I had to reiterate my concerns for the two investment banks and Wachovia.

He asked whether we thought Morgan Stanley could find a buyer, and I told him that, in fact, we might need to have him talk to China's president. Any such contact would have to be set up carefully, because the president of the United States should not appear to directly ask the president of China to invest in a U.S. institution. But if it looked like the Chinese wanted to do the deal, we might arrange a conversation. The president would thank Hu for the cooperation of the Chinese in working through the capital market issues with us. That should be enough to indicate how important this matter was to the U.S. Though the president did not commit to the plan right then, he told me to work with National Security Adviser Steve Hadley on it.

Kevin Warsh had begun an effort to get Wachovia to discuss a possible merger with Goldman Sachs, but he was making little progress. The North Carolina bank seemed to lack a sense of urgency. On Saturday afternoon I got involved.

Because he had only recently resigned as undersecretary for domestic finance, Wachovia CEO Bob Steel was not allowed to talk to Treasury on behalf of Wachovia, but I could speak with Wachovia's directors. I called Aramark CEO Joe Neubauer, who was on Wachovia's board. I'd worked with Joe and knew him to be financially sophisticated and a straight shooter.

"Joe, I just want to make sure you have the right sense of urgency," I said. "The Goldman Sachs people are waiting in their offices, and no one has showed up."

"Why does this have to be done so quickly?" he asked.

"Wachovia is likely to fail soon," I said. "The market is very nervous about your mortgage portfolio. It's much better to get ahead of this."

When Joe called me back later, it was clear that my message had sunk in. I also talked a number of times to Lloyd Blankfein to urge him to be aggressive and creative. I explained, though, that a Goldman-Wachovia deal could not be done if it required too much help from the Fed.

I was at home at about 9:00 p.m. on Saturday night, waiting to speak with my old friend Wang Qishan on the other side of the world, when I needed to squeeze in a call to Montana senator Max

Baucus. He wanted to speak with me about TARP and executive compensation. He had come up with an idea to use the tax code to control executive pay for TARP participants by eliminating corporate deductions for compensation above a certain income level.

It wasn't a bad idea, but frankly I was losing my patience. There I was, trying to save the markets and about to have a difficult conversation with the Chinese, and once again my ear was being chewed off about compensation. "If people are incompetent, I fire them. They don't get their golden parachutes. I've been tough on everyone," I remember telling Baucus. I said I didn't see the point in changing the tax laws to penalize the very banks that we wanted to entice into participating in our asset-buying program.

As I would discover in the coming days, the Democratic senator was not about to back down on this idea, which had its merits. Ultimately, we would accept it, but that night I was short with him because I needed to speak with Wang. It was a miracle I was on time for our 9:30 p.m. call.

I'd kept the Chinese vice premier briefed throughout the crisis, and although we were always friendly, on this night we kept pleasantries to a minimum. I talked about the market, and TARP, and my optimism that we would get the powers we needed. Then I brought up Morgan Stanley.

Wang had a high regard for John Mack and his company. As he knew, CIC was looking at increasing its 9.9 percent stake in Morgan Stanley. I said that we would welcome that. But Wang seemed lukewarm and concerned about the safety of any Chinese investment. I knew that CIC had lost heavily on its existing Morgan Stanley holding, and that had been a source of great controversy inside China. I told him that the U.S. government viewed Morgan Stanley as systemically important. But his unenthusiastic tone convinced me to drop the matter—China was already providing tremendous support to the U.S. by buying and holding Treasuries and GSE securities. If a deal for Morgan Stanley had been possible, Wang would have signaled it.

Later I called Steve Hadley at the White House and let him know that I didn't believe China was going to invest in Morgan Stanley, and that the president's call to Hu would be unnecessary. And when I got to John the next day and told him that the Chinese didn't seem to be interested, he wasn't surprised.

Sunday, September 21, 2008

All the Sunday talk shows had asked for me, and I had four interviews lined up. If there was ever a time to get a clear message out, it was now. Throughout my career I had made a point of answering questions directly. But it was different as a government official. You knew what you were going to be asked, but you had points you wanted to make, and you had to find a way to get them out no matter what questions came your way.

Even though she hadn't slept much herself on Saturday night, Michele Davis arrived at my house early on Sunday to prep me for my round of interviews. "You don't have to get your points out all at once," she said. "You'll have time to get them out over the course of the interview." Before I went on *Meet the Press*, Tom Brokaw said the same thing.

"I'm going to be tough," he said. "That's the way you want it—fair but tough. Just remember, Hank, let me come to you."

At the end of the interview, Brokaw noted that the problems with money market funds had spread to commercial paper and begun to threaten Main Street America. He asked, "The domino effect of this is going to be a no-growth economy, isn't it?"

"That is why we need these powers. That is why we need Congress to move quickly," I explained. "It pains me tremendously to have the American taxpayer be put in this position, but it's better than the alternative."

That afternoon Ben and I attended a well-intentioned but dysfunctional meeting in Tennessee senator Bob Corker's offices with several of his fellow GOP senators from the Senate Banking Committee (and a couple more patched in on speakerphone). Corker, a constructive force in the Senate, wanted Ben and me to educate the group, but Jim Bunning hijacked the meeting. I had occasionally locked horns with Bunning, a cantankerous conservative, and this meeting was no exception. The Kentuckian clearly believed that the American people were not worried about our financial institutions or economic collapse. Ben and I both became frustrated with Bunning. The meeting was a complete waste of time for us, when time was more precious than anything.

The prospects of merging either Morgan Stanley or Goldman Sachs looked dim, despite the efforts of Ben, Tim, Kevin Warsh, and me. Tim had tried to initiate talks between Goldman and Citigroup, on the theory that Goldman would strengthen the commercial bank's management team, but Citi was not interested. He had also taken the lead in promoting a JPMorgan acquisition of Morgan Stanley, but JPMorgan kept turning that suggestion down. Midafternoon, Ben and I joined Tim on a call with Jamie Dimon, and we unsuccessfully appealed to him again to acquire Morgan Stanley. Undaunted, we tried Mack, calling to ask him to approach Jamie Dimon one more time. Frustrated, John refused, explaining that he had already spoken with Jamie several times and wasn't about to try again.

"A fire sale to JPMorgan would cost thousands of Morgan Stanley jobs," he protested.

The fact is, had John called Jamie again, I'm sure the JPMorgan chief would still have said no. WaMu was Jamie's top priority, as I had known for some time. (Within the week, JPMorgan would announce it was buying the Seattle-based institution.)

Goldman and Wachovia were interested in merging, but Goldman, like Morgan Stanley, had found big embedded losses in Wachovia's real estate portfolio. A deal could not be completed without government assistance. The Fed was even considering a novel approach that might allow it to make a loan to support the deal that was secured not only with assets but with warrants to purchase equity in the combined company.

In the end, Ben, Tim, and I decided against supporting a Goldman-Wachovia merger. It would have been difficult to structure and would have presented complex and perhaps unresolvable legal and political challenges. My past association with Goldman would have created a problem with appearances.

More important, however, I couldn't back a Goldman Sachs–Wachovia merger for a fundamental reason. With no deal in sight for Morgan Stanley, a Goldman merger would have increased the likelihood of a Morgan Stanley failure. If the market believed that Goldman Sachs needed to merge with a bank to survive, it would have lost even more confidence in an unmerged Morgan Stanley. Similarly, a JPMorgan acquisition of Morgan Stanley would have been destabilizing to Goldman Sachs, leaving it to stand alone, with every other major investment bank having either failed or been forced to merge.

Our job was above all to reduce the risk of these investment banks' failing. After a weekend of frenetic activity, Ben, Tim, and I concluded that the course of action that would be the least likely to lead to the failure of either was our Plan B. The Fed needed to turn Morgan Stanley and Goldman Sachs into bank holding companies, with the expectation that both would find strategic investors to assure their survival. (Although this was far from clear at the time, I now believe we were very fortunate that we didn't succeed in merging either one of them, because the last thing we need today is an even more concentrated financial services industry.)

On Sunday evening, I talked with Mack and Blankfein. John, who had become increasingly optimistic about a Mitsubishi UFJ deal, told me he hoped to announce an agreement in principle the next morning to sell up to 20 percent of Morgan Stanley to the Japanese company. I pledged to do anything I could to be helpful. Lloyd said he had been looking for strategic investors in Japan and China and come up empty. Furthermore, he was frustrated to have wasted so much time on Wachovia only to find that Fed assistance wasn't available. Did I have any ideas?

"Lloyd, you need to find an investor. I won't have any ideas you don't have," I said. "Look everywhere in the world to find an institution where you have a good relationship with someone who is very credible. Leave no stone unturned."

He hesitated, considering the situation. Then he said quietly, "Just tell me: am I doing the right thing?"

A little while later, at 9:30 on Sunday night, September 21, the Federal Reserve announced that it had approved Morgan Stanley's and Goldman Sachs's applications to become bank holding companies.

The Wall Street I knew had come to an end.

CHAPTER 12

Monday, September 22, 2008

By Monday morning our $700 billion rescue plan had made news around the world. I got to the office early and went to the Markets Room to check the credit spreads on Morgan Stanley and Goldman Sachs. To my relief, the investment banks' CDS had steadied, although the LIBOR-OIS spread was still under pressure. But there was no question we were tiptoeing on the razor's edge. We needed to get this legislation done fast.

It would have been challenging enough to push TARP through in a nonelection year, but politics truly complicated our efforts. In the midst of a fiercely contested presidential campaign, Republicans were anticipating heavy congressional losses and were keenly sensitive to voter frustration with the Bush administration and with Wall Street. On Sunday, Senator Obama, who had made a number of public statements expressing his qualified support for our approach, indicated in a CNBC interview that he would want to make sure I was involved in the transition if he won. Senator McCain had also been relatively supportive.

But the economy had become the main issue in the presidential campaign, and Obama continued to hammer his rival for a comment he'd made on September 15 that "the fundamentals of our economy are strong." McCain and Obama were within a few percentage points of each other in the polls and fighting heated battles in swing states. Obama was creeping ahead, and McCain was trying to distance himself from the Bush White House. He was slinging populist rhetoric on the campaign trail, excoriating Wall Street, talking about protecting taxpayers, and using the word *bailout.*

At a town hall meeting on Monday morning in Scranton, Pennsylvania, McCain told the crowd, "I am greatly concerned that the plan gives a single individual the unprecedented power to spend one trillion—trillion—dollars without any meaningful accountability. Never before in the history of our nation has so much power and money been concentrated in the hands of one person."

I was concerned that McCain's rhetoric could inflame public sentiment against TARP, so I turned to South Carolina senator Lindsey Graham, the candidate's close friend and national campaign co-chairman. Lindsey called me midday to tell me John was at the tipping point, almost ready to come out against TARP. Was the plan necessary? he asked.

"Absolutely," I said.

I went through all the reasons, emphasizing that I knew McCain's support would be crucial in getting the Republicans to vote for the legislation. Lindsey urged me to speak directly with John, but I couldn't get through to him. I tried Lindsey again a few hours later, and he reiterated his point. A number of McCain's advisers disliked TARP and saw a political advantage in his opposing it.

"It's so important you get to John," I remember Lindsey telling me. "He has people pushing him the wrong way, and I'm trying to spend as much time as I can with him. I'll make sure he calls you back."

McCain called me within the hour, but it wasn't a good conversation. "Hank, you're asking for a lot of authorities," he said. "The American people don't like bailouts, and you know I've always been an advocate of the taxpayer."

"In any normal circumstance I'd be with you, but right now I can't tell you enough how fragile the system is," I said, emphasizing that several big institutions were on the edge. "I'm going to really need your support to get something done—your public support."

McCain was in a rush and had to hang up before I could get a commitment from him. I was so concerned about the conversation that I called Josh Bolten at the White House for advice. Josh assured me that Lindsey Graham understood the need for government action and was completely behind it.

"Stay close to Lindsey," he said. "Just keep talking to him, keep that as a bridge to McCain."

The uncertainty caused by Republican disenchantment with TARP helped drive the Dow down 373 points, wiping out Friday's gains. Shares of Washington Mutual and Wachovia dropped sharply. On the plus side, Morgan Stanley's and Goldman's CDS spreads had narrowed considerably, indicating that the plan to turn them into bank holding companies had given them a little breathing room. It helped, too, that Mitsubishi UFJ had announced its intention to buy 20 percent of Morgan Stanley.

Still, we needed to sell TARP hard. As Treasury staff negotiated with congressional Democrats on the particulars, we felt we could not show any doubts about our approach or any openness to other ideas. Whenever anyone on the Hill asked the Treasury team if they had any other plans, the response was: "This is the plan." If we had entertained other options, the process would have bogged down.

Executive compensation remained a sticking point. That evening when I met with my team—Kevin Fromer, Michele Davis, Jim Wilkinson, Neel Kashkari, and Bob Hoyt—to review the issue, we discussed the increasingly strident tone of the election campaign: "You hear what people are saying on the campaign trail. You listen to the candidates," Michele said. "To get the votes, we're going to need executive compensation restrictions."

I told them I believed that we should take very tough positions with top executives of failing companies, as we had when we fired the CEOs of the GSEs and AIG. But to my mind, restricting pay could put us on a slippery slope with Congress. The whole idea of TARP was to encourage the maximum number of institutions to participate in our auctions and sell their bad assets. Those taking part would clean their balance sheets and attract new capital from private investors.

As we walked out of our meeting, Kevin Fromer warned me, "This is going to be tricky."

I replied, "I would rather get nothing at all than get something that ties my hands so I know it won't work."

I held out for a few days, refusing to compromise and angering many on the Hill. But doing so allowed us to agree on a set of restrictions that the market accepted. Congress would make them much tougher after I'd left.

Tuesday, September 23, 2008

Ben Bernanke, Chris Cox, Jim Lockhart, and I were scheduled to appear before the Senate Banking Committee at 9:30 a.m. We knew it wasn't going to be an easy session, and we knew we had to be prepared. Ben called me two hours before that to say he was concerned that we hadn't been doing a good enough job of explaining what we needed. He wanted to make sure I was comfortable with the statement he planned to give.

Going into the hearing, I knew I had to choose my words carefully. We faced a real dilemma: To get Congress to act we needed to make dire predictions about what would happen to the economy if they didn't give us the authorities we wanted. But doing so could backfire. Frightened consumers might stop spending and start saving, which was the last thing we needed right then. Investors could lose the final shred of the confidence that was keeping the markets from crashing.

I described the roots of the crisis, the bad lending practices that had hurt homeowners and financial institutions and caused a chain reaction that had spread to Main Street, where nonfinancial companies were having trouble funding their daily operations. I stressed the need for swift action, but I resisted when I was asked to describe what a meltdown would look like and to provide details on what it would mean to lose a retirement account or a job.

Ben was less hesitant to present an alarming scenario. "The financial markets are in a quite fragile condition, and I think absent a plan they will get worse," he told the panel. "I believe if the credit markets are not functioning, that jobs will be lost, that our credit rates will rise, more houses will be foreclosed upon, GDP will contract, that the economy will just not be able to recover in a normal, healthy way."

The Senate is more civilized than the House, but this was a long, difficult session. I didn't get to speak until 90 minutes or so into the hearing, after the committee members had made their statements.

Over the course of the nationally televised, five-hour hearing, the senators expressed big concerns about moving too fast, about taxpayer protection, and about the broad powers I was requesting. This was understandable: we were asking for a lot—on short notice, and just weeks before Election Day. They fired questions at us,

and the senatorial rhetoric blew hot and heavy. Jim Bunning denounced TARP as "financial socialism" and "un-American." Richard
Shelby criticized our ad hoc approach and our rush. And these,
nominally, were our Republican friends.

As for the Democrats, Chris Dodd, whose advice we'd followed
in sending up a bare-bones outline of legislation, took the opportunity to say, "This proposal is stunning and unprecedented in its
scope and lack of detail. . . . It is not just our economy at risk, but
our Constitution as well."

Still, Chris was helpful in some ways. Reading the bill closely, he
noted, "There's nothing in here that would prohibit you from using the flexible notions and thoughts out there on how a better
approach might work—an equity infusion, for instance."

I responded, "Mr. Chairman, . . . you said it better than I did. I
didn't want to find myself in the position of being here, asking for
these authorities. But under the circumstances, I think they're better than the alternative. . . . Our whole objective here is going to
be to minimize the ultimate cost to the taxpayer."

To that point, we had put equity only in the GSEs and AIG, and
we'd basically killed the shareholders of those companies. We
didn't want to give a whiff of support to speculation that we would
inject equity, because we feared that such speculation would only
drive bank share prices to zero before Congress had had a chance
to vote on TARP. I left the hearing room knowing that we were still
a long way from getting something done.

Senator Obama called afterward to touch base. I told him that it
had been a tough hearing. He noted that the American people were
not happy to see big compensation packages for an industry need-
ing government help, and he warned me that I had to stay on top of
my party if we wanted to make sure TARP passed. The Democrats,
he said, were more inclined to support the legislation.

Meanwhile, I was getting reports from my people that the bill that was being worked on in the House and the Senate was getting longer and longer—and we hadn't yet seen any resolution on the major issues: executive compensation, taxpayer protection, and oversight.

One of my worries lifted Tuesday when Goldman Sachs—which had overnight Sunday become the fourth-biggest U.S. bank holding company—had finally found its strategic investor. And they'd found the most credible investor in the world, Warren Buffett, who announced that he would invest $5 billion in perpetual preferred shares yielding 10 percent, with warrants to buy $5 billion worth of common shares. What cemented his decision was the prospect of TARP's being passed. As he would say in an interview on CNBC the next day, "If I didn't think the government was going to act, I would not be doing anything this week."

But the markets were not as easily assuaged: stocks took another fall as the trading day closed, and the Dow finished down 162 points, at 10,854, as credit spreads continued to widen.

With investors like Buffett counting on TARP, we pressed ahead on our sales efforts. At 6:15 p.m. I sat down in John Boehner's office with House Republican leaders. They disliked TARP but knew something needed to be done, and they kept trying to come up with an alternative. Boehner had already warned me that things were not going well in the GOP caucus. About a third of the House Republicans were facing tough elections and worried about losing their seats. Another third were so ideologically driven that they would never vote for TARP.

"The group you're shooting for is the one-third in the middle," Boehner told me. "And you're fishing in a small pond."

Boehner's staff had set up a table with food in the back of the office, and people came and went as we grappled with how to deal with the crisis. I did more listening than speaking, trying to understand what Boehner was dealing with, and it dawned on me how difficult it was to reason with some people. The facts didn't seem to matter to some in this group. I looked around and wondered where the votes would come from. Florida's Adam Putnam was the most constructive—he suggested that I needed to tell people more explicitly how bad it would be if the financial system collapsed: massive unemployment, people living on the streets. Adam was right, but scaring the public to win support would only make things worse economically.

Virginian Eric Cantor, meanwhile, was pushing an insurance program. It wasn't particularly well developed, but it was meant to avoid big government intervention. The plan, as I understood it, would have provided insurance to companies holding the frozen mortgage assets, allowing them to limit their losses. The firms would have had to pay insurance premiums to the Treasury Department for the coverage. By that evening I was at the end of my rope, and I lost it a little, making a sarcastic remark to Cantor about dropping our whole plan in favor of his insurance idea.

"We've gone to the American people, we've gone to Congress, we've put forward the best idea to deal with this problem, and we've got a good number of people that are supportive," I remember saying. "And you want me now to go and say, 'Hey, I've thought about it some more. I got a better idea. I'm going to go with Eric Cantor's insurance program. That's the idea to save the day.'"

I left Boehner's office demoralized. A number of people pulled me aside, saying, in effect, "We believe this is a serious situation, but you're not going to get the votes for this. You're going to have to come up with another idea that works."

Wednesday, September 24, 2008

After the gathering at Boehner's office, I was not looking forward to meeting with the entire House Republican Conference the next morning. It was scheduled for 9:00 a.m. in the Cannon Caucus

Room. By then, too, I'd heard all about the fiasco of the morning before, when Vice President Cheney, Josh Bolten, Keith Hennessey, and Kevin Warsh had traveled to the same room to argue for TARP only to endure a long, ugly meeting with angry Republicans.

Before I left for the GOP conference, Michele Davis and Kevin Fromer told me to present the lawmakers with something they could understand. I would have to make them see that the esoteric numbers on the screens of Treasury's Markets Room translated into real danger for the average American. Credit markets were still in crisis. The squeeze in the Treasury market had become almost unimaginable. Fails to deliver had now reached a staggering total of $1.7 trillion—compared with $20 billion 12 days before.

Knowing how difficult this meeting was going to be, I asked Ben Bernanke to accompany me, and he readily agreed to do so. Speaking to the crowd in the grand meeting room with its deep red carpet and crystal chandeliers, we explained that the commercial paper market was nonexistent, and that financing was disappearing for big and small companies alike, endangering their ability to sustain normal activities. But it didn't make a bit of difference to this group, which opposed big government intervention as a first step on the path to socialism. They lined up ten deep on both sides of the room, waiting for a microphone, and blasted us. Certain that their constituents opposed bailouts, they could not be persuaded to support TARP.

Although Boehner had been firm and direct about his support in our September 18 meeting with congressional leaders, he was less friendly and eager to work with us in this setting. He limited his comments to a short pep talk on the previous day's tactical victory on offshore oil drilling. Then one member after another said the bill couldn't pass without House Republicans, and there was nothing we could do to change their minds. It was an untenable situation. Afterward one member of Congress came up to me and said, "I've been talking about deregulation and free markets my whole life. You're asking me to change my view, and there is no way I can do that." That response applied to many in the group that morning.

Shortly afterward, Boehner and I went to Pelosi's office and told her about the meeting. She wanted to get TARP passed, and she pressed Boehner: "What can you do? What ideas do you have?" He didn't have much beyond Cantor's insurance plan, which he acknowledged was not really well formulated. He mentioned the possibility of "pro-growth" ideas, but Pelosi said it was no time to be talking about "tax cuts for the wealthy."

The House Financial Services Committee convened at 2:30 p.m. Some House hearings could be terrible—you never knew what was going to happen. But Barney Frank's hearings were different. Always pragmatic and efficient, he made sure things moved along with a fair amount of decorum.

Nonetheless, Ben and I were besieged with questions from all sides. Why wouldn't the government take stakes in the companies it helped? Why wouldn't we put restrictions on executive pay? In fairness, this is how our representative government works. Some members were grandstanding, positioning themselves to help their reelection campaigns. But for the most part, the lawmakers were just doing their jobs, trying to understand in a very short amount of time a complex issue for which most had little preparation or background. And we were asking for a lot.

In the Senate hearing the day before, I had stood firm on the compensation issue, but I now realized that I would have to give some ground. I told the House panel that we would find a way to address executive pay.

Paul Kanjorski, the Pennsylvania Democrat who chaired the Capital Markets Subcommittee, said we still hadn't made a convincing case. "The average American people don't really know what you are really talking about when you say it is going to cost us far less than the alternative," he said, noting that I needed to clearly explain the ramifications of an electronic run on the money market system. "When I talk to average Americans in my district and across this country, the sun came up today, they went to work today, they stopped and picked up gas today," he went on, "and they are wondering what all the hullabaloo is about." What, he pointedly asked me, was the alternative I referred to?

I answered this question as best as I could, given that Barney kept hustling the hearing along. But there was no doubt about it—the session wasn't going well. Topping it off, Michele Davis got a message on her BlackBerry that John McCain was suspending his campaign to return to Washington to tackle the economic crisis. She passed me a note that said in part, "If you get a question, just say that you know that both Senators McCain and Obama recognize the seriousness of the situation."

I turned around and looked at Michele, stunned. This was crazy. Even more incredibly, I had spoken to Lindsey Graham just minutes before walking into the hearing, and he hadn't said a word about McCain's coming back.

When the hearing recessed, I went into Barney's office and called Josh Bolten to tell him in no uncertain terms that I thought it was dangerous for McCain to return. I was dumbfounded that the president had allowed it. Josh said the White House was equally frustrated. McCain wanted a meeting at the White House, and the president felt he had no choice but to accommodate him.

I called Obama right away. He said that he would try to be as constructive as possible but that the Democrats were doing their part and I had better keep in touch with McCain. The president was scheduled to give a major speech that evening making the case for TARP, but news of McCain's decision to suspend his campaign dominated the rest of the afternoon. After the House hearing, I walked over to the Senate side of the Capitol to answer questions from the Senate Democratic Caucus. They were meeting in the Lyndon Baines Johnson Room, a huge room with a tiled floor and an imposing ceiling fresco, where LBJ had once reigned as majority leader. Harry Reid and the Democrats were waiting for me, but before I went inside, Joe Lieberman approached me.

"You're doing great, Hank," the Connecticut senator said, confiding that the Democrats wanted to exclude him from this meeting because he was supporting McCain. "I'm going to walk beside you, because they won't throw me out if I go in with you."

Ben was already there, and upon my arrival (Lieberman had already disappeared into the crowd), Reid went to the podium and told the group that we would answer questions. The first person to speak was John Kerry of Massachusetts, whom I had found to be consistently on the right side of the issues about the financial crisis. He said he was unsure that he wanted Ben and me there because there was a political element to everything, and suggested that the group first meet alone. But Reid refused, saying that questions needed to be answered. From the look of it, the entire caucus was there, though some seemed no more eager to vote TARP through than were House Republicans. Many were unhappy. At least a third were irate that the crisis was happening and were unwilling to agree to anything unless there were major modifications to the bill. One after another they spoke, occasionally asking a question but usually just attacking our proposal. I felt fortunate that Chris Dodd was chairing the Banking Committee because many of these senators liked and trusted him. But he had his work cut out for him.

Halfway through the session, I hit the wall. I had been going for days with little sleep and no exercise, hustling from one difficult meeting or conversation to another, and I ran out of gas. I realized

I was going to get the dry heaves, and if I did that in front of people it would make for a bad news story, to say the least. So I made a poor joke.

"Excuse me," I announced, standing at the podium. "I have to go get rid of some Diet Cokes."

I rushed out of the room and into a bathroom stall, had a short bout of dry heaves, then returned to the meeting. Again, no one seemed to notice anything amiss, and I returned as Ben was responding to another irate senator.

Afterward Hillary Clinton told me to stick with Schumer if I wanted to get things done. I told her I would, but the fact was, Chuck and I had a serious disagreement about how the $700 billion should be allocated. I wanted Treasury to have access to the total amount right from the start, but Schumer wanted it doled out in tranches. I suspected he wanted to reserve part of the money for the next administration.

Before I went to bed that night, I watched President Bush address the nation from the State Floor at the White House. "Our entire economy is in danger," he said, carefully explaining how we had gotten to that point: foreign investment in the U.S., easy credit, a housing boom, irresponsible lending and borrowing. It was his most substantive address yet on the financial crisis, and it was well delivered, but the last thought I had before I fell asleep was that even a speech by the president wouldn't be able to sway the House Republicans.

Thursday, September 25, 2008

We'd devised TARP to save the financial system. Now it had become all about politics—presidential politics. The president, the leaders of both parties, and both candidates were scheduled to meet around 4:00 p.m. Thursday. I wondered what McCain could have been thinking. Calling a meeting like this when we didn't have a deal was playing with dynamite.

Democrats, I later learned, had moved into high gear to devise a strategy to ensure that they emerged as the winners from McCain's maneuver. They didn't want to take the blame for TARP's failure—and they didn't want McCain to be able to claim credit for its success.

By midmorning, Democrats and Republicans from both houses were haggling over the bill's provisions. Over the course of two hours or so, in the Foreign Relations Room, located below the vice president's office on the Senate side, the negotiators agreed on several big items, including setting the size of TARP at $700 billion. TARP funds would not be immediately available to the administration but could be drawn down in tranches. Senate and House negotiators agreed on the need to place restrictions on executive compensation and to give Treasury warrants to purchase equity in companies participating in the program so that taxpayers could share in any possible gains they made.

Enough tentative progress had been achieved for Utah Republican senator Bob Bennett to get caught up in the moment as he emerged from the negotiation sessions around midday. He grabbed a microphone and told the press, "I now expect we will, indeed, have a plan that can pass the House, pass the Senate, be signed by the president, and bring a sense of certainty to this crisis that is still roiling in the markets." Chris Dodd told reporters that he, too, was confident.

But there were problems with this scenario. It was a big stretch to say these negotiators had reached an actual agreement. And, in any case, House Republicans were not on board, and without them TARP was going nowhere. The math was simple. We would need 218 votes for House passage. Though the Democrats, with 236 members, held a clear majority, we weren't going to get 100 percent of their votes, so we had to have some Republicans. But the only House Republican attending the morning negotiating session had been Spencer Bachus, the ranking Republican on the House Financial Services Committee. Afterward, he allowed that progress had been made. But he wasn't in a position to deliver his colleagues.

Hour by hour the need for the legislation was becoming more urgent. The noose continued to tighten on the nation's credit markets: by the close of trading, LIBOR-OIS spreads had widened to nearly 200 basis points, up 30 basis points from the day before. By comparison, they had been about half that level just after Lehman failed.

Then Washington Mutual went down—the biggest failure in U.S. banking history. While the legislators were negotiating, Sheila Bair called me around 11:00 a.m. to break the news that the FDIC was going to seize the bank, and that JPMorgan would pay the government $1.9 billion for the company, which had $307 billion in assets.

WaMu's demise wasn't a surprise. It had been struggling for months and had taken a catastrophic turn for the worse: Its CDS rates, already shocking at 2,742 on September 15, had nearly doubled to 5,266 on Wednesday, September 24, as the bank was hit by a run on deposits. Customers had withdrawn $16.7 billion over the preceding ten days.

Back in March, JPMorgan had wanted to buy WaMu, but its regulator, the Office of Thrift Supervision (OTS), and management had opted instead for a $7 billion capital investment from a group led by the private-equity firm TPG. This decision proved to be a mistake: an acquisition by JPMorgan would have stabilized the bank. Still, I had kept in close touch with Sheila and Ben Bernanke on WaMu and periodically talked with JPMorgan CEO Jamie Dimon.

Unfortunately, the WaMu solution wasn't perfect, although it was handled smoothly using the normal FDIC process. JPMorgan's purchase cost taxpayers nothing and no depositors lost money, but the deal gave senior WaMu debt holders about 55 cents on the dollar, roughly equal to what the securities had been trading for. In retrospect, I see that, in the middle of a panic, this was a mistake. WaMu, the sixth-biggest bank in the country, was systemically important. Crushing the owners of preferred and subordinated debt and clipping senior debt holders only unsettled the debt holders in other institutions, adding to the market's uncertainty about government action. Banks were even less willing to lend to one another. In the future, I concluded, we were going to need to go beyond the standard FDIC resolution process for a failing bank.

At 2:25 p.m. I spoke with John McCain, who had just returned to Washington. The call did nothing to ease my mind.

"We have to protect the American taxpayers," he told me, pointing out that nothing would get done in Congress without the House Republicans. They didn't like our proposal and I needed to listen more carefully to them, he said.

"John, our system is on the edge," I told him. "WaMu barely got bailed out today. Several other institutions are on the brink. If we don't get something done soon, this economy is going to collapse."

I was so concerned that McCain would do or say something rash that I resorted to a veiled threat: "I'm not a politician, but if you or anyone else does something that causes this system to collapse, it is not going to just be on me. I am going to go and say what I think to the American people."

As soon as we finished up, I called Joel Kaplan at the White House to let him know that I'd had a tough conversation with the Republican presidential candidate. Not long after, Senator Judd Gregg called to confirm my worst fears about McCain's return.

"Hank," the New Hampshire Republican said, "I have just been in a meeting that took my breath away."

McCain, it seems, had come to Washington to save the day, and became livid when he got off the plane to learn that a deal had apparently been reached without him. As Judd told me, McCain, with Lindsey Graham at his side, had come in late to the Senate Republican Policy Committee luncheon, held weekly in the Mike Mansfield Room on the second floor of the Capitol. McCain sat through part of a presentation by Bennett and a short one by Judd. Lindsey told the assembly of 40 or so senators, "It's not right for any of you to reach an agreement, because there is no agreement unless John agrees."

Then, Judd related, McCain had declared, "I don't care what you people do, I am going to do what is right for the country." The Arizona senator subsequently stormed out, leaving the Republican senators to finish their lunches, whether or not they had any appetite left.

Now I knew why McCain had seemed so angry when we'd spoken half an hour before.

I'd barely gotten off the phone when Barney Frank called to tell me that Spencer Bachus had just blown up the deal. Bachus had put out a statement saying he had not been authorized to cut any deals and that that morning there had been "no agreement other than to continue discussions."

Bachus later insisted to me that he had been acting on orders from Boehner, who must have understood that any agreement that was not supported by a critical mass of House Republicans was doomed to failure.

Barney wanted me to speak with Nancy Pelosi; the three of us got on the phone, and the two Democrats reamed me about Bachus. They basically wanted to know how they could get anything done with, as they said, Republicans behaving that way.

Meantime, the Republican leaders of both houses, John Boehner and Mitch McConnell, had been putting out statements asserting that there had been no agreement on a deal with the Democrats.

None of this confusion and contentiousness boded well for the upcoming meeting at the White House.

Joel Kaplan asked me to meet with President Bush before the bipartisan gathering in the Cabinet Room. The three of us stood on the terrace outside the president's private dining room, and I watched George Bush chew on an unlit cigar on that damp, chilly afternoon. I told him of my exchange with McCain, and I saw a trace of a smile on his lips. He said that it was good that I had been firm. We were playing for big stakes. He said he sure hoped McCain knew what he was doing. As always, he tried to reassure me.

"Hank, we are going to get this done," he promised. "There has to be some way Boehner can work this, and maybe I can help with the House Republicans."

Any hope that conversation gave me was quickly shot down when we walked into the Oval Office, where GOP leaders had gathered. Everyone was trying to be cooperative. McConnell said we had to try to make this happen. But Boehner said nothing had changed; he didn't have the votes.

"We need to get there," the president said, pressing him.

"I'm trying," Boehner said, reflecting his caucus's reluctance. "I don't have the support."

All along Boehner had said he couldn't deliver the votes, and now it looked like he was falling down on the job. I think he blamed me for putting him in this position. He wouldn't speak to me again until October 3, when Congress finally approved TARP.

From the Oval Office we walked down the short corridor to the Cabinet Room to join the Democratic leadership, Obama, and McCain. It was quite an august group that had been assembled to hash out a solution to the financial crisis. Arrayed around the oval mahogany table with the president, the vice president, McCain, Obama, and me were the members of the House and Senate leadership: Reid and McConnell, Pelosi and Boehner, Dodd and Shelby, Frank and Bachus, Durbin and Hoyer. Staffers filled the chairs lined up along the walls and in front of the French doors that opened out onto the Rose Garden.

The president started the meeting by saying that we had a common objective and that we needed to work together to act as quickly as possible to reach our goal. As he spoke, I felt a sharp foreboding as I surveyed this group of politicians who represented disparate interests and were in some cases uncompromising in their positions. The president asked me to speak, and I once again described the dire conditions in the market and the need for emergency powers. When I finished, the president said he had a simple test for making a decision on this: "If Hank Paulson and Ben Bernanke say it's going to work and help stabilize the financial system, we are for it."

By protocol, the president turned to call on the Speaker of the House. And when Pelosi spoke, it was clear the Democrats had done their homework and had planned a skillful response for McCain. Pelosi said that Obama would represent the Democrats, who, she pointed out, had been working with me in good faith to formulate a deal. Harry Reid agreed that Obama would speak for the Democrats.

Then Obama delivered a thoughtful, well-prepared presentation, sketching the broad outlines of the problem and stressing the need for immediate action. He said the Democrats had been working closely with me; he ran through the rough terms of the morning's discussion on the Hill, then mentioned the need for adjustments on oversight and executive compensation, as well as help for homeowners. He spoke without notes—much less a teleprompter—and spoke eloquently. "The Democrats will deliver the votes," he asserted.

Then he sprang the trap that the Democrats had set: "Yesterday, Senator McCain and I issued a joint statement, saying in one voice that this is no time to be playing politics. And on the way here, we were on the brink of a deal. Now, there are those who think we should start from scratch. . . . If we are indeed starting over, the consequences could well be severe."

But, of course, there was no deal yet. Bachus had been maneuvered into giving credibility to the appearance of one. But he, Boehner, and McConnell had since issued statements disclaiming the idea that there ever had been a deal.

Now Obama and the Democrats were skillfully setting up the story line that McCain's intervention had polarized the situation and that Republicans were walking away from an agreement. It was brilliant political theater that was about to degenerate into farce.

Skipping protocol, the president turned to McCain to offer him a chance to respond: "I think it's fair that I give you the chance to speak next."

But McCain demurred. "I'll wait my turn," he said. It was an incredible moment, in every sense. This was supposed to be McCain's meeting—he'd called it, not the president, who had simply accommodated the Republican candidate's wishes. Now it looked as if McCain had no plan at all—his idea had been to suspend his campaign and summon us all to this meeting. It was not a strategy, it was a political gambit, and the Democrats had matched it with one of their own.

Boehner, who had just gotten through telling us in the Oval Office that he didn't have the votes, said he was trying to find a way to get House Republicans on board. "I am not talking about a totally new deal, but we do need to tweak the core part of the program," he said.

He raised the idea of including Cantor's unformed insurance

plan. Obama asked me if it was consistent with what we were trying to do elsewhere, and I said it wasn't.

Decorum started to evaporate as the meeting broke into multiple side conversations with people talking over each other. Shelby waved a sheaf of papers, claiming they were from more than 100 economists who all thought TARP was a bad idea. He said we needed time to consider this plan. The president jumped in to say, "No, this is a situation where we need to act. We don't have time to have hearings with a bunch of economists."

McCain still hadn't spoken. Finally, raising his voice over the din, Obama said loudly, "I'd like to hear what Senator McCain has to say, since we haven't heard from him yet."

The room went silent and all eyes shifted to McCain, who sat quietly in his chair, holding a single note card. He glanced at it quickly and proceeded to make a few general points. He said that many members had legitimate concerns and that I had begun to head in the right direction on executive pay and oversight. He mentioned that Boehner was trying to move his caucus the best he could and that we ought to give him the space to do that. He added he had confidence the consensus could be reached quickly. As he spoke, I could see Obama chuckling.

McCain's comments were anticlimactic, to say the least. His return to Washington was impulsive and risky, and I don't think he had a plan in mind. If anything, his gambit only came back to hurt him, as he was pilloried in the press afterward, and in the end, I don't believe his maneuver significantly influenced the TARP legislative process.

A number of people I respect on the Hill have a different view. They believe McCain ended up being helpful by focusing public attention on TARP and galvanizing Congress to action. And John later did try to find ways for House Republicans to support legislation. But Democrats absolutely did not want him to get any credit. They

wanted the economic issue as their own. Accusing McCain of blowing up a nondeal was just hardball political tactics. But when it
came right down to it, he had little to say in the forum he himself
had called.

Then Spencer Bachus chimed in to say that while he and House
Republicans had not endorsed a deal, he was proud that House
Republicans had been successful in including strong taxpayer protections. Pelosi jumped in, insisting vociferously that House Democrats were responsible for the taxpayer protections, not House
Republicans. They began speaking over each other, as the president tried to restore order, and before long Pelosi and Bachus
were yelling at each other. The room descended into chaos as the
House and Senate members erupted into full-fledged shouting
around the table. Frank started to loudly bait McCain, who sat
stony-faced.

"What's the Republican proposal?" he pressed. "What's the Republican plan?"

It got so ridiculous that Vice President Cheney started laughing.
Frankly, I'd never seen anything like it before in politics or business—or in my fraternity days at Dartmouth, for that matter.

Finally, the president just stood up and said: "Well, I've clearly
lost control of this meeting. It's over."

As everyone left the room, I was appalled and disheartened. Not
only had I witnessed conduct I could never have imagined before,
but we didn't even have a deal. If anything, people seemed further
apart than before.

The Democrats had gathered in the Roosevelt Room and I became concerned that they would say something inflammatory to
the press when they left. So I decided to approach them and urge
moderation.

Everyone was huddled around Obama at the west end of the

room, and when they saw me there was an uproar. They shouted at me to leave. I didn't know what to do. Then, in an attempt at levity, I walked over to Pelosi and dropped to my knees, genuflecting at the altar of the Speaker of the House.

"Nancy," I started to say.

She burst out laughing. "Gee, Hank, I didn't know you were Catholic."

"Don't blow this up," I said. It had been a difficult meeting, I acknowledged, but we all needed to come together.

"We're not the ones trying to blow this up," she said.

CHAPTER 13

Friday, September 26, 2008

The run on Wachovia began Friday morning, September 26. The North Carolina bank had been struggling for months, but once the FDIC had seized WaMu the day before, traders began treating Wachovia as if it were next in line to fall. Overnight its credit default swaps soared, and loyal institutional and corporate customers fled, emptying transaction accounts. By day's end, $5 billion would be gone and shares of the bank would fall by 27 percent, to $10.

The collapse of WaMu was awful, but Wachovia was another order of magnitude altogether. With branches all over the country, from California to the Carolinas and up through the Northeast, it was the fourth-largest bank in the U.S. by assets, and the third by domestic deposits. Wachovia had grown rapidly through acquisitions. One of those purchases had proven to be its undoing: Golden West Financial, a big California savings and loan stuffed with option adjustable-rate mortgages. Wachovia had bought the thrift in 2006 at the peak of the housing boom.

With Wachovia's long-term customers pulling their money, we at Treasury knew it was only a matter of time before it failed. That was unthinkable; our financial system could not have withstood its demise. But I had decided to keep at a distance from any negotiations. My former colleague Bob Steel had left in July to steer Wachovia through this crisis, and he would be breaking the law if he talked to me or anyone at Treasury on behalf of his bank.

I had reviewed Wachovia's plight with Tim Geithner early in the morning, and it was very much on my mind at my regularly scheduled Friday breakfast with Ben Bernanke at the Fed. We were optimistic that Wells Fargo or Citigroup would step up and buy Wachovia. If not, the regulators had the necessary powers to deal with a failing bank, although I was confident that everyone understood the necessity of avoiding such an outcome.

I was still mulling over the strange events of the previous day, and what they might mean for TARP. After the disastrous Cabinet Room meeting, I had wondered if we'd ever get lawmakers to agree. It was a good thing, as Obama had said when we spoke by phone late Thursday evening, that the public hadn't seen the indecorous partisan brawling, or there would have been no confidence left in the market.

Yet some good had come from that difficult day. As Ben had told me the night before, "I don't know what you said to McCain, but whatever it was, it's working. He's now saying all the right things."

I had also seen the beginnings of a bipartisan spirit at work on Thursday evening in a crowded, closed-door negotiating session on the Hill. We'd gone there after the Cabinet Room debacle, determined to make progress. The meeting was surprisingly productive, and I had left mildly optimistic.

But with WaMu's collapse and the run on Wachovia, it was clear that the markets weren't going to pause to see how TARP made out before punishing their next victim. Banks had stopped lending to one another, and the money markets remained all but frozen.

John McCain called midmorning. He sounded upbeat though apologetic about the previous day's fracas. "Boy, what a difficult meeting," he said. "The reason I didn't say anything at the end was because it's pretty hard to say anything with Barney Frank screaming at you."

McCain struck a positive note, saying that the House Republicans were willing to talk if some of their ideas—he stressed the insurance plan in particular—were considered. "We need to come up with some way to let them get something," he said.

Still, McCain had put himself in a sticky spot. The first presidential debate was scheduled for that night, and the Obama campaign appeared to have outmaneuvered John. When he'd suspended his campaign on Wednesday, McCain had called for the debate to be postponed to focus on cutting a rescue package deal. Obama had refused, scoring points by questioning why someone who wanted to be president couldn't manage to both negotiate a compromise and run a campaign. Shortly after we spoke, McCain's team announced that he would fly down to Oxford, Mississippi, for the debate.

All day I worked the phones, talking with Senate and House leaders, trying to get some traction on the issues in dispute while a Treasury team entered into a negotiating and drafting session with staff from multiple congressional committees. Wachovia's shares fell relentlessly while its credit default swaps more than doubled to 1,560 basis points. Morgan Stanley moved back into the danger zone: its CDS had soared past the 1,000-basis-point mark.

I caught only part of the first presidential debate that night, but I was pleased to see that neither Obama nor McCain tried to score political points at TARP's expense. Maybe, I hoped, the polarized parties would be able to come together long enough to do what was needed to save the system.

Saturday, September 27, 2008

I had planned to return to Treasury early Saturday morning, but Kevin Fromer told me to stay home. "Rest up," he said. "We've got to narrow the open issues down and get the agreements on paper." He was certain that however rough it might still be, we had the makings of, as he said, "a piece of legislation." His self-assurance rubbed off on me.

I was working in the sitting area of my bedroom when Nancy Pelosi phoned to raise a potentially contentious issue. The Speaker didn't like the idea of taxpayers' being on the hook for any part of this bailout, and she suggested taxing the financial industry so the government could get back any money it spent. This was the first I'd heard of this idea, but I could tell Nancy wasn't trying to complicate the negotiations—clearly, she was having trouble with her caucus. But there was no way that the markets would accept her proposal. It would be like trying to save and punish someone at the same time. I told her I strongly disagreed with her idea but that I would work with her to find a solution. I hung up confident that we could do just that.

We were scheduled to work through the major open issues with congressional leaders that afternoon, but both the composition of the group and a free-for-all format spelled trouble. The key to legislation is getting the right people in the room. I wanted to keep it small and simple, and the Republicans agreed to send one representative from each chamber. But Senate Democrats were clamoring to be involved, and House Democrats also wanted their key players on hand. As the Banking Committee chair, Chris Dodd was the lead Senate negotiator. But Max Baucus wanted to weigh in on compensation; an increasingly assertive Chuck Schumer was taking the lead on TARP tranching; chairman of the Senate Budget Committee Kent Conrad was focused on oversight and insurance; and Rhode Island senator Jack Reed pushed the Democrats' idea of taking equity warrants in companies that sold illiquid assets.

We arrived at the Dirksen Senate Office Building at about 2:00 p.m. and gathered in the vice president's office for last-minute preparations before we headed up to Nancy Pelosi's conference room and that same long table where, little more than a week before, Ben Bernanke, Chris Cox, and I had made our case for quick congressional action. Kevin Fromer, Neel Kashkari, Bob Hoyt, and I sat between Judd Gregg and Roy Blunt, the lead negotiators on the Republican side, facing House and Senate Democrats. Perhaps 30 staff members lined the walls.

Mitch McConnell had put Gregg in charge of Senate GOP negotiations when Richard Shelby elected to sit out the debate. It was a fortunate, and inspired, choice. Judd was a respected New Hampshire conservative who possessed one of the sharpest minds in the Senate, knew the issues cold, and was a superb negotiator; he commanded the respect of Senate Republicans. He understood that the system was endangered and wanted results. Roy Blunt had taken Spencer Bachus's place at the table, and this, too, pleased me. The Missouri congressman was a careful listener with a smooth manner, who would do a good job of representing House Republicans. Like Gregg, he knew we needed to get something done.

Chris Dodd opened with remarks about the importance of bipartisanship. I began by noting the increasing length of the proposed legislation and made clear we would not accept a bill that couldn't work. The three-page outline we had sent up to the Hill had turned into a 40-page bill under Dodd and Barney Frank the previous weekend. Now it was more than 100 pages.

"We want to adopt something that works, but there is resistance within our caucuses," Barney said diplomatically. He represented House Democrats, along with Rahm Emanuel. Charlie Rangel also attended.

It didn't take long for the meeting to start getting out of hand. There were frequent interruptions, and people seemed unwilling to negotiate. We began with a contentious issue: executive compensation. Baucus and Frank were the main proponents of the Democratic view, but everyone had an opinion. Some, like Baucus, wanted to limit tax deductibility on the executives' pay. Others wanted to be able to claw back compensation that was awarded on the basis of inaccurate financial statements. Schumer led the attack on golden parachutes, those generous payouts often given to fired or retiring executives.

I wasn't about to defend golden parachutes, but we needed a solution that worked. Our priority was to buy assets quickly from as many banks as possible. To help make that happen, we wanted clear, easy-to-execute rules that would encourage participation. So I pushed to exempt smaller institutions from the rules while resisting the more complex compensation formulations that might deter bigger banks or be difficult to execute. I thought our stand made sense: we had been tough so far, forcing the CEOs of Fannie Mae and Freddie Mac to leave without their golden parachutes. By contrast, the Democrats were understandably looking for something that they could trumpet to reduce the political backlash they saw coming.

Two nights before, Chris Dodd had run an orderly meeting, and we'd made real progress on many thorny issues. This meeting, however, was becoming increasingly loud and chaotic. Soon, perhaps in frustration at my stance—or just to be heard above the din—Baucus began yelling at me.

"Hank, you're alone on executive comp. I'm not one to threaten, but you have to listen."

We got word from outside the room that the press was already reporting on the scene inside. It was outrageous. Here I was dealing with a room full of Senate Democrats competing with one another to pound on me, while their staffers leaked to their press contacts, oblivious as to how that might affect the markets we were trying to save. We complained, and Rahm Emanuel acted quickly, confiscating the staff members' BlackBerrys. It reminded me of the Old West, where everyone had to check their guns in at the saloon.

Rahm was looking for a solution, and he bluntly summed up the dilemma on executive compensation. "You need your market to work, and we need ours to work," he said. "Golden parachutes are a problem."

Rahm was right, as was Kent Conrad, who added, "We need something to go back and sell on executive comp."

But there were too many competing voices to make progress. There was a similarly wide range of opinion on oversight matters, as well. Baucus wanted an inspector general specifically for TARP. Others wanted a congressional overseer; Conrad was pushing a Financial Stability Oversight Board, comprising me, Ben Bernanke, Chris Cox, Jim Lockhart, and HUD Secretary Steve Preston. We debated how closely this board would be involved in day-to-day activities. Everyone conceded that there were too many oversight bodies being proposed, but no one wanted to give up his favorite.

"We trust you," Conrad assured me. "This isn't aimed at you personally. We need more oversight."

"I welcome it," I responded. In fact, I thought strong oversight would protect TARP, and I was fine with Conrad's idea of a board, although I pointed out that it ought to be consultative. If it got involved in micromanaging executive decisions, nothing would get done. "Let's get oversight that works," I said.

I wish now that I'd put my foot down and insisted on dropping one of those redundant oversight bodies, if only to save taxpayers money and make the program more workable. We would end up getting them all, and TARP was already under the eye of the Treasury's existing inspector general's office—not to mention the Government Accountability Office (GAO), Congress's investigative arm, as well as numerous congressional committees.

In the middle of the meeting, House members had to leave to vote on a nuclear cooperation agreement between the U.S. and India. (It passed.) The senators, meanwhile, probed the specifics of the TARP plan, pressing on the $700 billion figure. How did we arrive at that number? I said it was the best estimate we could come up with, and the market would accept no less.

When the House members returned, we turned to the stickiest issue of the afternoon: the timing of the release of the TARP money. The Democrats were fairly certain Obama would win the election, and they didn't want the Bush Treasury to be able to use all the money. They wanted to give us $250 billion or $300 billion and leave the new administration a say over the rest.

Chuck Schumer didn't believe Congress would be willing to give the Bush administration $700 billion. I told him the markets needed to know the money was available, but he didn't seem convinced. Treating our back-and-forth like a run-of-the-mill negotiation, he kept saying, "You probably won't be able to use more than $100 billion." I was trying hard to communicate with this group, and they with me, but we couldn't seem to break through to one another, and tensions were rising.

I asked what would happen if we urgently needed more funds and didn't have time to go back to Congress to ask for them. Barney quipped, "Then you'll go back to Uncle Ben." His one-liner broke the tension and gave us all a much-needed laugh.

Then Schumer said: "If you need more than $350 billion before January 20, you'll use the Fed or call us back and ask for more."

"You're raising a congressional concern, but we need to protect the American people from financial disaster," I said. "Geithner, Bernanke, and Warren Buffett will say your way won't work."

"You keep asserting that, but I don't hear persuasive reasons. Explain to us why," Max Baucus said.

I described again the terrible state of the markets. It was clear to me that we would need at least as much money as we were asking for and that it was crucial we send an unambiguous signal to the markets that the funds would be available unimpeded by any political concerns.

After a couple of hours, we broke for dinner, without having made progress on a single issue. Dodd wanted to return to this bargaining format later, but once away, I didn't want to go back. In truth, the meeting seemed like a setup: these weren't negotiations, they were just arguments. We were getting nowhere on the release of TARP money, and I felt that we were getting beaten up by a leaderless group of posturing Democratic senators. The fact that they had suggested that this same group should reconvene later meant to me that they either didn't want, or didn't know how, to reach a deal. We needed to break the logjam.

We adjourned to John Boehner's conference room. I called Pelosi, Obama, and Reid, who was out of the building. There were just too many cooks in the kitchen, I said. The compensation proposals were unreasonable, and I believed they would backfire. I told Obama that his guys were blowing the negotiations, seemingly trying to one-up each other. He told me he would talk with Chris

Dodd, then called me back about 45 minutes later to tell me that Dodd was optimistic that there had been progress.

A few days earlier, Obama had said to me, in one of our frequent calls, "Hank, I intend to be president, and I don't want to preside over an economic wasteland. So let me know if we ever get to the point that I need to step in." With TARP—and the safety of the financial system—on the line, I believed we had reached that point and I told him so. "These negotiations are a disaster," I said. "The Senate Democrats aren't taking them seriously. They don't seem to understand the gravity of the situation." I learned later that Obama called Harry Reid, who joined the negotiations later that evening.

My team and I decided to approach Barney Frank, who understood how important it was for TARP to be approved and that we would need GOP votes to get it done. Dan Meyer and Kevin Fromer found him on the third floor having dinner with his partner, Jim Ready, and asked him to meet with us.

Barney said he thought the two sides had been making progress, but when Dan and Kevin explained our view that it would be counterproductive to restart the previous meeting, he agreed to come to Boehner's office to meet with me.

The discussion with Barney was much more productive than the afternoon session. With Keith Hennessey and Judd Gregg, we tackled the issue of tranching and quickly reached a breakthrough on the release of funds. Congress would release an initial $250 billion that could be increased to $350 billion if the president certified to Congress that it was necessary. To release the remaining $350 billion, Treasury would have to submit a report to Congress with details of its plans for the money. If Congress did nothing, the money would be released automatically after 15 days. To withhold the funds, Congress would have to pass legislation denying the release, then override a presidential veto.

Building on that success, we decided to try a new strategy for the night. We would separate the Democrats, treat each like a king, and hammer away in private on individual issues. We began a night of shuttle diplomacy. Negotiators crisscrossed the elegant marble expanse of the Capitol's National Statuary Hall, once the meeting place of the House, to reach Boehner's personal office, where we had set up our base.

While we were on Capitol Hill negotiating, FDIC and Fed officials were scrambling, as they had been all day, to find a buyer for Wachovia. The big bank was going down, and as I said to Judd Gregg during a break in the talks: "We're doing this, but I can't help thinking about Wachovia." I knew that Wells Fargo and Citi had emerged as leading contenders for the North Carolina bank. Just before 8:00 p.m., I spoke to Sheila Bair to find out what was happening. She was optimistic, but nothing was going to be announced that day. Like Tim Geithner, she thought Wells Fargo was the most likely buyer.

Rahm Emanuel, playing a hugely constructive role, rushed back and forth between Pelosi and us on the industry tax issue, which we knew would defeat the point of our intervention. Charging the industry for the cost to the government of buying bad assets would only saddle banks with the very losses we knew they couldn't bear. Rahm obviously didn't like the idea, either. But when he tried to reach a compromise with us, a Pelosi staff member said no. At one point Rahm thought we were going to have to give in, and he tried to go around me to Josh Bolten, who told him the White House wouldn't undercut me. We held firm.

At times, it felt like a three-ring circus that night, as senators, representatives, and staffers ducked in and out of meetings to hash out their differences. Some crowded into the narrow corridors outside of Boehner's or Pelosi's offices. As it got later, Boehner's office all but turned into a pizza parlor. Just about everyone seemed to be eating a slice: plain, pepperoni, sausage, anchovy. I had never seen so many greasy cardboard boxes in my life.

Though tired, members and their staffs drove themselves hard. Clever retooling of language helped us bridge the gap between Democrats and Republicans on the proposed plan to insure bad assets. That was no easy matter. Kent Conrad had earlier called it "the worst idea ever." But Barney Frank opened the door to a compromise by saying, "If a plan is acceptable to the secretary, the House Democrats will support it."

We got to work on it. House Republicans wanted to be for something other than our approach. They insisted that we not only include the authority for insurance in the bill, but that we put an actual plan in place. But Conrad threatened to kill TARP if it included a workable insurance program, which he feared would saddle the government with huge unknown liabilities. Republicans wanted the law to require us to implement an insurance program.

We didn't think the insurance idea was terrible, per se. It had just not been thought through. House Republicans asked us to draft the language, and Neel Kashkari explained to their staff the different ways you could price and score the insurance: you could limit it to $700 billion worth of assets, less premiums received, or you could limit it to $700 billion worth of premiums, which would be a very powerful program capable of insuring trillions of dollars in assets. Republicans chose to limit it to covering $700 billion in assets, aiming to protect the taxpayers through the premiums collected on the insurance.

Our compromise was to word the bill to require Treasury to set the insurance premium at a level that would ensure that "taxpayers are fully protected." In other words, we would have to price the insurance at such an expensive rate that no one would use it. I explained how this language would work to Conrad and he was comfortable with it.

Harry Reid, responding to my earlier calls to him and to Obama about the lack of progress, had returned to the Capitol later that evening and spent time alone with Nancy Pelosi. Shortly after 11:00

p.m. the principal negotiators reconvened in the Speaker's office, having worked out our major differences, with two exceptions. One was Nancy's industry tax; the other was executive compensation. It was late and everyone was tired, but Nancy pushed us all to compromise.

"We can't leave here," she said. "The American people expect a deal. The markets expect a deal."

Judd Gregg stayed to work on the tax with Nancy, Rahm, and Barney Frank, and the trio of Democrats agreed to his idea of making the language open-ended: if after five years of TARP taxpayers ended up behind, then the president at that time could propose that Congress enact a tax to have the industry pay for any losses generated by the program. We knew this would not unsettle the markets, which would see the provision as toothless.

Neel Kashkari and I met with Schumer, Dodd, and Baucus in Nancy's conference room to find a solution for the impasse over executive pay. Schumer had been pushing to force banks to retroactively cancel all their golden parachute contracts. We said that was practically impossible. Finally, Schumer suggested, "What about no 'new' golden parachutes?" We hadn't thought of that option, and we all took a break to discuss it.

Exhausted, I went back to the small office I was using and had a bout of the dry heaves in front of Judd Gregg. I wasn't that sick, but I made a lot of noise, which seemed to galvanize Rahm Emanuel.

"We need to get everyone back together again and get this thing done," he said.

Harry Reid came in and asked if I needed a doctor. I said no, I was just tired. It was around midnight, and I was sitting down and talking with Neel and Kevin Fromer when Schumer, Baucus, and Dodd entered the office. We agreed to Baucus's provision to cap tax deductions on executive pay above $500,000 and to ban new golden parachutes for executives of failed companies. We took care to specify that firms needing special assistance should have tougher compensation restrictions than firms that were simply participating in TARP-related sales of assets. Neel grabbed a sheet of Nancy's letterhead stationery, wrote out the basics of our agreement, and later made copies for everyone.

Finally, we had the framework of a deal: workable language on tranching; compensation restrictions for the executives of companies participating in TARP; multiple levels of oversight that nonetheless allowed us flexibility to act effectively; a provision for the government to receive warrants that could be converted into the stocks of participating companies; and a vague nod at recoupment through a potential industry tax. The language would be finalized that night, and the House would vote on the bill on Monday.

In a celebratory mood, Pelosi, Reid, Dodd, Frank, Schumer, and I walked together to Statuary Hall to announce the deal. As we approached a bank of microphones set up amid the marble images of famous Americans, Schumer put his arm around me, and I put my arm around him. Although I took this as a sign of camaraderie, he later told the press that he had had to steady me. I must have looked very tired.

I was pleased with our progress, but while I felt some relief, I knew that as yet nothing was finished. We still had to design the program, hire people, implement it, and do all of this in time to help the market. But things seemed better than they had in weeks. TARP was moving along, and Wachovia looked like it would soon be in new, safer hands.

Perhaps I should have foreseen the problems ahead, but for a moment that night, as I fell asleep, I just felt good.

Sunday, September 28, 2008

When I rose a few hours later, I learned that Wells Fargo chairman Dick Kovacevich had spoken that morning over breakfast with Bob

Steel and wanted to buy Wachovia outright. Wells appeared to be willing to pay a price above the market, which surprised me, considering the dire circumstances surrounding Wachovia. I was hopeful a deal could be reached by the end of the day. Wells was a rare exception in an industry littered with struggling banks. Although Wells had taken losses on credit cards and mortgages, it had maintained high lending standards when its competitors relaxed theirs. As a result, it was in a relatively strong position.

Meanwhile, up on the Hill, Kevin Fromer, Bob Hoyt, and Neel Kashkari were working against the clock to negotiate the many remaining details and turn them into legislative text. Getting the language just right was our most important task.

On Sunday evening I asked Ben Bernanke to make calls to help me drum up support for TARP from the House Republicans. I thought they were getting tired of hearing my voice—and of hearing the Democrats praise me. People had told me that Ben and the president might be more effective. The president gladly pitched in, but the exercise would prove very discouraging to him, because most of those he called ended up voting no. Ben had much the same experience with his list.

That night I briefed the president and Josh Bolten on Wachovia. I told them that I was cautiously optimistic that Wells would buy Wachovia, but noted that without a buyer, the bank would fail unless it received government support. The weakened market needed us to stand behind our major institutions.

I explained that for the first time in U.S. history, the government might have to invoke the imminent danger of systemic risk to bail out a bank. By law the FDIC could provide financial assistance to failing banks and thrifts as long as whatever method it used—a loan, say, or a cash contribution—cost less than outright liquidation. Congress had wanted to make sure that shareholders of these troubled institutions did not benefit from taxpayer money, and the FDIC Improvement Act of 1991 allowed only one way around the "least cost" requirement: if the FDIC believed that the institution's failure would seriously hurt the economy or financial stability, it could invoke the "systemic risk" exception. Doing so required the approval of the Treasury secretary (after consultation with the president), two-thirds of the Federal Reserve Board, and two-thirds of the FDIC's board of directors. Congress intended the exception to be used only in the most dire of circumstances, and it had never been invoked before.

Wachovia, however, was so large, and the system so fragile, that I knew the time had come, and I made this very clear. Josh replied that the administration was not afraid to make big decisions.

Before I went to bed, I had instructed my Treasury team to call me about a Wachovia deal regardless of the hour. I fell asleep without receiving news and awoke in the middle of the night, worried because I still hadn't heard anything. I spoke to my team the next morning, and what they told me took my breath away.

I had assumed Wells Fargo would be the buyer, but on Sunday it decided not to make an offer. Early that evening the government concluded it should invoke the systemic risk exception. Because I wasn't at Treasury, it fell to David Nason to get the president's approval to take this action for Wachovia, and at 11:00 p.m. David called Josh Bolten to do so.

The FDIC told Wachovia it was going to use its powers to provide open bank assistance and invited proposals from Citigroup and Wells. As it turned out, everyone was up all night as Sheila Bair went back and forth trying to get the Federal Reserve or Treasury to bear the risk of any losses resulting from any government assistance. Treasury staff carefully questioned the FDIC's assumptions in a series of conference calls. Wells finally came back in the wee hours with a very unattractive offer. By 4:00 a.m. FDIC staff concluded they expected no loss to the government under Citi's proposal. That ended the debate on loss sharing between government entities, and Sheila agreed to accept Citi's offer.

Monday, September 29, 2008

Early Monday morning, September 29, the FDIC announced that Citigroup would acquire Wachovia. All depositors would be protected. But unlike with the WaMu failure, all creditors would also be protected, a hugely important step that signaled to the markets the government's willingness to support our systemically important banks.

Under the terms of its complicated offer, Citi would pay $2.16 billion in stock and assume $53 billion of Wachovia's senior and subordinated debt. Wachovia would be split up, with its money management and stock brokerage arms left to shareholders in a stub company still called Wachovia. Citi would acquire the commercial and retail banking businesses and agree to absorb up to $42 billion in losses from Wachovia's $312 billion pool of loans. The FDIC would guarantee any remaining losses. In exchange, the FDIC would get $12 billion in Citigroup preferred stock and warrants, giving it a way to potentially recoup money for its fund.

Although the FDIC emphasized in a statement that Wachovia had not failed, the truth was that without intervention the big bank certainly would have collapsed. Many in Congress, however, didn't understand how precarious the situation was. All weekend as we had negotiated the fine points of TARP on the Hill, I had warned that another huge bank was about to go down. Now, even as we struggled to get $700 billion for the entire financial system, the FDIC had guaranteed nearly $300 billion worth of assets for one bank and no one had blinked an eye. We said, "It's urgent we get

TARP—look at Wachovia," and they said, "Wachovia was just acquired." They didn't seem to get it.

The news that poured out of the Markets Room on Monday about Europe's hard-pressed institutions proved unrelentingly bad. The U.K. seized lender Bradford & Bingley and sold most of it to Banco Santander, while giant Hypo Real Estate, Germany's number two commercial real estate lender, received a 35 billion-euro ($50 billion) guarantee from the government and a group of private banks. These actions followed Sunday's 11.2 billion-euro ($16.3 billion) bailout of the Belgian financial services firm Fortis by the governments of Belgium, Luxembourg, and the Netherlands.

European stocks dove, while credit markets deteriorated further. LIBOR-OIS spreads climbed to record levels. Banks continued to be afraid to deal with one another—a sure sign of panic.

Throughout the morning, I spoke with members of Congress who voiced their support for TARP while raising their own specific concerns. Maxine Waters, the Democratic congresswoman from California, called to push for minority hiring and to get reassurance that we would do something about foreclosures. I told her we would. "That's good," she replied, "because I'm going to vote for it. And if you don't come through, my ass is grass."

Despite the positive calls, I was getting reports that the bill wouldn't pass. House Minority Whip Roy Blunt warned me that he didn't have enough Republicans on board. Minutes before the vote started, Josh Bolten and Joel Kaplan told me that they weren't optimistic, either. We could only hope for the best.

When the voting began, I was shut in my office with Michele Davis and on the phone with Russian finance minister Alexei Kudrin. It was an odd time for a call, but Russia was an important investor in U.S. and GSE debt, and I knew I needed to assuage Kudrin's fears. He said he was starting to see signs that the banking crisis was spreading to Russia from Europe, and I could tell that his problems were much bigger than he was letting on. He was concerned about Friday's run on Wachovia and our rescue of the bank, and wanted to know more about TARP. He wasn't alone. Earlier I had spoken with Jean-Claude Trichet at the European Central Bank, and Saudi Arabian finance minister Ibrahim al-Assaf. Everyone hoped Congress would pass TARP to restore confidence. When I got off the phone, Michele started to prepare me for a postgame victory lap with the press.

"When this is done," she said, "you're going to need to walk out there and give a clear-eyed statement where you thank Congress for giving you this. You are going to need to emphasize that this isn't just about buying illiquid assets. This is about market confidence. Don't talk about mechanics."

I nodded. My key advisers came in and out of the office as the total of negative votes kept rising. Michele and Jim Wilkinson assured me that the nays usually went first, while the yeas held back. But the roll was called quickly, and well before 2:00 p.m. the nays had passed the 218 total that meant defeat. Michele told me not to worry: "The whips will get people to reverse themselves."

As the voting went on, Obama called to say, bluntly: "Hank, you're going down. Your guys aren't doing it. Your Republicans aren't doing what they're supposed to do."

I had never heard him sound so partisan.

"We need more Democrats," I said.

"From what I hear, there are only a few more. Even if I give you six or seven, it won't be enough."

It surprised me to hear Obama, normally calm and cool, sounding as agitated as I felt at that moment.

Next, I spoke with McCain, who said, "I'm doing everything I know how."

In the end, of course, TARP was voted down, by a margin of 228–205. Pelosi phoned to deliver the bad news, blaming the defeat on the Republicans, who didn't want to approve anything that looked like a bailout. Two-thirds of them had voted against TARP, compared with 40 percent of the Democrats. Republican leaders, including Boehner, blamed Pelosi for driving away GOP votes with a floor speech that had denounced the Bush administration's "right-wing ideology of anything goes." There was plenty of blame to go around, and neither side, unfortunately, fully understood the consequences of failure.

The camera crews waiting in the Media Room to conduct interviews with me were sent away. Instead, accompanied by Michele Davis and Jim Wilkinson, I walked over to the White House for a meeting with the president, the vice president, and key advisers. On the way, I called Roy Blunt to thank him for everything he had done. He was disappointed but said he wasn't going to give up; he was confident we could eventually get the votes. So was I, but nonetheless, it was a devastating defeat.

"Isn't there something we can do without this?" Vice President Cheney asked. Though a free-market advocate and highly skeptical of government intervention, he had understood from day one how essential our actions were. He was not content to sit back and watch the economic devastation that might result from congressional inaction. "Doesn't the Fed have some power? Don't we have some power?"

"No, we don't," I said.

"We'll figure out how to get it," the president said.

Josh Bolten took me aside and reassured me once more: "We'll get this done."

Before I returned to my office, I stepped out onto the White House lawn and spoke to the press. For once, I was less concerned about reassuring the markets than about delivering a strong message to Congress. "We've got much work to do," I said. "This is much too important to simply let fail."

My stomach sank when I returned to my office and looked at the Bloomberg terminal behind my desk. Stocks had begun the trading session down sharply, then gone into free fall as the vote mounted against TARP. The Dow had posted its largest one-day point decline ever, almost 778 points, or 7 percent, while the S&P 500 suffered an 8.8 percent drop, for its worst day since the October 1987 crash. Overall, more than $1 trillion in stock market value was wiped out—a jarring one-day record.

Though I often focused on what many people might consider the esoteric aspects of finance—commercial paper funding, credit default swap rates, or the triparty repo market—I cared deeply about the loss of value in the equity markets. It meant so much to the average citizens—to their retirement security and to their sense of confidence.

Credit market functions are crucial but somewhat abstract to most Americans. How often does anyone hear about LIBOR-OIS spreads on the evening news? But if credit stopped flowing, businesses would shut down across America and many, many jobs would be lost. It's like clogging the arteries of a human body. Soon critical functions become impaired, and then, with a heart attack, they cease suddenly.

That afternoon and evening, I talked with a number of people whose positive attitudes helped to buck me up. Lindsey Graham was particularly inspiring. "Hank," he said, "you have both presidential candidates supporting you in an election year. You have the support of the leadership in Congress. All you need is 13 more votes in the House. You need to project confidence publicly and privately."

That night I spoke again to Josh Bolten, who was already thinking of new approaches. "Hank, you've done what you can do," he told me. "Give me the ball for a few days, and let's see if we can corral the votes."

Tuesday, September 30, 2008

September 30 marked the Jewish holiday of Rosh Hashanah and the markets were open, but Congress was not in session. I woke up early and went to the gym for the first time since the day after Lehman fell. I felt out of shape, and as I attempted to follow my routine I tried hard not to dwell on the House defeat.

The markets were in great distress Tuesday. Overnight, LIBOR had jumped to 6.8 percent, more than double the week before and the highest level in years. The crisis was spreading rapidly through Europe. That morning the French-Belgian bank Dexia had become the fifth big European financial institution to succumb to a bailout or nationalization in the past two days. Governments around the world, from France to India and South Korea, were taking action to stabilize, and in some cases to prop up, their weakened financial institutions. Ireland said it would guarantee payments on as much as 400 billion euros ($574 billion) in bank debt. The figure guaranteed nearly the entire Irish banking system and amounted to twice the country's gross domestic product.

Almost every hour I got an update from Josh Bolten or Joel Kaplan about TARP's progress. They were feeling optimistic again. Rahm Emanuel had helped concoct a strategy with Harry Reid to push the legislation through the Senate first. Senate Republicans were more secure in their seats than their House counterparts and more sympathetic. Prepared to move boldly and quickly, Reid said he could schedule the vote as soon as the next day.

There were two options for getting TARP through the House on a second try. One was to assume that the Republicans would never sufficiently support the legislation and therefore try to win over as many Democratic votes as possible. And one way to get those votes might be to offer a second stimulus spending plan, as

Pelosi had once suggested. But doing that would drive away the Senate Republicans.

A second option was to try to gain broader support and attract Republicans by combining TARP with energy-related tax credits that were set to expire and a patch on the Alternative Minimum Tax, the unpopular levy that perennially had to be adjusted to protect the middle class from a tax increase. Other sweeteners included raising FDIC deposit insurance limits and addressing mark-to-market accounting in some way.

The leadership chose the second route and included these provisions. But, as Josh Bolten pointed out, one big reason some Republicans were proving more receptive was that they had gone home to find their constituents upset that TARP's failure had wiped out 10 percent of their retirement accounts—and they were blaming Congress for it. As a result, Monday's stock slide meant a lot more cooperation.

During this difficult time, Ben Bernanke told me that he thought that solving the crisis would demand more than the illiquid asset purchases we had asked for. In his view, we would have to inject equity capital into financial institutions. Dan Jester and Jeremiah Norton came to see me and made the same point. I agreed that they were probably right, but we had no plan in place, and the concept made me uncomfortable, even though we had been careful to make sure that TARP's language allowed it as an option. I was philosophically opposed to any action that might smack of nationalization—government interventions always come with some undesirable influence or control—and I also knew that we would sabotage our efforts with Congress if we raised our hands midstream and said we might need to inject equity. I believed that illiquid asset purchases would be the biggest part of whatever we did, and told Ben this.

Still, I had also talked with a number of investors I trusted, and they all told me the same thing: the system's problems were too big and immediate to be fixed by anything other than capital injections. I asked Dan, Jeremiah, and David Nason to give this some thought.

We had a meeting Tuesday morning and then a conference call to discuss raising the FDIC cap on insured deposits from $100,000 to $250,000 per account as part of the TARP sweeteners. We turned to another key issue—guaranteeing all bank transactional accounts—and picked it up again that afternoon in a conference call with Ben Bernanke, Tim Geithner, Kevin Warsh, Joel Kaplan, and David Nason.

This idea was being pushed by Larry Lindsey, a former economic adviser to the president and onetime Fed governor. To pay their bills, companies routinely kept sums of cash in their checking accounts that far exceeded the $100,000 FDIC insurance limit. That left them prone to pulling their money at the first sign of danger and, as with Wachovia, thereby fueling bank runs. We discussed the idea of unlimited guarantees to stabilize these accounts, but we worried that in the midst of a panic, foreign depositors would move their money to the U.S. to take advantage of this new protection, sparking retaliatory actions by other countries and weakening the global financial system.

None of us liked Lindsey's idea, and Tim, in particular, was concerned. He rightly noted that it could lead to all kinds of distortions. No one wanted to incite a harmful round of global "beggar thy neighbor" policies.

Despite such concerns, the idea of government guarantees to stabilize the banks was appealing: just announcing, as we had ten days before, that we would guarantee money funds had calmed that critical corner of the market.

"What you really need is for the president to get the authority to guarantee any liabilities for financial institutions," Tim said. He was probably right about this bold idea, but those of us dealing with Congress knew it would be impossible to get it approved. We were having enough difficulty winning temporary authority to invest in assets.

Later Tuesday afternoon, during another conference call, Sheila Bair weighed in. The FDIC chair also worried about the destabilizing impact of big transaction accounts' leaving banks—after all, that was exactly what had happened to Wachovia—and she, too, strongly supported the idea of an unlimited transaction account guarantee.

Before the Senate took up TARP the next morning, the administration pressed for and received an increase in deposit insurance to $250,000.

Wednesday, October 1, 2008

On Wednesday, I joined Ben for his monthly lunch with the president. There was no agenda, and we spent much of the meeting talking about TARP's legislative prospects and the fragile markets. I always told President Bush what was on my mind, and that day I said that even though Congress had not yet approved the asset-buying plan, Ben and I were beginning to think we might also need a program that would let us take direct equity stakes in financial institutions.

"You're still going ahead with your illiquid asset purchase plan?" the president asked.

"Of course," I said, adding, though, that we might have to move more quickly to stabilize the financial system.

President Bush knew that we weren't exaggerating. Since September 18, when we had first presented our plan to buy toxic assets to him, the markets had deteriorated badly—far worse, and on a far wider scale, than any of us could have imagined.

Harry Reid pulled out all the stops in the Senate to get TARP approved on Wednesday night, October 1. Emphasizing the gravity of the occasion, he required all senators to vote while in their seats, and the bill, which was sweetened with tax extenders, energy provisions, and a mental health parity bill, passed by a solid bipartisan margin of 74 to 25.

With Senate approval, TARP's success now depended once again on the House, where Barney Frank was working hard to push things along. To win Democratic votes, he pressed us to do something about homeowner relief. We were committed to foreclosure mitigation and pointed out that to the extent we bought illiquid assets we'd have more leverage in working with banks to that end. But I declined to give Barney a letter he requested explaining our position that he could use to reassure his caucus. There wasn't much I could say in writing that I hadn't said all along, and I was concerned a letter would annoy House Republicans, who opposed foreclosure mitigation, and end up costing us more votes than we gained.

Thursday, October 2–Friday, October 3, 2008

Even as we pushed to gain House support, we got hit with a surprise when the Wachovia deal with Citi was suddenly thrown into doubt. I had heard from Ken Wilson that Wells might enter the picture again, and I had given Sheila and others a heads-up. Then on Thursday afternoon, while I was running on the treadmill at the gym, Ken phoned to tell me it was definite: Wells had called to say it was going to make a new offer for Wachovia. Wells had determined it would reap significant tax benefits from the deal.

"They're coming in," he said.

"Ken, first of all, they shouldn't be coming to us, they should go to the Fed. I don't want them calling me directly. Second, they jacked around with us before. They missed their chance. This deal has already been announced."

"I'm just telling you that Wells Fargo is coming in, and as I understand it, they don't want any government money," Ken said. The bank was prepared to make a firm offer without any contingencies.

I stopped my workout and went to a small office in the gym. I quickly called Kevin Warsh, Tim Geithner, and Joel Kaplan to alert them to what had suddenly become an extraordinarily complex situation. Tim was furious. He believed that if the Wells proposal was accepted and the Citi agreement scrapped, it would undermine confidence in the government's ability to make deals and would potentially destabilize Citi. These were real concerns. I knew Citi had problems of its own. However, the Wells offer was better for taxpayers—it required no public money.

Later, back in the office, I spoke again with Kevin Warsh and said, "I've got to tell Sheila."

She hadn't yet heard the official news. I knew she would take the new offer seriously and do what she had to do, placing a high priority on reducing the cost to the government. But I reminded her that she needed to be careful: the Wachovia-Citi deal had already been announced, and Wells had walked once before. She thanked me, and the next thing I heard, Wachovia had a new deal—with Wells.

Later I met with Neel Kashkari, Jim Wilkinson, and Joel Kaplan to tell them that in anticipation of TARP's passing the next day, I was going to name Neel interim assistant Treasury secretary, in charge of running the new program. Though I was concerned that he might be perceived as just a junior Goldman Sachs banker who had come to Washington to work with me, naming him was an easy decision. Neel was well suited for the job: he was tough and brave, and knew how to get things done quickly.

On Thursday night, Wells Fargo made a bold offer of $15.4 billion that Wachovia's board accepted. Wells Fargo planned to keep Wachovia intact, and though it estimated that it would take lifetime losses of $74 billion on Wachovia's loan portfolio, it would seek no government assistance. To seal the deal, Wachovia issued Wells Fargo preferred stock worth 39.9 percent of its voting power.

The next morning, Citi responded with a statement saying that the transaction breached an exclusivity agreement Wachovia had signed the previous Sunday. Citi threatened to sue, but there was little that the Fed or the FDIC could do, as this was a private takeover and taxpayers were not at risk.

I had been exchanging calls with Tim, Sheila, and Kevin Warsh on the Wachovia situation when Nancy Pelosi called to say that although it had been a long fight, the prospect of TARP's passing the House on Friday looked good.

The Speaker was right. At 1:22 p.m. on a sunny autumn afternoon, the House passed the Emergency Economic Stabilization Act of 2008 by a margin of 263 to 171, with 91 Republicans voting for the legislation. The yes votes included 32 more Democrats and 26 more Republicans than the first vote had.

Indeed, it was remarkable that in the closing days of its session, one month away from a hotly contested national election, a Democratic-controlled Congress had responded so quickly to the pleas of an outgoing, and unpopular, administration for a combination of spending authorities and emergency powers that were unprecedented in their scope and flexibility.

For the rest of the day, I took a host of congratulatory calls, but they all came with the same warning: move fast. French finance minister Christine Lagarde jarred me when she emphasized how shaky the European markets were. Europe's banking problems had been building day by day. Ireland's decision earlier in the week to guarantee bank deposits had caused money to flee the U.K. for safer Irish accounts; on Friday, Britain was forced to raise the limit on its own deposit insurance. French president Nicolas Sarkozy was convening an emergency minisummit in Paris the next day to deal with the financial crisis.

There was no time to savor our legislative victory. At home TARP's passage failed to console the market: the Dow dropped 157 points, for a total of 818 points lost over the week.

Late on Friday, as I sat in my office, I told Michele Davis, "To put it mildly, I don't feel ecstatic." If anything, I believed we were still almost as vulnerable as when we first submitted TARP. The markets, after all, were much worse.

Acting on Michele's advice, I emphasized in my public comments that it would take time to put a comprehensive plan together and that we would still need to use the combined powers of all the regulators.

I needed time to think in a quiet setting, so Wendy and I had decided to get away for the weekend—my first respite in weeks. Before I left Treasury, I asked Neel to figure out how soon we could begin to buy the banks' toxic assets. And I made sure to tell Dan Jester and the rest of the team: "Figure out a way we can put equity in these companies."

Chapter 14

Friday, October 3, 2008

I flew out of Washington Friday at 4:00 p.m. for a weekend break, knowing only too well that the legislation signed by President Bush at 2:30 p.m. that afternoon had bought us little time. If anything, the financial markets and the economy were in worse shape than they had been before TARP's passage.

Congress and the markets expected immediate results, but it was going to take weeks to launch a program to buy toxic assets from banks. Since Monday, world financial markets had taken a drastic turn downward. European banks were teetering, the credit markets remained frozen—with the vital commercial paper business all but shut down—and stock prices had fallen sharply. The SEC's ban on short selling would expire in a few days. I had directed my team to craft a plan to provide capital to banks, but we didn't yet know how such a program might work.

No doubt about it, this would be a working weekend. But at least I would be working on Little St. Simons Island, one of my favorite places on earth. For 27 years Wendy and I, and our family, had come regularly to this narrow stretch of land off Georgia's Atlantic coast. It had changed little in that time. Never developed, its beautiful forests and marshes were blessed with an abundance of wildlife.

We touched down on neighboring St. Simons Island and drove five miles to the marina. Most folks traveled to Little St. Simons Island by motorboat—you can't reach it by car—but Wendy and I preferred to kayak, and we left Washington's concerns behind for an hour as we paddled the three and a half miles to the island, arriving just in time to see the sunset. Walking to our lodge through the refreshing salt air, Wendy assured me that I would sleep well that night, and I began to unclench a little. If nothing else, I had made it to the weekend.

Saturday, October 4–Sunday, October 5, 2008

The next morning at dawn I headed out with my fly rod and fishing gear to Bass Creek to catch some redfish. Standing in warm, knee-deep water, surrounded by shorebirds, I caught and released half a dozen redfish on a clouser minnow fly. I felt like myself for the first time in a long while—just Hank Paulson, out fishing.

But I was soon back to business. Tim Geithner called after I returned to the lodge and told me that we needed to make a strong, unequivocal public statement backing our financial institutions.

I agreed. But how could we do so in terms that the market would believe? The President's Working Group gave us an excellent platform, we decided. The Treasury, Federal Reserve, FDIC, and SEC could stand together and commit themselves to coordinated action in the crisis.

Tim and I set Treasury and New York Fed staff to work. We

wanted to outline clearly the powerful tools that government agencies now possessed to deal with the crisis, specifically highlighting the broad authorities—and deep pockets—granted Treasury by the TARP legislation, as well as the FDIC's ability to protect depositors and guarantee liabilities by invoking systemic risk, as it had with Wachovia.

All weekend, drafts of a statement moved back and forth. I managed to wedge in a little more fishing, but I spent three or four hours at a crack on calls with Ben Bernanke and Tim, and my team at Treasury.

I also kept a wary eye on the Citigroup–Wachovia–Wells Fargo triangle, discussing the increasingly complicated situation with Ben and Tim. Citi was demanding that Wells Fargo drop its $15.1 billion offer for Wachovia, claiming it breached Citi's own deal. News reports quoted Citi CEO Vikram Pandit as calling the deal illegal, so I assumed a lawsuit was forthcoming.

On the plus side, Wachovia, despite its abundant problems, had attracted two major banks and would be saved from failure. But one of those banks, Citi, had troubles of its own, having written down $19 billion of bad assets in the first six months of the year. We were concerned that Citi might be hurt if its deal with Wachovia disintegrated—and this time the institution under attack would be one of the biggest financial services companies in the world.

I flew back to Washington Sunday evening and got on a conference call with my staff about 7:00 p.m. Among other things, Dave McCormick filled us in on developments in Europe, and it was clear we needed to move fast on the PWG statement as well as on our capital and illiquid asset purchase programs.

Over the weekend, French president Nicolas Sarkozy's summit of European leaders had failed to produce the desired unity that would calm the markets. Quite the contrary: participants squabbled publicly over how far they should go to support their most important financial institutions. Then on Sunday night, continental time, while Germany arranged a $68 billion rescue for troubled lender Hypo Real Estate, Chancellor Angela Merkel had said her country would guarantee personal savings accounts, a proposal that by some calculations would have affected $1 trillion of savings.

Dave had been talking to his counterparts overseas, trying to get a grasp on the German situation. We hoped that Merkel's comment was just a "moral guarantee" intended to reassure her markets, not a hard, two-year guarantee like the one the Irish parliament had approved the previous week.

"This is going to move quick and force us to do some things we may or may not want to do," I said.

Monday, October 6, 2008

Usually when I got to Treasury in the morning, I stopped in the Markets Room. On Monday, though, I went straight to McCormick's office to check on Europe.

"Things are in complete disarray," he told me.

The U.K. was fuming. The British press was reporting that the country's financial officials were upset that Merkel had given no indication of her plans. The U.K. feared Merkel's "beggar thy neighbor" policy could cause a domino effect, potentially destabilizing banking systems across Europe as each country enacted its own guarantees to prevent money from leaving to seek safer havens. It wouldn't be long before we had to follow suit.

President Bush's deputy chief of staff Joel Kaplan echoed Dave's concerns when I spoke to him later that morning.

"Hank, it seems to me we're going to have to do something to match the Europeans," he said.

"You're probably right," I said.

That morning we released the PWG statement. We affirmed our commitment to coordinated forceful action, vowing to move with "substantial force on a number of fronts." Alluding to the FDIC authorities on Wachovia, we asserted that we would stand behind our systemically important institutions. Though the statement was intended to reassure the markets, it fell flat.

However, I'm not sure any statement would have made a difference that day. Asian and European markets plummeted in reaction to European banks' problems and concerns that TARP would not provide a quick enough fix in the U.S. Once our markets opened, the reports were equally frightening: the Dow fell sharply—in little more than an hour it was off 578 points, or 5.6 percent. The LIBOR-OIS spread would hit a near all-time high of 288 basis points before contracting slightly; a month earlier, it had stood at 81 basis points.

The disarray prompted the White House to debate whether President Bush should call a meeting of world leaders to tackle the crisis. I believed the key was to quickly find a solution to prevent a meltdown, but I did not think a summit was the way to do that— it could expose political divisions among countries, and this would further destabilize the markets. Over lunch on Monday I told Steve Hadley, Keith Hennessey, and Dan Price, the president's talented and energetic assistant for international economics affairs, that any such meeting with world leaders should be held after our presidential election, albeit as soon as possible.

"This crisis will only get worse before it gets better," I said.

Instead of meeting with his peers, I suggested President Bush call his fellow heads of state to urge them to send their finance ministers to the upcoming G-7 gathering ready to forge a solution. The International Monetary Fund and the World Bank were holding their annual get-togethers in Washington the next weekend. This meant that the G-20, which included representatives of both developed and emerging nations—including China, India, and Russia—would be in town. We decided to ask the chairman of the G-20, Brazilian finance minister Guido Mantega, to gather the group on Saturday.

On Monday I announced that Neel Kashkari would lead our TARP efforts as interim assistant Treasury secretary for financial stability. I made this an interim appointment because we were working to identify and vet permanent candidates acceptable to Obama and McCain.

Neel, who combined toughness with an engineer's precision, was doing a typically fine job building a staff and organizational structure to move things forward. That morning he and his team had finished a 40-page PowerPoint presentation, outlining a massive undertaking. He had teams working on everything from hiring asset managers to figuring out how to conduct the auctions.

Although the Dow rallied late on Monday, it ended up below 10,000 for the first time in four years. Worldwide, more than $2 trillion in stock market value had evaporated. The uncertainty surrounding the fight for Wachovia hurt all financials. Early in the day Citi had reacted to its jilting by filing a $60 billion lawsuit, but agreed midday to freeze the litigation until Wednesday. Wachovia dropped nearly 7 percent, while Citi fell more than 5 percent, and Wells Fargo almost 3 percent. Credit default swaps on Morgan Stanley hit 1,028 basis points.

After the close, Bank of America reported a 68 percent drop in earnings for the third quarter and announced plans to raise $10 billion in equity. I knew that the next day would bring a fresh attack on bank stocks.

Tuesday, October 7, 2008

Early Tuesday morning I walked to the White House for a conference call with President Bush and British prime minister Gordon Brown, who told us that his government planned to inject capital into U.K. banks. He wanted our support and promised to coordinate with us. Brown also told the president that he should consider gathering the leaders of the G-20 together to deal with the problem. The president took in that suggestion, but his first priority was to ensure a good G-7 finance ministers' meeting and come up with a coordinated plan of action.

Europe continued to suffer. Iceland, facing default on its obligations, had taken over two of its three largest banks and was negotiating a loan from Russia. Despite the country's small population of some 300,000, its commercial banks had expanded aggressively to the point where their assets were several times greater than Iceland's GDP. Now the entire country was caught in a liquidity squeeze, adding to the general jitters about Europe.

Something had to be done. The credit markets remained locked up, endangering businesses—and employment—around the world. On Tuesday, the Fed made another attempt to thaw the markets, unveiling its new Commercial Paper Funding Facility. The Fed's first venture into the commercial paper market had been directed toward asset-backed paper issued by financial institutions. This new approach created a special purpose vehicle to buy three-month paper from all U.S. issuers, vastly improving the liquidity in the market. The new facility represented a radical move by the Fed, but Ben Bernanke and his board knew that extraordinary measures had to be taken.

That afternoon I moved a capital program one step further when Neel, Dan Jester, and I met with President Bush and a large contingent of White House staff in the Roosevelt Room. I had kept the president and his people up to date on equity investments, so he wasn't surprised when presented with our thinking in greater detail.

From the start of the credit crisis, I had been focused on bank capital, encouraging CEOs to raise equity to strengthen their balance sheets. TARP had continued this focus. Banks were stuffed with toxic assets that they could unload only at fire-sale prices, which they were reluctant to do. By buying such assets at auction, we reasoned, we could jump-start the market, allowing banks to sell those bad assets in an orderly fashion, getting better prices and freeing up money to lend.

Initially, when we sought legislative flexibility to inject capital, I thought we might need it to save a systemically important failing institution. I had always opposed nationalization and was concerned about doing something that might take us down that path. But now I realized two crucial things: the market was deteriorating so quickly that the asset-buying program could not get under way fast enough to help. Moreover, Congress was not going to give us any more than the $700 billion we had, so we needed to make every dollar go far. And we knew the money would stretch much further if it were injected as capital that the banks could leverage. To oversimplify: assuming banks had a ten-to-one leverage ratio, injecting $70 billion in equity would give us as much impact as buying $700 billion in assets. This was the fastest way to get the most money into the banks, renew confidence in their strength, and get them lending again.

David Nason, Jeremiah Norton, and Dan Jester were working on a capital program, sorting through a variety of issues, from the type of instrument we might use to matters of pricing and other terms. They were moving quickly, but I wanted them to move even faster, and they grew accustomed to my asking for updates several times a day.

Because we were focused on supporting healthy institutions as opposed to rescuing failing ones, we considered a program in which the government would match any money the banks raised from private investors. We also explored different ways of taking an equity stake. Buying common stock would strengthen capital ratios, but common shares carried voting rights, and we wanted to avoid anything that looked like nationalization.

So we were leaning toward preferred stock that did not have voting rights (except in very limited circumstances) and could be repaid in full even if common shares substantially declined in value. Preferred is senior in priority to common stock and receives higher dividends, another bonus for the public.

We laid all of this out for the president, who listened with his usual attentiveness and concern.

"Are you still going to buy illiquid assets?" he asked.

"That's the intent," I said.

"You need to recognize where Congress and the American people are," he said. "You are going to need to communicate this well."

President Bush was right, but this dilemma haunted me throughout the crisis—how to make the public understand the grave situation we faced without inflaming the markets even further.

Certainly, we appeared to be facing an all-out run on the system. On Tuesday, fueled by concerns over bank stocks, the Dow tanked again, falling 508 points, or 5.1 percent, to 9,447; while the S&P 500 dropped below 1,000 for the first time since 2003. Bank of America's shares plunged 26 percent, to $23.77. Morgan Stanley fell another 25 percent, to $17.65, raising the question of whether Mitsubishi UFJ would still want a deal.

I didn't know how much more stress the system could bear.

Wednesday, October 8, 2008

It turned out that Angela Merkel's Sunday night statement that Germany would stand behind its bank deposits was intended only as a confidence-building pledge, not as an announcement of government action. Germany would not authorize a guarantee as Ireland had. On Wednesday, the British government announced its own plan, a £500 billion ($875 billion) program to shore up its banking system. Eight banks, including the Royal Bank of Scotland and HBOS, had initially agreed to participate in the program.

The markets needed all the help we could give them. On Wednesday, in an unprecedented action, six central banks, including the Fed, the Bank of England, and the European Central Bank, all reduced policy interest rates. This was the first time in history that the Fed had coordinated a rate reduction with other banks; its federal funds rate target now stood at 1.5 percent.

European markets briefly rallied, but U.S. stocks opened lower despite these moves. LIBOR-OIS spreads soared to 325 basis points from 289 basis points the day before. And we could see the problems spreading to the emerging markets: on Wednesday, Indonesia's stock exchange stopped trading after its main index fell 10 percent.

Given the global sweep of the problem, I knew there weren't going to be any silver bullets for solving it. Rather, we would need to take a range of actions on a sustained basis.

While Jester and Nason worked through the details of a plan to make direct equity investments in banks, I watched the Europeans warily. We thought they might turn to a wave of defensive actions, including guarantees, not only for depositors but for unsecured bank borrowings. With fear rampant, such guarantees might help restore confidence in their banks, but they would put our banks at a disadvantage unless we did something similar.

We were seemingly watching a run on the global banking system, and we needed a blunt instrument to stop it the way our earlier guarantee of the money market funds had halted a panic in that sector. A week earlier Tim had suggested trying to get legislative authority for even more sweeping guarantees in the TARP legislation. That would have been impossible. But, as we'd noted in the PWG statement, the FDIC had the power to guarantee the debt of an individual bank.

We needed to know what the FDIC was prepared to do. After consulting with Tim, I called Sheila Bair.

We were facing a national emergency, and the Europeans were almost certain to act, I told her. Their economies were all dispro- portionately dependent on their banking systems: European bank assets were more than three times the size of the euro zone's GDP, while U.S. bank assets were roughly the same size as our GDP. I asked Sheila if there was any way the FDIC could publicly commit to backing unsecured bank borrowings.

While Sheila understood the gravity of the situation, she wor- ried that the FDIC didn't have enough resources or the ability to assess the risk to its fund. She said she was prepared to work with me on this issue. I decided to strike while the iron was hot and proposed a meeting in my office with her and Ben, who was also eager to have a broad-based FDIC guarantee.

It was midmorning on that overcast fall day when Ben, Sheila, and I sat down together in my office, with Tim plugged in on my speakerphone from New York. I told Sheila that what she had done with Wachovia had been incredibly important. What if we applied elements of that approach more broadly?

"We're looking to make a strong statement that we are not go- ing to let any systemically important institutions go down," I said.

I asked if the FDIC would be prepared to guarantee the debt of any such institution. Tim added that a broad guarantee was neces- sary to demonstrate a forceful commitment to protect our financial system.

I knew we were asking a lot. By law the FDIC had to use the least costly method to provide financial assistance to a failing bank, unless it invoked the systemic risk exception because it believed that an institution's failure would seriously hurt the economy or financial stability. Now we were looking for an action that applied to all banks, not just an individual bank, and a guarantee that applied to new unsecured borrowings for bank holding companies, not just the insured institutions they owned. We weren't going to reach an agreement today, but we needed to make progress.

Understandably, Sheila was very protective of the FDIC fund. "We only have about $35 billion, Hank."

"If we don't act, we are going to have multiple bank failures," I said, "and there won't be anything left in your fund."

"This is vital," Ben said.

We talked about the need for a broad guarantee of bank liabilities. Sheila finally indicated that she would keep working with us. After the meeting, I immediately sent her some draft language suggesting that "the FDIC, with the full support of the Fed and the Treasury, will use its authority and resources, as appropriate to mitigate systemic risk, by protecting depositors, protecting unsecured claims, guaranteeing liabilities, and adopting other measures to support the banking system." I called Joel Kaplan with an encouraging update. "We may be getting there," I said.

But I'd spoken too soon. Before long I got an e-mail from Sheila saying that she wasn't certain she could move forward on this plan. I knew that I had overreached a bit and that my suggested language on an FDIC guarantee was too broad and general. When I called Joel again, however, I told him that I would keep working on Sheila, and that I had faith that she would come around.

In the meantime, I was determined to make a more definitive public statement about the need for capital injections, and with Michele Davis's help I drew up a detailed update on the financial markets since TARP's passage. I didn't want to be too explicit—after all, we still didn't have a program—but I wanted to build on the PWG's statement on Monday.

"The markets want to hear that we are going to inject capital, but the politicians and the public don't want to hear it," she advised. "We should let the air out of the balloon a little bit at a time."

At 3:30 p.m., during a live news conference, I released a four-and-a-half-page statement that, in describing our powers under TARP, made a point of listing first the ability to inject capital into financial institutions. I also noted that it probably would be several weeks before we made our first asset purchase. Because we still didn't have a capital program in place, I didn't allow a Q-and-A period. I'm sure that annoyed the press, which hadn't had a chance to grill me since TARP had passed.

Neither my financial markets update, the British bank bailout, nor the central bank rate cuts cheered the morose markets. The Dow fell another 189 points to 9,258, and bank stocks suffered most. Bank of America's shares dropped 7 percent, and Morgan Stanley's fell 4.8 percent to $16.80; its CDS were above 1,100.

Adding to market woes, AIG was again bleeding. A few days earlier the company had said that it would sell everything but its property/casualty businesses to pay off its government debt. Now, it had run through most of its $85 billion loan—in barely three weeks. On Wednesday afternoon, the Federal Reserve announced it would lend an additional $37.8 billion to the company, secured by investment-grade bonds. It astonished me that not even $85 billion had been enough to stabilize the insurer.

I spoke to John Mack, and he was beside himself that the SEC's short-selling ban would expire at midnight—before he could complete his deal with Mitsubishi UFJ. He wanted to know what Chris Cox planned to do. I agreed that the timing was terrible, but the fact was that Cox had painted himself into a corner during his TARP testimony when he promised that the SEC would lift the ban right after the legislation passed. I wondered how Morgan Stanley would pull through. The bank's position had weakened since September 22, when it announced the investment from Mitsubishi UFJ. Its shares were now barely half that day's price of $27, depressed by market fears that the deal would never happen. I, too, had my doubts.

Thursday, October 9, 2008

With the G-7 coming to town, Ben Bernanke and I knew we would be very busy all weekend, so we moved our Friday breakfast ahead a day. In the small conference room off my office, we grimly reviewed the dire situation in the U.S. and the need to move quickly. We agreed that we needed to outline a bold, credible plan to restore market confidence.

I briefed Ben on Treasury's progress with the capital program and guarantees. He filled me in on the Fed's progress in fashioning a more expansive commercial paper funding facility that would be available to all highly rated issuers, including industrial companies. Days earlier, Ben had suggested using TARP money, but I had declined. I hadn't wanted the revamped commercial paper facility to be TARP's first program, and we needed to save the funds, not use them for programs the Fed could fund itself. But Ben's idea had set me thinking, and I had asked Steve Shafran to work on a facility for the frozen consumer loan market using a structure similar to what Ben had suggested, a facility in which TARP would bear the risk of the first losses.

During our quick meal, we previewed the G-7 meeting, and Ben gave me a thoughtful memo listing nine specific actions we could take to support our critical institutions. The ideas Ben suggested had already been under discussion or were in earlier drafts of our planned G-7 communiqué. This didn't surprise me given how closely Treasury and the Fed had been working together on these issues—including the previous weekend when we were drafting the PWG statement.

I thanked him and after breakfast asked Dave McCormick to see if he could use any of Ben's words in the draft communiqué for the G-7 meeting. He incorporated Ben's ideas into the appendix, which we titled "The Action Plan."

That morning I met in my small conference room with Mervyn Davies, chairman of Standard Chartered Bank. He proudly told me that Standard Chartered would not participate in the U.K. plan. It did not need government capital, he said.

Afterward he took me aside and asked in a low voice about Citigroup and GE. "Are either of those two going down?" he asked. "What we hear isn't good."

This jolted me. Obviously Citi had problems, but this was the first time I'd heard the chairman of another major bank speculate that it might fail. And even though I'd had concerns about GE, I had assumed that with the Fed now buying commercial paper, the company would weather the crisis. I had a high regard for Mervyn; I trusted his judgment and greatly appreciated his candor. It also occurred to me that he might be viewing GE as a concerned counterparty.

That day Treasury was consumed with preparations for the G-7 meeting starting the next afternoon. Dave McCormick headed the effort, and in a stroke of diplomatic inspiration, he suggested that I invite Sheila Bair to the group's Friday dinner, where we would be discussing the Swedish and Japanese experience in dealing with massive bank failures. I called her that morning and told her how important the G-7 was going to be: the Europeans needed reassurance about the U.S. government's commitment to our important financial institutions. I asked if she would give a presentation to all the assembled central bankers and finance ministers, take them through the FDIC's powers, and explain how she had used these to solve the Wachovia crisis. She readily agreed.

At noon Dan Jester and David Nason came to my office to review their progress on the capital program to help domestic financial institutions. They took several of us through their proposed term sheet, soliciting my decisions on a few sticky issues. They had chosen to abandon the idea of the government's matching the capital raising of the banks, and I agreed. Matching made great political sense, but the market was effectively closed for bank equity offerings, and there was no point in trying something the market would not accept. I also approved their recommendation that we take preferred stock to balance the sometimes inconsistent goals of stabilizing the system while protecting the taxpayer: banks would get needed capital without raising the specter of nationalization.

We also debated limits on executive compensation. I agreed with my political advisers—Michele Davis, Kevin Fromer, and Bob Hoyt—that TARP's most stringent restrictions should apply. This meant, for example, that rather than just eliminating golden parachutes in the new contracts of certain executive officers, the top officers of banks accepting capital would have to forgo any such payments in existing contracts as well; they would also have to provide for clawbacks of pay if financial statements were found to be materially inaccurate.

There were a few outstanding issues. We needed to get bank regulators to sign off on the treatment of the capital for regulatory purposes, and I also wanted to nail down a pricing mechanism that would ensure widespread participation while keeping the program voluntary. But overall I felt confident we finally had the framework for a workable approach.

In any case, we needed to get a capital program together immediately to help the financial system. The short sellers had wasted little time justifying John Mack's worries, returning to the market on Thursday to drive shares of both Morgan Stanley and Merrill Lynch down 26 percent. Morgan Stanley's CDS still hovered around 1,100 basis points.

The bad news continued to pour in from around the world. By Thursday morning, Iceland had shuttered its stock market and seized the country's biggest bank, Kaupthing. The two next-biggest banks were also now under government control. LIBOR-OIS spreads had ballooned to a new record of 354 basis points.

I had a very long, difficult call with the president that afternoon, partly to discuss his role in the G-7 and G-20 meetings that weekend. He was looking for any ray of hope on the financial front. He had done everything that I had recommended, including politically unpopular actions that went against Republican principles, and here we were, worse off than ever. He pressed me about the capital program and asked, "Is this what it's going to take to end this thing?"

"I don't know, sir," I admitted, "but I hope it's the dynamite we've been looking for."

I felt unhappy that nearly a week after TARP's passage, I still had mostly bad news to deliver. Europe had big problems; seven countries had already had to rescue banks. I continued to be concerned about Citigroup, GE, and, most of all, Morgan Stanley, with the Mitsubishi UFJ deal still in question. Even though President Bush always encouraged me to be candid, this was a low moment for me. Later that day Josh Bolten called to empathize, and to reiterate the president's support.

"I just wonder, Hank, why, after all the steps we've taken to stabilize the market, are the markets not responding?"

"Josh, I wonder exactly the same thing," I said.

Late in the day Citigroup dropped its bid for Wachovia, saying it would not block a merger with Wells Fargo (though its $60 billion lawsuit would continue). On the surface this provided a shred of good news, but after my conversation with Mervyn Davies I had to wonder what would happen to Citi now that its problems were harshly illuminated.

Friday, October 10, 2008

As the demands of the crisis grew, I had made Dave McCormick, the undersecretary of international affairs, my point man on Morgan Stanley. Though only in his early 40s, Dave was a seasoned manager and great communicator, able to work with finance ministers as well as their deputies.

First thing Friday morning, I went to Dave's office. "We are really going to have to get something done with Morgan Stanley," I told him.

Dave had been working with Japanese finance officials to try to move the Mitsubishi UFJ deal along. The Japanese bank appeared to be pulling back from its agreement. The U.S. bank's shares had fallen so far that Mitsubishi UFJ was worried that if it invested, the U.S. government might step in and wipe out its position.

"I know it may not be the most dignified thing in the world," Dave said, "but you're going to have to lean on them. The market doesn't think this deal is going to close."

The G-7 ministers were arriving in Washington as we spoke, and, as was customary, I had a bilateral meeting with the Japanese finance minister, Shoichi Nakagawa. It was scheduled for noon, and I told Dave I would broach the Morgan Stanley issue then.

The session in my small conference room with Finance Minister Nakagawa dealt mainly with the major issues we were confronting; among other things, he strongly believed that the U.S. should inject capital into our banks, as Japan had done in the 1990s.

Then I turned the conversation to Mitsubishi UFJ's agreement with Morgan Stanley. "We believe," I said, "that this transaction is very important to the stability of the capital markets."

Friendly and dynamic, Nakagawa was Japan's fourth finance minister in two years, and like all of us he carried a heavy load. He didn't commit to pushing the Mitsubishi UFJ deal along, but he agreed to focus on the issue, and that was the most I had hoped for.

The G-7 ministerial meeting began at 2:00 p.m. that afternoon. We gathered in the Cash Room, which was adorned with the flags of our respective countries. Ben and I sat side by side facing our counterparts from the world's major economies. They were arrayed around a huge rectangle of tables: central bank head Masaaki Shirakawa and Finance Minister Nakagawa from Japan, Axel Weber and Peer Steinbrück from Germany, Christian Noyer and Christine Lagarde from France, Mario Draghi and Giulio Tremonti from Italy, Mark Carney and Jim Flaherty from Canada, Mervyn King and Alistair Darling from Britain. Jean-Claude Trichet from the European Central Bank was also there, along with World Bank president Bob Zoellick and Dominique Strauss-Kahn, managing director of the IMF. As a group we had wrestled with difficult challenges, but the stakes had never been so high, nor our collective mood so dark.

Before the meeting both Ben and Dave McCormick had warned me that the Europeans were angry about Lehman Brothers; many attributed their deepening problems to its failure. Nonetheless, I was surprised to see Trichet pass out a one-page graph that illustrated the dramatic increase in LIBOR-OIS spreads post-Lehman. Then, using uncharacteristically forceful language, he said that U.S. officials had made a terrible mistake in letting Lehman fail, triggering the global financial crisis.

Trichet was not alone in his sentiments—other ministers, including Nakagawa and Tremonti, pointed to the problems caused by Lehman in their opening remarks. It was the first time, though far from the last, that I heard global political leaders use this sort of rhetoric to blame the U.S. government for their financial systems' failings as well as our own. It was obvious to me that AIG and some other financial institutions had been on their own paths to failure, independent of Lehman. So, too, were banks in the U.K.,

Ireland, Belgium, and France. Lehman's collapse hadn't created their problems, but everyone likes a simple, easy-to-understand story, and there was no doubt that Lehman's failure had made things worse.

Not wanting to seem defensive, I kept my response simple. My goal was not to justify our actions, but to be sure we left this meeting unified in our desire for a coordinated global response to our problems.

"Lehman," I said, "was a symptom of a larger problem." I noted that the U.S. had not had the ability to put capital into Lehman and that there had been no buyer for the firm. Now, with TARP, I pointed out, we had the power to act.

Mervyn King would pick up on this theme, reminding the ministers that "Lehman is the proximate cause, but it's not the fundamental cause" of the current market crisis. Mervyn was as keen, I think, as I was to move from pointing fingers to linking hands to get out of the mess we were in.

During our discussions, Mervyn and some of the others suggested that to help give the market confidence we should do something different and more forceful with the communiqué. Business as usual would not create the impact we wanted.

Mervyn thought that the draft communiqué lacked punch and that we should shoot for something much briefer that could fit on one page. I agreed.

As the speakers went on, I watched Dave McCormick, who was sitting next to me, scribble out a new draft communiqué. He handed it to a staff member, who quickly brought back a typed version that I thought was just right. I suggested to my colleagues that we try this shortened version, and they agreed. Dave disappeared with his fellow deputies, returning in less than half an hour with a new draft.

The deputies had drawn up a concise, powerful statement—so

concise and powerful that it went through only one round of changes by the ministers. In a few brief sentences including five bullet points, we showed our resolve:

> *The G-7 agrees today that the current situation calls for urgent and exceptional action. We commit to continue working together to stabilize financial markets and restore the flow of credit, to support global economic growth. We agree to:*
>
> *1. Take decisive action and use all available tools to support systemically important financial institutions and prevent their failure.*
>
> *2. Take all necessary steps to unfreeze credit and money markets and ensure that banks and other financial institutions have broad access to liquidity and funding.*
>
> *3. Ensure that our banks and other major financial intermediaries, as needed, can raise capital from public as well as private sources, in sufficient amounts to re-establish confidence and permit them to continue lending to households and businesses.*
>
> *4. Ensure that our respective national deposit insurance and guarantee programs are robust and consistent so that our retail depositors will continue to have confidence in the safety of their deposits.*
>
> *5. Take action, where appropriate, to restart the secondary markets for mortgages and other securitized assets. Accurate valuation and transparent disclosure of assets and consistent implementation of high quality accounting standards are necessary.*

Once we had the five-point plan, the group's mood changed. We'd started out with gloominess and finger pointing, but suddenly we felt ready for action. This handful of words solidified our resolve and set the stage for our future moves.

Energized, we walked out onto the steps of the Treasury's Bell entrance, facing the White House visitor center, for our customary "class photo." It was midafternoon, the sun was shining, and even the sound of a group of demonstrators chanting "Arrest Paulson!" couldn't dim my mood. Peer Steinbrück leaned over and said to me, "It sounds like we're in Germany."

As if to underscore the importance of our meetings, Friday was astonishingly volatile in the markets. The Dow plunged 8 percent, or 680 points, to below 8,000 in the first seven minutes of trading, then rebounded by 631 points in the next 40 minutes. After slumping again, it roared up 853 points to 8,890 just after 3:30 p.m. before plummeting to 8,451, for an overall loss of 128 points on the day. It was the culmination of a terrible week: the Dow and S&P 500 both closed down 18 percent, while the NASDAQ fell 15 percent. It was the worst week for stocks since 1933.

In the credit market, the LIBOR-OIS spread had reached a shocking 364 basis points, and investors fled once more to safe Treasuries. Morgan Stanley ended the day in single digits, at $9.68, with its CDS topping the 1,300 mark.

Considering the day's horrific numbers, I realized two things: One, if it didn't close its deal with Mitsubishi UFJ, Morgan Stanley was dead. Two, we would have to work through the weekend to get the capital program going. The markets would not be satisfied by general statements and encouraging words. We needed to show real action—and fast.

Fortunately, I was making progress with Sheila on the bank guarantee. After a couple of conversations, she had sent over a good proposal, and we were nearly there. She was prepared to guarantee new liabilities, not existing ones.

But we needed Sheila to stretch further. She wanted to guarantee the debt only of banks, not of bank holding companies, and she wanted to limit coverage to 90 percent of the principal. But many of these institutions issued most, if not all, of their debt at the holding company level. A guarantee would allow them to roll existing paper into more-secure longer-term debt and gain some breathing room. Sheila was concerned that the breadth of the holding company guarantee would increase the risk to her fund. We argued that this view was too narrow. If the big banks' holding companies defaulted on their unsecured debt, the stress on the entire banking system would be enormous, leaving her with the very same unattractive choices that she was trying to avoid.

Saturday, October 11, 2008

Early the next morning President Bush met with the G-7 finance ministers and central bankers at the White House. This was a great gesture. The president had never attended, or participated in, a G-7 event before, but he had a gift for setting people at ease, and he was warm and friendly, speaking with bracing humility and frankness.

"This problem started in America, and we need to fix it," he said. He talked about going back to his hometown of Midland, Texas, where people would ask why he was bailing out Wall Street. He didn't like it any better than they did, but he said he had answered: "We have to do it to save your jobs." Now he told the finance ministers and central bankers that he wanted to fix the problem while he was still president, to make things easier for his successor, regardless of who that was.

The president's directness clearly pleased the group in the Roosevelt Room; we followed him to the Rose Garden and stood behind him as he delivered a short speech acknowledging the severity of the crisis and outlining the government's efforts to solve it.

While I spent the day on phone calls and one-on-one meetings with finance ministers, the Treasury team plugged away on the capital purchase program. At 3:00 p.m. I met in the large conference room with Ben, Joel Kaplan, Tim Geithner, and my Treasury people. Tim had come to Washington Friday evening at my request—not in his capacity as head of the New York Fed, but as a superb organizer who would work with Treasury and help us put forward some specific proposals.

Sheila was there as well. As we worked to finalize the FDIC debt guarantee, she had begun to push for another new guarantee, this one of bank transaction accounts, the non-interest-bearing accounts companies keep.

These were radical steps—ones that I would never have considered in other times—but we needed action this weekend. Tim was visibly impatient, and I felt a great sense of urgency. I pushed so hard during the meeting that afterward, both Kaplan and Jim Wilkinson took me aside and said I was moving too fast. These steps needed to be analyzed more carefully, and they felt my approach had discouraged dissent. I told them that if I had waffled one bit, we wouldn't have a program to debate.

To be frank, I hated these options, but I didn't want to preside over a meltdown. I asked Tim to lead the group in developing programs we could implement immediately, and, typically, he rolled up his sleeves and dug right in. We also asked David Nason, who had the most thorough knowledge of bank guarantees at either the Fed or Treasury, to act as devil's advocate on the plan to ensure a thorough vetting.

Shortly after the meeting, Dave McCormick and Bob Hoyt came into my office. Dave said, "We're having trouble buttoning down the Morgan Stanley situation with the Japanese. I think Mitsubishi still wants to make the investment, but they are going to need more assurance." McCormick had been talking with representatives of Mitsubishi UFJ and the Japanese government to let them know we were watching the situation closely. He'd learned that the Japanese bank was worried that if the U.S. bought equity in Morgan Stanley, we would dilute its investment. It was a reasonable concern, and he had indicated that Treasury would structure any subsequent investment to avoid punishing existing investors. Dave and Bob suggested writing a note on Treasury letterhead to reassure the Japanese.

The G-20 summit wouldn't take place for another month, but we had asked its members to meet in Washington that weekend to discuss the financial crisis. At 6:00 p.m. these finance ministers and central bankers met at IMF headquarters, a few blocks from the White House. I made the first presentation, striving to be direct and humble about our failings, while emphasizing the very positive outcome at the G-7 and the U.S.'s commitment to fixing our problems. Jean-Claude Trichet followed me and echoed the success of the G-7.

I left the room for a few moments, and as Guido Mantega delivered his prepared remarks, I surprised everyone by striding back into the room accompanied by President Bush. It was astonishing for a U.S. president to drop in like that on a group of finance ministers and central bankers. Mantega paused to let the president speak.

As he had that morning, the president acknowledged America's role in the problems we faced, adding, "Now is the time to solve this crisis." Then he stepped aside to let Mantega resume. The Brazilian minister said, "If you don't mind, I'm going to speak in Portuguese, my native language."

President Bush replied, "That's okay, I barely speak English."

The group laughed appreciatively, and I knew the surprise visit had been a good idea. People needed to be reassured of our resolve, and the president had done just that in his own disarming way.

When I got home, Wendy told me Warren Buffett had been trying to reach me. I intended to get back to him right after dinner, but I could barely keep my eyes open and went straight to bed afterward, falling into a deep sleep. When the phone rang later that evening, I fumbled to pick it up.

"Hank, this is Warren."

In my grogginess, the only Warren who came to mind was my mother's handyman, Warren Hansen. *Why is he waking me up?* I thought, before realizing it was Warren Buffett on the other end of the line.

Warren knew I was working on a capital program, and he had an idea. We had been struggling with the issue of pricing. We needed to protect the taxpayer while encouraging a broad group of banks to participate; our objective was not to support particular institutions but the entire system, which was undercapitalized. Warren suggested asking for a 5 or 6 percent dividend to start on the preferred shares, then raising the rate later.

"The government would make money on it, it would be friendly to investors, and then you could step up the rate after a few years to encourage the banks to pay back the government," he explained.

I fought back my exhaustion and sat for a half hour or so in the dark on a chair in my bedroom, mulling over this idea. I knew, of course, that as an investor in financial institutions, including Wells Fargo and Goldman Sachs, Warren had a vested interest in this idea. But the truth was I was looking for an approach just like his: an investor-friendly plan that would protect the taxpayer and stabilize the banking system by encouraging investments in healthy institutions. Considering two-tier structures similar to Warren's, my team had been leaning toward a 7 or 8 percent dividend. But as I went back to sleep, I was convinced Warren's was the best way to make a capital purchase program attractive to banks while giving them an incentive to pay back the government.

This Warren turned out to be quite a handyman, too.

Sunday, October 12, 2008

Shortly after 9:00 a.m. Sunday, I called Jeff Immelt at GE to feel him out about the government guarantee on bank debt that we'd been debating. Because it was not a bank, GE would not be eligible for such a program and might be disadvantaged competitively.

"I don't think we can do anything for GE," I said, "but would you rather we do it or not do it?"

"That's an easy question," he said. "Maybe a lot of my guys would disagree with me, but the system is so vulnerable you should do whatever you can do, and we'll be better off than if it hadn't been done. And if we're not, it's still something you've got to do."

Jeff's answer impressed me. How many other CEOs in his position would have taken such a broad perspective?

The Treasury team had once again worked late into the night— this time on the capital purchase and guarantee programs, and at 10:00 a.m. a weary but highly focused group gathered in my large conference room. We were joined by Ben Bernanke, Tim Geithner, Sheila Bair, Joel Kaplan, and Comptroller of the Currency John Dugan. For the next three hours, we sweated out the details of the plan we would unveil the next day.

I briefly recounted my conversation with Buffett, saying that I now favored using preferred stock with a dividend starting at 5 percent and increasing eventually to 9 percent. The regulators agreed to tweak their rules to allow this to qualify for tier-1 capital treatment for bank holding companies that already had substantial amounts of preferred stock.

Now that we had a plan, I was ready to debate it. Playing his assigned role as devil's advocate, David Nason argued that the FDIC guarantee would distort the market. Every time you put the U.S. government behind one group's paper, he said, you made it harder for another. In this case, we would crowd out industrial firms, or financial institutions that weren't bank holding companies, making it harder for them to raise money. In the end, all of us, including David, believed that this was a step we needed to take.

Sheila continued to express doubts—the FDIC, after all, was plowing new ground. She wondered how appropriate it was to extend the guarantee to the debt of bank holding companies, rather than just to FDIC-insured banks. And she pressed to charge banks more to insure their unsecured debt. Tim maintained that the fee had to be low enough to encourage participation. Because I had a good working relationship with the FDIC chair, I met with Sheila alone several times that afternoon when the tension between Tim and her got too high or to reassure her that she was doing the right thing.

"Our whole financial system is at risk, and if everything goes down, so will your fund. The last thing everybody will ask is, 'What happened to the FDIC fund?'" I remember saying. "Your decision will prevent a financial calamity, and Ben and I will support you 100 percent." I also pointed out, "If we price this properly, you will make a lot of money."

Extending the guarantee to the liabilities of bank holding companies was absolutely essential but a very difficult decision for Sheila. I told her that Treasury would use TARP to prevent bank holding companies from failing.

"I know how important this is. We've done a lot of work on it at the FDIC," Sheila said. Despite her wavering, she finally agreed, acknowledging the support from Treasury and the Fed.

We decided to gather again late in the afternoon to nail down details as well as our plan for implementation. The capital and the guarantee programs had to be clear, easy to understand, and attractive. News was circulating that the U.K. would formally announce Monday that it was taking majority stakes in the Royal Bank of Scotland and HBOS. We had received a copy of the U.K.'s capital plan, and its terms were more punitive than the ones we were discussing.

The key for us was how to get as many institutions as we could to sign up for the capital purchase program (CPP), which is what we called our plan to inject equity into the banks. We settled on equity investments of 3 percent of each institution's risk-weighted assets, up to $25 billion for the biggest banks; this translated into roughly $250 billion in equity for the entire banking system.

We wanted to get ahead of the crisis and strengthen banks before they failed. To do this, we needed to include the healthy as well as the sick. We had no authority to force a private institution to accept government capital, but we hoped that our 5 percent dividend—increasing to 9 percent after five years—would be too enticing to turn down.

We had designed the equity program so that banks would apply through their individual regulators, which would screen and submit applications to a TARP investment committee. But rather than wait for these applications to come in, we decided to preselect a first group, advising them as to how much capital their regulators thought they should take.

After the disastrous week we'd just finished, we needed to do something dramatic. So I thought we should launch the program by bringing in the CEOs of a number of the biggest institutions, getting them to agree to capital infusions, and quickly announcing this to the markets. Public confidence required that they appear well capitalized, with a cushion to see them through this difficult period.

We reasoned that if we got these major banks together, other banks would follow. The weaker institutions would not be shamed, and the stronger institutions could say they did it for the good of the system. If only weaker banks took capital, it would stigmatize—and kill—the program.

Treasury played no role in picking the first group of banks. That was done by the New York Fed, aided by the OCC. They chose systemically critical banks that together held over 50 percent of U.S. deposits. These were the four biggest commercial banks, JPMorgan, Wells Fargo, Citigroup, and Bank of America; the three former investment banks, Goldman Sachs, Morgan Stanley, and Merrill Lynch; and State Street Corporation and Bank of New York Mellon, two major clearing and settlement banks that were vital to the infrastructure. We thought it would be great news for the market to hear on Tuesday morning that these banks had agreed to accept a total of $125 billion in capital, or one half of the CPP.

It was up to me to call the bank chiefs and invite them to Treasury the next afternoon: Ken Lewis, Vikram Pandit, Jamie Dimon, John Thain, John Mack, Lloyd Blankfein, and Dick Kovacevich, who, as chairman of Wells Fargo, was the only non-CEO invited. We also invited State Street's Ronald Logue and Bank of New York Mellon's Robert Kelly. I wouldn't tell them what the meeting was about—I simply said that it was important, that the others were coming, and that it ultimately would be good news. Kovacevich hesitated a bit—he had to come from San Francisco—but like everyone else agreed to meet on very short notice.

Through all the discussion and planning, we hadn't lost sight of Morgan Stanley's plight. Dave McCormick had raised the idea of sending a letter to the Japanese that would highlight the principles underlying any policy actions we might take and indicate our intention of protecting foreign investors. This would give the Mitsubishi UFJ leadership and board some needed reassurance.

I liked the idea, so Dave called the CEO of Mitsubishi UFJ and ran the idea of a letter by him. Dave reported that the Mitsubishi UFJ executive seemed positive, if noncommittal. He and Bob Hoyt then drafted the letter. It did not mention Morgan Stanley by name, nor did we offer any specific commitments. In essence, it simply restated the signals we had been sending publicly, but it was on letterhead from the U.S. Treasury and that did the trick. Once I had approved the draft, Dave sent it to the Japanese Ministry of Finance, which promptly sent it on to Mitsubishi UFJ. We received word an hour or so later that this would get the deal done.

Monday, October 13, 2008

Columbus Day was a holiday for many Americans, and it brought good news to the tired teams at Treasury. Mitsubishi UFJ and Morgan Stanley had finally completed their deal. The terms had been adjusted to reflect a lower value for the U.S. bank. For its investment, Mitsubishi UFJ would now receive convertible and nonconvertible preferred stock, giving it 21 percent of Morgan Stanley's voting rights. Previously Mitsubishi UFJ would have acquired common and preferred. That morning a check for $9 billion was hand-delivered to the New York investment bank.

Europe delivered its own share of encouraging news. Anticipating our actions, leaders of the 15 euro-zone countries had agreed late Sunday night to a plan that would inject billions of euros into their banks through equity stakes; they also vowed to guarantee new bank debt through 2009. Monday morning, the U.K.'s FTSE 100 shot up nearly 325 points, or 8.3 percent, while German and

French markets rose more than 11 percent. The three-month London interbank rate dropped 7 basis points to 4.75 percent, while the LIBOR-OIS spread narrowed slightly to 354 from Friday's 364, reversing a monthlong steadily upward trend.

Before the London markets opened on Monday the U.K. government had effectively nationalized the Royal Bank of Scotland and HBOS, injecting billions of pounds of capital and taking seats on the banks' boards. The U.K. program came with much greater government control and stiffer terms than ours: the British government fired the banks' top executives, froze bonuses for executives, and imposed a 12 percent dividend on its preferred stock.

As a result, the U.K.'s biggest banks and healthiest banks—HSBC, Barclays, and Standard Chartered—all turned down the capital. We did not want that to happen in the U.S. To the contrary, we designed our plan to entice banks so that the broadest possible range of healthy institutions would accept capital.

Before the U.S. markets opened, Treasury staff and I sat down with General Motors CEO Rick Wagoner and a number of his executives, who hoped to get some government money for their struggling company. Rick had been calling me, trying to set up a meeting for some time, but I had declined to do so. I believed that TARP was not meant to bolster industrial companies but to prevent a collapse of the financial system. Commerce secretary Carlos Gutierrez attended the meeting in my office.

No one questioned that America's automakers were in trouble. On September 30, President Bush had signed a $25 billion loan package to help the Big Three build cars that would meet federal fuel economy standards. Reports had recently surfaced that General Motors and Chrysler were discussing a merger.

Now the GM contingent brought dire news that the company faced a banklike run from creditors and suppliers who had not been paid on a timely basis. This liquidity squeeze, they contended, would result in GM's failure—right, as it turned out, around the time of the presidential election. They were looking for a total of $10 billion: a $5 billion loan and a $5 billion revolving line of credit.

"We need a bridge loan to avoid a disaster and we need it quickly," Wagoner said. "I don't believe we can make it past November 7."

He and his team may have sincerely believed this, but I knew better. I had worked with companies like GM long enough to know that they did not die quickly. A financial institution could go under immediately if it lost the confidence of creditors and clients, but an industrial company could stretch out its suppliers for quite a while. In any case, I was loath to do anything that might appear to reflect politics.

I told Wagoner that we took his situation very seriously but that he should continue to work closely with Carlos. "I have no authority to make a TARP loan to General Motors," I said.

As soon as the GM delegation left, we went into high gear to prepare for the afternoon meeting with the banking CEOs. I was concerned about Jamie Dimon, because JPMorgan appeared to be in the best shape of the group, and I wanted to be sure he would accept the capital. I asked Tim to soften Jamie up ahead of time. To my relief, Tim had already done so, soliciting Jamie's support without briefing him on our program. Jamie, he believed, would back us. The government principals—Ben, Tim, Sheila, John Dugan, and I—met one final time to go over the plan, deciding who would say what.

When the nine bankers arrived at Treasury for the 3:00 p.m. meeting—walking up the Treasury steps past a phalanx of TV cameras and photographers—we had our plan down cold. Once inside, they were directed to my large conference room. I'd had so many meetings in this room that its splendor and idiosyncrasies— the 19th-century furniture and chandeliers, the framed currency and tax seals on the oiled walnut walls—had become almost as familiar as my living room. But I wondered if our visitors found it strange to be working out 21st-century problems in such a historic setting and beneath the portraits of George Washington and Abraham Lincoln.

We took our seats at the long table, with Ben, Sheila, Tim, John, and me on one side, and the CEOs sitting across from us, arranged alphabetically by bank. Fortunately, given their dispute over Wachovia, this meant that Citi's Pandit and Wells's Kovacevich were at opposite ends of the table.

The men facing us constituted the top echelon of American banking, but their circumstances varied. Some, like Dimon and Kovacevich, represented comparatively strong institutions, while Pandit, John Thain, and John Mack had been struggling with losses and an unforgiving market. But I knew that even the strongest of them had to be worried about their futures—and they needed to realize that they were all in this together.

I opened the meeting, making clear that we had invited them there because we all agreed that the U.S. needed to take decisive action. Together, they represented a significant part of our financial system and thus had to be central to any solution.

I briefly described the use of the systemic risk exception to guarantee new senior debt, and the Treasury's $250 billion capital purchase program. And I pointed out that we wanted them to contact their boards and confirm their participation by that evening.

"We plan to announce the program tomorrow," I said, adding that we wanted to say publicly that their firms would be the initial participants.

When I was done, Ben emphasized how important our program was to stabilizing the financial system. Sheila explained the Temporary Liquidity Guarantee Program (TLGP), addressing issues of structure, pricing, and what types of debt would qualify. The FDIC, she said, would guarantee new unsecured senior debt issued on or before June 30, 2009, and would protect all transaction accounts, regardless of their size, through 2009.

Tim subsequently announced the capital amounts that regulators had settled upon just hours before: $25 billion for Citigroup, Wells Fargo, and JPMorgan; $15 billion for Bank of America; $10 billion for Merrill Lynch, Goldman Sachs, and Morgan Stanley; $3 billion for Bank of New York Mellon; $2 billion for State Street Corporation. In total, the nine banks would receive $125 billion, or half of the CPP.

In answer to a question, Tim emphasized that the capital and debt programs were linked: you couldn't have one without the other.

David Nason took the bankers through the basic terms of the capital, explaining how much they would have to pay on the preferred, noting that there could be no increases in common dividends for three years, and describing limitations the program would impose on their share repurchase programs. Treasury would also receive warrants to purchase common shares with an aggregate exercise price equivalent in value to 15 percent of its preferred stock investment. Bob Hoyt outlined how executive compensation would work; the limitations would apply as under TARP, with no golden-parachute payments and no tax deductions on incomes above $500,000.

The CEOs listened intently, plying us with questions throughout. Some were more clearly enthusiastic than others. Dick Kovacevich indicated his discomfort, arguing that Wells Fargo was in good shape. It had recently acquired Wachovia and planned to raise $25 billion in private capital—exactly the amount regulators now wanted him to take from the government.

"How can I do this without going to my board?" I remember him saying. "What do I need $25 billion more capital for?"

"Because you're not as well capitalized as you think," Tim calmly replied.

I knew as well as anyone how this worked. Right up until they failed, even the weakest banks claimed that they didn't need capital. But the fact was that in the midst of this crisis the market questioned the balance sheets of even the strongest banks, including Wells, which now owned Wachovia with all of its toxic option ARMs. Our banking system was massively undercapitalized, though many banks did not want to acknowledge it. Every bank in the room would benefit when we restored confidence and stability.

"Look, we're making you an offer," I said, jumping in. "If you don't take it and sometime later your regulator tells you that you are undercapitalized and you have to raise private-sector capital but you are unable to do so, you may not like the terms if you have to come back to me."

Ben joined in to say that the program was good for the system and good for everyone. He said the meeting had been very constructive and that it was important for us all to work together.

Later press reports would highlight the difficulties of the meeting, but it went much better than our expectations. These CEOs were smart people used to negotiating and raising issues. But for some, there was no discussion necessary.

"I've just run the numbers," said Vikram Pandit. "This is very cheap capital. I'm in."

"I don't really think that all of us are the same, but it's cheap capital," Jamie Dimon pointed out. "And I understand it's important for our system."

John Thain and Lloyd Blankfein raised a number of issues concerning such matters as share buybacks, the size of the warrants, and the redemption of the preferred. John also asked a number of questions about executive compensation. "Will these terms change when a new administration comes in?" he asked. I told him that the CPP was a contract he could count on and that we were including all of the pay requirements specified in the TARP legislation. But we did note that there was no protection against any new legislation.

At this, Ken Lewis, who had been silent throughout the meeting, finally spoke up.

"I have three points," he said in his soft-spoken way. "One, if we spend another second talking about executive compensation, we are out of our minds. Two, I don't think we should talk about this too much. We're all going to do it, so let's not waste anybody else's time. And three, let's not focus on how this hurts or helps each of our institutions, because it's going to have strengths and weaknesses for some—for example, the unlimited guarantee for transaction deposits is going to hurt us significantly. But let's just cut the B.S. and get this done."

Each CEO was handed a sheet of paper with our basic terms on it. The banks were asked to agree to issue preferred shares to the Treasury; to participate in the FDIC guaranteed-debt program; to expand the flow of credit to U.S. consumers and businesses; and to "work diligently, under existing programs, to modify the terms of residential mortgages, as appropriate." There were empty spaces on the sheet where the CEOs were to write in the names of their institutions and the amount of capital they were getting from the government, as well as lines where they would sign their names and fill in the date.

John Mack signed his agreement right then, in front of all of us.

"You can't do that without your board," Thain said.

"I've got my board on 24-hour call," Mack assured him. "I can get this done, no problem."

Kovacevich, for his part, said he couldn't get approval from his board that quickly. I said I wanted him to try.

The meeting ended by 4:10 p.m., just after the market had closed. We had arranged things so that each CEO could go off to an office in the Treasury Building and make the necessary calls to his board and top staff to analyze the offer and get the necessary approvals. David Nason and Bob Hoyt visited each of them and answered questions. I went back to my office and started calling the congressional leaders and the presidential candidates so they wouldn't hear about the meeting through leaks.

On the whole, the Hill leaders were encouraging. Barney Frank understood immediately as I explained our action to him. Spencer Bachus had raised the idea of equity purchases in the early days of TARP and supported us, as did Chris Dodd. Nancy Pelosi couldn't resist pointing out that the Democrats had wanted this all along. Roy Blunt, who had worked hard to rally Republicans behind TARP, noted, however, that "this is going to be a surprise to the country and to a lot of Republicans."

After lending his support the day before, Jeff Immelt now called to tell me that the capital program would hurt GE. "We are actually lending, we're bigger than most of these banks, and we're being left behind," he said. He told me his people were nervous. "I'm not trying to make you feel bad; I stand by what I said. We are better off with this program than without it. I just have to tell you, I'm worried about my company and our ability to roll over paper in the face of this."

While I went through my calls, people came in and out of my office giving me reports on the CEOs: Pandit had signed; Kovacevich signed but refused to fill in the dollar amount Wells would receive—a protest, I suppose, at being forced to take the money. Jamie Dimon gave his signature, but, I later learned, he told Bob Hoyt to hold his acceptance in escrow until everybody else had signed. (He also gave Bob his personal cell phone number, saying,

"Call me and tell me when everything is done. Then throw this number away after you use it.")

As we had hoped, each of the nine CEOs signed on that day, and we never had to reconvene.

And the day kept delivering good news. The torrid start overseas had spread to the U.S., reflecting market optimism about government actions to solve the global financial crisis. Even as we were meeting with the financial industry's most important CEOs, the Dow posted its biggest-ever point gain, jumping 936 points, or 11 percent, to 9,388.

Shortly after I got the word that all the CEOs were on board for the CPP, Wendy called me from the White House. She was at the Columbus Day state dinner for Italian prime minister Silvio Berlusconi, and I had to strain to hear her voice over the background noise. She said that the cast of the Broadway show *Jersey Boys* was going to be singing some of my favorite Frankie Valli songs.

"The president wants you to get over here," she said.

I told Wendy I would see her soon.

CHAPTER 15

Tuesday, October 14, 2008

Sitting back and letting out a long deep breath is not what I do best. But on Tuesday, October 14—after we'd all been working nonstop since August to keep disaster at bay—I finally had a chance to exhale and let down my guard for a moment. Things were finally looking up. The day before, the nine biggest U.S. banks had agreed to accept $125 billion in capital from the government, European leaders had announced plans to fix their own banking problems, and no critical institution appeared to be on the verge of failure.

Early that morning, Ben Bernanke, Sheila Bair, John Dugan, and I held a press conference in the Treasury Building's Cash Room to explain the previous day's moves. I tackled the controversial issue of government intervention head-on, pointing out that we had not wanted to take such actions—arguably the most sweeping in banking since the Great Depression—but that they had been needed to restore confidence to the financial system.

World markets had responded enthusiastically. Japan's Nikkei index soared by 14.2 percent, while the U.K.'s FTSE 100 rose 3.2 percent. In early trading, the Dow had jumped 4.1 percent to 9,794. Credit markets were stronger as well, as the LIBOR-OIS spread narrowed slightly to 345 basis points.

But no sooner had I returned to my office than one thorny issue I believed had been settled reared its head. Ken Lewis was on the phone, concerned about his deal with Merrill Lynch. With the markets stabilizing, the Bank of America CEO was worried that John Thain, who had sold Merrill only to prevent its failure, might now want to back out: after our weekend actions, Thain might have stopped believing that his firm's survival depended on BofA. If that were the case, Ken wanted regulators to remember just how crucial to the country his decision to buy Merrill during the height of the crisis had been and to insist that Thain honor his contract.

"Ken," I asked, "has John or anyone at Merrill indicated to you that they might want out?"

"No, I just have a concern."

I heard him out and told him that I believed John would stay committed to the deal, but that I would pass his concerns on to Tim Geithner, and I did. I never mentioned them, however, to Thain.

In making critical decisions, finding the right mix of policy considerations, market needs, and political realities was always difficult. I tended to put politics last—sometimes to our detriment. To my mind, the bank capital program struck a perfect balance. It was designed to meet a market requirement, it addressed the problem of bank undercapitalization while safeguarding taxpayer interests, and it had been, I thought, brilliantly executed.

I expected the program to be politically unpopular, but the intensity of the backlash astonished me. Though the criticism from Republicans was muted, some conservatives, who had resisted TARP initially, felt betrayed, and their vocal dissatisfaction made me nervous. I knew that if the program turned into a political football and became an issue in the presidential campaign, the banks would get spooked and back away from the capital. Our efforts to strengthen the fragile system would collapse.

Fortunately, the candidates did not politicize the issue. On October 13, the night that the banks agreed to accept the money, I'd had a long phone conversation with an angry John McCain, who complained that we weren't doing enough to deal with mortgages. He was also upset about the equity investments, but after we talked it out, I was confident he would not publicly attack our plans—and to his great credit, he did not, even though he was behind in the polls and might have been tempted to try to energize his campaign that way.

Democrats liked the program—some even took credit for it—but, joined by an ever-growing populist chorus, they began griping that banks were hoarding their new capital, not using it to increase lending. Before long it seemed that almost every member of Congress or business leader was directing his or her anger at the banks and their regulators. And this was before even one dollar of government money had landed on bank balance sheets.

John Thain didn't help matters. Merrill reported a $5.1 billion third-quarter loss on Thursday, October 16. Referring to Merrill's $10 billion government injection, he told analysts on a conference call that "at least for the next quarter, it's just going to be a cushion."

The day after he made his remarks, Nancy Pelosi and Barney Frank complained to me about Thain's insensitivity. I got John on the phone, and I told him that although he was right in that Merrill wasn't slated to get the capital until after its merger with BofA closed at year-end, he needed to be more politically aware. I asked that he clarify his statement publicly. He said he would look for an opportunity to do so, but would only comment if he was asked about it. I would have preferred a more proactive effort on Thain's part. Then I heard that Chris Dodd planned to call the nine big-bank CEOs before the Senate Banking Committee to grill them about lending at an upcoming hearing. I managed to persuade him not to, arguing that if he did, he would so stigmatize and jeopardize the capital program that those first nine banks might back out.

I understood the need to get credit flowing again. In the Cash Room I had made sure to say that "the needs of our economy require that our financial institutions not take this new capital to hoard it, but to deploy it." By requiring Treasury consent for share buybacks and increases in dividends, our program contained built-in incentives for the banks to retain capital, repair their balance sheets, and resume lending. But that would not happen overnight—after all, many businesses were reluctant to take out loans in an economic downturn. I didn't think I could tell the banks how much to lend or to whom.

But politicians and the public became increasingly agitated in the midst of a hard-fought presidential campaign. They expected that our actions—meant to prevent bank failures—could also avert the recession and slow the wave of foreclosures already under way. Obama and McCain both denounced Wall Street's greed as they traveled around the country. And no single issue inflamed people more than revelations of excessive executive pay—and perks. New York State attorney general Andrew Cuomo launched a high-profile probe of AIG's corporate expenses, including a notorious post-bailout retreat for insurance agents at a California spa that generated a lot of fiery press coverage. People were outraged that banks that had received government aid were still planning to dole out lavish pay packages.

I empathized with their anger. People had seen the values of their homes and their 401(k)s plunge. We were in a deep recession, and many had lost jobs. Frankly, I felt the real problem ran deeper than CEO pay levels—to the skewed systems banks used that rewarded short-term profits in calculating bonuses. These had contributed to the excessive risk taking that had put the economy on the edge. I was convinced, for policy reasons and to quell public anger, that regulators needed to devise a comprehensive solution. I encouraged Ben, Tim, Sheila, and John Dugan to work on policy guidance for compensation, lending, foreclosures, and dividends that would apply to all banks, and not just those that took capital.

Jeff Immelt had come to my office on the 16th to make the case that the FDIC should guarantee GE Capital's debt issues. He believed our new programs put GE at a huge disadvantage, making it difficult for the company to fund itself. Nonbanks like GE could tap the Fed's Commercial Paper Funding Facility, but they weren't eligible for TARP funds or the FDIC's new debt guarantee, known as the Temporary Liquidity Guarantee Program. Why would investors buy GE debt when they could purchase the debt of other financial institutions with an FDIC guarantee?

"We are the ones out there making the loans that the banks aren't, and we need help," Immelt said. I knew he was right, and I said we would explore it with his finance team and the FDIC.

Following the success of the G-7 and the coordinated actions that had calmed the market, the White House revived plans for a summit at which President Bush could discuss the financial crisis with a broad range of leaders. I had made outreach to the developing world a priority and felt strongly, as did deputy secretary Bob Kimmitt, that if we were going to host a summit, it should include the members of the G-20. The president agreed. I asked Dave McCormick to work with the finance ministers to find common ground for the meeting, while the president put Dan Price in charge of preparations, including negotiating the summit communiqué with the other leaders' representatives.

Then French president Nicolas Sarkozy made an impromptu call to President Bush requesting a meeting, along with European Commission president José Manuel Barroso, after the October 17 European Union–Canada Summit in Quebec City. Sarkozy and U.K. prime minister Gordon Brown had been sparring over which of them would lead reform efforts in Europe. Brown envisioned a new Bretton Woods–style gathering to overhaul the world economic order set in place during World War II. Sarkozy, who held the presidency of the European Union, had called for replacing the failed "Anglo-Saxon" model of free markets and advocated a major summit in New York, which he considered the epicenter of the problem.

The White House suspected that Sarkozy was looking to pull off a publicity coup on our home turf. President Bush invited him to a sit-down at Camp David, where a meeting could be better shielded from the media glare. The two agreed to get together on Saturday, October 18. French finance minister Christine Lagarde and I would join them, along with Secretary of State Condi Rice, who canceled a trip to the Middle East to attend.

On Friday afternoon, Wendy and I left by helicopter from the South Lawn of the White House, with the president and Laura Bush, Condi, and Steve Hadley and his wife, Anne. *Marine One* carried us over the Washington Monument and off to Camp David in half an hour. At about 4:00 p.m. Saturday, Sarkozy, Barroso, and Lagarde arrived. Thirty minutes later we were sitting down in the main lodge, Laurel, in the same homey wood-paneled conference room where I had made my first official presentation to the president back in 2006. While we met, Wendy took the opportunity to go looking for warblers.

Inside, Sarkozy was singing a sweet song of his own. Lively and articulate, the French leader used every bit of charm at his disposal to try to persuade President Bush to agree to a summit in New York on the order of the G-8, reasoning that the small group's shared values would make it easier to agree on a plan.

Selling hard, Sarkozy said that hosting the summit would demonstrate President Bush's leadership. The president agreed on the need for a meeting but insisted on a more inclusive group, such as the G-20, which included China and India. He wanted to focus on broad principles and a blueprint for regulatory and institutional reform. By contrast, Sarkozy was looking to put his stamp on a host of specific topics like mark-to-market accounting and the role of the rating agencies.

"That is not for us," President Bush said. "We're going to have our experts do that."

The French leader came right back at him. "These experts are the ones that got us in trouble in the first place," Sarkozy said, looking directly at me. He would later suggest that finance ministers shouldn't even be in the room at the summit.

Sarkozy dominated the hour-long meeting in Laurel, but he must have left frustrated. He'd won agreement on a meeting—which we had already decided to hold—but little beyond that. In the end, President Bush, Sarkozy, and Barroso released a joint statement that said the U.S., France, and the European Union would reach out to other world leaders to hold an economic summit shortly after the U.S. elections.

As preparations for the summit got under way, the Europeans, with the exception of Gordon Brown, resisted meeting with the entire G-20. As a concession, President Bush agreed that Spain and the Netherlands—which were not members of the G-8 or G-20—could attend the gathering of the bigger group as guests of the EU presidency. Chinese president Hu Jintao was the first world leader to sign on. The Saudis expressed their reluctance, worried that they would be blamed for high oil prices, and pressed to make a big financial contribution to a fund for poorer countries, but I called Finance Minister Ibrahim al-Assaf and reassured him. On Wednesday, October 22, the White House was able to announce that President Bush had invited the leaders of the G-20, representing some 85 percent of the world's GDP, to a November 15 summit in Washington to discuss the crisis.

That day brought other, much less welcome news when Tim Geithner told me that AIG would need a massive equity investment. I was shocked and dismayed. On September 16 the New York Fed had loaned the company $85 billion; then in early October it had extended an additional $37.8 billion. Now, Tim said, the company would soon report a dreadful quarterly loss, which would trigger rating downgrades; the resulting collateral calls would be disastrous. Initially, AIG had confronted a liquidity crisis; now it faced a severe capital problem. Tim believed the only solution was an injection of TARP funds.

AIG was systemically important and could not be allowed to fail, but I was distressed at the prospect of using TARP money. Not only would this drain our limited funds, reducing our capacity going forward, but the insurer was so obviously unhealthy—and politically tarnished—that it would enflame public resentment of bailouts and make it harder to get Congress to release the final $350 billion of TARP when we needed it. Furthermore, the taxpayers might never get their money back from a capital injection in AIG.

With the November elections just a couple of weeks away, foreclosure relief was another hot-button issue. Housing advocates complained that the government wasn't doing enough, but much of the public strongly opposed bailing out people who had run into trouble on their mortgages. Some of the hardest-hit states happened to be key battlegrounds in the presidential election: Florida, Nevada, Ohio, and Arizona.

I soon found myself at odds with Sheila Bair, even though I

admired her energy and her efforts to deal with problem mort-gages. Following IndyMac's July failure, the FDIC, working off the principles for a fast-track systemic approach pioneered by Trea-sury's HOPE Now program, developed an innovative plan in which the thrift's loans were modified to cap monthly mortgage pay-ments. Initially the limit was set at 38 percent of pretax income. (Subsequently it was cut to as low as 31 percent.) To make this work, banks could either lower interest rates or extend the life of loans. The FDIC applied the so-called IndyMac Protocol to every failed bank or thrift that it took control of.

But Sheila wanted to dramatically broaden the scope of the relief efforts. She had called me at Camp David before Sarkozy's visit to argue that language in the TARP legislation gave Treasury the authority to guarantee mortgages the government didn't own to prevent foreclosures—and that the cost of doing so didn't have to come out of TARP funds. Nor was there a limit on the funds the government could use.

It was the first I'd heard of this argument, and I strongly dis-agreed, questioning its legal validity. I could only imagine the public outrage if we declared that Treasury's authorities included the power to insure mortgage modifications to the extent we deemed appropriate! But I told Sheila I would study her plan.

Sheila was very effective at taking an idea, simplifying it to make it broadly understandable and appealing, and then driving hard through any objections that stood in the way. Her plan would give an incentive to lenders to modify loans by offering downside pro-tection when they agreed to use the IndyMac Protocol. If a loan modified under her program went into default and foreclosure, the government would cover half of the loss suffered by the lender. Eventually, she would propose using some of TARP's $700 billion to fund that guarantee.

Sheila's plan would soon put us on the spot. On October 23,

the Senate Banking Committee held a hearing to examine the government's regulatory response to the financial crisis. Shortly before the session, Chris Dodd called me to advocate Sheila's foreclosure relief proposal. I assumed she had been talking to him. I said it was promising but that it raised serious questions, some of them legal.

We at Treasury would later call this the "ambush hearing." Sheila told the committee that the FDIC and Treasury were working together to stem foreclosures, describing her program to provide insurance to banks handling problem mortgages. Dodd indicated during the hearing that he had spoken to me and believed I was on board. When pressed on the issue, Neel Kashkari, whom I'd sent to testify, could say only that Treasury was considering the idea.

In fact, we favored mortgage relief, but as we did more work, we questioned Sheila's plan's economics and effectiveness. First, more than half the loans modified in the first quarter of 2008 were already delinquent again within six months. It wasn't just the interest on mortgages that was causing the problem: people who fell behind on their house payments tended also to have auto and credit card debt they could not afford. The IndyMac Protocol considered only the first mortgage, not home equity loans or other debt. It was one thing to apply the protocol to mortgages the government already owned but quite another to mortgages owned by banks, which would be paid only if there was a redefault. Given the high occurrence of such redefaults, we felt Sheila's proposal would provide the wrong incentives and put the government on the hook for way too much money.

Ignoring these concerns, Sheila was aggressively promoting the use of TARP funds for her loss-sharing plan and had everyone leaning on us, from the press to Congress. Our critics asserted that Treasury was funneling taxpayer money into the big Wall Street banks while Sheila wanted to put it into the hands of struggling homeowners.

Truth is, the critics had the argument backward. We initially opposed Sheila's idea because we viewed her loss-sharing insurance proposal as leading to precisely what we were accused of trying to promote—a hidden bailout for big financial institutions. If a modified loan went sour, the government would have to write a large check to the bank, not to the homeowner, and there was likely to be a messy foreclosure after the redefault.

Sheila kept pushing Treasury, though, and we kept analyzing her idea. Our chief economist, Phill Swagel, came up with suggestions for improvements, including factoring home-price declines into the insurance payments, an idea similar to one later adopted by the Obama administration. Compared to Sheila's plan, Phill's approach gave more of any subsidy to homeowners, not the banks. Finally, I made it clear that we could not participate in any foreclosure spending program outside of TARP and that we wouldn't be able to do it with TARP funds until the last tranche was taken down.

Meantime, I knew that we needed to get money out through the capital program faster, before banks, responding to rising political pressure over their lending, compensation, and foreclosure mitigation practices, refused TARP money at all. We had established a procedure under which a bank's application was screened by its regulator, which submitted it to Treasury if the bank was healthy. At Treasury a team of bank examiners hired from the regulators reviewed each application before making a recommendation to Treasury's TARP investment committee.

I pushed my TARP leadership team to speed up the postapproval closing and funding process to get the money into the system as quickly and efficiently as possible. At one point I instructed them to call each regulator and approved bank and lean on them to hurry up.

Still, we remained vigilant about the screening process; we did not want to put taxpayer dollars into failing banks. If we had questions about a bank's viability, we sent the application to a peer review council comprising senior representatives from all four regulators—the Fed, FDIC, OCC, and OTS—to decide whether the institution should receive funds.

With the presidential election fast approaching, our most pressing challenge was how to use most effectively the remainder of the first $350 billion in TARP, even as we wrestled with the question of how to work with the winner's transition team to access the last tranche of TARP and deploy those funds. I felt that any decision involving the last tranche—particularly programs that would be implemented after we left office—was so crucial we needed to involve the incoming administration. Michele Davis finally said, "We need to stop trying to guess what they'll want to do and instead act as if we will be here for the next year. We should be prepared to show them a plan the day after the election."

She was absolutely right. And for the next two weeks we concentrated on how to balance policy, politics, and the markets as our time at Treasury wound down.

Over the October 25 weekend, we split up to work on different projects. Neel Kashkari and Phill Swagel went to New York to meet with officials from the Bank of New York Mellon, which Treasury had hired to serve as the trustee for the reverse auction program that we planned to use to purchase the illiquid assets. Dan Jester and David Nason stayed in Washington to work on closing the $125 billion capital investment in the first nine banks; I wanted to make sure that none of them backed out in the face of the political backlash.

Steve Shafran would focus on consumer credit, a concern since markets had begun to freeze in August 2007. It was a crucial assignment. About 40 percent of consumer loans were packaged and sold as securities, but that market had all but shut down, making it much harder for American families to buy cars, pay for college tuition, or even purchase a television with a credit card.

Steve began work with the Fed on a program in which TARP funds would be used to help create a Fed lending facility that would provide nonrecourse senior secured funding for asset-backed securities collateralized by newly made auto loans, credit card loans, student loans, and loans guaranteed by the Small Business Administration. The risk to the government was expected to be minimal, as losses would be borne by TARP only after issuers and investors had taken losses. This work would lead to what became known as the Term Asset-Backed Securities Loan Facility, or TALF.

Another group—including Dave McCormick, Bob Hoyt, Kevin Fromer, Michele Davis, Jim Wilkinson, Brookly McLaughlin, Deputy Assistant Secretary for Business Affairs Jeb Mason, Public Affairs Officer Jennifer Zuccarelli, Deputy Executive Secretary Lindsay Valdeon, and Christal West—accompanied me to Little St. Simons Island. For some time, I had been planning to bring some Treasury people down for a visit, and although this wasn't conceived as a working weekend, no one was surprised that it ended up that way. We flew down on Thursday afternoon.

Outdoors—kayaking, fishing, birding, or biking—we managed to avoid talking business. Inside was another story. TARP dominated our discussions, and I was still stewing about the need to make a big investment in the tainted AIG. On a Friday call, Ben Bernanke empathized with my concerns. The AIG rescue had been a Fed deal, and he appreciated our support. "I'll help in explaining this to Congress," he said.

The Fed expected AIG to lose a mind-numbing $23 billion pretax in the third quarter, and I knew that I would need to think differently about how we would use and take down the TARP money going forward. With the markets so uncertain, it was impossible to predict how many companies might produce AIG-like surprises that would require government intervention. I began to worry about having enough money available to deal with any emergencies that might arise.

That weekend we took a hard look at our priorities and our TARP funds, trying to find a way we might convince Congress to release the last tranche. Certainly the math argued for doing so. Of the first $350 billion, we had already allocated $250 billion to the capital purchase program; half of that was committed to the nine big banks. We estimated that AIG could require a whopping $40 billion. That brought us up to $290 billion. And we could easily tally a list of potential demands on our resources, from the increasingly distressed commercial real estate market to the monoline insurers. We would need funds to help restart the consumer side of the asset-backed securities market. After what we'd gone through in the past few weeks, I could easily invent doomsday scenarios that would require hundreds of billions of dollars.

On Saturday evening, after dinner, we gathered in a small room in the main lodge that doubled as a natural history museum—complete with mounted ducks and tarpon, turtle shells, and the skeletons of alligators and dolphins—to hash out the policy and political considerations. My political advisers—Jim, Kevin, and Michele—explained how difficult it would be for Congress to give us the last $350 billion. I wouldn't take no for an answer; the danger of being unprepared was too great. The questions were: What would it take for us to get it? And what commitments would we have to make to demonstrate a credible plan for using the money so that we could bring Congress on board?

Everyone agreed we would need to offer a plan for foreclosure relief. Partnering with the Fed on TALF was a top priority, but the idea had not yet been unveiled, was difficult to explain, and would be seen as a change in our strategy. We also took a hard look at our plan to buy illiquid assets, which was proving more difficult to develop and taking longer than any of us wanted. Kevin, Jim, and Jeb argued that the criticism would be severe if we backed away from asset purchases. But Michele countered that if we announced a program we couldn't execute effectively, we'd eventually take even more heat.

We were entering a period in which anything I said would be viewed through the prism of election-year politics. So we decided that I should avoid making public comments until after November 4, even though this meant I could not lay the groundwork for any future change in strategy.

I left the island leaning toward developing targeted programs dealing with asset-backed consumer loans, foreclosures, and the troubled monoline insurers, as well as illiquid assets. And I wanted to move as soon as possible after the election to ask Congress to release the last tranche.

I knew how hard this would be, but I was convinced we would need all the TARP funds, despite how much the American people and their elected representatives loathed bailouts. I would spend much of the next two months debating with my colleagues and inside my own head exactly when to ask Congress for the money, and how to do it.

We flew back to Washington on Sunday afternoon and went straight to the office. At 8:00 p.m. I met in my large conference room with senior staff and White House deputy chief of staff Joel Kaplan. We wanted to compare our notes from the weekend and make a decision about how to proceed.

Steve Shafran reported on the consumer lending program he was working on. One challenge was that he and the New York Fed agreed on a different approach than the Washington Fed, but he expected a solution would be found. Dan Jester and David Nason said they had been working throughout the weekend to finalize the equity deals with the nine big banks and expected to complete them soon. (The paperwork was finished just after midnight.) Neel reported that 20 additional banks had applied for the capital program, including such important names as Capital One and Northern Trust.

Neel and his team had spent Sunday at Bank of New York Mellon. Under our reverse auction plan, Treasury would determine a specific amount of TARP money to spend on illiquid assets, then hold an auction in which financial institutions would bid to sell their assets to Treasury. The government would buy the assets at the lowest price, helping to improve liquidity and create a market, which private-sector buyers had been unwilling to do.

That was how it was meant to work, anyway. Right after TARP passed, Treasury had asked potential custodians to submit proposals, and they indicated they would be able to start auctions quickly. But after discussing with Bank of New York Mellon the unique requirements of the legislation—allowing thousands of firms to register to sell their assets and making sure they had signed off on executive compensation restrictions, for example—Neel learned that it could take two months, not two weeks, to set up an auction. And because the auctions would have to start small to allow for any necessary adjustments, we might be able to buy only about $5 billion of assets by the end of the year.

"It's just too small in terms of the volumes that we need to move," Neel explained.

There was another problem. A bank owning a small amount of a security might decide to unload it at any price, no matter how low, just to be rid of it. But that could trigger big write-downs at other banks that owned a lot of the same security.

We didn't have time to ramp up the reverse auctions, so I told Neel to concentrate on a different idea we had for moving the assets:

hiring professional money managers and giving them each a certain sum of money to buy eligible assets in the market.

Though it was getting late, and everyone was tired, we had a lively discussion, and as usual nobody held back. We debated whether we should go ahead with the direct purchase of illiquid assets, the program most visibly associated with TARP. Neel, Jim Wilkinson, and Jeb Mason argued in favor of staying the course, with Jeb making the case that we should focus on buying whole mortgages, as TARP allowed, instead of the more complex securitized mortgages. David Nason and Dan Jester thought we should focus on executing our $250 billion capital purchase program and that the regulators should assess the health of the banks before proceeding with a new program. Both Dan and David believed we should consider expanding the CPP to insurance companies. And everyone agreed we would need to designate a big portion of the last $350 billion for future capital programs.

Shafran said we had to include a foreclosure program in TARP; otherwise we would be on the wrong side of history—and of politics.

"You'll live to regret it if you don't," he said.

I told him all I needed was to see a program that would succeed.

As the clock ticked toward 10:00 p.m., I began to seriously doubt that our asset-buying program could work. This pained me, as I had sincerely promoted the purchases to Congress and the public as the best solution. But in addition to the problems Neel had outlined, it appeared the magnitude of the crisis was outstripping our ability to deal with it by directly buying troubled assets, even with the last $350 billion. Housing prices continued to decline, while mortgage troubles had spread beyond subprime to prime residential loans and, more recently, to commercial real estate. Problems were mounting in the market for asset-backed consumer loans, as the deepening recession crimped individuals' ability to repay debt.

Still, I held off making a final decision, hoping that we could devise a plan that would work faster than the reverse auctions. I concluded that any new capital program should wait until our existing program was further along. I gave the go-ahead to look into buying whole loans and to continue to work on foreclosure relief plans. I also wanted to address the troubled monoline insurers, if only to separate their viable municipal finance business from the failed structured finance business so that state and local governments would be able to tap the public markets for desperately needed funds.

But the big question was whether we would have enough TARP money to deal with unforeseen emergencies—like AIG.

In fact, no recipient of government aid had caused more public ire than AIG—and it once again stood on the brink of failure. I needed someone to manage the situation, but everyone seemed to shy away from it. It was a thankless task that came at an awkward time, at the end of the administration, when people were already searching for new jobs. Some told me point-blank that they didn't want to do it.

As it happened, though, I had just the right person on staff in Jim Lambright, who had arrived just days before—on October 22— to manage TARP's investments. Still in his 30s, Jim had been appointed by President Bush to be chairman of the Export-Import Bank in 2005. I'd met him while working on the Strategic Economic Dialogue with China. Now I asked Jim to work with the Fed to structure what would become Treasury's TARP investment in AIG. I could tell that the former Golden Gloves boxer had the fortitude and capability to handle the problem.

By late October, AIG was in dreadful shape, partly because of deteriorating conditions in the insurance business and partly because of its leveraged capital structure. The financial mess inherited by AIG's new CEO, Ed Liddy, had turned out to be even worse than the Fed had expected. And the Fed's $85 billion loan, with its high interest rate of LIBOR plus 8.5 percent, had imposed a heavy financial burden on a badly wounded company. But those terms, while intended to protect the taxpayer, were undermining the government's investment. At the time of its rescue in September, we had not had the authority to put equity capital into AIG. Now we did. With the company expecting to announce a whopping loss on November 10, it would go down without a capital investment and a new financial plan in place.

Treasury needed to establish new TARP guidelines for an investment in a failing company, including stricter executive compensation guidelines than those in force for capital investments for healthy institutions. The Fed and its adviser, Morgan Stanley, also worked with AIG and its rating agencies to avoid a downgrade that would lead to crippling collateral calls.

Meantime, the automakers continued to struggle. The White House's hopes of redirecting the $25 billion in low-interest fuel-efficiency loans to bail out the companies had hit a wall. It couldn't legally be done unless Congress changed the language of its legislation, but Nancy Pelosi refused. She was unwilling to change the bill's environmental focus. Instead, she insisted that I had the authority to use TARP funds to rescue the car companies, which had been pleading their case in Washington with some success.

On October 27, Moody's downgraded the credit rating on GM's and Chrysler's debt, and the Dow fell 203 points to close at 8,176. The VIX, the Chicago Board Options Exchange's volatility index, posted its second straight record day.

One day later, however, the Dow shot up 889 points, to 9,065, with nearly half the gain coming in the last hour of trading. Some analysts credited bargain hunting, while others attributed the rise to increased confidence resulting from Treasury and Fed actions. Though delighted to see the jump in share prices, I cautioned everyone not to overreact to one or two days in the market.

The imminent election contributed to the volatility in the markets. Obama had pulled well ahead of McCain, and although the Democratic candidate and I had enjoyed a frank, respectful relationship, he had begun to make pronouncements that distressed me, hitting hard on the issue of bank lending. I was concerned that McCain would pile on, making our efforts to get capital out to the banks even more difficult. On Tuesday evening, October 28, I called Rahm Emanuel to talk about it. I knew that Rahm was close to Obama and, as a former investment banker, understood the intersection of politics and markets as well as anyone. I also believed he was likely to hold a prominent position in the next administration.

"You should call Barack and deal with him directly," Rahm said. "He likes you."

That evening, Obama and I had an extensive conversation.

"Everyone is talking about making the banks lend more, but 'more' than what?" I asked. "I expect them to lend more than they would have without the program, but the government should not make lending decisions."

"I recognize that this is not a simple issue, but the banks need to understand their responsibilities," Obama replied, adding that compensation was even more explosive politically. He agreed to tone down his rhetoric but warned me that I should also be talking to McCain: if the Republican candidate jumped on either the lending or compensation issue, Obama would have to do likewise.

On October 30, I took the opportunity to deliver a pep talk to my staff, just before we began a lengthy strategy session in which

I would lay out the assignments for the next few days. "I am so proud of this team, and all you have done in such a short amount of time," I said. "I know you're tired."

But the capital purchase program had to be flawlessly executed, so I went on: "If you have family obligations, forget them. I'll help you get jobs, I'll kiss you on all four cheeks, but we've got one more big push before Thanksgiving."

They burst out laughing—they had such extraordinary dedication and camaraderie. And of course everyone already expected that they were going to be on the job all weekend. That's what we did. I had to fly to Chicago with Wendy to babysit our granddaughter—but I, too, knew that I would spend most of the weekend working.

Saturday, in fact, found me talking on my cell phone with Ben about foreclosure relief. He knew that the White House had never seen a mortgage mitigation plan that it favored, but like me, he believed that devising one would be critical to getting congressional approval to release the final tranche of TARP.

"The Fed will support you, if it's one that makes sense," Ben said.

I returned on Sunday evening and went directly to a meeting at Treasury where we once again discussed taking down the remaining $350 billion of TARP. To do so, we would need to explain how the funds would be used. After yet another discussion of potential strategies, I reluctantly concluded that a direct purchase program for illiquid assets was not a good use of our limited TARP dollars. The markets were getting worse, and every program I looked at either took too much time to implement or would not be big enough to make a difference. Capital investments were more powerful, and we had decided to reserve $150 billion for future bank capital programs and to set aside funds to expand beyond banks to insurance companies. To make this work politically, we would need to deal with foreclosures.

The next afternoon, at a meeting in the Roosevelt Room with a large group of senior White House staff and economic advisers, I decided to address the controversial mortgage relief issue directly. I said I didn't think we should spend time debating the pros and cons of the issue.

"I know many of you strongly oppose government spending for foreclosures, and I can't find a program that isn't flawed," I told them. "I'm just going to make the assertion that we need the second half of TARP, and we can't get it without foreclosure relief."

If we agreed on that, I said, I would go to the president and tell him that foreclosure relief was a political reality. I also dropped a bomb when I informed them we had decided against buying illiquid assets.

The White House staff didn't argue with me, but I could see they were taken aback. Although they understood my reasoning, they knew that dropping the asset purchases would create a political and communications problem. Neither did they disagree with the need for the last tranche, but they pointed out the political difficulty of going to Congress to ask for the money without the asset-purchase plan in place.

I explained that we did have a purchase plan in mind, though not for toxic mortgages. I outlined the work Steve Shafran had been doing with the Fed to use TARP money to unlock the consumer credit markets, explaining how the new Fed lending facility would essentially guarantee a minimum price for asset-backed securities.

As soon as the questions about securitization started, I realized what we were up against. Ed Gillespie, who as counselor to the president oversaw communications, was a smart guy, and he asked very basic questions to help him figure out how to sell the program as a good use of TARP. He was echoed by Dan Meyer, the president's assistant for legislative affairs.

"Hank, explain to me again this TALF securitization plan and why government intervention is necessary," Ed said.

This wasn't an encouraging sign. If these wise White House insiders had a hard time grasping the proposed program, how would lawmakers and the public get it? Even more important, would they understand and accept the surprise move away from buying illiquid assets?

I had hoped to get the last tranche for emergencies, and to have it in place for the new administration, but Joel Kaplan, Dan Meyer, and Ed Gillespie believed that we would have to clearly demonstrate a need for the money to persuade Congress to give it to us. Dropping the asset-buying plan would undermine our credibility, and I was beginning to understand that unless I faced an emergency, I might never be able to get the rest of the TARP money without the full support of the president-elect. I realized we needed to rethink our approach. At the same time, I decided to keep Neel working on options for asset purchases for the time being, because I knew that giving up on it would shock the market and subject us to a great deal of criticism.

I stewed over these issues all evening, through a dinner at the Brazilian ambassador's residence and into the night. I saw no way around the political obstacles, but I dreaded being caught without money if another crisis arose. I tossed and turned a lot that night, thinking of the stricken look on Ed Gillespie's face after I said I was dropping the plan to buy assets.

Despite the rain that covered the city, Washington thrummed with excitement on Election Day. Every election riveted the nation's capital, of course, but this one carried particular historic resonance for the city's African American majority. I had already voted by absentee ballot, so I went straight to my office. At 8:00 a.m. I called Joel Kaplan at the White House.

"I've been thinking about it," I said, "and I don't think we should try to take down the second half of TARP."

Joel was hugely relieved, as was my team, who feared I was leading them into the second Battle of Little Big Horn. The president and vice president were also relieved when I met with them later that day in the Oval Office. I was convinced I had made the right decision, but I also knew that we had only a thin cushion to carry us through the long transition period leading up to January 20.

On Tuesday the Dow saw its biggest presidential Election Day rally ever, jumping 305 points, or 3.3 percent, to 9,625. The London interbank rate fell to its lowest level since November 2004. Market watchers credited the optimism to speculation that the government might extend its capital program to nonbank financial companies like GE.

Wendy stayed up to watch the election results, but I went to bed early. Obama was ahead, and I figured the election was a foregone conclusion. After the Democratic candidate was declared the winner at 11:00 p.m., Wendy woke me up to tell me the historic news. I went back to sleep comforted by the knowledge that our president-elect fully understood the threat our economy still faced. I was also relieved that the election was over and that I would no longer have to worry that our actions might become campaign issues. Now I would need to talk with the transition team to find out how they wanted to work with us.

In the meantime, Treasury still had plenty of business to take care of. On November 5, the day after the election, Jim Lambright and I sat down in the Oval Office with President Bush, Vice President Cheney, and Keith Hennessey. It was five days before AIG would release its third-quarter earnings.

Jim carefully explained the situation. AIG's problems had been exacerbated by the crumbling financial markets; since the deal had been made, the global insurance business had slumped. Now the company's credit default swaps had neared 2,400 basis points. That meant that it cost almost $24 to insure $100 of AIG credit—an extraordinarily high amount.

The market could see that AIG's capital structure was unsustainable. The Federal Reserve's loan had saved it, but the company still had too much debt. The loan's high cost strained interest coverage, and its short, two-year duration created pressure to sell assets quickly in a soft market. Meantime, the company was still weighed down by substantial market and credit risks from its holdings of residential mortgage-backed securities and the credit default swaps it had written on residential MBS. It had even used its securities lending program to purchase residential MBS.

It turned out AIG's third-quarter losses were going to be $24.5 billion pretax—even worse than we had expected. We needed to act quickly to inject $40 billion of TARP capital into AIG to avoid a rating downgrade that would trigger $42 billion in collateral calls and finish the company off.

The Fed's restructuring plan would shift AIG's worst mortgage-related assets and credit default swaps into two new Fed vehicles, called Maiden Lane II and Maiden Lane III, which together would hold $52.5 billion. That way any collateral calls triggered by a future downgrade would hurt the company less. More than 20 subsidiaries would be sold; AIG would become a much smaller, more narrowly focused property/casualty insurer.

Under the New York Fed's plan, Treasury's $40 billion would purchase senior preferred shares in AIG; in return we would receive a 10 percent dividend and warrants for 2 percent of the company's shares. The Fed would scrap the $85 billion two-year loan, substituting a five-year $60 billion loan and cutting the interest rate from 8.5 to 3.0 percentage points over LIBOR. Under the New York Fed's creative restructuring, the $150 billion deal would not increase the government's 79.9 percent stake.

President Bush, frustrated with both the incompetence of the company's prior management and the rating agencies that had failed to catch AIG's problems earlier, once more found himself in the position of supporting a philosophically unpalatable bailout for reasons of necessity. After Jim had laid out the revised rescue plan, the president asked him, "Are you asking me or telling me this is going to happen?"

New to his job, Jim looked to me to answer.

"I'm telling you this is going to happen, Mr. President," I said.

"Will we ever get the money back?"

This time Jim responded. "I don't know, sir."

"We need to be very clear that we're doing this because it's a systemically important company and we need to keep it from failing," the president said.

President Bush's anger quickly echoed across the country when taxpayers learned the government was revamping its September bailout plan and giving AIG easier loan terms along with much-needed capital. To the public, AIG symbolized everything that had gone wrong with the system—incompetence rewarded with big bonuses and lavish spending. While I shared their disgust, I told the president that AIG's new CEO, Ed Liddy, was working his tail off for a salary of one dollar a year. But like the president, I understood that we had to hold our noses and save the company in order to protect the frail financial system.

The jittery markets didn't maintain their elation about Obama's triumph for long. Wednesday was another wild ride, with the Dow dropping 486 points, or 5 percent, to 9,139—the worst plunge on record for the day after a presidential election. Bank stocks were hard-hit, and though no institution appeared to be in immediate danger, Citigroup fell 14 percent to $12.63.

As we worked to bolster the banks, commercial real estate became a growing source of concern. I got a glimpse of just how bad the situation was when Wendy and I had dinner on November 8 with our friends *New York Times* columnist Thomas Friedman and his wife, Ann. Her father, Matthew Bucksbaum, had co-founded General Growth Properties in Des Moines with his brother Martin in 1954. The company was the second-largest mall operator in the U.S., but its stock had been tanking and I knew that it was struggling to avoid bankruptcy.

Ann was stoical, and we didn't talk much about the situation that evening. But it seemed that everywhere I went, I encountered another grim reminder of the pain this crisis was inflicting on our nation and of how much we needed to repair our markets—not for the banks, but for Americans who depended on companies like General Growth for their livelihood.

The day after my dinner with the Friedmans, Ben Bernanke, who had flown back overnight from a G-20 meeting in São Paulo, met me in my office for a TARP oversight board meeting to approve the AIG investment and to make some joint calls to congressional leaders to prepare them for the AIG announcement. None of the leaders we contacted that Sunday afternoon and evening objected, other than Richard Shelby. As John Boehner said, "You've got no choice."

On Monday, as AIG revealed its breathtaking third-quarter loss, Treasury announced TARP's first one-off investment when it unveiled the revised package for the company. Though the Dow slipped nearly 1 percent, AIG's shares rose 8.1 percent, to $2.28.

The rescue package took care to apply TARP's strictest provisions on golden parachutes and froze the size of the bonus pool for the company's top 70 executives. But that did not satisfy an increasingly angry public.

The same day we announced the AIG deal, Dan Tarullo, the head of Obama's economic transition team, arrived at Treasury with Lee Sachs, a former Clinton Treasury official who was under consideration to run TARP for the new administration. Tarullo said his team wanted to monitor what we were doing with TARP but didn't expect to be included in policy decisions. After all, there could be only one president at a time. I told them that I would be making a major speech on November 12 and that they would like it, because we wouldn't be announcing new programs and we wouldn't ask for the remaining TARP money. They both were visibly relieved. I had accepted that it wouldn't be realistic to get Sachs nominated and quickly approved for the permanent post, but I'd hoped he would take up residence at Treasury and work side by side with Neel. As it turned out, we didn't see much of him or Tarullo.

Between collapsing insurance giants, dying shopping malls, bailed-out banks, and all-but-bankrupt automakers, the American people had watched one institution after another totter. I'd kept my public comments to a minimum in the weeks before the election. But I knew the markets and the press were growing impatient, and I began working hard on the speech I planned to deliver on November 12 at Treasury, in which I would make clear my decision to move away from buying illiquid assets.

I had struggled with this decision, and up until a few days before the speech I would stop by Neel Kashkari's office every morning to talk over possible asset-purchase programs. He had lined up several big money managers, including Western Asset and Black-Rock, to work on the government's behalf, but we concluded that we couldn't design a program big enough or execute it quickly enough to make a dent in the problem in any reasonable period of time.

On November 11, the Federal Housing Finance Agency, the regulator for Fannie Mae and Freddie Mac, announced that the GSEs would adopt parts of Sheila Bair's IndyMac Protocol to simplify mortgage modifications. The FHFA program targeted people who had missed at least three mortgage payments and used the property as their primary residence; like the IndyMac Protocol, it limited mortgage payments to 38 percent or less of the household's gross monthly income. The program had built-in flexibility, and reductions in monthly payments could come from cutting the interest rate, extending the life of the loan, or deferring principal payments. Fannie and Freddie owned or guaranteed 31 million mortgages, so this would extend foreclosure relief to many more homeowners—and, I hoped, assuage those who complained that the government had not done enough.

But Sheila Bair did not show much enthusiasm for the FHFA program and continued to push Treasury to back her loss-sharing plan. I called Sheila to let her know I had decided against trying to get the last tranche of TARP, and as a result would not be announcing any new foreclosure efforts, such as her insurance program, beyond FHFA's new initiative. This news did not please her, but she said she understood.

My round of calls to congressional leaders included a conversation with Barney Frank. I mentioned the FHFA program and explained to Barney that we couldn't do more on foreclosures without a final tranche of TARP money, and we weren't going to ask for that. I also pointed out that we hadn't told Congress or the public that the TARP funds would be used for a spending program. Although he didn't like my message, he didn't push back as hard as I'd expected. But I heard from him again early the next morning.

"You need a housing program," he said. "We sold TARP to our caucus because owning mortgages would help you deal with the foreclosures, and this is going to cause a big problem with them." He added that if we came up with a foreclosure plan, we could get the last tranche of TARP.

He was optimistic that President-elect Obama would support the effort and that we would get Democratic votes. If we didn't like

Sheila's insurance program, we should come up with something different, he said. I liked Barney's attitude, but I told him he was more optimistic than anyone else on this issue, and that I'd had no indication that the new administration wanted to work with us.

Getting my speech right was tricky. I hadn't provided any public update on our progress since late October, and I was concerned about unsettling the markets and discrediting our efforts. Everyone expected me to announce my intent to request the rest of the TARP funding. Saying definitively that we weren't going to would not be well received, so I decided it was better not to mention it at all. I knew, though, that the market participants would do the math and wonder if I had enough money left to deal with emergencies. I would have to communicate that I was comfortable with the funds I had and with the procedures for getting the rest, and hope for the best.

Similarly the markets were expecting me to unveil the details of a program to buy assets. And buyers and sellers of illiquid assets had been frozen waiting for our program, so silence was not an option. I needed to explain our rationale for not purchasing the toxic securities and to describe the other priorities for TARP dollars. I focused on Treasury's ongoing efforts with our bank capital program and our plans to help the consumer loan market.

Michele Davis and I were going over last-minute preparations for my speech when Jeb Mason burst into my office to make a final plea for a small-scale asset program in which Treasury would buy whole mortgages and get foreclosure relief for the homeowners.

"Hank, I want to say one more time, you shouldn't be going out there and saying you're not going to buy illiquid assets directly," Jeb said. "We should have some program, even if it's a small program."

I always encouraged give-and-take, but that morning, knowing that I was about to make a controversial announcement to a roomful of reporters, I was not in the mood for it. The program he wanted would have been a nightmare to administer. "I've heard you multiple times on this, and I've made my decision," I snapped.

Jeb was right that the speech was risky, but I'd rather get politically lambasted than knowingly develop a program only for show. If I said anything but the truth, I couldn't look at myself in the mirror.

Shortly afterward, I walked into the bright lights and chattering voices of Treasury's Media Room, and delivered what I considered to be a terrific, if complicated, speech. In my six-page statement I covered everything the government had done to ease the crisis, from our ongoing HOPE Now mortgage modification program, which each month was helping 200,000 homeowners avoid foreclosure, to the GSE rescue.

I also brought the public up to date on our TARP efforts. I said that after much consideration we had decided that the asset-buying program was not an effective way to use TARP money, though we would continue to study possible targeted purchases. We were working to quickly get capital to participating banks, I added, and emphasized that those institutions had responsibilities when it came to lending, compensation and dividend policies, and foreclosure relief. I noted that Treasury and the Fed were working on a program to improve the availability of consumer credit by improving liquidity in the asset-backed securitization market, and that the facility might be extended to new commercial and residential mortgage lending.

I also tackled the issue of foreclosure relief, applauding Sheila's IndyMac Protocol and mentioning Fannie and Freddie's new modification program. I conceded that Sheila's insurance idea was important and said we would evaluate it, but pointed out that we would have to figure out how to finance it.

The reporters were polite, asking a lot of questions about the securitization program. But just as I feared, the markets focused on the facts that there wouldn't be a program to purchase mortgage-related assets and that we weren't going to be moving ahead quickly with any new programs that would require us to ask for the remaining $350 billion. The reaction was immediate and brutal: the Dow fell by 411 points, to 8,283, and the S&P 500 and the NASDAQ each dropped by 5.2 percent. Public criticism and plenty of negative press followed.

November 12 was a day of major announcements. Treasury, the Fed, and the FDIC put out a comprehensive joint statement dealing with the hot-button issues of lending, executive compensation, dividends, and foreclosure mitigation. Since the compensation and lending controversies exploded in mid-October, I had encouraged Ben, Tim, John Dugan, and Sheila to address these issues in strong, clear language. The resulting regulatory guidance pleased me: it said in no uncertain terms that banks must fulfill their fundamental role by lending to creditworthy borrowers and must work to avoid preventable foreclosures. It also warned against compensation plans that "created perverse incentives that jeopardize the health of the banking organization" and called for programs that were "aligned with the long-term prudential interests of the institution."

Also that day, the FDIC agreed to guarantee up to $139 billion of debt issued by General Electric's finance subsidiary, GE Capital, under the temporary program the regulator had established in October. Though not a bank, GE Capital was systemically important, and David Nason and I had worked hard to get Sheila comfortable with making this decision. The FDIC said it would extend the Temporary Liquidity Guarantee Program to nonbanks on a case-by-case basis, using criteria like size, credit rating, and connection to the economy. GE Capital, along with Citigroup, would become one of the two biggest users of TLGP, issuing some $70 billion of government-guaranteed debt. (The GE parent company agreed to indemnify the FDIC against any losses for GE Capital.)

But none of this news mattered to the markets, whose earlier volatility seemed to have turned into a full-fledged slide. The Dow was down nearly 40 percent from the start of the year, and companies from General Motors to Genworth Financial were coming under enormous pressures.

January 20 was a long way off, and I felt very exposed. Between AIG and the banks, we'd allocated all but $60 billion of our $350 billion. I had exhausted my political capital and credibility in an effort to keep the system from collapsing, and now I would have to rely on the incoming Obama administration to help me.

CHAPTER 16

Wednesday, November 19, 2008

Just one week after I had delivered a speech meant to reassure the markets, I headed to the Oval Office to tell the president that yet another major U.S. financial institution, Citigroup, was teetering on the brink of failure.

"I thought the programs we put in place had stabilized the banks," he said, visibly shocked.

"I did, too, Mr. President, but we are not out of the woods yet," I said. "Citi has a very weak balance sheet, and the short sellers are attacking."

It was just after 1:00 p.m., and world markets were again in disarray, pummeled by investor worries about banks, automakers, and the overall U.S. economy. The U.K.'s FTSE 100 Index and the Frankfurt Stock Exchange's DAX 30 Index had ended their trading sessions down nearly 5 percent, and the Dow was on course for a 5 percent slide of its own, to 7,997, its first close below 8,000 since March 2003.

All financial companies were under pressure, but Citi was being hammered the hardest. Its shares had already sunk 13 percent, on their way to a full-day plunge of 23 percent to $6.40, a fall of 88 percent from May 2007. Its credit spreads were also starting to balloon—they would hit 361 basis points that day, up from about 240 basis points the day before.

Arguably the best-known bank in the world, Citi had operations in more than 100 countries and more than $2 trillion in assets on its balance sheet. But the sprawling New York–based giant, built through multiple acquisitions, struggled with an unwieldy organizational structure and lacked a single unifying culture or clear business strategy. I'd long believed it had become almost too complex to manage.

In the boom years, Citi had built a substantial exposure to commercial mortgages, credit cards, and collateralized debt obligations tied to subprime mortgages. It carried more than $1.2 trillion in assets off its balance sheet, half of these related to mortgages.

I knew that Citi was the weakest of the major U.S. banks. For its size, the bank had a modest retail deposit base, particularly on its home turf. This made it more dependent on wholesale funding and foreign deposits, and hence more vulnerable to panic.

The market's fears had intensified earlier that morning when Citi announced that it would wind down the last of its SIVs, bringing $17.4 billion worth of risky assets onto its books. This news followed the disclosure two days before that the bank was laying off 53,000 employees and had dropped plans to sell $80 billion of marked-down assets. Investors worried that Citi couldn't find buyers for its toxic assets or might not be able to afford the write-down from a sale.

Notwithstanding Citi's shakiness, I had been falsely reassured by the fact that the market had supported the bank for so long. Its sinking share price had tracked the decline in other financials, and

Citi's regulators had indicated that they were keeping close tabs on it.

But now the market had turned on Citi, and we would have to act quickly. Like that other troubled financial colossus, AIG, the New York bank was deeply enmeshed in a complicated web of ties to financial institutions and government entities all over the world.

"A collapse would be horrific," I told the president. "We've said we will let no systemically important bank fail. We can't let it happen now."

"Aren't there things you can do to save it?" the president asked.

I explained that we had the resources in TARP, but if Citi came unglued, it could trigger a chain reaction among the hundreds of financial institutions that were its customers and counterparties, and we didn't have the wherewithal to deal with another run on the banking system. The Citi crisis proved that we needed to get Congress to release the rest of the TARP money, I said.

"It's politically difficult, but we're going to have to figure out how to do it," I told him.

"Just don't let Citi fail," he replied.

With the president's admonition on my mind, I flew to Los Angeles later that day. I was hesitant to leave Washington, but Nancy Reagan had long ago invited me to speak at the Ronald Reagan Presidential Library. I knew the markets were watching my every move: canceling the trip could spark rumors that might further endanger Citi. I arrived at the Westlake Village Inn in Simi Valley at about 9:30 p.m. and went to bed almost immediately in order to be rested for the morning.

Of all the rough nights I'd endured throughout the crisis, this one was by far the worst. Surrounded by photos of Ronald Reagan in the White House and at his Santa Barbara ranch, I lay awake, tormented by self-doubt and second-guessing.

November had been one rough month. Democrats were excoriating us over foreclosure relief and our decision not to buy toxic assets, while conservative critics continued to carp at the bailouts we'd been forced to undertake, which they slammed as nationalization or, worse, socialism. The markets were falling relentlessly. In the barely two weeks since Senator Obama's election, the Dow had lost 17 percent.

But I felt we could point to any number of successes, from securing TARP's passage to the money market fund guarantee, our efforts at international coordination, and the bank capital program. But that night as I tossed and turned, I wondered if my recent decisions had only added to the confusion, suspicion, and fear that so many citizens felt. In spite of all we had done, the country was heading deeper into an ugly recession, and one of its biggest banks was on the verge of collapse.

The rare bright spot in recent days had come with the G-20 leaders' meeting on November 15. It was a signal achievement of President Bush's to have brought together countries as diverse as Germany, Saudi Arabia, and Mexico to address the global financial crisis and shape a communiqué that embraced free-market principles while recognizing the need for financial reform. Even as some leaders of the developed countries apologized for the mistakes of our free-market system, their counterparts among the emerging nations warned of the dangers of overregulation. But overall, the meeting had been marked by earnest cooperation, with all the leaders rejecting protectionism and agreeing that reform efforts would be successful only if there were a commitment to free-market principles.

Once the leaders left, however, I had returned to unpleasant political realities, and on November 17 Ben and I were once again sitting at Nancy Pelosi's long conference table, surrounded by Democratic representatives and senators. Looking around the room, I saw no friendly faces.

"Don't you want to show those of us who voted for TARP that some of the money is going to foreclosure relief?" Nancy asked pointedly.

Although I assured the lawmakers I would keep working to find ways of reducing foreclosures beyond our loan modification plans, they weren't convinced. This wasn't political theater. It didn't matter that TARP had been created as an investment program to prevent the collapse of the financial system or that we needed to conserve our limited resources in such a volatile market. They all wanted a spending program and a piece of me.

The next day, November 18, Ben, Sheila Bair, and I testified before Barney Frank's Financial Services Committee. I had endured some rough hearings on Capitol Hill, but this was the toughest one chaired by Barney. He displayed four pages of excerpts from the TARP legislation that he said authorized aggressive action on foreclosures. New York Democrat Gary Ackerman said, "You seem to be flying a $700 billion plane by the seat of your pants."

Maxine Waters piled on. "You, Mr. Paulson, took it upon yourself to absolutely ignore the authority and the direction that this Congress had given you," she intoned.

Then, just a few hours later, Bob Rubin, now a board director and senior counselor at Citi, called to tell me that short sellers were attacking the bank. Its shares had closed the day before at $8.36 and were sinking deeper into single digits. I had known Bob for years, first as my boss and the former head of Goldman Sachs, then as Treasury secretary under President Bill Clinton. Always calm and measured, Bob put the public interest ahead of everything else. He rarely called me, and the urgency in his voice that afternoon left me with no doubt that Citi was in grave danger.

Thursday, November 20, 2008

Exhausted and demoralized, I gave up on sleeping and switched the hotel room television on to CNBC. Normally I didn't pay much attention to the talking heads, but that morning I listened glumly as market participants and traders blamed the ongoing financial crisis on me and my decision to drop the asset-buying plan.

Feeling low, I made my first call of the day, at about 5:30 a.m. Pacific time, to Tim Geithner in New York.

"I feel responsible for this mess," I told him.

"Hank, you're doing your best. Don't look back," he said.

Tim's steady, no-nonsense manner quickly braced me, focusing me on the crisis we faced. Speculators were pushing Citi's credit spreads wider, while short sellers continued to drive its stock down. We needed to get our teams together. Ninety minutes later, Tim and I held a conference call with Ben, Sheila, and John Dugan.

"We've told the world we're not going to let any of our major institutions fall," Tim asserted. "We're going to have to make it really clear we're standing behind Citigroup."

I left the inn for the Reagan Library. It was a beautiful Southern California morning, but I was too tense to enjoy it. Before my 11:00 a.m. speech, I toured the library, where the president's writings were framed on the walls. I stopped to read his words, neatly written in longhand, and I reflected on what an extraordinary communicator he had been. He understood the immense power of a clear message, delivered simply and straightforwardly. And his message had been clear and simple. More than any other president,

Ronald Reagan represented the free-market principles I had long believed in.

As I was about to address an audience of Reagan conservatives, I was struck by the irony of my situation. To protect free-enterprise capitalism, I had become the Treasury secretary who would forever be associated with government intervention and bank bailouts. The speed with which the crisis hit had left me no other choice, and I had set aside strict ideology to accomplish the higher goal of saving a system that, even with all its flaws, was better than any other I knew—I had been forced to do things I did not believe in to save what I did believe in. Now here I was, about to deliver a speech explaining these government bailouts to a gathering of conservative true believers in a shrine of free-market capitalism. And if that weren't irony enough, I knew that if our rescue of Citi failed, all of our efforts to date would have been in vain.

A short while later I addressed the group, taking them through each step of the crisis and stressing the need for global regulatory reform. But I realized straightaway that my speech was too defensive and complex—and too long. The audience was friendly and supportive, but these were staunch Republicans who just hated bailouts. The one big round of applause I got came when I said we shouldn't use TARP money to bail out the automakers.

Afterward, I touched base briefly with Bob Rubin. "Things aren't good," he said in his typically low-key way. As its shares sank and the press speculated about a government bailout, Citi's customers were increasingly nervous.

At lunch I listened to some of the members of the audience talk about the losses they and their friends had taken on their houses and in the market. They weren't criticizing me—on the contrary, they thanked me for my hard work. But my doubts from the night before returned. I felt responsible for their suffering and for all that had gone wrong.

Uneasy, I spoke to Ken Lewis and Jamie Dimon at the airport before boarding my 4:00 p.m. flight. Both reported that the markets were tough and that everyone was watching Citi, whose shares ended the day down a further 26 percent, at $4.71. The broader markets were taking their worst hit in years. The Dow dropped 5.6 percent to 7,552, and the S&P 500 fell to its lowest close since 1997.

I buckled my seat belt before takeoff and began to sketch out a plan of attack for the next day. We had so much riding on a Citi rescue, and we had to find a way to discourage short sellers from turning on another bank. My mind churned. But the strains of the day had taken their toll on me, and I fell asleep before takeoff. I didn't wake up until almost midnight, as we circled before landing. When we touched down on the runway, I remembered the president's last words about Citigroup before I left the Oval Office a day earlier: "Don't let it fail."

Friday, November 21–Saturday, November 22, 2008

All day Friday, Citi's regulators worked flat out, floating ideas to stave off disaster, from selling parts of the bank to strengthening its deposit base by combining it with another bank. Some wanted to replace Citi's management and directors. I had strongly advocated installing new leadership at failing institutions and had even chosen the new CEOs for Fannie, Freddie, and AIG. But I wasn't looking for scalps; I wanted to find solutions. And at Citi, Vikram Pandit had been CEO only since December 2007. Unless we had someone in mind who was better qualified and willing to take the job, I saw no point in discussing the matter.

"We can pound on Citi all day long," I told my team. "But you know what? If they go down, it's our fault. We've got to deal with it, and if we don't, the American people will pay the price."

During the last hour of trading, we got some uplifting news when NBC announced that Obama had picked Tim Geithner as his Treasury secretary. The markets exploded upward, with the Dow jumping 7.1 percent to close at 8,046, up 6.5 percent for the day. Citi surged by 19 percent, though it still closed down for the day at $3.77. Its credit default spreads were approaching 500 basis points, while those of JPMorgan, Wells, and BofA were all comfortably below 200 basis points.

Obama's decision gratified me. Apart from reassuring investors, it meant, I felt, that many of our policies would be pursued, even if they were modified and rebranded. Indeed, I took the market's rebound as a vote of confidence in what we'd been doing: the markets saw Tim's nomination to succeed me as a sign of continuity.

When I called Tim to congratulate him, he said that the Obama transition wanted him to disengage from day-to-day activity at the New York Fed as soon as possible. The new economic team was meeting in Chicago that weekend, and the president-elect wanted him there. I pressed him not to go. We needed to come up with a rescue plan before Monday, and his presence was crucial as the bank's primary regulator.

"I'll do everything I can to be helpful," I said. "But we need you on the job this weekend."

To my relief, Tim agreed to remain in New York. But given his future position, he wouldn't speak to Citi or any other bank.

By the time Tim, Ben, Sheila, John Dugan, and I conducted our first conference call, on Saturday at 10:30 a.m., Citi had submitted a two-page proposal to the OCC. The company wanted the government to insure more than $300 billion of toxic assets, including residential- and commercial-mortgage-related securities and troubled corporate loans.

We knew we couldn't assume that Citi's request would be enough to stabilize the markets. We needed to design a plan that would both appeal to investors and protect the taxpayer. And, in my opinion, we needed to put more equity into the company. Capital was the strongest remedy for a weak balance sheet, and the markets needed to see that the government was supporting Citi.

The OCC, FDIC, and New York Fed had set up offices at Citi's headquarters and were scouring the $300 billion of assets to determine their true value. Jeremiah Norton, who happened to be in New York that Saturday, joined the on-site examiners. After he arrived, regulators handed him a memo that they had prepared after an all-night session with bank executives that said Citi, by its own estimates, would become illiquid by the middle of the next week. Regulators were frustrated, complaining that Citi executives were disorganized and unable to provide necessary information on the assets they wanted insured.

No one seemed more frustrated than Sheila, who at first suggested using the FDIC's normal procedures for handling Citi. She proposed other, less costly strategies, such as closing Citi and putting the remains in the hands of a healthy bank. Clearly, she didn't want the FDIC to pay for the losses at Citi, which had significant operations that were not insured by her agency.

I respected Sheila, who improved most programs we worked on together. But sometimes she said things that made my jaw drop. That morning she had said she wasn't sure that Citi's failure would constitute a systemic risk. She felt that Citi had enough subordinated debt and preferred stock to absorb the losses. She spoke as if Citi were just another failing bank and not a world leader—with $3 trillion in assets, both on and off its balance sheet—imploding in the midst of the worst economic conditions since the Great Depression.

"So," she said, "why not let them go through the receivership process?"

Although I believed she was simply posturing, I replied, "If Citi isn't systemic, I don't know what is. And if we do anything less than a powerful response, it will send jitters through the whole market, and people could really put us to a test. I don't have a lot left in TARP."

We also had to consider Citi's $500 billion of foreign deposits. Because foreign deposits were not protected by FDIC insurance, that money was more likely to run to avoid the risk of a bank failure, a major reason Citi's liquidity was likely to evaporate in a few days.

I asked hypothetically if the FDIC could insure foreign deposits in an emergency; Tim believed it could, but Sheila didn't think so. In my view, we couldn't wait to find out. We needed to make another equity infusion in the company. I believed that if we acted forcefully now we had enough TARP capacity to prevent a Citi failure. But if the market's confidence evaporated and the giant bank had to start unwinding all of its $3 trillion in assets in a hurry, the losses could spiral and shake the entire banking system down to its smallest players.

Sheila and I spoke one-on-one after the morning conference call broke up. "Hank, this is hard for me," she said. She was dealing with a board that was skeptical about rescuing Citi and exposing the FDIC's $35 billion fund to the company's potential losses. And to do her job right, Sheila had an obligation to get answers to all the questions she was posing.

Through the afternoon, the New York teams made progress in valuing Citi's problem assets and began work on a plan to insure potential losses, but this was no easy task given the large number of complex assets. Moreover, the FDIC had reservations about some of the valuations, because they used a different process from other regulators'. But Sheila promised to keep working toward a deal, and I felt sure we would have her support in the end.

That evening, British ambassador Nigel Sheinwald had invited Wendy and me to a dinner at his residence, adjacent to the British

Embassy and just a short distance from our house. As we circulated during cocktails, friends and strangers approached, saying things like "I hope you're getting some sleep." This made me uncomfortable; I didn't want to be thought of as poor Hank, the victim. I said to Wendy, "Do I look that bad?" She replied, "You should be grateful that people are being so supportive."

As the hundred or so guests began to take their seats for dinner, I ducked into an empty room to check in with Ben Bernanke. We talked for about half an hour before I returned to the dining room. We agreed that Citi needed an equity investment from TARP, but I demurred when Ben raised the possibility of buying common stock; the idea was good corporate finance but bad public policy. Citi's market value was only about $21 billion, and I pointed out that if we invested any meaningful amount in common stock, we would not only dilute shareholder equity and reward the short sellers, but also leave the government owning a large part of the bank. I could all too easily envision headlines about the nationalization of Citi. I told Ben I was leaning toward buying preferred stock.

Sunday, November 23, 2008

Early Sunday morning, I returned to Treasury and was not surprised to learn that we still had plenty of work to do. Once again, surrounded by the empty soda cans and half-eaten sandwiches of another frantic weekend, we raced against time to announce a deal before the Asian markets opened.

Still, progress was painfully slow. Some of the regulators complained that Citi lacked a sense of urgency. Bob Rubin called to say that Citi was not being given clear direction. The confusion came in part because Tim would not talk directly with the bank—

we had lost a key negotiator. I asked Dan Jester and David Nason to take the lead on all calls with Citi from then on.

By evening, thanks in large part to Dan and David, we had made it work. We all agreed on the loss sharing on the $306 billion in identified assets. Citi would absorb the first $29 billion in losses in addition to its existing reserves of $8 billion, with the government taking 90 percent of the hit above that. The first $5 billion of government exposure would come out of TARP, and the FDIC would take the next $10 billion. The Fed would fund the rest with a nonrecourse loan. To bolster Citi's capital, the U.S. would invest $20 billion in return for perpetual preferred shares yielding 8 percent. It would receive an additional $7 billion in preferred shares as a fee for the guarantee, in addition to warrants equivalent to a 4.5 percent stake in the company.

Citi would face tough restrictions, including limits on executive compensation more stringent than those in our capital program. The bank would be prohibited from paying more than one cent per quarter in dividends on common stock for three years without U.S. government approval. Citi would also implement the FDIC's IndyMac Protocol on mortgage modifications.

I was quite pleased with our solution, as I felt it validated my decision not to use TARP money to directly purchase illiquid assets. With another bank on the brink, we had needed a quick solution that used up as few of our scarce resources as possible. Had we bought Citi's $306 billion of bad assets directly, we would have had to write a check from TARP's fund. Instead, we creatively combined powers with other agencies and shared the risk of losses with the FDIC and the Fed.

Kevin Fromer and I called to update congressional leaders, who were glad to hear we'd averted disaster. But the Democrats made it clear I would now have to do something to help the automakers.

Their message: "You can't just take care of fat-cat Wall Street bankers and ignore the plight of working Americans."

Early that evening, I called the president. I explained that we had fashioned a plan we believed the market would accept, enabling us to avoid a chain reaction of failures.

"Will it work?" he asked.

"I think so, but we won't know until the morning."

Monday, November 24, 2008

At 7:35 a.m. on Monday, I spoke again to the president, and I had good news to report. Asian stocks were flat overnight, but European markets were soaring, on their way to 10 percent gains. Now President Bush turned one of my favorite expressions on me.

"How many sticks of dynamite are you going to need to break this crisis?"

"I don't know, sir," I answered. "But the way things are going, I may have to put one in my mouth and light the fuse."

After the president stopped laughing, I told him that I sometimes felt like Job. If something could go wrong, it would. But he told me, "You should welcome the challenge, Hank. Thank goodness the crisis happened when it did. Imagine if it had hit at the beginning of a new administration, when they were just learning how to work together."

It was the start of a great morning. Citi's shares jumped by more than 60 percent at the opening of trading. I was pleased that our rescue plan had punished the short sellers and thereby averted similar attacks on other banks.

Feeling as good as I had in weeks, I took a brief break from Washington to support Wendy. That evening, the Randall's Island

Sports Foundation in New York City was honoring her for her work in environmental education. Late in the afternoon, I flew to New York to attend the benefit dinner at the Plaza Hotel.

Wendy had been a great source of strength for me, bucking me up through the long string of crises, but the lengthy workdays and nonstop stress had robbed us of any quality time together. I went to the office early every morning and came home late, and if I didn't get right on the phone, I often went straight to bed. Wendy and I rarely had dinner together, and when we did, I was distracted. Worst of all were the times I was physically present but mentally elsewhere. Wendy said she felt as if she'd lost her husband and best friend.

The evening also gave me a chance to reconnect with old friends, but during the predinner cocktail party I had to duck out of the room a few times to take calls, including two from Nancy Pelosi, who told me point-blank that it was politically impossible to rescue Citi and not help the automakers. She had until recently opposed bailouts for the car companies, which she considered poorly managed and which had done themselves no favors when their CEOs flew to Washington by private plane to beg for money. I reiterated my position that Congress should rescue them by amending earlier legislation that provided a $25 billion loan for fuel-efficiency improvements. I was worried that we didn't have enough resources to take care of the financial system, much less the automakers, which couldn't seem to come up with a plan for their long-term viability. Then I switched to the foremost issue in my mind—getting Congress to release the remaining tranche of TARP.

"We're going to need more money from TARP," I told her. "Do you realize what we just escaped with Citi?"

"It's going to be very hard," she said. "The American people don't support it, and I don't have the votes."

I hoped Nancy would bite on my implied offer—agree to help release the remaining tranche, and we'd use some of it on the auto companies. But it was obvious that the politically astute Speaker didn't want to do it. She knew that an auto bailout would depend on the Democrats—the Republicans were lined up against it—and she wanted me to fall on my sword by using TARP money for a very politically unpopular act.

At dinner, Wendy and I sat next to Mike Bloomberg, who was also receiving an award. When he spoke, the New York mayor graciously mentioned me, asserting that "no magic wand" existed to fix the financial crisis and that I had the support of everyone in the room. Wendy spoke so eloquently on teaching kids about nature that I wished I had taken some public speaking lessons from her.

The next morning, we caught an early flight to Washington. Back at Treasury, I stopped in the Markets Room and saw that the markets were reacting favorably to the Fed's announcement of powerful new programs. One was the Term Asset-Backed Securities Loan Facility, or TALF. This program was the culmination of the efforts of the Fed, working with Steve Shafran at Treasury, to unclog the market for securitized consumer loans for cars, credit cards, college expenses, and small businesses. It was designed to pump $200 billion into the credit markets through a one-year loan facility set up by the Fed and backed by $20 billion of TARP funds.

The Fed also announced that it would buy up to $100 billion worth of debt issued by Fannie Mae, Freddie Mac, and the Federal Home Loan Banks, as well as $500 billion of mortgage-backed securities guaranteed by Fannie, Freddie, and the Government National Mortgage Association, better known as Ginnie Mae. Treasury had been purchasing GSE-guaranteed debt at a much more modest level, and the Fed's announcement had an almost instantaneous effect: rates on 30-year mortgages dropped by as much as half a percentage point, while Fannie and Freddie securities increased in value, cheering capital markets. The Dow appeared set for another strong session. Over the past three days, it had surged 927 points, or more than 12 percent.

Tuesday, November 25, 2008

Joel Kaplan kept a block calendar on the wall of his modest White House office that showed the days left before the new administration swept in on January 20. Kevin Fromer, Dave McCormick, and I had come to the White House late on the afternoon of November 25 to talk about getting Congress to release the second half of TARP. Joel, Josh Bolten, and Keith Hennessey used the calendar to demonstrate how little time remained to get anything accomplished between annual government spending bills and dealing with the automakers.

Joel believed that the best course was simply to wait and let Obama take down the rest of TARP when he came into office. But since I had strongly advised both Joel and President Bush that this would be imprudent, he suggested that we try to link arms with the Obama team to act on TARP and autos in December. Joel, who doubled as the White House's point man on autos, said we needed to deal with the carmakers, either through a TARP loan or separate legislation. We all understood that GM would file for bankruptcy by year-end if it didn't get financial assistance.

To me, a 76-day transition period between administrations was a barbarically long time to be without adequate resources. Earlier in the afternoon I had called Rahm Emanuel to tell him we needed to take down the last $350 billion. "That is not good news," he said, and he recommended that I call Larry Summers.

I got home shortly after 7:30 p.m. and was buoyed by the sight of my daughter, Amanda, her husband, Josh, and little Willa, my granddaughter. The next day we were all going to Little St. Simons Island for Thanksgiving. I only needed to hear Willa say, "Boppa, I want to cuddle," then climb onto my lap with her blanket, to forget the credit crisis for a few minutes.

But soon I needed to call Larry Summers to explain that we didn't have enough approved TARP money left to protect the system.

"What do you think you will need to get the rest?" he asked.

"I think we'll have to give Congress some clarity on what we're going to use it for," I answered. "We're going to have to commit to a mortgage relief program and a solution on autos."

"Do you think it would be sufficient to say that there's going to be a program spending up to $50 billion for mortgage relief and that Obama will determine what the program is?"

"I would far prefer that to proposing a program ourselves," I said, knowing full well President-elect Obama would want to choose his own program.

Overall, Larry was noncommittal, but he asked whom on my staff the transition team could work with. I was hopeful the Bush and Obama teams would work together successfully on a plan.

By midmorning on Wednesday, Wendy and I were kayaking toward Little St. Simons Island, while Amanda, Josh, and Willa rode the ferry. The day was windy and refreshing, and the brisk salt air and exercise relieved much of my tension. We picnicked on the beach that afternoon, and I made a few more calls before turning off my phone for the first time since August.

I had one of my best Little St. Simons fishing days on Thanksgiving, followed by a turkey dinner on the beach. Standing on one of my favorite spots on earth—beside the ocean, surrounded by birds—and watching Willa spot a bald eagle, I felt for a moment that my problems weren't that huge.

Friday morning, however, I turned my phone back on and spent much of the day on the phone. Josh Bolten had invited the

Obama economic team to sit down with us on Sunday to discuss getting access to the rest of the TARP funds and to devise a solution for the automakers.

That weekend, Joel came up with a proposal: Car companies seeking government loans would present detailed plans for their future to a financial viability adviser, or "auto czar," whose appointment would be agreed upon by President Bush and Obama. While the czar assessed the plans, Treasury would make a short-term bridge loan to the companies—say, to March 31. If an automaker failed to provide an acceptable plan, the adviser would create one, with options including a Chapter 11 reorganization. Joel's proposal required that Obama publicly support the Bush administration's policy that the automakers needed to be on a path for viability before they could get TARP money.

Sunday, November 30, 2008

Getting the Obama team to meet proved to be a challenge. Rahm Emanuel declined to attend, and the president-elect's people wanted the meeting to take place at Treasury rather than the White House, presumably so as not to appear to be working too closely with the Bush team.

The meeting was set for 4:00 p.m. the Sunday after Thanksgiving, in my office. Larry Summers arrived early, accompanied by Dan Tarullo, Obama's economics adviser. As the former Treasury secretary walked around the anteroom of his old office, he paused in front of a large photograph of a gathering of former Treasury secretaries taken at a dinner George Shultz had given in my honor in 2006. Larry liked the picture so much we later made him a copy.

The Bush contingent consisted of Josh, Joel, Keith Hennessey, Commerce secretary Carlos Gutierrez, Dan Meyer, and me. The

Obama team also included Mona Sutphen, future deputy chief of staff for policy, and Phil Schiliro, legislative affairs specialist. After a few pleasantries—and Larry's request to keep these exploratory discussions confidential—Josh opened by saying I wanted Congress to give us access to the rest of TARP, and that would happen only if Obama led the effort. I laid out my suggestions for using the last tranche, which included a foreclosure program, the TALF, and funds for contingencies and future Obama programs. Joel outlined the plan for automakers.

Other than Larry, Obama's people were quiet and seemed on guard. They asked a lot of questions but offered no suggestions for how we might work together. Though the meeting was polite, I quickly realized that we weren't getting anywhere. Larry clearly didn't like our idea for the car companies, preferring not to be bound by the Bush administration's viability test and an independent auto czar. When the meeting ended, so did my hopes of getting Obama's people to support me on getting the final tranche.

Monday, December 1–Sunday, December 7, 2008

The next day, the markets turned ugly again, as the National Bureau of Economic Research announced that the U.S. was officially in a recession and had been for the past year. The Dow plunged 680 points, or 7.7 percent; frightened investors piled into 10-year Treasuries, pushing the yield down to 2.73 percent, the lowest point since the 1950s.

On Tuesday, GM and Chrysler sent letters to Congress asking for emergency loans of $4 billion and $7 billion, respectively. (Two days later the auto executives themselves would arrive, in fuel-efficient hybrids this time.) But House and Senate Republicans remained adamantly opposed to bailing out the automakers. That didn't bode well for getting the final tranche of TARP. Democrats would not release it without an auto provision, and Republicans would not approve it if it contained an auto bailout.

The streets of Washington were cold and grim on the afternoon of December 2, when I left for Beijing to attend my final Strategic Economic Dialogue as Treasury secretary. We had two days of productive sessions, which included announcing a number of programs for the U.S. and China to cooperate on energy and the environment. We had selected these initiatives knowing they would hold bipartisan appeal in the U.S. and would help ensure the continuation of the SED into the next administration.

In my concluding meeting with President Hu Jintao in the massive Great Hall of the People, he emphasized the important contribution SED had made to strengthening U.S.-China relations, and he encouraged me to come back soon after I left Treasury. As was our custom, Hu and I then adjourned to a private meeting, where I assured him that the relationship between our countries would only improve and advised him to avoid protectionist moves on currency and trade.

"China stands to gain more than anyone in the world by freeing up trade, and it stands to lose more than anyone by backsliding," I said.

"We didn't move as fast in a number of areas as you wanted us to," Hu said. "But we don't vacillate, and we will continue with reform and opening up."

I left Beijing pleased with the success of the SED, but I was returning to an increasingly troubled economy. On December 5, the government reported November job losses of 533,000, for a total of almost 2 million jobs lost in the past year. The unemployment rate stood at 6.7 percent, versus 4.7 percent a year before. And the latest news from the auto industry was bleak. That morning, United Auto Workers president Ron Gettelfinger testified before Congress that "GM could run out of funds by the end of the year, and Chrysler soon thereafter."

Wendy and I spent a restful day together on Saturday and attended the Kennedy Center Honors the next evening. A reception in the East Room of the White House preceded the event, and there I ran into Nancy Pelosi. I told her that circumstances might force us to notify Congress that we needed to draw down the last TARP tranche, perhaps over the holidays. She took my hand, which she always did when she was trying to charm.

"Please don't," she told me. "We don't have the votes."

While Nancy and I were chatting, I was surprised to see Clint Eastwood walking toward us. The actor, a friend of Nancy's, would be speaking on behalf of honoree and fellow actor Morgan Freeman, and he said, "I don't know what she's talking to you about, but she's stronger than you, Mr. Treasury Secretary. I suggest you do whatever she wants."

I chuckled appreciatively. By then, no one understood Nancy Pelosi's power better than I did.

Thursday, December 11–Wednesday, December 17, 2008

I wanted a chance to talk through the auto situation in a small setting, so Joel Kaplan and I had lunch alone with the president on December 11. The day before, the House had approved an emergency plan to speed $14 billion to the car companies without dipping into the TARP funds, but the administration-approved measure faced serious opposition among Senate Republicans. Vice President Cheney had joined a group of White House staff led by Josh

Bolten that tried to persuade them to help the automakers. He said the GOP risked being labeled the party of Herbert Hoover if it allowed the companies to fail. But they refused to budge.

This would be one of our last lunches together. As usual, we ate in the president's private dining room off the Oval Office. In my two and a half years at Treasury, I had noted how little these lunches varied. I normally ordered soup and either a chicken- or a tuna-salad sandwich. The president always ate the same thing: a little bundle of carrots, a chopped apple, and a hot dog in a bun. Wendy frequently accused me of inhaling my food, saying she had never seen anybody eat faster than I did. Then again, she had never eaten alone with the president—his food would be gone in five minutes. Sometimes we'd have low-fat soft frozen yogurt for dessert; other times the president would take out a cigar and chew on it.

For President Bush, an auto bailout was a bitter pill to swallow, especially as the last major economic decision of his administration. He disliked bailouts, and he disdained Detroit for not making cars people wanted to buy. But we were in the midst of a financial crisis and a deepening recession, and he recognized that if the giant companies were to declare bankruptcy, they would be doing so without advance planning or adequate financing for an orderly restructuring. The consequences for the economy would be devastating. It would create more panic, and it would crush auto suppliers and other carmakers—not just Chrysler and Ford, but also Honda's and Toyota's U.S. operations. Although the president didn't explicitly say he would jump in to save the automakers, I knew he recognized—once again—the need for quick, decisive action.

Senator Bob Corker had tried to make legislation palatable to Senate Republicans but his efforts fell apart that night, largely because the auto unions refused the wage cuts that he proposed. When Democrats and Republicans failed to reach agreement, they went home for Christmas break having done nothing to bolster either automaker. Harry Reid was quoted as saying on the Senate floor, "I dread looking at Wall Street tomorrow. It's not going to be a pleasant sight."

He didn't have to wait for Wall Street. Asian markets opened first and were sharply down: Japan's Nikkei index fell more than 7 percent in midday trading, as did Hong Kong's Hang Seng.

I had just arrived at the office at 7:00 a.m. the following morning when Joel called me. President Bush had decided to announce that he would consider using TARP funds to help the car companies. He was flying to Texas on *Air Force One*, and he wanted to get his statement out immediately, well before the U.S. markets opened. The statement had already been written; Joel wanted to make sure I was comfortable with it. I had just a few minutes to read it over, and I quickly said it was okay.

The statement did calm the markets, giving the White House some time to debate the next steps. Josh told me that the White House would control the process but that Treasury should run the negotiations with carmakers. I assigned Dan Jester, Steve Shafran, and Jim Lambright to develop the terms for the loans to GM and Chrysler. I encouraged the White House to make a quick decision. Since Congress had failed to act, TARP was the only tool we had before the companies ran out of funds, and there was nothing to be gained from dragging the process on.

Another big problem erupted early in the afternoon on December 17, when Ken Lewis called to tell me that Bank of America's board had concerns about whether to go ahead with its $50 billion deal to buy Merrill Lynch. He said he had recently learned that Merrill Lynch's fourth-quarter losses were expected to run to about $18 billion, pretax—way out of line with what he or anyone had expected. As a result, his board was considering invoking the material adverse change (MAC) clause to get out of the deal with Merrill Lynch. Common in merger arrangements, a MAC allows the buyer to break the agreement under extraordinary circumstances. But I knew that shareholders from both companies had already approved the deal, and I had never heard of a buyer successfully invoking a MAC after a shareholder vote. Moreover, this MAC clause was unusually favorable to Merrill Lynch in that it could not be invoked for a general deterioration in market conditions.

While I understood that December was shaping up as a bad month for banks, the $18 billion number shocked me. "This is a very serious matter," I told Ken. "You need to come to Washington and meet with the Fed immediately."

"I sure hope you'll be there," he told me.

We set up a meeting for 6:00 p.m. that evening at the Fed. Bob Hoyt, Jim Lambright, Jeremiah Norton, and I arrived early and conferred with Ben Bernanke, Don Kohn, and general counsel Scott Alvarez in Ben's conference room. Surrounded by the portraits of former Fed chairmen that lined the walls, I learned that the Fed knew nothing about the expected size of Merrill Lynch's losses but was aware that BofA was expecting to lose money in the fourth quarter and had a weak capital ratio. Ben and I agreed that we should take a tough line on the MAC, asking BofA for its legal justification. I shared my concerns about the market reaction to an $18 billion pretax Merrill Lynch loss for one quarter. If Merrill's losses were truly of this magnitude, we faced a serious problem.

Ken Lewis arrived promptly at 6:00 p.m. with his chief financial officer, Joe Price, and newly minted general counsel, Brian Moynihan. Ken explained that BofA had recently learned that Merrill was expected to lose $18 billion in the fourth quarter and raised the possibility of invoking the MAC. Ben strongly pushed back on that, saying that doing so might lead to a run on the bank. Ken asked if he was talking about Merrill Lynch, and Ben replied, "No, both Merrill and Bank of America—out of a loss of confidence in management for putting themselves in this position."

Someone raised the possibility of the government's giving BofA a support package similar to Citi's. Ben replied that Citi had received federal assistance because of systemic risk, not to facilitate the close of a merger. If a systemic risk existed after BofA's merger with Merrill closed, we should address it at that time, Ben said.

Ben and I indicated that Treasury and the Fed were committed to preventing the failure of any systemically important institution. By the end of the meeting, BofA had agreed to work closely with the Fed to provide the necessary information so that we could better understand the situation; we, in turn, would give them more details of the structure of the Citi bailout. We left the meeting knowing we had a lot of work to do to get all the facts about the nature of the losses and what had caused them.

With the U.S. falling further into recession, I was deeply concerned about being caught short of funds. Merrill Lynch's staggering fourth-quarter losses now threatened the viability of two huge institutions, with combined assets of $2.7 trillion, and raised the specter of a costly rescue of Bank of America. Add to that the impending auto bailout, and TARP would be drained even further. January 20 was only 33 days away, but that would seem an eternity if I didn't have sufficient funds to deal with any crisis that arose.

I arrived at the office on Friday, December 19, at 7:15 a.m. with renewed determination to get Tim Geithner or Larry Summers to persuade Obama to work with us to take down the last tranche right after the holidays. The previous afternoon the president had given me his final instructions on the autos, and I had asked my Treasury team to negotiate through the night so that we could announce a deal before the market opened.

We had expected President Bush to announce his auto deal at 10:00 a.m., only to learn he would now do so an hour earlier. That left us scrambling to finalize the term sheet, which we did only two minutes before the president went on air from the White House. The government would loan Chrysler $4 billion and GM a total of $13.4 billion from TARP—with $4 billion of the GM loan dependent on Congress's releasing the last tranche.

Although we wanted the car companies to restructure to increase their long-term viability, we would not be around to oversee these changes. So we crafted terms that would put the automakers on a path to reorganization through bankruptcy proceedings and would make it difficult for President Obama to avoid that outcome. We did this by requiring the companies to submit in mid-February restructuring plans to demonstrate how they would achieve financial viability and repay the loans. They would have to come up with a competitive product mix and cost structure; our terms required significant concessions by labor and creditors. If the conditions were not met by March 31, the government would call in the loan, forcing a restructuring under bankruptcy. We knew it would be almost impossible to win major concessions from all parties without this pressure.

After all the activity of the past few months, this was the first time Treasury had worked so closely with the White House, and I was very proud of my team for executing such a crucial deal so well in such a short period of time.

That same day, December 19, I learned from Ben that Bank of America had gone back to the Fed to say that the Merrill Lynch situation was getting worse: its estimated losses now stood at $22 billion pretax. Midafternoon I called Ken Lewis to find out how the losses had increased by $4 billion in two days. He said he was trying to understand that himself. I remained adamant that he needed to close the Merrill deal.

An hour later, Ben and I got on a conference call that included Ken and his BofA team and what seemed to be dozens of Fed officials from the Washington, Richmond, and New York Reserve banks. The New York Fed was represented by senior vice president Art Angulo and general counsel Tom Baxter.

Ken said that his board was still considering invoking the MAC, but the New York Fed officials pushed back hard, questioning its enforceability. I weighed in, offering my belief that invoking the MAC would pose a risk to BofA and the entire system. Ken raised the idea of using the clause to renegotiate the terms of the deal with Merrill, and I answered that this would cause the same concerns as invoking the MAC to get out of the deal: it would create an extended period of uncertainty in a market that already was being driven by fear. We agreed that we needed to learn more and that we would talk again early the following week.

The next afternoon, I flew to Colorado for a few days of skiing with my family over Christmas. On Sunday morning, Ken Lewis called me. The usually calm CEO sounded shaken. He reiterated that his board was concerned about Merrill's losses and was still weighing the MAC. They needed to make a decision before the deal closed on January 1, he said. I told him that Treasury and the Fed were committed to saving any systemically important institution and reminded him that we would work on a support package, if needed. "You know how strongly we feel about this," I said.

Since we had been so clear about our commitment to a government support program, I doubted that Ken was just testing us. Indeed, I concluded from earlier conversations that Ken himself was unsure about what kind of government help was appropriate or needed. He seemed to be having a difficult time with his board.

I got back to Ken later and again emphasized to him that the government would not let any systemically important institution fail; that exercising the MAC would show a colossal lack of judgment by BofA; that such an action would jeopardize his bank, Merrill Lynch, and the entire financial system; and that under such circumstances, the Fed, as BofA's regulator, could take extreme measures, including the removal of management and the board.

"I understand," Ken said. "Let's de-escalate."

The next day, Ben called me to tell me he had confirmed that Ken and BofA's board were going ahead with the Merrill deal, but the board wanted a letter from the government committing to a support package.

"Ben," I said, "that doesn't make any sense."

"I know," he said.

"I will call Lewis back and handle it," I said.

I called the BofA CEO and told him straightaway: "Ken, we can't give you a letter."

We had not yet committed to a plan for helping BofA, let alone worked out all the details of such a plan, I explained. Ben and I had already said publicly that we wouldn't let a systemically important institution fail. A letter could only reiterate that stance. But Treasury would have to disclose the letter publicly, and that would only raise more concerns in the market. Ken said he understood and would tell his board.

On New Year's Eve, I got another call from Ken. He said he was closing the Merrill Lynch deal the next day and told me that he trusted me to make sure the government would come up with a program for BofA.

The deal closed on January 1.

Last Days

Though we had worked out the TARP loans to the automakers, their stressed financial units presented another problem. GMAC Financial Services lacked sufficient capital, and Chrysler Financial had liquidity issues—as a result, neither unit could provide the credit that dealers and customers needed to get sales moving again. On December 29, Treasury announced a $5 billion capital infusion from TARP into GMAC, which had become a bank holding company, along with an additional $1 billion for GM to invest in GMAC. On January 16, Treasury committed $1.5 billion of TARP funds to Chrysler Financial, to make new loans to car buyers.

We worked hard to make sure the Obama team would have some breathing room when they settled into the White House, and no one cared more about this than President Bush. He went out of his way to make things easier for the new administration.

President-elect Obama understood that he would need the second half of TARP, but congressional opposition remained high, and he waited until the last possible moment to ask the president to notify Congress. He waited so long, in fact, that my colleagues in the White House had begun to hope that President Bush might be able to avoid having to ask for the money.

When Obama finally called on January 8, he asked if President Bush would be willing, if necessary, to issue a veto, because Obama didn't want his first act as president to be a veto of Congress's TARP disapproval. The president replied, "I don't want my last action to be a veto. Let's make sure a veto is unnecessary."

On January 12, President Bush formally requested the second $350 billion from Congress. On January 15, the Senate voted to give the president-elect those funds.

Later that night, the Bank of America deal was completed, and the president gave his farewell address to the nation. It bothered me, and I am sure it bothered the president, that the administration's final rescue would be made public in the same news cycle as his speech. The president's staff was unhappy about the timing, but we could not delay the BofA announcement.

Bank of America's deal closely resembled Citigroup's. The government would invest $20 billion of TARP money in preferred stock

paying an 8 percent dividend. BofA would absorb the first $10 bil-
lion of losses on a $118 billion pool of loans and mortgage-backed
securities. Losses beyond that would be split 90/10 between the
government and BofA. Like Citi, BofA would commit to mortgage
modifications and more-stringent restrictions on executive compensation.

The deal was announced in the wee hours of January 16. Then
at 7:00 a.m. BofA released its fourth-quarter earnings: a $1.79 billion
loss for itself and a $22 billion pretax loss for Merrill. BofA shares
would fall 14 percent to $7.18 on the day. Despite the damage, I was
reassured. BofA was stable and Merrill had not failed.

That day was no less noteworthy—or busy—than its predecessors. Aside from BofA's earnings announcement, we unveiled our
investment in Chrysler Financial. Both of these deals were finalized in the early hours of the morning, concluding the last all-
nighter at Treasury my team would endure. Citigroup also reported
a shockingly high $8.3 billion loss for the fourth quarter, as well
as a plan to split into two entities: Citicorp to serve as the global
bank and Citi Holdings to hold an estimated $301 billion in trou-
bled assets.

Although fourth-quarter earnings at the nation's banks were as
bad as I had feared, I was encouraged by what appeared to be a light
at the end of the tunnel. Bankers throughout the country were telling me that the earnings environment had improved significantly
in January. It didn't surprise me that the banks could make good
money with the government support programs and low interest
rates. What surprised me was that it had taken so long.

Friday, January 16, was my last working day at Treasury. I am not a
particularly sentimental man, and though we had all enjoyed an
extraordinary camaraderie at Treasury, I had planned no parting

words or special ceremony. Jim Wilkinson and Neel Kashkari came by in the later afternoon; they wanted to be with me in the last moments I was in the office. They seemed to expect some memorable valediction, but I told them, simply, I was never emotional about moving on.

Looking back now, I can't help but be awed by the hard work and incredible dedication of the Treasury team, and those at the Federal Reserve, and in the many other government agencies, who gave selflessly in some of the darkest moments they or this country had ever seen.

As I prepared to leave office, I knew that we had succeeded in averting the collapse of the system. As controversial as TARP and our other actions had been, they had prevented a much greater disaster that would have caused far more pain to the American people.

I understood that many of my fellow citizens viewed the bailouts—if not the whole financial industry—with bitterness and anger. Though I shared some of their feelings, the crisis did not shake my faith in the free-market system. Yes, our way of doing things occasionally needs repairs and overhauls—that is true now more than ever—but I've yet to see an alternative to our system that can provide as many people not only with their needs but also with the promise of much better lives.

How many weekends and holidays did my team at Treasury give up during the crisis? What would have happened had I not been able to rely on their devotion, talent, and creativity?

As with my Treasury team, so with my colleagues in government. Ben Bernanke, Tim Geithner, Sheila Bair, Chris Cox, John Dugan, Jim Lockhart—at times we differed on philosophy and strategy, but I never doubted their dedication to this country or their commitment to taking the bold actions necessary to save the system. I was able to leave Treasury confident that, with Tim as my successor and Ben continuing to chair the Federal Reserve, many of our plans and programs would continue into the next administration.

I'd often found the political realities of Washington frustrating, but I had also met politicians willing to make unpopular decisions to serve the greater good. No one showed more courage than President Bush, who not only unstintingly supported me but set aside ideology, and often the preferences of some of his own staff, to do what needed to be done. This must have been personally difficult for him on many occasions, but he never let me see it.

As I left Treasury that last time and drove by the White House, which was busy with preparations for a new president, I took a moment to feel good about what we had accomplished.

We had been on the brink, but we had not fallen.

Afterword

I don't wake up mornings wishing that I were still Treasury secretary. For one thing, I am finally getting a good night's sleep again. I hope as the markets settle down and the economy begins to recover that that is also true for the millions of people in America—and throughout the world—who have been living through this long nightmare of home foreclosures, job losses, and tight credit since the onset of the financial crisis in 2007.

Certainly I miss my team at the Treasury Department and my other colleagues in government. Even on the worst days, I took comfort from knowing that I was working with some of the sharpest and most creative minds in the country—men and women who had chosen public service over personal enrichment. And I do regret that I am unable either to help with the "exit strategy" to end the emergency programs we put in place to save the financial system or to work within the government for urgently needed regulatory reforms.

When I became Treasury secretary in July 2006, financial crises weren't new to me, nor were the failures of major financial institutions. I had witnessed serious market disturbances and the collapses, or near collapses, of Continental Illinois Bank, Drexel Burnham Lambert, and Salomon Brothers, among others. With the exception of the savings and loan debacle, these disruptions generally focused on a single financial organization, such as the hedge fund Long-Term Capital Management in 1998.

The crisis that began in 2007 was far more severe, and the risks to the economy and the American people much greater. Between March and September 2008, eight major U.S. financial institutions failed—Bear Stearns, IndyMac, Fannie Mae, Freddie Mac, Lehman Brothers, AIG, Washington Mutual, and Wachovia—six of them in September alone. And the damage was not limited to the U.S. More than 20 European banks, across 10 countries, were rescued from July 2007 through February 2009. This, the most wrenching financial crisis since the Great Depression, caused a terrible recession in the U.S. and severe harm around the world. Yet it could have been so much worse. Had it not been for unprecedented interventions by the U.S. and other governments, many more financial institutions would have gone under—and the economic damage would have been far greater and longer lasting.

By early 2009, it was clear that our actions had prevented a meltdown. Coupled with initiatives from the Federal Reserve and the Federal Deposit Insurance Corporation, the programs we designed and implemented at Treasury—along with those advanced by the Obama administration, which were largely continuations or logical extensions of ours—had stabilized the financial system, restarted credit markets, and helped to limit the housing collapse. Even before I left office in January 2009, the major banks were gaining strength, and many would soon have access once again to the equity and debt markets.

Among these actions, an innovative guarantee staved off a meltdown of money market funds. The Term Asset-Backed Securities Loan Facility, which Treasury conceived and designed jointly with the Fed, has been successful in reestablishing the securitization marketplace for consumer finance in areas such as credit card and auto receivables. And our decision to put Fannie and Freddie into conservatorship ensured the availability of affordable loans for new homebuyers and for those refinancing their mortgages. This was by far the single most important step taken to counter the price declines in housing, a sector critical to our recovery.

We also had a significant impact on foreclosure mitigations by mobilizing and coordinating the private sector to adopt common loan modification plans. We encouraged fierce competitors to co-operate with one another and to work closely with financial counselors to get troubled homeowners to pick up the phone to contact their mortgage servicers. Overall, we ramped up the pace of loan modifications and spared hundreds of thousands of families from the hardship of losing their homes. (The counseling group we supported, known for its 888-995-HOPE toll-free line, was integrated by the Obama administration into its own program.)

And, of course, our decision to take preferred-equity stakes in financial institutions through the capital purchase program—paired with debt guarantees from the FDIC—succeeded in stabilizing the reeling banking industry. Altogether nearly 700 healthy banks, big and small, took advantage of the program, which invested $205 billion in these institutions. I believe the taxpayer will make money on these bank investments. We had originally estimated that up to 3,000 banks might participate, bolstering their capacity to lend. Unfortunately, the political backlash that erupted against institutions' taking TARP money led many banks to withdraw their applications and discouraged others from submitting theirs.

I came to Washington as an advocate of free markets, and I remain one. The interventions we undertook I would have found abhorrent at any other time. I make no apology for them, however. As first responders to an unprecedented crisis that threatened the destruction of the modern financial system, we had little choice. We were forced to use the often inadequate tools we had on hand—or, as I often remarked to my team at Treasury, the duct tape and baling wire of an outdated regulatory regime with limited powers and authorities.

Our actions were intended to be temporary. If we don't get the government out as soon as is practical, we will do grave harm to our economy. Yes, our first priority has to be recovery. But it is equally important that we exit these programs. This is critical to our own continued economic success.

The history of capitalism in America has been one of striking the right balance between profit-driven market forces and the array of regulations and laws necessary to harness these forces for the common good. In recent years, regulation failed to keep pace with rapid innovations in the markets—from the proliferation of increasingly complex and opaque products to the accelerating globalization of finance—with disastrous consequences.

In my time in Washington, I learned that, unfortunately, it takes a crisis to get difficult and important things done. Many had warned for years of impending calamity at Fannie Mae and Freddie Mac, but only when those institutions faced outright collapse did lawmakers enact reforms. Only after Lehman Brothers failed did we get the authorities from Congress to inject capital into financial institutions. Even then, despite the horrific conditions in the markets, TARP was rejected the first time it came up for a vote in the U.S. House of Representatives. And, amazingly enough, as I write this, more than one year after Lehman's fall, U.S. government regulators still lack the power to wind down a nonbank financial institution outside of bankruptcy.

I am not sure what the solution is for this ever more troubling political dysfunction, but it is certain that we must find a way to improve the collective decision-making process in Washington. The stakes are simply too high not to. Indeed, we are fortunate that in 2008 Congress did act before the financial system collapsed.

This took strong leadership in both the House and the Senate, because all who voted for TARP or to give us the emergency authorities to deal with Fannie and Freddie knew they were casting an unpopular vote.

Since I've left Treasury I'm often approached by people eager to hear about my experiences. Most often they have two basic questions for me: What was it like to live through the crisis? And what lessons did I learn that could help us avoid a similar calamity in the future?

I hope the book you've been reading answers the first question. The answer to the second question is obviously complex, but as I have thought about this over the last year or so, I would narrow down the many lessons into four crucial ones:

1. *The structural economic imbalances among the major economies of the world that led to massive cross-border capital flows are an important source of the justly criticized excesses in our financial system.* These imbalances lay at the root of the crisis. Simply put, in the U.S. we save much less than we consume. This forces us to borrow large amounts of money from oil-exporting countries or from Asian nations, like China and Japan, with high savings rates and low shares of domestic consumption. The crisis has abated, but these imbalances persist and must be addressed.

2. *Our regulatory system remains a hopelessly outmoded patchwork quilt built for another day and age.* It is rife with duplication, gaping holes, and counterproductive competition among regulators. The system hasn't kept pace with financial innovation and needs to be fixed so that we have the capacity and the authority to respond to constantly evolving global capital markets.

3. *The financial system contained far too much leverage, as evidenced by inadequate cushions of both capital and liquidity. Much of the leverage was embedded in largely opaque*

and highly complex financial products. Today it is generally understood that banks and investment banks in the U.S., Europe, and the rest of the world did not have enough capital. Less well understood is the important role that liquidity needs to play in bolstering the safety and stability of banks. The credit crisis exposed widespread reliance on poor liquidity practices, notably a dependence on unstable short-term funding. Financial institutions that rely heavily on short-term borrowings need to have plenty of cash on hand for bad times. And many didn't. Inadequate liquidity cushions, I believe, were a bigger problem than inadequate capital levels.

4. *The largest financial institutions are so big and complex that they pose a dangerously large risk.* Today the top 10 financial institutions in the U.S. hold close to 60 percent of financial assets, up from 10 percent in 1990. This dramatic concentration, coupled with much greater interconnectedness, means that the failure of any of a few very large institutions can take down a big part of the system, and, in domino fashion, topple the rest. The concept of "too big to fail" has moved from the academic literature to reality and must be addressed.

There are a number of steps we should take to deal with these issues. To start, we should adjust U.S. policies to reduce the global imbalances that have been decried for years by many prominent economists. If, as a consequence of our current economic problems, American citizens begin to save more and spend less, we ought to welcome and encourage this change. We should go further and remove the bias in our tax code against saving—in effect moving toward a tax code based on consumption rather than income. The system we have today taxes the return on savings, giving incentives to spend rather than to save. Moving to a consumption tax would remove the bias against saving and help boost investment and job creation while reducing our dependence on foreign capital.

Our government needs to tackle its number one economic challenge, which is reducing its fiscal deficit. Our ability to meet this
challenge will to a large extent determine our future economic success. We are now on a path where deficits will rise to a point at
which we may simply be unable to raise the necessary revenues
even if significant tax increases are imposed on the middle class.
Dealing with this problem requires moving quickly to reform our
major entitlement programs: Medicare, Medicaid, and Social Security. Any such reform needs to be done in a manner that recognizes
and addresses the $43 trillion of built-in deficits that the GAO is
projecting over the next 75 years. These will only become more
difficult to deal with as time goes by. The longer we wait, the greater
will be the burden on the next generation.

Striking the right balance to achieve both effective regulation
and market discipline is another huge challenge we face. The recent
crisis demonstrated that our financial markets had outgrown the
ability of our current system to regulate them. Regulatory reforms
alone would not have prevented all of the problems that emerged.
However, a better framework that featured less duplication and that
restricted the ability of financial firms to pick and choose their own,
generally less-strict, regulators—a practice known as regulatory
arbitrage—would have worked much better. And there is no doubt
in my mind that the lack of a regulator to identify and manage systemic risks contributed greatly to the problems we faced.

We need a system that can adapt as financial institutions, financial products, and markets continue to evolve. Before the crisis
forced us to shift from making long-range recommendations to
fighting fires, Treasury conducted a thorough analysis of the proper
objectives of financial services regulation, and this exercise led us
to sweeping proposals for fundamental reforms. These recommendations were controversial when they were issued in March 2008,
but in retrospect seem quite prophetic.

Among other things, we proposed a system that created a government responsibility for systemic risk identification and oversight. We recommended strengthening and consolidating safety and soundness regulation to eliminate redundancy and counterproductive regulatory arbitrage. Acknowledging the proliferation of financial products—and the abuses that have accompanied them—we also proposed a separate and distinct business conduct regulator to protect consumers and investors.

There is a well-recognized need for a global accord requiring banks to have higher levels of better-quality capital. This will be more difficult to achieve for some of the more highly leveraged European banks, but consistency here is important, and a stronger capital position will allow the banks to lend more in a downturn, when credit is most needed. Regulators must also require bigger liquidity cushions, and these, too, must be harmonized globally. A simplistic one-size-fits-all model will not work for liquidity. Bank managements and regulators need to have a better understanding of the potential liquidity demands, which will vary bank by bank, under adverse conditions.

With a $60 trillion global economy and a $14 trillion U.S. economy, it is inevitable that we will have a number of very large financial institutions whose increasing size and complexity are driven by customer demands in a global marketplace. Inside the U.S., which still has 8,000 relatively small banks along with its many big institutions, competitive pressures will also force the industry to continue to consolidate. Just as many people shop at Wal-Mart while mourning the disappearance of their local retailers, so, too, will they find their way to bigger commercial banks offering a wider range of lower-cost services and products than smaller banks do. The institutions that are emerging to satisfy all of these needs are complex, difficult to manage and regulate, and pose real risks that must be confronted.

There is no question that tighter, and one trusts better, regulation is coming. I hope and expect that big institutions will be regulated in a way that considers the risks resulting from their size and from acquisitions or new business lines that make them riskier and further complicate the already difficult task of managing them effectively.

However, regulation alone cannot eliminate instability, and we will inevitably be confronted with the failure of another large, complex institution. The challenge is to strengthen market discipline as a tool to force institutions to address problems before they become impossible to solve and to design a means of absorbing a large failure without the entire financial system's being threatened. As I have said repeatedly, we need more authority to deal with, and wind down, failing institutions that are not banks. The current bankruptcy process is clearly inadequate for large, complex organizations, as the failure of Lehman Brothers demonstrated.

I shudder at the thought of any future administration's having to cope with another crisis hobbled by the constraints that we faced. For this reason, I favor broad authorities to deal with the failure of a systemically important institution—including the power to inject capital and to make emergency loans. Some critics may say that such powers would only increase the risk of moral hazard, but I am confident that procedural safeguards can be put in place to help manage such concerns and to mitigate market distortions.

Wind-down authority must be constructed to impose real costs on creditors, investors, and the financial franchises themselves so that market discipline can continue to be a constructive force in the regulation of large, complex firms. However wind-down authority is devised, it will affect market practices and credit decisions. To minimize uncertainty in the market, the government should provide clear guidance as to how it would use this enhanced authority. And a very high bar should be set before it is used, similar to the constraints that are placed on the FDIC before it liquidates—or, in technical terms, "resolves"—commercial banks.

The successful management of large, diversified financial institutions also demands the presence of strong, independent risk and control functions as well as compensation policies that do not promote excessive risk taking. Risk management, compliance, control, and audit functions are underappreciated and very difficult jobs that must be considered to be as important as those of the revenue-generating traders within an organization. These risk professionals must hold the upper hand in any dispute. This can only be accomplished if the organization has a culture that respects these essential jobs and demonstrates as much by offering a career track and compensation structure that attracts and keeps outstanding talent.

There is now a recognition that regulators need to work with the financial industry to set pay standards, but this can and should be done without regulators' determining specific compensation levels. Instead, pay should be aligned with shareholder interests by ensuring that as an employee's total compensation grows, an increasing amount of it is given out as equity that is deferred—vesting and paying out later—and subject to being clawed back under certain circumstances.

Senior executives should be prevented from selling most, if not all, of the shares they are paid; when they retire or leave, their deferred shares should be paid out on a predetermined schedule and not accelerated. It is critically important that those running financial institutions today recognize the understandable outrage about the costs that have been inflicted by the crisis on the public and the taxpayer. It is incumbent upon these executives to show real restraint in their own compensation as an example of leadership that will strengthen the culture of their firms.

Determining the future of housing policy will be among the most difficult political issues, and it will require a decision on the future of Fannie Mae and Freddie Mac. These institutions, which were at the heart of the U.S. policies that overstimulated housing in the past, cannot stay in conservatorship forever. They remain the primary source of low-cost mortgage financing in the U.S. But as the housing and mortgage markets recover, the Fed's support for the GSEs will end, and private capital will return. Fannie and Freddie should not then be allowed to revert to their old form, crowding out private competition and putting taxpayers on the hook for failure while shareholders benefit from success.

At a minimum, the GSEs should be restructured to eliminate the systemic risk they posed. An easy way to address this is to shrink them by reducing their investment portfolios—and their huge debt loads. I also believe that their mission should be curtailed significantly to reduce the subsidy for homeownership that helped create the crisis. It is important to leave room for a robust private-sector secondary mortgage market that serves the taxpayer and homeowners equally well.

Realistically, these enormous entities won't be allowed to simply disappear. Focusing on the function of the GSEs as mortgage credit guarantors, Congress could replace Fannie Mae and Freddie Mac with one or two private-sector entities that would purchase and securitize mortgages with a credit guarantee explicitly backed by the federal government. These entities would be privately owned but set up like public utilities and governed by a rate-setting commission that would establish a targeted rate of return. This approach would address the inherent conflicts between private ownership and public purpose that are unresolved in the current GSE structure.

The stress in this case would come from mortgage originators' looking for new ways to put risky loans into the pool to get a government-backed guarantee. In this model, safety and soundness regulation would be essential, as would be supervisory oversight to make sure that the quality of conforming loans remained high.

An obvious issue is whether such a utility approach leaves room for the private sector in the secondary mortgage market. The size of the loans subject to the government-backed guarantee, as well as the price charged for the guarantee, would determine the extent of the private sector's role. This should frame the debate and force policy makers to determine the government's proper role in stimulating and subsidizing housing.

There is much other work to be done. Not only must we update our woefully inadequate regulatory architecture to better deal with large, interconnected financial institutions, we must also strengthen oversight of complex financial products, reform credit rating agencies, maintain fair-value accounting, change the way money market funds are structured and sold, and reinvigorate the securitization process. Underlying all of these actions is the need for greater transparency. Complexity is the enemy of transparency—whether in financial products, organizational structures, or business models. We need regulation and capital requirements that lead to greater simplicity, standardization, and consistency.

Contrary to popular belief, credit default swaps and other derivatives provide a useful function in making the capital markets more efficient and were not the cause of the crisis. But these financial instruments do introduce embedded and hidden leverage into financial institutions' balance sheets, complicating due diligence for counterparties and making effective supervision more difficult. The resulting opacity, which should be unacceptable even in normal markets, only intensified and magnified the crisis. This system needs to be reformed so that these innovative instruments can play their important role as mitigators, not transmitters, of risk.

Standardized credit default swaps, which make up the vast majority of CDS contracts, should be traded on a public exchange, and nonstandardized contracts should be centrally cleared, subject to more regulatory scrutiny and greater capital charges. The key to this solution is for regulators to encourage standardization, require transparency, and penalize excessive complexity with capital charges. There will still be a role for customized derivative contracts, but only accompanied by appropriate supervision and increased costs.

One of the most glaring problems to emerge from the crisis was the poor quality of the rating of debt securities provided by the three major credit rating agencies: Moody's, Standard & Poor's, and Fitch. All have been granted special status as Nationally Recognized Statistical Ratings Organizations (NRSROs) by the SEC.

When I came to Washington in July 2006, only nine private-sector companies in the world carried a triple-A rating. Berkshire Hathaway and AIG were the only financial institutions so rated; GE, a major industrial company with what is essentially a large embedded financial institution, also had the top rating. Today there are only five triple-A-rated companies; AIG, Berkshire Hathaway, and GE have all been downgraded (as was Toyota). Yet as recently as January 2008, there were 64,000 structured financial instruments still rated triple-A, and many others had investment-grade ratings. As the credit crisis intensified, more than 221,000 rated tranches of asset-backed securities were downgraded in 2008 alone.

The agencies are enhancing the transparency, rigor, and independence of their ratings of structured products. But in the future, financial institutions and investors need to do more of their own homework, and regulators should no longer blindly use a high credit rating as a criterion for low capital requirements.

To reduce investor and regulator laxness resulting from over-reliance on a few monopoly researchers, I would like to see a further review of how to increase competition among rating agencies. In addition, banking and securities laws and regulations should be amended to remove any reference to credit ratings as criteria to be relied on by regulators or investors to assess risk and capital charges.

Some people have also blamed the use of fair-value accounting for causing or accelerating the crisis. To the contrary, I am convinced that had we not had fair-value—or as it is sometimes known, mark-to-market—accounting, the excesses in our system would have been greater and the crisis would have been even more severe. Managements, investors, and regulators would have had even less understanding of the risks embedded in an institution's balance sheet.

We need to maintain fair-value accounting, simplify the current implementation rules, and ensure consistency of application both globally and among similar institutions. The U.S. and international accounting standards setters must be allowed to get on with this important task without being pressured to make short-term, piece-meal changes that mask honest reporting by financial institutions.

It is critical to have an accounting system that shines a light on any securities with impaired value for which there is not an active market. These difficult-to-value assets need to be identified and their valuation methodology described in a clear and open manner.

There are more than 1,100 money market mutual funds in the U.S., with $3.8 trillion in assets and an estimated 30 million-plus individual customers. This is a concentrated yet fragmented industry with the top 40 funds managing about 30 percent of the assets. These funds invest for the most part in commercial paper instruments with a top credit rating or in government or quasi-government securities. Before the crisis, investors had come to believe that they would always have liquidity and would be able to get 100 percent of their principal back, because funds would always maintain a net asset value (NAV) of at least $1.00.

In the immediate aftermath of the Lehman failure, money market mutual funds came under intense pressure. A number were on the verge of "breaking the buck." This dramatically eroded investor confidence, causing redemption requests to soar. In turn, the money funds pulled back on their funding of the many large financial institutions that depended on them for a big portion of their liquidity needs. It was a development that we were not well equipped to address.

We stepped in to guarantee the money market funds to prevent the crisis from getting worse, but the fundamental problems in the industry's business model remain. Many of these funds charge investors very low fees, often as little as 5 basis points—or 0.05 percent—while offering interest rates that are higher than those available on insured bank deposits or on Treasury bills. If something looks too good to be true, it almost always is. In this case, it was the money fund industry's soft or implicit guarantee of immediate liquidity and full return of principal with a premium yield and a low fee. Many, if not most, of these funds simply did not have the financial capacity to maintain their liquidity or a 100 percent preservation of capital for their investors in the midst of the credit crisis.

This expectation of complete liquidity with no fear of loss is a problem that should be addressed. Money funds are investment products, not guaranteed accounts. For years, the SEC has tried, unsuccessfully, to address this misperception. The SEC should explore whether fund managers should move from a fixed NAV, which makes money market funds resemble insured bank accounts, to a floating NAV. The funds would still be great products and could offer attractive returns, liquidity, and very low volatility and principal risk. But, as clients saw slight variations in principal, they would have a tangible indication that they were not investing in a bank account.

The credit crisis also exposed the erosion in mortgage underwriting standards, particularly in the originate-to-distribute securitization chain. To strengthen the underwriting practices and better align the interests of all parties, sponsors of these securities should be required to keep a continuing direct economic stake in the mortgages so that they have some "skin in the game," with exposure to any future credit losses.

As I finish this book, the G-20 has just completed another summit, in Pittsburgh, and has successfully pivoted from crisis management to macroeconomic coordination. Building on the principles and action plan for reform we established in Washington at the first G-20 summit, in November 2008, and on the results of the meeting in London in April 2009, the G-20 will now serve as the major forum at which leaders of developed and emerging markets address global financial and economic issues.

Although the preeminence of the G-20 leaders' forum rightly gives the emerging-markets countries a greater voice, it is also clear that the strength of the relationship between the U.S. and China will be critical to the functioning of the G-20 and global cooperation. Global problems cannot be solved by the U.S. and China alone, of course, but agreement with China makes it much easier to make real progress on any major issue.

The G-20's role in tasking and reviewing the work of the international financial bodies will be among its enduring contributions. The creation and expanded role of the Financial Stability Board (FSB), which comprises central bankers, finance ministers, and securities regulators, has been an important outgrowth of the G-20 process. The FSB will have the lead role in establishing the rules of the road for capital, liquidity, and financial products that will need to be implemented by national legislatures. And on politically sensitive matters such as compensation, the FSB has already shown an ability to develop nuanced and constructive proposals. Together with other international standards setters such as the International Organization of Securities Commissions (IOSCO), the Basel Committee, and the International Accounting Standards Board (IASB), the FSB must play a crucial role in ensuring that the G-20 reform agenda is implemented in a coordinated and cooperative way that leads to convergence rather than fragmentation. None of this takes away from the preeminent role of the U.S. in the world economy, but simply recognizes the vital fact of our interdependence.

While much progress has been made, real risks remain, including those of trade and financial protectionism. At each G-20 summit, the leaders condemn protectionism, but they do so against the backdrop of increasing political pressures at home that have resulted in a variety of measures that are inconsistent with their repeated pledges. The U.S.'s own commitment to trade liberalization remains in question. As I complete this book, no action has been taken on pending free-trade agreements, and no progress has been made on completing the World Trade Organization's Doha round of multilateral trade talks.

In a world where virtually everyone agrees we have had inadequate regulation of banks and capital markets, there is a very real danger that financial regulation will become a wolf in sheep's clothing, rivaling tariffs as the protectionist measure of choice for those nations that want to limit or eliminate competition not only in financial services but also in any other sector of their economy. Though this is not a new development, the risks are greater today because the U.S. model of capitalism appears more vulnerable than in the past, even as the economic crisis pushes nations toward short-term measures to protect jobs. One of the lessons of the Great Depression is that protectionist actions by industrial nations seeking to wall off their countries to protect their jobs and industries were self-defeating and made that awful downturn longer and more painful.

The European Union has already introduced regulation that mandates that certain securities can count toward regulatory capital only if their credit ratings are issued by an agency located in the EU. The EU proposal on alternative investment funds similarly would require fund managers to have established offices in the EU or operate under "equivalent" regulations; otherwise they would not be allowed access to the EU market. And the EU is requiring that credit default swaps be cleared through clearing parties located in its member states. As a result, a number of other countries have indicated that they are considering similar territorial restrictions.

The potential fragmentation is not limited to Europe. The U.S. has prohibited banks receiving certain federal funds from issuing H-1B visas to hire highly skilled foreign nationals, even though such people would add value to the economy. The February 2009 U.S. stimulus bill contained a "Buy American" provision that has led to similar protectionist language in other bills. Both federal and state officials are seeking to insert protectionist restrictions even where they are not required by law.

The best way to combat protectionism, whether by tariff or regulation, is with strong leadership from the U.S. We must keep our markets open for trade and investment, enact previously negotiated trade pacts, work toward a successful Doha round, and forge new trade agreements and investment treaties. We must also demonstrate our commitment to rebuilding our economy, fixing our regulatory system, and getting the government out of the private sector as soon as possible. The world needs to know that we are serious about reducing our budget deficit and cleaning up our other messes.

I am quite hopeful that we will put in place the necessary reforms for the financial system. There is finally a broad consensus among policy makers in the U.S. and internationally as to the causes of the crisis. I also remain optimistic about the economic future of the U.S. and its continued leadership role in the global economy. I don't mean to minimize our troubles, but every other major country has more-significant problems. As the richest country on earth, with the biggest, most diverse, and most resilient economy, we have the capacity to meet our challenges. Though what happened over the past few years was a difficult chapter in our nation's economic history, it is just one chapter, and there will be many more that are marked by economic gains and rising prosperity if we learn from our mistakes and make the necessary corrections.

If we don't lose our sense of urgency, and if the needed reforms are put in place domestically and internationally, markets will adapt and continue their positive trend of the past 25 years. Let's not forget that these markets helped tear down the Iron Curtain, lifted hundreds of millions of people out of poverty, and brought great prosperity to our nation. Efficient, well-regulated capital markets can continue to provide economic progress around the world. That inevitably leads to more political freedom and greater individual liberty.

ACRONYMS USED IN THE TEXT

ABCP: asset-backed commercial paper
AIG: American International Group
AMLF: Asset-Backed Commercial Paper Money Market Fund
   Liquidity Facility
ARM: adjustable-rate mortgage
ASF: American Securitization Forum
BofA: Bank of America
CDO: collateralized debt obligation
CDS: credit default swap(s)
CIC: China Investment Corporation
CPP: capital purchase program
ECB: European Central Bank
ESF: Exchange Stabilization Fund
FDIC: Federal Deposit Insurance Corporation
FHA: Federal Housing Administration
FHFA: Federal Housing Finance Agency
FSA: Financial Services Authority
FSB: Financial Stability Board

GAO: Government Accountability Office

GDP: gross domestic product

GSE: government-sponsored enterprise (Fannie Mae, Freddie Mac)

HERA: Housing and Economic Recovery Act

HUD: U.S. Department of Housing and Urban Development

IASB: International Accounting Standards Board

IMF: International Monetary Fund

KDB: Korea Development Bank

LIBOR: London Interbank Offered Rate

LIBOR-OIS: London Interbank Offered Rate–overnight indexed swap

LTCM: Long-Term Capital Management

MAC: material adverse change

MBS: mortgage-backed securities

MLEC: Master Liquidity Enhancement Conduit

NAV: net asset value

NEC: National Economic Council

OCC: Office of the Comptroller of the Currency

OFHEO: Office of Federal Housing Enterprise Oversight

OTC: over the counter

PDCF: Primary Dealer Credit Facility

PWG: President's Working Group on Financial Markets

S&P 500: Standard & Poor's 500 Index

SARS: severe acute respiratory syndrome

SEC: Securities and Exchange Commission

SED: Strategic Economic Dialogue

SIV: structured investment vehicle

TAF: Term Auction Facility

TALF: Term Asset-Backed Securities Loan Facility

TARP: Troubled Assets Relief Program

TIAA-CREF: Teachers Insurance and Annuity Association of
   America and College Retirement Equities Fund
TLGP: Temporary Liquidity Guarantee Program
TSLF: Term Securities Lending Facility
WaMu: Washington Mutual

Acknowledgments

Writing *On the Brink* required me not only to live through the crisis the first time, but also to live through it again. Both times I was aided by my team at Treasury, and by the White House staff. They dedicated an enormous amount of time to helping me remember and reconstruct events that took place at warp speed. We didn't always have notes or paper to rely on, but I had many, many hours of help from Dan Jester, David Nason, Michele Davis, Kevin Fromer, Neel Kashkari, Bob Hoyt, Phill Swagel, David McCormick, Dan Price, Steve Shafran, Joel Kaplan, Josh Bolten, Jim Lambright, Jim Wilkinson, Ken Wilson, Bob Steel, Taiya Smith, Karthik Ramanathan, Jeremiah Norton, Keith Hennessey, and Christal West. My chief of staff, Lindsay Valdeon, who worked around the clock organizing much of our effort and sharing her sound judgment, deserves special praise. And I extend my thanks to my former boss, President George Bush, for his support on this project.

I was very fortunate to have as a collaborator Michael Carroll, formerly editor of *Institutional Investor*, whose understanding of finance and narrative helped my story come alive. His discipline, thoroughness, and talent were invaluable. He assembled a very able and dedicated team, including Deborah McClellan, Ruth Hamel, Katherine Ryder, and Will Blythe, who worked long hours to complete this book.

I am grateful to my attorney, Robert Barnett of Williams & Connolly, and my able editor, Rick Wolff, for their spot-on advice, steady support, and encouragement throughout the project. My thanks also to the Business Plus team, including Dorothea Halliday, Mark Steven Long, Tracy Martin, Harvey-Jane Kowal, Bob Castillo, Tom Whatley, Ellen Rosenblatt, Barbara Brown, Jimmy Franco, Rob Nissen, Deborah Wiseman, Susan Benson Gutentag, Lynn von Hassel, and Stephen Callahan.

FactSet Research Systems Inc. and Credit Market Analysis Ltd. provided us with market research. The assistance of Monica Boyer and David Wray was also helpful.

I thank Jessica Einhorn, dean at the Paul H. Nitze School of Advanced International Studies at Johns Hopkins University, for bringing me to this great institution, which benefits from her strong leadership. I am appreciative of the fact-checking and research support I received from SAIS students and from Seth Colby.

And to my wife, Wendy, in particular, I extend my gratitude for her support throughout my tenure as Treasury secretary and for enduring what turned out to be an all-consuming eight-month project—the writing of this book.

INDEX

Pandit, Vikram, ix
  appointment to Citigroup, 79, 409
  Bear Stearns and, 116
  Lehman and, 191–93, 202
  TARP and, 359, 362–68
  Wachovia and, 332
Paulson, Amanda (daughter), 20, 31, 42,
    418–19
Paulson, Dick (brother), 21, 23
Paulson, Heather (daughter-in-law), 31
Paulson, Henry (grandfather), 21–22
Paulson, Henry Merritt (father), 20–23
Paulson, Marianna Gallauer (mother),
    19–21, 23, 24, 41–42
Paulson, Merritt (son), 20, 31–32, 42
Paulson, Rosina Merritt (grandmother),
    21–22
Paulson, Wendy Judge (wife)
  at Beijing Olympics, 159–60
  at British Embassy dinner, 412–13
  at Camp David, 44, 374
  dating, 25–26
  environmentalism of, 36–37, 47, 53–
    54, 89, 106, 415–16
  at Friedman dinner, 395
  at Gridiron Club dinner, 89
  as Hillary Clinton supporter, 20, 26, 47
  at Kennedy Center Honors, 423
  Little St. Simons Island vacations, 329,
    331, 419
  move to Barrington, 29
  at National Geographic Society, 105–6
  presidential election results and, 392
  proposal and marriage to, 26
  Randall's Island Sports Foundation
    dinner, 415–16, 417
  as source of strength, 215, 416
  Treasury secretary nomination and,
    19–21, 38–39, 41, 42
  at White House dinners, 53–54, 154,
    368
Pelosi, Nancy, viii
  AIG and, 239
  automakers and, 387, 416–17
  Citigroup and, 416
  economic stimulus of 2008, 85–86
  emergency response to crisis, 255,
    258–59, 261
  housing legislation, 145–46, 153
  impressions of, 258–59
  TARP and, 287, 294, 296, 299–300,
    304, 311–14, 319–20, 328, 367, 371,
    406, 416–17, 423
Pentagon, 20, 26–27
Peregrine Fund, 37
politics vs. policy, 370, 408
Porat, Ruth, 157
Portland Beavers, 31
Portland Timbers, 31
Portman, Rob, 45
prayer, 25, 40, 215
predatory lending, 65, 246
Preferred Stock Purchase Agreement,
    167–68
presidential campaign of 2008, 181,
    225–26, 388
  AIG and, 226, 240
  Election Day, 391–92
  Fannie/Freddie and, 13–15
  first debate, 303–4
  McCain's suspension of, 288–91,
    293–94, 303
  TARP and, 278–81, 288–91, 293–99,
    319, 371, 372, 380, 383
President's Working Group on Finan-
    cial Markets (PWG), 50–52, 90,
    235–37
  public statement, 331, 332, 334, 341
Preston, Steve, 156, 307
Price, Dan, 334, 373
Price, Joe, 199–200, 202, 426
PricewaterhouseCoopers, 230
Primary Dealer Credit Facility (PDCF),
    116, 135–36, 142, 218
Prince, Chuck, 69–70, 79
Principia College, 22
protectionism, 55, 451–52
Purdue University, 25
Putin, Vladimir, x, 140–41
Putnam, Adam, 285

Quetico Provincial Park, 23

Ramanathan, Karthik, xi, 73, 78–79,
    247
Randall's Island Sports Foundation,
    415–16, 417
Rangel, Charlie, 150, 154, 306

About the Author

Henry M. Paulson, Jr., served under President George W. Bush as the 74th secretary of the Treasury from July 2006 until January 2009. As Treasury secretary, Paulson was the president's leading policy adviser on a broad range of domestic and international economic issues.

Before joining the Treasury Department, Paulson had a 32-year career at Goldman Sachs, serving as chairman and chief executive officer following the firm's initial public offering in 1999. He is involved in a range of conservation and environmental initiatives, having served as chairman of the Peregrine Fund, chairman of the board of directors for the Nature Conservancy, and co-chairman of its Asia-Pacific Council.

Prior to joining Goldman Sachs, Paulson was a member of the White House Domestic Council, serving as staff assistant to the president from 1972 to 1973, and as staff assistant to the assistant secretary of Defense at the Pentagon from 1970 to 1972.

Paulson graduated from Dartmouth in 1968, where he majored in English and was a member of Phi Beta Kappa and an All-Ivy, All-East football player. He received an MBA from Harvard in 1970.

**BUSINESS
PLUS**

Recognized as one of the world's most prestigious business imprints, Business Plus specializes in publishing books that are on the cutting edge. Like you, to be successful we always strive to be ahead of the curve.

Business Plus titles encompass a wide range of books and interests—including important business management works, state-of-the-art personal financial advice, noteworthy narrative accounts, the latest in sales and marketing advice, individualized career guidance, and autobiographies of the key business leaders of our time.

Our philosophy is that business is truly global in every way, and that today's business reader is looking for books that are both entertaining and educational. To find out more about what we're publishing, please check out the Business Plus blog at:

www.businessplusblog.com